LOVE FOR SALE

LOVE FOR SALE

and other essays

Clifford Thompson

Autumn House
Press

PITTSBURGH

"Autumn House" and "Autumn House Press" are registered trademarks owned by
Autumn House Press, a nonprofit corporation whose mission is the publication and
promotion of poetry and other fine literature.

Autumn House Press Staff

Editor-in-Chief and Founder: Michael Simms
Managing Editor: Caroline Tanski
Production Editor: Adrienne Block
Co-Founder: Eva-Maria Simms
Community Outreach Director: Michael Wurster
Fiction Editors: Sharon Dilworth, John Fried
Assistant Editors: Giuliana Certo, Christine Stroud
Media Consultant: Jan Beatty
Publishing Consultant: Peter Oresick
Tech Crew Chief: Michael Milberger

Autumn House Press receives state arts funding support through a grant
from the Pennsylvania Council on the Arts, a state agency funded by the
Commonwealth of Pennsylvania, and the National Endowment for the Arts,
a federal agency.

ISBN: 978-1-932870-78-7

Library of Congress Control Number: 201292081

ACKNOWLEDGMENTS

I HAVE MANY people to thank, but the following stand out: Phillip Lopate; the gracious Michael Simms and Caroline Tanski of Autumn House Press; the editors of *Cineaste*—Dan Georgakas, Leonard Quart, Cynthia Lucia, and the founder, Gary Crowdus—for sharing their knowledge of film and letting me write for their great magazine; Wendy Lesser, for plucking my work from among a sea of envelopes and giving it a home in her wonderful journal, *The Threepenny Review*; and my wife, Amy Peck, for being a great sounding board and a loving and encouraging voice.

for

Amy

CONTENTS

PART FOUR: IN YOUR EAR

PART FIVE: DISPATCHES FROM TELLCLIFF.COM

LOVE FOR SALE

– Preface –

A COLLECTION OF essays is an odd thing. Generally speaking, there is no sense of movement toward an illuminating conclusion, as there is or should be in a novel; usually there isn't even a single subject followed all the way through, as in a biography, say, or the history of a war. Even the best essay collections, from James Baldwin's *Notes of a Native Son* to Jonathan Lethem's *The Disappointment Artist*, can seem to have a hodgepodge quality. What, for example, does Baldwin's tale of being arrested on charges of stealing a hotel sheet ("Equal in Paris") have to do with his take on the film *Carmen Jones* ("The Dark Is Light Enough")? The answer lies in that innocuous possessive pronoun, "his." The essays in a collection, whatever they concern, represent *his* (or her) views. Taken together, and given a broad enough array of topics—suddenly, variety becomes an advantage—they demonstrate a sensibility; they are like a porcupine's quills, extending in different directions but, collectively, revealing a shape, helping define their source.

What, or who, is the source of the essays you're about to read? I am a middle-aged black American; I'm a husband and father; for close to two decades I've made my living as an editor; but in my heart, I'm a writer—the author of several dozen published essays, some of which are now in your hands. I love several forms of art—literature, film, painting, jazz—and these are the subjects I often write about, sometimes separately, sometimes together.

I'm not sure that jazz is the most important of these for me, but it's the one that offered a way of thinking and writing about the others; it is jazz that helped me make sense of my cultural identity and served as one safe place in the world from which to contemplate the rest. As a younger man I struggled to figure out who and what I was. I was black, and I had grown up in America, but I didn't know how to reconcile those two things. Individual instances of black achievement aside, the history of blacks in America seemed to me one long tale of woe, not one that could sustain me emotionally and intellectually in the largely white circles where I've often found myself since my college days. How could I make sense of my life and presence in this country without renouncing blackness, which I was unwilling (not to mention unable) to do? And yet how could I embrace America, the source of so much misery for people who looked like me? The answer I found was that jazz—which I had already begun listening to—not only represented a major, positive black contribution to American culture; it embodied an element central to Americanness: improvisation, or making a new way to achieve an end. The Founding Fathers did it with the Declaration of Independence and the US Constitution; black American slaves did it with the Underground Railroad; jazz musicians do it every time they solo.

Secure in my cultural identity, and my love of jazz, I began to explore the connections between that art form and others: the novels I've long read, starting with my random discovery of *The Sun Also Rises* in a bookstore the summer I was seventeen; films, which I've watched devotedly since boyhood and began to study seriously as a freelancer for *Cineaste* and other movie publications; and visual art, for which I have a late-blooming affection and which, in my spare time, I try to create myself.

The essays that follow are divided into five sections; except for the first and last sections, the pieces are grouped according to the art forms they cover, but often a piece about one form will discuss another. Those connections among the arts, and the connections between art and life (the latter explored particularly in the first section), are what truly excite me. It is with great enthusiasm that I discover, say, how Zadie Smith is like Clint Eastwood; what the sax great Coleman Hawkins has in common with Thomas Hardy; how the bassist/composer Charles Mingus is like the Roman statesman/philosopher Marcus Aurelius. It is that enthusiasm I wish to share.

PART ONE

ON MY MIND

THREE FUNERALS AND A WEDDING

The Threepenny Review, 2012

THE WORST FUNERAL I ever attended, by far, was my friend Gerald's. Half a generation older than me, Gerald took me under his wing when I arrived, at twenty-three, as an editorial assistant at Doubleday in 1986; he was one of few blacks there and tended to gravitate toward the others. A married father of two, Gerald was also on what is known as the Down-Low—that is, he secretly slept with men. He certainly kept that a secret from me, until one day in the spring of 1994, when he called from his hospital bed to tell me in a trembling voice that he had AIDS. I went to visit him soon afterward. Before I could make a second visit, he died.

The funeral was held at a Seventh Day Adventist church in Harlem, a couple of blocks from the apartment where I had once lived. Conducting the service was a sort of tag team of two ministers—maybe there were three—who seemed to know very little about Gerald and who soon proved to be poor choices for other reasons as well. After congratulating each other for having shown up, they made remarks hinting that they had done so reluctantly (because, one assumes, of the cause of death); they added that they had agreed to perform the funeral after talking with Gerald's widow, whom they kept calling "the wife." Later in the service one of them made a homophobic joke. At another point several people, including me, rose one by one to give spontaneous testimonies about what Gerald had meant to them, or how much he had helped them in their writing or publishing careers; after the last of us had sat down, one of the minister-clowns returned to the podium to inform those gathered that Gerald was clearly "one of the most important people in literature in the history of this nation."

Gerald was many things. He was a great supporter of black endeavor, especially in literature and music. He was easy to make laugh, and he did so from his rather ample belly. He was quiet-spoken, a quality that, like his laugh, seemed at odds with the anger that ran not far below his surface— anger at racism and at white people, anger that made him, to speak the unvarnished truth, a bit of a racist himself. There are, it seems to me, two logical ends of the spectrum of black people's attitudes toward whites. At one end is the belief that every person of every color should be evaluated individually, that the failure to observe this rule is the very cause of black people's miserable history in America; at the other end is the belief that since so many white people have treated so many black people so abominably, it makes good old-fashioned sense not to trust them. Gerald and I were friends despite my being at one end of the spectrum and his being pretty near the other. Our debates on the subject were usually friendly and usually won by him; it didn't help my arguments that while I rejected the opposing point of view on moral grounds, I felt the pull of its logic. (I've wondered more than once if I would be a match for him now.) What I admired about Gerald was that, unlike so many who defend their own kind, he stood up for others, too. One day, after a couple of years of hearing him support blacks and disparage whites, I was floored when he said something to the effect of, "Lately I've been more into feminist issues than black issues." Gerald, I say again, was many things. He cannot be called—and I write this as someone who had a lot of respect for him—one of the most important people in literature in the history of this nation, and to say that he was is to admit to a profound ignorance. For that reason I'm glad, in retrospect, that the minister said so: it means that the farce that constituted the world's goodbye to my friend was not a triumph of prejudice and meanness but a result of something a little easier to forgive.

LIKE MANY work environments, Doubleday seemed a good place to be if you knew why you were there and what you were doing. I barely had a handle on either. I wanted to be a writer and so had sought a job that had to do with books—an idea that made sense in a vague sort of way but had very limited application to my day-to-day work. I wrote great reports on manuscript submissions (at least my boss said so), but most of my time was spent fielding phone calls from impatient authors, typing copy from my boss's nearly illegible handwritten notes, or filling out forms whose connection to the literature of the age I failed to grasp. What might've helped me was a sense of where I wanted to go in the company and what I needed to do to get there, but I was ambivalent about the obvious goal— becoming an editor—because it wasn't clear to me what the editors at Doubleday *did* that amounted to anything. From what I could tell, they talked on the phone; they went to lunch; they had what were called focus meetings and pre-focus meetings; they yelled at their assistants. What did any of it have to do with the shaping of great writing? When did these editors *edit?* And if they edited at home after leaving the office, instead of spending time with their loved ones—instead of writing—what kind of life would that be?

The one bright spot for me in all this was Gerald. He knew that what I really wanted was to be a writer, so one day he arranged a lunch for the two of us and a female literary agent he knew well. I tried, earnestly, to convey to the agent what I wanted to accomplish, tried to find out from her how I could do so. At one point Gerald laughed and said in his usual cut-through-the-bullshit fashion, and speaking the absolute truth, "My boy's so nervous." Nervous or not, with Gerald's help I got the agent sufficiently interested in me to place a short story of mine in an anthology edited by Terry McMillan. It was my first published piece. To Gerald's horror, it was about a young black man who dates a white woman.

IRONICALLY, BECAUSE so much of Gerald's funeral was so appalling, I remember it more clearly than I do some others. There was, for example, James Baldwin's funeral. When Baldwin died, in December 1987, I was working at Doubleday for Marshall De Bruhl, the editor who headed the imprint Anchor Press. Marshall was very friendly with Doubleday's consultant Gloria Jones, the widow of the novelist James Jones, one of Baldwin's confreres during his fabled years in Paris. So it was that one morning, as I was sitting at my desk, Marshall walked in and announced that Baldwin's funeral was to be held at Manhattan's Cathedral of St. John the Divine and added, "You and I are going." And we did, getting picked up by limousine on that gray day at Doubleday's Midtown Manhattan offices, riding in the back next to Mrs. Jones, sitting in that enormous cathedral surrounded by the literati. I am sorry to say that that event, for all its grandeur, solemnity, and sadness, was largely wasted on me—partly because, for all my supposed devotion to the world of books, the Baldwin I'd read amounted to one short story ("Sonny's Blues") whose details I barely remembered. Just as scandalously, the funeral failed to inspire me, bone-headed twenty-four-year-old that I was, to go on a Baldwin-reading tear.

No, it was Gerald who did that. By then Doubleday had become part of Bantam Doubleday Dell, whose imprint Laurel came out with paperback editions of Baldwin's books. One day, months after Baldwin's funeral, Gerald stopped by my desk with an armful of them. It's not going too far to say that his gift changed my life. That summer, 1988, after leaving Doubleday, taking a part-time job, and starting work on an ill-fated novel in my mouse-ridden Brooklyn apartment, I consumed those books. I felt as if the voice in them, in all its wisdom, intimacy, humility, pain, rage, exasperation, wistfulness, and affection—in short, its humanity—was speaking directly to me, and the fact that Baldwin was black was the icing on the cake. (He was also, of course, gay; I have to think that meant something to Gerald.) I fell in love with Baldwin's work and with Baldwin himself, who seemed to me to have set the high-water mark for American letters.

In 2005, forty-two years old and less wide-eyed, I read quite a few of Baldwin's books again. As an insightful woman once wrote, nothing remains the same, and Baldwin's writing did not strike me this time around as being unquestionably the work of the greatest, most capable writer America had ever produced. There was too much to get past, structurally and stylistically—from the near-plotlessness of some of the novels to what amounted to tics: the frequency of the adverb set off by commas, for example, or of certain words, with "terrifying" high on the list. To be fair, that word must have accurately summed up the way the world often appeared to him. Baldwin was born in 1924 and grew up poor, one of many children, in Harlem—at a time when being black was an unarguable hindrance, when being gay was unspeakable (to use another favorite Baldwin word) and made him a minority within a minority, when being as intelligent as he was must have felt like a curse, one that let him see exactly the predicament he was in. And what came through more powerfully than before in the re-reading of even the most loosely structured of his novels (*Tell Me How Long the Train's Been Gone*, say) were the lessons about humanity learned through the sheer terror of having been James Baldwin, terror that even at its worst was laced with guilt, for being better off than others he knew, for refusing to partake in the depths of their suffering. A onetime boy preacher, Baldwin had left the Christian church but did not seem to have left behind its belief in sin—one's own or one's country's—or its belief in there being a reckoning. (Hence the title and message of *The Fire Next Time*.) The burden of those beliefs and of his fear, guilt, and hard-won wisdom come through in every sentence he wrote, as does his humanity.

And to give Baldwin his due, it is necessary to recognize the beauty of many of his essays. Every so often I re-read the long title piece of his 1955 collection *Notes of a Native Son*, and surely it is a measure of the depths of that work that it seems to be about something different each time. It is mainly about Baldwin's going on his nineteenth birthday to his father's funeral, where the eulogy "presented to us . . . a man whom none of us had ever seen—a man thoughtful, patient, and forbearing, a Christian inspiration to all who knew him, and a model for his children"; then again, the essay chiefly concerns Baldwin's discovery, in the segregated New Jersey town where he'd found work in defense plants, of what his father had long warned him about—"the weight of white people in the world"; or is its real focus the way to conduct oneself in the world responsibly? "Notes of a Native Son" is, of course, about all of those things, and more.

In much of his work Baldwin argued that blacks and whites, for all the animosity between them, must accept each other, for their mutual salvation. In "Notes of a Native Son," he wrote:

> In order really to hate white people, one has to blot so much out of the mind—and the heart—that this hatred itself becomes an exhausting and self-destructive pose. But this does not mean, on the other hand, that love comes easily: the white world is too powerful, too complacent, too ready with gratuitous humiliation, and, above all, too ignorant and too innocent for that. One is absolutely forced to make perpetual qualifications and one's own reactions are always canceling each other out. It is this, really, which has driven so many people mad, both white and black. One is always in the position of having to decide between amputation and gangrene. Amputation is swift but time may prove that the amputation was not necessary—or one may delay the amputation too long. Gangrene is slow, but it is impossible to be sure that one is reading one's symptoms right. . . .

In an age when most people seem to be yelling most of the time, dead-certain of the rightness and simplicity of their arguments—and when the certainty, simplicity, and volume seem to increase along with the complexity of the issue—how one yearns for the acceptance of ambiguity that Baldwin expresses here about that most complex of issues: race. Simplicity is certainly one of the active ingredients in prejudice, key to what Baldwin calls "blot[ting] so much out of the mind"; indeed, dismissing whole groups of people as having this or that insufferable trait requires a kind of self-lobotomy that is particularly dangerous in an era with so much to absorb. Each of us has, of course, gone under his own knife to some extent: I concluded long ago that the world is divided not between the prejudiced and the nonprejudiced but between those who work to overcome their prejudices and those who don't give a damn. Those who accept the challenge embrace complexity as a condition of their lives.

I GOT MARRIED in 1992 to a woman who is, among other things, white. Roughly equal numbers of black and white people came to the building in Brooklyn's Prospect Park to witness our union and dance together to songs by acts as varied as Talking Heads and Otis Redding, The Romantics and James Brown. By the day of our wedding I had long come to take for granted the racial aspect of the union between my wife and me, but, as I should have realized, it was a slightly bigger deal for some of the old friends and seldom-seen relatives who came in from various parts of the country. I heard later from some of the guests what a good feeling it gave them to see such a festive mix of blacks and whites. There was, on the other hand, one of my groomsmen, a black man, who—given flak by some of his other black friends for having participated in my wedding—drifted for a time toward their point of view.

And then there was Gerald. He was at the wedding, sitting at a table with two women, former Doubleday colleagues, one of whom would call me two years later with the news of his death.

I went up to him when he was about to leave the wedding. If he had any negative thoughts about what he had just witnessed, he kept them to himself. Maybe, in the end, we can't expect more than that. He asked me, "Are you happy?"

"Yes," I said.

He replied, in all sincerity, "I hope you stay that way."

LOVE FOR SALE

for Juanita

The Threepenny Review, 2011

On a Thursday in late August of 2007, when I was forty-four and she was eighty-two, I saw my mother for what seemed sure to be the last time. (It was. She died the next night, when I was two hundred miles away.) The hospital bed where she lay was in Washington, DC; I had taken the bus from New York that morning, having talked by phone the night before with my sisters, who told me how bad things looked. Over the previous two years my mother had been in and out of the hospital with a bewildering series of infections, lung ailments, and more, and her stays often disoriented her. Lately, even when visiting her in the home she shared with one of my sisters, I could see that her mind was not what it had been. So as I walked into my mother's hospital room, I did not have high expectations for our final time together.

I was in for a surprise. My mother had tubes in her nose and a plastic breathing device over her mouth, but for someone who couldn't talk, she did a lot of communicating that day. When I smiled and said, "Remember me?", her eyes lit up and her eyebrows rose as she shook her head no; she was, on her deathbed, joking with me, as we had done with each other my whole life. I fought back tears as I told her that any generosity in me had come from her; soon, though, the lightness of her spirit got to me, and I was cheerfully reminiscing about all manner of things, such as the time she had to come to the hospital in the middle of the day—when she should have been sleeping before sorting mail on the night shift at the post office—because I had, rather uncharacteristically, ripped my hand open while putting it through a window in my high school. Now, my hand, with its prominent, twenty-eight-year-old scar, took hers, and I sang to her, songs we both liked: "Up on the Roof" by the Drifters, "If I Didn't Care" by the Ink Spots. I squeezed her hand. She squeezed mine. Her eyes smiled up at me. It's what I like to remember about my last moments with her.

I ENJOY SINGING. I'm a whistler, too. (So is my older daughter. Recently, to my considerable satisfaction, she told me about an exchange with a high-school classmate of hers: "You're, like, the best whistler I know," the classmate said, to which my daughter replied, "That's because you haven't met my dad.") In my kitchen is a clock/radio/CD player my mother gave us years ago, and on it I like to play a jazz recording that I whistle along with while washing dishes: the version of "Love for Sale" on *'58 Miles*, studio sessions of that year from a sextet led by Miles Davis. A shade under twelve minutes, it is one of the loveliest jazz performances ever committed to disk. Like a host, Miles—on muted trumpet—introduces the song's theme at the beginning and plays it again at the end, taking subtle, supple liberties with the bent-note wistfulness of the melody, in the only parts of the tune I can keep up with. Between those two passages come solos by the alto-sax luminary Cannonball Adderley, who had not only the sweetest sound in jazz but one of the fastest, and the tenor-sax god John Coltrane, whose signature wails are all that separate his bursts of breakneck virtuosity. Getting into the spirit, the pianist Bill Evans delivers a solo as linear as a horn player's.

Like a host: I remember once watching *The Tonight Show* with Johnny Carson when one of his guests was Steve Martin, then in the "wild and crazy guy" phase of his career. In contrast to the genial laughter Carson inspired, the audience went crazy over Martin, who was outrageous from the beginning of his appearance to the end. At the time, in my teens, I wondered how Carson felt during those eight or ten minutes, as Martin's over-the-top performance so dominated the show. But for years afterward, and more years after that, as Martin's career entered valleys between his acts of self-reinvention, millions continued to watch Carson every night, welcoming his familiarity and the way he made what he did seem so easy. On "Love for Sale," Miles performs a feat similar to Carson's: hosting, preceding and following the saxophone pyrotechnics of two of the most gifted jazz musicians who ever lived, Miles employs the art of deceptive simplicity; his outchorus, echoing his introduction, given added resonance by our memory of what came in between, is straightforward, moving, beautiful. I whistle along to the end, Miles's solo echoing in my head when the others have faded.

EACH AUTUMN I do some hosting of my own: my college friend Tracy comes to visit for a weekend. Tracy is a big, warm-hearted man, a world-class talker, an enthusiastic consumer of music, movies, and dessert, and, like me—and like every man named Tracy I have ever met—an African-American. A Baptist, he doesn't drink, but he doesn't mind when I do. We spend at least part of Friday evening at my Brooklyn apartment, where he catches up with the members of my (interracial) family; on Saturday, he and I set out to conquer Manhattan.

This past year our jaunt fell on what would have been my mother's eighty-sixth birthday. I thought from time to time of that, and of her, as we wound our way in the crisp mid-October air through the Manhattan streets. To be sure, ours is the nerd's tour of New York: between long talks at this restaurant and that coffee house, we spent no small part of our time among the redwood-high shelves of Strand Books and the comics and sci-fi paraphernalia of Forbidden Planet (Tracy's idea). That night we were seeing a jazz performance at a place I'd heard of but knew next to nothing about; the club was on the Upper East Side, so we headed up there early to look for a place to eat dinner before the show. Gazing through the windows of one bar-restaurant, using my hands for blinders, I searched for black faces—

just to make sure this wasn't the kind of place where friendly conversation would give way to cold stares the moment we entered. I said to Tracy, "I see a couple of brothers." Then I said, as we were walking in, "I never talk like that." Tracy smiled and said, "I bring out the best in you." Soon we were shooting the breeze over a good meal.

One of the things Tracy and I have in common—is there a way to say this without seeming self-congratulatory?—is that our deep interest in things black co-exists with an openness toward all kinds of people. For that reason we laughed, not with scorn but with appreciation, when we went around the corner to the performance. To begin with, one might reasonably guess that a jazz club called The Miles Café was named in honor of Miles Davis, but this one was named (at least in part) after the owner, the bald Japanese man who greeted us in the front room. From there we went to the performance area, which was not dim and catacomb-like in the way of many jazz clubs but fairly large, square, and well-lit, more like a room in a community center; about half of the seats were filled, many if not most by East Asians. Then there was the band. On drums was Jimmy Wormworth, a black man who was seventy if a day; on alto sax, Elijah Shiffer, a very young-looking white guy; on piano, Charles Sibirsky, a white man in middle age or beyond; and on tenor sax, the featured performer, a young man named Tacuma Bradley, who was obviously East Asian but, to me and Tracy, looked black as well. Later a female singer, Niranjana Shankar, who appeared to be Indian, made an appearance, and a tall, older East Asian woman, whom Tacuma introduced as his mother, sat in for a bit on piano. This UN-like band did wonderful renditions of jazz standards—"In a Mellowtone," "Daahoud," "Easy Living." And then Shankar took the stage and let me have it, singing "Love for Sale."

I am a fan of instrumental jazz. I have a passing familiarity with the lyrics of some of the songs that inspired my favorite nonvocal tunes; there are others I don't know at all. And so it was not until Shankar began to sing that I learned what you surely know already, what I might've figured out if I'd given two seconds' thought to that lovely song's title: the actual subject of "Love for Sale." *If you want to buy my wares / Follow me and climb the stairs*

/ Love for sale . . . I'm not puritanical, and I don't think of myself as naïve (then again, who does?), but for just a moment, in my forty-seven-year-old heart, I felt like that kid of 1919 who shouted at the disgraced slugger Shoeless Joe Jackson, "Say it ain't so!" Then the moment passed, and I began to think of the song's lyrics as the mildest possible example of—really, more of a metaphor for—something I've become increasingly aware of over the years: the unpleasantness, misfortune, and plain evil that we don't see even when it's in front of our faces, the actual or potential chaos beneath everyday life's smooth surface; the things, simply put, that we just don't want to think about. Brooding about that led me to remember the very last thing that occurred between me and my mother.

When I walked out of her hospital room there were two people standing outside it: my niece, Elinor, then twenty one, and my mother's caregiver, Brenda, who had come to seem one of the family. I talked with them briefly and hugged them both, and then I turned to go—whether in search of my siblings or straight to the bus station, I can't recall now. What I do remember is that while I was talking to Elinor and Brenda, I had the damnable luck to glance through the doorway of my mother's room. The expression on her face was sadness itself, and she seemed to be looking right at me. Our eyes met for an instant, at least I think they did, and then I turned away and finished talking. After that I left. The next time I saw my mother she was in a casket.

It was the right thing to do: by walking away from my mother's room, I ensured that the memory of our last time together—the one she would take to her grave, the one I would carry forward—was a good one, much better than anybody could have expected. It was a better memory, surely, than one in which I returned to her room and we both cried, helpless together in the face of her imminent death, which would come—when? In two hours, two days, two weeks? How long could I, should I, have cried with her? What was left to say?

It was the wrong thing to do: however futile the effort to comfort her might have been, I should have gone back in there and tried, no matter how long it took. That was what I owed the woman who brought me into the world, who raised me by herself beginning when I was eleven, who paid

for my college education on her postal clerk's salary, who welcomed anyone of any race I brought home, who came to stay with my wife and me
for a week when our first child was born. What kind of son, what kind of
man, would not do that much?

I left the hospital without knowing which view was right. I didn't know
as I sat in The Miles Café, and I don't know as I write this.

AFTER THE GROUP'S performance I had the warmest interaction with jazz
musicians I have ever experienced. I chatted with Shankar, who was very
approachable; I talked with the friendly Sibirsky about the lyrics of "Love
for Sale." Tracy and I both talked to Wormworth, who turned out to be a
comedian. "C.C. Sabathia!" he said, shaking Tracy's hand—a reference to
Tracy's size and that of the black Yankees pitcher. He joked with us for
another minute, then said he had to go get paid: "Time for *dinero*," he informed us, "and I don't mean Robert!" Then Tracy and I talked to Tacuma
and his mother. I told them that that day would've been my mother's birthday and added, truthfully, that it had done me good to see their mother-
son interaction. Tacuma smiled in appreciation, and, tapping his chest
with his fist, thanked us for coming out, saying that it warmed his heart to
see us all.

As we left them, Tracy suggested, kindly, that my seeing Tacuma and
his mother had not been an accident, because it was what I had needed. He
believed that because he's a Christian; I didn't because I'm not. I am sometimes tempted to think that there is a reason for everything that happens,
but I think my believing would be based on my very desire to do so, not on
objective reality.

Each of us, I feel, has a duty to try to see things as they are, not as we
would like to think they are. But each of us must also, of course, make it
through the day. It is possible, where my mother is concerned, that I failed
at the very last moment. But I had a good relationship with her, and she
knew I loved her. I had to remember the first fact without losing sight of
the other two, and without forgetting what all of them together signified:
that I was merely human. I tried to take all that with me as I left the warmth
of the jazz club and headed out into the New York night.

15

DREAMS OF LAURA

The Threepenny Review, 2009

CARTOONING IS LARGELY the province of the shy loner. That was certainly true for me during the decade or so, beginning when I was eight years old, that I aspired to be a professional comic-book writer and illustrator. Shyness is no crime, but it can present a large obstacle to getting what one wants in life. An intriguing chicken-or-the-egg question about cartoonists might be: are they shy people attracted to imagining and illustrating alternate worlds as a way of creating what they only dream about in the worlds they inhabit, or does cartooning, a solitary pursuit, make people less social beings? Whatever the answer with regard to me, I felt what is often called the shock of recognition, saw a reflection of my own well-mannered but antisocial younger self, when I read this passage by another ex-would-be cartoonist and comic-book fan, John Updike, in his beautiful collection of memoirs, *Self-Consciousness*: "If I'm nice and good, you'll leave me alone to read my comic books."

I imagine the "you'll" in that passage to refer to adult relatives and family friends, of whom there was no shortage in my own case: they were the aunts and uncles who lived in very close proximity to the house in Washington, DC, where I grew up. The memory of their collective presence is a warm and pleasant one, but one of my regrets is that I did not get to know them better as individuals—particularly the two uncles who lived closest, good-hearted but rough-hewn, country-raised men, exemplars of rural self-sufficiency whose like, in this age of MapQuest, Weather.com, and Internet grocery shopping, seems increasingly rare. There was the boisterous Uncle Manson, of the sudden and startling, rooster-like laugh and bone-jarring backslaps; there was the smaller, quieter, darker-skinned Uncle Nay, of the manliness that was almost shaming—the more so because he never consciously projected it: it emanated, rather, from the extreme competence he brought to everything from fixing his car to building his back porch, tasks at which he shrugged off the occasional accident, continuing to work as blood dripped from his arm. In retrospect they were compelling figures, but in the 1970s I was much more interested in drawing than in asking my uncles questions about their days as young men in the sticks of Virginia.

There was one social aspect of my cartooning days, though, owing to the placement of the drafting table I received one Christmas. Rather than in my shoebox of a bedroom, where it wouldn't have begun to fit, the table —the greatest gift I ever got as a boy—went against the partial wall separating our family's living room and dining room. There, I had a view (albeit sideways) of our TV and could talk with my mother, grandmother, and sisters as I drew; I have very fond memories of doing so.

And if shyness is a trait common to many cartoonists, so is another, seemingly opposite one: a desire for control. As a child I had an aversion to what is now called imaginative play when it involved other children; the whole point, to me, was to exercise my creativity, not have it thwarted or compromised by some stupid kid from around the corner. At my desk, with my pen, pencil, markers, ruler, and thick white paper, I was in command. And when I drew the superhero who was my alter-ego, I gave him— i.e., myself—what in all my shyness I didn't have: a girlfriend. She was as pretty as my limited skills could make her. Her name was Laura.

UNBEKNOWNST TO ME then, "Laura" was also the name of a famous 1944 movie, directed by Otto Preminger and starring Gene Tierney as the title character, a beautiful and virtuous young ad executive. Dana Andrews plays the brave, laconic Lieutenant Mark McPherson, who steps in to investigate Laura's apparent murder. In doing so he meets the men in her life: Waldo Lydecker (Clifton Webb), a cultured, pompous columnist and radio commentator, and Shelby Carpenter (Vincent Price), a man smooth to the point of being slippery, who by his own account doesn't know "a lot about anything" but knows "a little bit about practically everything"—a "vague sort of a fellow," as McPherson calls him to his face, who had no visible means of support until Laura gave him a job at her agency. The more McPherson learns about Laura, and the more he gazes at the portrait of her, painted by yet another of her suitors, the more he falls in love with her. Meanwhile, his investigation appears to go nowhere. In one scene, alone in Laura's apartment with a view of her portrait, McPherson is a surrogate for many an adult: adrift, melancholy, with no clear goal beyond what life and his own lousy timing have conspired to place beyond his reach.

Sitting in Laura's chair, McPherson has a drink and falls into a light sleep, one that, in my interpretation, comprises the rest of the movie. The word "dream" is spoken several times in *Laura*; Lydecker asks McPherson at one point, "Have you ever dreamed of Laura as your wife?" He has, and he does. McPherson has not been asleep long when Laura returns and finds him; she has been away at her country house and only now hears the reports of her death. (It turns out that the face-disfiguring shotgun blast thought to have killed Laura in her home actually took the life of another woman, when Laura wasn't there.) With Laura before him in the flesh, McPherson has a fair chance to compete against his rivals for her affections, to pit his inner qualities against the outer charms of these more talkative fellows, whose other advantage was having met Laura in time. McPherson, in effect, cheats time—a powerless element in the world of dreams, in which the *what* of our fears and desires trumps the *when*. (During the movie's climax another errant shotgun blast destroys a hall clock, killing time.) *Laura* is a story of winning, through the power of imagination, of dreams, some semblance of what you otherwise cannot have.

LAURA'S MEMORABLE MUSICAL score was composed by David Raksin. In 1950 the great jazz alto saxophonist Charlie "Bird" Parker recorded a highly popular version of it. In a way Bird seems the musician least likely to have taken on the score of that movie, with its theme of hopeless longing; he was a man who let nothing—not timing, certainly not shyness—come between him and what he wanted. For Bird, no desire was too large or small to indulge, and no time was wrong to indulge it, whether the desire involved sex (many and amazing are the stories); money (which he sometimes got by cheerfully cheating the members of the bands he led, and which he just as cheerfully shared with others); drugs (only alcohol got in the way of his heroin addiction); or food (one night, in a club packed with people waiting to hear Bird play, the club's manager found the saxophonist in the kitchen eating sandwiches and pleaded almost tearfully with him to go on stage— to which Bird replied, "Man, why don't you try one of these sandwiches? They're crazy"). At about the time he recorded "Laura," Bird began living with Chan Richardson, the last of his four wives. To put it another way, romantic notions about women glimpsed across a great divide were not the stuff of his life. Surprisingly, then, Bird's version of "Laura," available on *Charlie Parker with Strings* and elsewhere, retains the wistfulness of the original. Unlike other Bird recordings—even others of his ballads—his "Laura" does not find him jumping chords like a hurdler or producing cascades of sixteenth- and thirty-second-notes; he plays it almost as straight melody, putting no intellectual distance between himself and tune's theme of melancholy. It is as if Bird, the man who took whatever he wanted, reached down to find an object of longing of his own, or as if he discovered something pure and deeply human, something inevitable, in longing itself.

IN 1992 I married Laura, whose name turned out to be Amy. This past Christmas Amy's present to me was an easel. I long ago gave up drawing comics, but I've flirted with paint from time to time over the years, and recently I've become enamored of it. I've produced still lifes, landscapes, and paintings of real and imaginary people; I'm just good enough to be able to enjoy it. (A guy I was once friends with, looking at a painting of mine, put it this way: "You're no Degas, but you've got a touch.") Sitting at the easel in my Brooklyn apartment, as I once sat at my drafting table, I come closer than I ever thought I would again to the joy of producing visual work that I knew as a teenager. And the social element is there again: I like nothing better than working on a painting while Amy and the girls are in the room chatting with me, maybe watching the Mets on TV, maybe indulging me by listening to a Charlie Parker record. Some things, of course, are gone forever. Maybe that is why the real-life people whose likenesses I have tried to capture include Uncle Nay and Uncle Manson. I am like McPherson, whose dream of knowing another is crushed by his own wretched timing. A picture is the best I can do.

MY CITY, MY COUNTRY

Notes of an American in the Age of Terror

Written in late 2002

I WAS BORN and raised in Washington, DC; in 1986, at age twenty-three, I moved to New York City, where, except for seven months spent in Europe in 1991, I have lived ever since. What that means is that on the morning of September 11, 2001, terrorists attacked the two places I think of as home. Like most Americans, and all New Yorkers, I remember what I was doing when I heard the news—in my case, standing at a photocopy machine at the Bronx-based reference-publishing company where I head an editorial staff. A colleague walked up to tell me that she had gotten a call from an acquaintance, who said that a plane had flown into one of the towers of the World Trade Center. The order of events after that is a bit jumbled in my memory, but I do recall two things clearly: standing with my staff on our company's sixth-floor wooden deck, where, craning our necks, we could see black smoke billowing from the Trade Center, a few miles downtown; and feeling my surprise turn to creeping dread when I learned that the second tower and the Pentagon had been hit, too. Not long before that morning, a lot of time and ink had been spent in arguing about whether the twenty-first century would start on January 1, 2000, or a year later. I know when it started for me.

The emotions I have felt most powerfully where 9/11 is concerned are confusion and fear. The following story doesn't make me look heroic, but it does reveal something about my state of mind in the wake of the attacks. Late one night, not more than a week after 9/11, my wife and I were lying in bed in our Brooklyn apartment when we were awakened by very loud noises. I ran to our bathroom window, which a week earlier had afforded a view of the twin towers; I now saw fresh smoke coming from where they had stood, and that, together with the noise, convinced me that the city was under attack. Heart racing, I went back to my bedroom, where my wife was sitting up and thinking the same thing I was. "What can we do?" she said, in what, considering the circumstances, was a calm voice. "I don't know if there's anything we can do," I told her. Then one of us, probably my wife, noticed that it was raining, a realization that triggered two others. The smoke I had seen was probably steam, a result of rain falling on Ground Zero, where fires were still burning; and the loud noises were not bombs going off, but thunder.

Since that period my fears about terrorist attacks have moved to the back of my mind—though, like cold sores, they tend to reappear occasionally and hang around awhile, usually called up by newspaper headlines about smallpox or the latest "credible threat." I have two children, the older of whom was not yet eight on the day the towers fell. The thought of losing them or my wife is one I don't even like to speak out loud, for fear of tempting fate, and the idea of dying myself and leaving them behind is not much better.

Fear is fear, and there is only so much to be said about it; its power—like that of death—derives in part from its very simplicity. Confusion is different. While fear can be a powerful motivator, confusion often brings on paralysis, and for quite a while after 9/11 I knew neither what to do nor how to think about the terrible events of that day. The confusion existed on many levels; even now, for example, stepping out of the shower in the mornings, I occasionally gaze at where the towers stood, not knowing which fact seems less real—that they're gone, or that they were ever there. On a deeper level, the confusion, rampant as it was for so long, boiled down to one question: Who is responsible?

★　★　★　★　★

I HAVE A cousin who is five years, eight months, and twelve days younger than I am. His name (which he shares with the unarmed African immigrant who died in a barrage of police gunfire in 1999) is Amadou Diallo. As a boy in Washington I saw Amadou when our families visited each other, maybe six or eight times a year. He was a cute kid, and after I grew up and left the area, I continued to think of him that way—until the day in the early 1990s when he spotted me on a Brooklyn sidewalk and we discovered that we lived nine blocks apart. He had grown into a multitalented man with a great sense of humor and a formidable intelligence, and in the years since then we have developed a close friendship. We share a curiosity about the world and an amused—sometimes not so amused—skepticism about the society we live in, born in part of our experiences and observations as black men in America. A musician as well as a photographer, Amadou has contributed immeasurably to my understanding of jazz; I have turned him on to several novels that have affected him deeply; we have investigated different areas of film together. On many nights in Park Slope coffee shops we have gone on talking about literature, music, movies, race, what I was writing, what he was composing, and other topics too numerous to mention, while chairs were being stacked on tables around us. But for all that, there is one major difference between us, and it came roaring to the surface not long after 9/11.

For many a thinking black person in America, there comes a day when it seems crucial to figure out his or her relationship to this country. Is it self-debasement to call yourself an American when the country is still rife with racism, when so much of its history involves—when, in fact, its economy once rested on—injustice toward people who look like you? Does it make sense to say that you are an African, even if you've never lived in Africa and don't know which African tribe you're descended from, let alone what its traditions are? Should you declare yourself a "citizen of the world," whatever those pretty words mean? I emerged from that quandary with the conviction that I was an American, by virtue of the sacrifices many blacks (and others) made so that I could participate fully in this society— and by virtue of the contributions made to this country by blacks as a people, ranging from the performance of slave labor, to service in every war dating back to the Revolution, to scientific inventions, to the development of America's indigenous music. The designation "American" was not one that would be slapped on me like a shackle, but one that I would claim proudly, even defiantly, despite—in part because of—racists who thought I did not deserve it. But with thirty million or so blacks living in the United States, it is not surprising that some of us would reach a different conclusion, and one who did so was Amadou. The history of the United States of America, for him, was a long, continuing tale of subjugation, hypocrisy, reprehensible acts committed all over the globe, and, on the part of most of the citizenry, a willful ignorance of conditions past and present. You could have America, as far as Amadou was concerned.

And so after the terrorist attacks, while I was still struggling to form a personal response that went beyond being, well, terrorized, Amadou was already angry over the injustice that would no doubt characterize the US response to the events. For while his heart went out to the victims of 9/11, he believed that the United States, through the evil it had sown elsewhere in the world, had brought this catastrophe on itself. "What do you expect?" was his refrain—"you" referring to Americans who were either responsible for, or oblivious and indifferent to, the suffering that the US has caused, chiefly through the propping up of oppressive regimes. For a time my telephone conversations and coffee-shop sessions with Amadou took on a decided edge. At their best, they found me articulating the reasons that I call myself an American, the reasons I find the concept of America a valid one and my heritage as a black American an inspiring one—while Amadou gave well-informed accounts of the sins committed by this country I had chosen to identify with; at their (frequent) worst, they found Amadou spouting half-thought-out condemnations of the United States while I made counter-arguments that I knew were weak even as they came out of my mouth. ("Deterrence?" I said, when Amadou asked what good I thought the US campaign in Afghanistan was doing—as if the kind of person who would knowingly fly an airplane into a skyscraper could be deterred by any power under the sun.) I confess that during that time I found Amadou, whom I love like a brother, to be irritating. I thought his stance reeked of self-righteousness; and, much more disturbingly, I wasn't sure that in his attacks on the United States—and, by extension, on my identification with it—he was altogether wrong.

Another good friend of mine, my old college mate Charles Hawley, has a PhD in history and taught for a time at Mount Holyoke. After 9/11 his students asked him why so many people hated the United States; the question itself, he told them, suggested an answer. I, too, thought that the question reflected naïveté, and yet I wondered if, in Charles's place, I could've given an informed and intelligent response. I didn't want to be lumped together with those students, even in—especially in—my own mind. Less still did I want to be equated with the people I have always held in contempt: those whites who lived in the time of slavery and thought, if they thought anything, It's not *my* problem. And so I began to read more about the actions of the United States on the international stage. Like many people, to judge from the best-seller lists, I was suckered into buying Noam Chomsky's book *9-11*. Coming in at 128 pages, including endnotes; bearing a title that consists of four characters, including the hyphen; and having no subtitle, this volume would appear to be a concise analysis of the causes behind the horrific events of September 2001. Instead, it consists of interviews Chomsky gave to various journalists, in which he free-associates about American atrocities everywhere and ends his half-explanations of events with such coy phrases as, ". . . for reasons that are familiar to anyone who has paid any attention." Gosh, thanks, Mr. Chomsky. (What's the return policy for your book?)

Still, there are useful snippets of information in *9-11*, even if you need a dental instrument to extract them; and facts about US foreign policy are available through the Internet and in other books, including Chomsky's

The Umbrella of U.S. Power. I found such information to be illuminating without being particularly helpful. In my reading about the US's questionable-at-best acts and outright atrocities not only in the Middle East but in The Congo/Zaire, Nicaragua, and elsewhere, I found concrete examples of what I more or less knew already: that my country has a lot to answer for. Now what? Did this knowledge make it a moral necessity for me to sever my identification with America, a connection that took the first three decades of my life to establish successfully? And if I did so, then what?

I found it somewhat helpful to draw an analogy between the American ideals of freedom and equality and the beautiful works by individuals whose personal conduct was less than exemplary. Long ago I decided that I could not allow the facts of artists' private lives to interfere with my enjoyment of their art. Should I remove the large photograph of Miles Davis from my office, should I never again listen to *Miles Ahead*, because Davis treated the women in his life like toilet paper and was unapologetic about having once been a pimp? Should I never again read the delightful "Love Song of J. Alfred Prufrock" because T. S. Eliot is reputed to have been an anti-Semite? If the answer to these questions was "no," then could I not still embrace America's stated commitment to freedom, even if its actions often did not match that sentiment? I call this idea "somewhat" helpful because while it made sense to me in theory, I wasn't too sure what it called for in practice.

I became more sure, ironically, after reading a work that on its surface had nothing at all to do with US foreign policy. In my second-hand copy of the 1950 volume *The Liberal Imagination*, by the critic Lionel Trilling, I discovered an essay on Sherwood Anderson, which led me to dust off Anderson's classic *Winesburg, Ohio*, a book I had loved when I read it in college. There, I found the following passage, which had struck me forcefully when I was twenty-one but faded from my memory in the intervening years:

> [I]n the beginning when the world was young there were a great many thoughts but no such thing as a truth. Man made the truths himself and each truth was a composite of a great many vague thoughts. All about in the world were the truths and they were all beautiful.

. . . .There was the truth of virginity and the truth of passion, the truth of wealth and poverty, of thrift and profligacy, of carelessness and abandon. Hundreds and hundreds were the truths and they were all beautiful.

And then the people came along. Each as he appeared snatched up one of the truths and some who were quite strong snatched up a dozen of them.

It was the truths that made the people grotesques. . . . the moment one of the people took one of the truths to himself, called it his truth, and tried to live his life by it, he became a grotesque and the truth he embraced became a falsehood.

It was Trilling's point that Anderson himself had become something of a grotesque. As a middle-aged man he had broken away from his workaday existence and begun life anew as a writer. The works that resulted, Trilling found, amounted to one long celebration of that break, beyond which, however, Anderson never progressed intellectually. What should have been the starting point of Anderson's journey thus became its end. Reading Trilling's take on what had befallen Anderson, I began to think that something similar had happened to me. I had ended a dark night of the soul by declaring myself an American, and I had mentally coasted on that decision afterward. I was like a man celebrating at the starting line of a race he has yet to run; having figured out that I was an American, I had neglected to think about what such a person *does*.

★   ★   ★   ★   ★

THERE ARE EIGHT million stories in the Naked City—so went the voice-over at the end of the old TV crime drama about New York. It might have been more accurate to say that there are eight million Naked Cities; New York, in other words, is a different place for everyone who lives here. Once, in my New York, a perfect day found me sipping coffee and writing in my notebook in a place called Café Lucca, where the pretty waitresses let me sit as long and spend as little as I liked, where the windows looked onto the intersection of Sixth Avenue and Bleecker Street, whose bustle perfectly balanced the café's calm, low-lit interior; from there, I would catch an afternoon showing of a classic film at Theater St. Mark's. Those things are not possible now, because Theater St. Mark's no longer shows movies, and Café Lucca no longer exists. Such days can still be had, though. Other places show classic films, and there are plenty of other cafés (I am writing this in one of them), even if none of them ever truly takes Lucca's place in my heart. Now, as then, I love the moments when, walking in Central Park or (much more likely) in Brooklyn's Prospect Park, I see tall buildings rising above the trees, reminders of the industry and creativity surrounding me, the mix of leaves and grand architecture suggesting the marriage of energy and poetry that is New York. The point is that the city is not, as some have said, a place that changed forever after 9/11; rather, New York City, everyone's New York City, is always changing, and always the same. Nine-eleven, symbolized by the absence of the towers from the skyline, is in a way just one example—albeit a colossal and tragic one—of a process that is happening all the time. New York, I think, will always be. More terrorist attacks here, as frightening as the idea is, as horrible as the reality might be, will not change that. Knocked down, it will be rebuilt. Parts of it, gone from sight, will live on in memory.

None of this is to say that I excuse those who visited such havoc on my city. I do not. I was glad in the fall of 2002 when a US missile destroyed a vehicle carrying several Al Qaeda members, and if I could send the rest of them to the same end with the push of a button, the temptation would be great. But I make a distinction between a person who is out to kill me and one who, while he would stop short of taking a life, hates my country for valid reasons. It is the latter person I would like to reach, to help.

In most ways my life is an average one. As I write this, I am staring my fortieth birthday square in the face. I have a job that entails some responsibility and, with my wife's, pays enough for my family and me to get by, not much more. A typical day for me goes something like this: in the shower in the morning my thoughts are a blend of what I have to do in the next twelve hours and what I want to do in my life; standing up on the subway train to the Bronx, I pull out whatever novel I am reading; at work, I marvel at how slowly I am progressing through my "to do" list; at lunch, if I'm not facing a publication deadline, I scribble fiction or nonfiction in my notebook while listening to jazz on my headphones; in the evening I pick up my daughter from day care; after dinner I play with her and her older sister; when they're in bed I glance at the newspaper, talk to my wife, watch *The West Wing* if it's Wednesday or, if it isn't, read an essay by a master, maybe Trilling, maybe Mary McCarthy or Robert Warshow, over which I may fall asleep. Somewhere in that schedule, in some fashion, I plan to start voicing my objections when I feel my country is overstepping its bounds.* That is my right under the First Amendment; more importantly, it is my responsibility. It is what an American does.

*Even if those objections seem to have no measurable effect—as was the case with the 2003 invasion of Iraq, a criminal act that somehow proceeded despite my presence at more than one anti-war rally.

DON'T CRY FOR ME

Racial Condescension in Coverage of Pop Culture

The Reading Room, 2002

THE WAR AGAINST racial inequality in America seems in some ways to have been largely won, and in other ways to have reached a permanent stalemate. Happily, no black American in the 21st century will need to face down police dogs and fire hoses in order to be able to vote, or walk into a predominantly white school accompanied by federal troops. But at least in the era of Martin Luther King Jr., the enemy had the common courtesy to operate in plain view. Today, when a significant number of black children still live in poverty, when a black man is statistically much more likely than his white counterpart to spend some part of his life in jail, who or what is to blame? Is it a black failure to strive sufficiently? Is it simple white racism, still pervasive but now largely hidden? Is it a self-perpetuating dance between the two? Or is it a class issue that is only tangentially connected to race?

In such confusing times, it seems more important than ever to tackle race-related problems whose origins are clear. One example is the police practice—widespread, long-suspected, and only recently acknowledged— of using race as a basis for stop-and-search procedures on roadways.

30

I am concerned here, however, with another, seemingly benign form of race cancer. Some call it liberal racism; I prefer to call it racial condescension. Instances of racial condescension occur with noticeable frequency in coverage of the arts and popular culture, perhaps because those are among the few areas in which individuals are evaluated on a public basis.

Consider, for example, Terrence Rafferty's *New Yorker* review of the 1989 film *Lethal Weapon 2*, the second in the series starring the white actor Mel Gibson and the black actor Danny Glover as cop-buddies. Glover is "mostly called upon to react with horror to [the Gibson character's] dangerous antics," Rafferty wrote. "The effect, sometimes, is of a white guy doing heroic stuff while his black pal shuffles along beside him. Glover, a good actor, deserves better." I couldn't put my finger on what about this passage bothered me, until I realized that whoever Glover deserved better *from*, in Rafferty's opinion, it wasn't Glover himself—who, as a highly successful man in his forties at the time of the movie's release, was certainly capable of looking out for his own interests. (When I saw that the white performer Jeff Daniels—"a good actor"—was playing second banana to Jim Carrey in the aptly titled *Dumb and Dumber*, my reaction was not, "How can they do that to Jeff Daniels," but "What in the world is Jeff Daniels doing?") To absolve Glover of blame—if one feels that wrong has been done—is also to deny him captaincy of his own life, which is every adult's due. (Incidentally, what if Glover weren't a good actor? Would he then deserve to play a demeaning stereotype?)

In other examples of racial condescension, critics take steps in the right direction, but the faltering nature of those steps is revealing. Two of these examples involve the black poet Maya Angelou. For John Singleton's 1993 film *Poetic Justice*, Angelou wrote the verse credited in the story to the young main character, played by Janet Jackson. Reviewing the film in the August 2, 1993 issue of the *New Yorker*, Anthony Lane wrote, "When I heard [the main character reading her poetry aloud], I thought that Singleton had made it up for the movie. Then I decided that it must be a bunch of old, unused lyrics that Jackson had borrowed from her brother Michael. At the end of the movie, however, I discovered that every single word of verse had been written by Maya Angelou. Whoops."

Lane's "whoops" is shorthand for, "I've committed the sin of criticizing the work of a figure held in high esteem by an oppressed minority group." The "whoops" both pokes fun at and contributes to the problem. Obviously, the word is meant ironically, since by the time it appears, Lane has already, quite reasonably, decided to criticize Angelou. But ironic or not, it comes across as apology—mock remorse for having picked on someone not quite his own size. Thus with "whoops," Lane takes Angelou to task while at the same time denying her the respect that is usually the flip side of honest criticism. Angelou read her poem "On the Pulse of Morning" in 1993, at the inauguration of Bill Clinton. Commenting on it, the poet David Lehman said, "She read the poem very well. . . . But if you ask me as a poet to be as ruthless on this poem as I would be on any other, I would have to say it's not very memorable." Why would anyone be asking anything else? Because Angelou, as a black poet, is assumed to be held to a lesser standard?

To cite yet another example from the *New Yorker*, there is David Denby's take on Jonathan Demme's film *Beloved*, based on Toni Morrison's novel and produced by—and starring—Oprah Winfrey. "Part of one's dismay at the results is caused by the sure knowledge that everyone involved in this right-minded project . . . worked with an acute, even excruciating sense of responsibility," Denby wrote for the October 26/November 2, 1998 issue. "There's no gravy in attacking a woman [Winfrey] who has done so much to promote reading, but one can ask—can't one?—whether some novels shouldn't be left in peace as mere books, unredeemed by the movies." The novel *Beloved* is considered by many—including Denby, to judge from his review—to be a modern classic. Denby praised the book while lambasting the movie based on it. This is all that is necessary. So why call the film project "right-minded," as if Winfrey and company were engaging in charity by focusing attention on the work of the poor suffering Nobel laureate Morrison? (Were Demi Moore et al credited with "right-mindedness" when the screen adaptation of *The Scarlet Letter* was released?) And yes, one can ask whether some books should not be filmed. But one shouldn't. One should *say*, unapologetically, that some books should not be filmed, and whatever else one has to say.

But to return to the subject of "right-mindedness" for a moment: this term reminded me of when I first began to be aware of the phenomenon I am describing—in the mid-1980s, around the time I read the December 30, 1986 *Village Voice* review of the movie *Native Son*, based on Richard Wright's novel. The review was negative, but that did not stop J. Hoberman from writing that the white actor Matt Dillon "deserves some recognition for donating his image to a worthy project." One imagines Dillon dropping coins into Wright's wrinkled paper cup. Who would think, reading this, that *Native Son* is one of the most celebrated American novels of the twentieth century, that an actor benefits from its reflected glory and not the other way around?

Don't get me wrong. I admire the work of the above-mentioned writers and critics, particularly Rafferty, Lane, and Denby. Far from considering them racists, I believe that the passages I have quoted are the results, at worst, of a fear of appearing racist, and at best of a genuine desire not to offend. But I think they and others should resist the urge to tread gingerly when discussing the work of black artists, and should, in particular, refuse to be cowed by the mounting of these artists on pedestals, no matter by whom or for what reason. The results of this refusal could include wrongful charges of racism; but such are the risks of being an honest critic.

DON'T CRY FOR ME

ON MASKS

The Threepenny Review, 2010

I AM A BLACK American. For that reason I take pride—you can argue over whether I should or not—in the fact that Picasso found inspiration for his work in the African tribal masks he saw at the Musee de l'Homme in Paris in 1907. Picasso was taken with the masks' simplicity of form and, because he was a superstitious man, with their being intended to ward off evil. But while Picasso was inspired by the masks, and while the faces he painted could themselves be said to look like masks, his work performed the opposite function: not hiding but showing the person—revealing the subject not as a fixed entity but as its true, ever-changing, impermanent self. With the African masks, on the one hand, and Picasso's paintings, on the other, we have a dichotomy: masking versus unmasking.

Or do we? We think of masks as closing off identity, but often they serve, or are intended, to expand it. They can open doors for the self, give the wearer new ability. Some of the traditional masks made in Liberia and the Ivory Coast were meant to evoke a spirit called Gunyege; they were worn by foot racers to help them in competitions. In Central Africa masks were worn in rituals tied to boys' emergence into manhood. In Western culture, the most prominent setting for masks may be the pages of superhero comic books, in which the costumed characters use masks for much the same purpose as young Central African males: making the transition from relative weakness (boyhood) to strength (manhood). The retiring Bruce Wayne becomes the fearsome Batman; the milquetoast Clark Kent becomes the nearly invulnerable Superman. (Kent does not put on a literal mask, of course—his inexplicably successful disguise is a face without glasses.)

For those who don't read comics or believe in the power of a mask to speed a runner along, there are "real" examples. Here, the masks tend to be figurative. In his 1895 poem "We Wear the Mask," the black American poet Paul Laurence Dunbar writes, "We wear the mask that grins and lies, / It hides our cheeks and shades our eyes,—/ This debt we pay to human guile. . . . / We smile, but O great Christ, our cries / To thee from tortured souls arise . . ." The "we" refers to oppressed blacks a generation after the end of slavery, and the "mask" might not seem to be particularly empowering—until we consider that the "grins and lies" and "human guile" allowed blacks to survive in the world until the great unmasking that was the civil rights movement. Really, though, what Martin Luther King and others offered was more of a trading of masks: a person who submits without violence as fire hoses, police dogs, and clubs are used on him is wearing a mask of sorts, one that helps him win his freedom.

I wear masks—one, at least. For over a decade I have run a department in a privately owned company, a capacity in which I have supervised numerous workers not long out of college and thus unused to office life. A little over a year ago, as I lectured two young workers on the importance of punctuality, the serious looks on their faces made me laugh inside—since the lecture, as they had no way of knowing, came from a man who sees himself more or less as the five-year-old he was in the late 1960s. My self-perception notwithstanding, the boss-mask lets me run the department with some degree of effectiveness. It allows me to be a manager, which I have not always been. My identity is expanded.

Which in turn raises some questions. Whoever I consider the "real" me to be, for half of my waking hours I am an office worker. During that time, the mask is the self. My wife and children see more or less what I consider to be the real me, but individually they see slightly differing versions, and the three of them together are outnumbered by the dozens of people I've worked with over the years, people who saw a different man or men when they looked at me. So who am I in the world? A picture of the totality might look like one of Picasso's works, with each perspective, as valid as all the others, fighting for domination. To return for a moment to the super-heroes: in the second *Spider-Man* movie, the hero lies unconscious in a subway car, surrounded by people he has just saved. They peek under his mask, and one of them says, "He's just a kid." But in the world of the movie, he's not *just* a kid—he's also Spider-Man, which is the only reason everyone is standing around talking about him.

No visual art—not comics, not even the work of Picasso—can capture the self in the fullness of its complexity and contradiction, with masks on and off. But how glorious the attempt can be. I have a fantasy of a portrait: abstract or, at most, semi-representational, painted on a very large canvas. The artist would aspire at once to the fluidity of Jackson Pollock, the color-ful boldness of Wassily Kandinsky or Maurice de Vlaminck, and the som-ber blacks and whites of Willem deKooning. This artist would depict a grown man confidently charming a large crowd while he is also a six-year-old boy too shy to answer his teacher; show him yelling at the top of his lungs not *although* but *because* he knows he is guilty and wrong; show him getting wet but refusing to put up his umbrella, because if he were going to do that he should have done it already, it being silly to get wet and *then* put up an umbrella you held the whole time; show him reading to his chil-dren in an animated voice while mentally calculating what's about to come out of his checking account; show him, in short, doing the impossible, crazy human dance that each of us does every moment of every day.

NOTES ON NOTES

or

Plugged in at the Party of Art

The Threepenny Review, 2007

IF YOU WANTED to pick the number whose very sound best and most comically captures middle age in all its dust-bunny grayness, it would be hard to top the number of years I have been alive as of this writing: forty-three. Yes, forty-eight and fifty-six are older than forty-three, but somehow they just *sound* cooler. And I am living proof that forty-three is old enough for some of the less savory trappings of middle age: once-bionic eyes that now strain to make out what's on the nearest street sign; prescriptions for three—three!—different kinds of medication; and the nine-to-five schedule of the working stiff ("stiff" being an allusion to the state of my lower back). There are compensations, though. My wife and children come to mind. There is also a certain indifference to mass opinion, one that lets me, for example, do a couple of things casually that I wouldn't have dared do at all as a teenager: (1) dance and (2) wear shorts or swimming trunks that reveal the skinniest legs anyone has ever seen. And there is one benefit I couldn't have foreseen twenty years ago.

For the past few years I have kept a succession of notebooks in my right hip pocket. The notebook is there from the time I get dressed in the morning until I get undressed at night, whether I am sitting or standing, at work, at a funeral, or at the local flea market. (The notebook is usually a 3½ by 5½ inch, forty-eight-sheet Clairefontaine; I tried a Moleskine someone gave me, but the wear and tear reduced it to shreds within five months, and the Clairefontaines hold up for the six to ten months it takes me to fill them.) The notebooks are repositories for the titles of books, records, and films that I read or hear about and want to investigate. (There's also usually a page devoted to my blood-pressure readings, but enough about that stuff already.) The notebooks are less important than what they signify, which is a thing I feel more and more as I age and wish I'd had more of when I was younger: curiosity—a feverish desire to learn, particularly about the arts. When I'm feeling "plugged in," as I like to call it—and I feel that way very often—I can forget that I am not a twenty-year-old, newly minted adult waking up to the wonders of the world.

Of course, the world, even the world of the arts, is an awfully big place. One person, even if that person's name is Harold Bloom, Susan Sontag, or Cornel West, can learn only so much, and only so much at a time—and if you open yourself to everything, the sheer amount of *stuff* out there can lead you beyond exhilaration into bewilderment.

As for the solution, I came across an eloquent expression of it—actually, two—in my job. I come across many things in my job. I am the editor of a magazine of biographical articles, which appears eleven times a year; the biographees are living people in a wide variety of fields. Most months, reading over the proofs of the articles, I am struck by connections between and among people who would seem to have little in common. One of the issues, for example, included articles on the theologian Stanley Hauerwas and the nonfiction writer Susan Orlean, two people whose ideas, you might think, wouldn't necessarily intersect much. But here is the surprisingly salty-tongued Hauerwas talking in an on-line interview about religion: "Being a Christian gives you something to *do*. It means your life is not just one goddamned thing after another." And here is Orlean writing in her book *The*

Orchid Thief: "[T]he reason it matters to care passionately about something is that it whittles the world down to a more manageable size. It makes the world seem not huge and empty but full of possibility."

What have been my tools for "whittling the world down" are my passions for learning about (in no special order) books, jazz, and film. Living in a world where I can immerse myself in these things is like being at an ongoing party, to which all trumpeters, novelists, cinematographers, directors, essayists, and saxophonists, great and minor, have been invited. Some of the guests turn out to be more interesting than others, but that's a party for you. The notebook helps here. Several years ago I read (for my job) an article about the writer Andrea Lee, which quoted her as saying that her "favorite book of all time" is Mikhail Bulgakov's *The Master and Margarita*. Into the notebook it went. As sometimes happens, I transferred that information from notebook to notebook until, having written it down two or three times without reading the book, I concluded that I never would, and stopped the transfers. Then—three weeks before this writing—I was in the Strand bookstore, at 12th Street and Broadway in New York, when I overheard two men talking. "I was on the subway and saw a guy reading *The Master and Margarita*," one of them said. "So I checked it out. I couldn't put it down." The Strand didn't have a copy that day, but back in the notebook it went . . .

A month or so ago I bought a jazz CD called *Boss Tenor*, a 1960 recording by the saxophonist Gene Ammons. The writer of the liner notes, Leroi Jones (who was not yet Amiri Baraka), listed some of the saxmen who were influenced by either Coleman Hawkins or Lester Young (whereas Ammons had synthesized the influences of both, in Jones's view). Among the names mentioned were Ike Quebec and Wardell Gray. Now, I prided myself on being able to recognize, blindfolded, sax solos by Hawkins or Young, or Benny Carter or Ben Webster or Charlie Parker or Johnny Hodges, or even such slightly lesser lights as Charlie Rouse or Don Byas—but Ike Quebec? Wardell Gray? *Who?* Into the notebook went their names, and off I went, to the Virgin Megastore at Union Square . . .

Last winter I picked up Phillip Lopate's *Totally, Tenderly, Tragically*, practically a one-book course on great films—one that I almost couldn't read for writing down movie titles in my notebook, many of them works by Japanese directors I didn't know: Yasujiro Ozu, Mikio Naruse, Kenji Mizoguchi . . .

In this state of being plugged in, I enjoy each book, film, and record for itself, but what truly fascinates me, and what I hope for with everything I read, watch, or put on my stereo, is a work's connection to something else. I have coined a word for this: *plugdinism*. It occurred to me as I listened to the music of the bassist-composer Charles Mingus, for example, that it bears similarities to the films of Robert Altman: that the films, with their many characters crowded into a single shot and their simultaneous conversations, might be mere exercises in cacophony but are instead works of power and beauty—pulling off a feat similar to that accomplished by Mingus's polyphonous compositions. In another example, it seemed to me that New Journalism, as practiced by Tom Wolfe, has features in common with a musical movement that came along at roughly the same time: Free Jazz, as ushered in by the saxophonist Ornette Coleman. The decidedly eccentric Coleman, instead of tossing out songs' original melodies and playing new ones based on existing chord progressions, as had the groundbreaking Charlie Parker before him, based his melodies on his individual response to the totality of a piece of music—lending even more freedom to an art form already characterized by improvisation. Similarly, Wolfe, in his essays and nonfictions books, is not bound by point of view, shifting between his own and that of his subjects to marvelous overall effect. These connections make the party of art feel smaller, more intimate to me, while adding new dimension to the things in it.

Recently I've tried to expand my focus, just a little. On the same day as the overheard conversation in the Strand bookstore, I went to the Guggenheim to see an exhibit of Jackson Pollock's drawings. The entry in my notebook from when I stood in front of Pollock's "Untitled, 1943" refers to the "simultaneity" the drawing has in common with Charlie Parker's music. For better or worse, I can't remember what I meant by that. Maybe, though, there is a link to be found between the works of those two self-destructive artists, who both died in the mid-1950s. Maybe I will find it. I have time. I'm only forty-three.

PART TWO

ON THE PAGE

ALMOST THERE

The Novels of Colson Whitehead

The Threepenny Review, 2002

THE YOUNG NOVELIST Colson Whitehead has emerged as a kind of mad literary geneticist, conducting experiments with genre that are, if not wholly successful, then exceedingly interesting. *The Intuitionist* (1999), his debut, shares DNA with a disparate set of books. Its reveling in the workings of the mundane echoes the so-called novels of Nicholson Baker ("so-called" referring not to their quality but to their place on the fringe of the novel form). One of *The Intuitionist*'s characters, a light-skinned black man passing for white, can find ancestors in works including William Wells Brown's 1853 work *Clotel* (the first novel published by a black American), Charles Chesnutt's 1900 novel *The House Behind the Cedars*, and James Weldon Johnson's *The Autobiography of an Ex-Coloured Man*, from 1912. (Not to mention a contemporary in Philip Roth's 2000 book *The Human Stain*.) And then there is the dominant gene in this pool: the detective story.

The Intuitionist concerns Lila Mae Watson, the second black person— and the first black woman—to become an elevator inspector. The novel's setting is unspecified, though the city almost has to be New York, given certain clues, and the time seems to be roughly the middle of the twentieth century (it is definitely before the advent of touch-tone phones). The world of elevator inspectors, we learn, is composed of two mutually exclusive, mutually antagonistic groups: the Empiricists, who perform their jobs through exhaustive review of elevators' mechanical workings; and the Intuitionists, whose technical knowledge, while thorough, serves merely as a point of departure for their sensing of elevators' well-being or lack thereof. Lila Mae, an Intuitionist, must clear her name after the crash of an elevator she has inspected, an occurrence that may have been the doing of the Empiricist, mob-connected head of the Department of Elevator Inspectors. Meanwhile, someone has been anonymously circulating fragments of a design by the deceased founder of the school of Intuitionism—plans that hint at a blueprint for the perfect elevator.

A joke central to *The Intuitionist* is the emotion the characters feel over the dry details of elevator inspection. More subtly humorous is the tension Whitehead creates between his technically informed passages on elevators, on the one hand, and on the other the school of Intuitionism, which—as embodied by Lila Mae—is almost certainly an allusion to black people's perceived inclination toward nature and emotion rather than intellect. (A less subtle joke is the part that elevators play in racial uplift. Tee hee.) But the dichotomy between the technical and the sensory, once established, has no place in particular to go, and the same is true for the passing-for-white theme; the novel's mystery element thus overrides everything else in the end. All the same, how many mystery novels not written by Raymond Chandler can boast writing like this?: "Pompey looks down, scowls and clenches his sons' shoulders. In unison their heads incline toward his hands, a common response to shoulder pinching, Lila Mae has noticed, instinct ushered in aeons ago by the opposable thumb of some slope-browed hominid patriarch."

In *The Intuitionist* the above-mentioned Pompey describes the difficulty inherent in being the first black person to do something, whatever that something is. In his second novel, Whitehead in a sense circumvents that issue, by focusing not on the first black this or that but on an American prototype who is himself black: the mythical steel-drivin' man John Henry.

John Henry. To wax personal for a bit: as an elementary-school student in the mid-1970s, I sang the version of the John Henry ballad that was in our music books—each line belted out by half the class and then echoed by the other half. ("O John Henry / told his captain / Well a man's got to / act like a man / and before / steam drill beats me / I will die / hammer in my hand.") We were all black, my classmates and I. As I got closer to adulthood, I realized that many of the icons our community held dear meant much more to us than to the larger American society; I'll never forget, for example, meeting kids at the mostly white college I attended who had never heard of James Brown. Eventually I came to expect this to be the case. And so I was surprised when one evening during my college years, or possibly later, as I was watching a TV sitcom with an all-white cast, one of the characters made a reference to John Henry. That was when I learned that the man I had sung about as a sixth-grader was not just the property of the black community; he was a legend embraced by all of America.

With *John Henry Days* (2001), Whitehead ups the ante not just with his decision to take on a national myth, but with his approach. The novel contrasts the story of John Henry, whose heart gave out after he won the contest with the steam drill, with that of J. Sutter, a hack journalist trying to beat the record for consecutive junketeering—an endeavor that lands him at a small-town celebration of John Henry in 1996. In drawing parallels between a mythic figure and a modern-day schlub, Whitehead follows the example of another novelist: one James Joyce, author of *Ulysses*. (There is even a Cyclops in *John Henry Days*—a patch-wearing journalist by the name of One Eye.) What saves this from being merely a cute idea is that Whitehead puts a black American spin on the Joycean model, "black" because of John Henry and "American" because of the structure of the book.

In *The Beer Can by the Highway*, John Kouwenhoven's 1961 work on the Americanness of American culture, the author notes the repeatability of many of the things born in the USA. Chewing gum: you can continue chewing it until your jaws ache. Jazz: the band can go on playing a number until the last soloist has keeled over dead. Skyscrapers: they can just keep going up. Similarly, like a magician with an endless supply of rabbits in his hat, Whitehead presents character after character with some connection—however tenuous—to John Henry. There is the Tin Pan Alley songwriter who composes a ditty about John Henry; the black scholar who journeys to a small, racist town, putatively the home of John Henry, to do his research; Paul Robeson, preparing to play John Henry on Broadway; the young woman reluctantly thinking of selling her late father's collection of John Henry memorabilia, which he assembled while growing more and more distant from his family; and several others. Whitehead gives you the feeling he could just keep going, though by the end no angle seems to be missing.

Missing, however, are descriptions of the novel's key events (including the steel-driving contest), which occur off-stage. This is not laziness on Whitehead's part; rather, it is his way of (1) commenting on the unknowable nature of human events, historical or otherwise, and (2) making the point that in our society, facts themselves are less important than what the consumer culture, and individuals, consider them to be. Consumer culture, indeed; by the time publicity machines and the masses have finished feeding on a person or a thing, the original is either unrecognizable or lost altogether. (Bobby Figgis, the holder of the junketeering record J. Sutter tries to break, ended his streak by simply disappearing one day, having been "devoured by pop.") *John Henry Days* begins with correspondence from anonymous individuals who all claim knowledge of the real John Henry, each letter contradicting all of the others. From this point of view, the individuals are the ones who matter; John Henry is almost beside the point.

What ultimately prevents this approach from succeeding is that the individual to whom Whitehead devotes the most attention, J. Sutter, is less a character than a set of clever observations, none of which provides many clues as to what makes him tick. The decidedly unheroic Leopold Bloom of *Ulysses* is made sympathetic by his love for his unfaithful wife and his grieving for his dead son; even Lila Mae Watson of *The Intuitionist*, herself a sketchily rendered character, cares about elevators, if little else that we can see. But it is difficult to say what animates J., beyond the possibility of breaking the junketeering record—and he pursues even that dubious distinction only after realizing that he's well on his way there already. As a result, the ending of *John Henry Days* is not only ambiguous; it is unimportant.

On the other hand, getting to it is certainly fun. Its shortcomings aside, *John Henry Days* contains many passages that may leave the reader open-mouthed at their virtuosity. Whitehead's description of an infamous Rolling Stones concert and his dissection of a small-town fair are self-contained masterworks. And some of his sentences are literary versions of bebop solos, making wild, impossibly quick side trips in the course of a longer journey. There is this take on late-night, crack-addicted frequenters of a bodega in a dicey Brooklyn neighborhood: "Those dynamic men on the flying trapeze, Gordy and Morty, who zoom on leave from gravity through alkaloid extracted from cocoa leaves, death defying, without a net worth, falling to earth only at dawn, when this team is too exhausted to perform any trick except attempting sleep while wired to the limits of human endurance." Or this observation of an interaction at a book-publishing party: "The recently liposucked found their palms falling farther than usual to pat new and improved thighs and at this sensation their eyes widened in astonishment, which was taken for animated interest by the food critic, who continued to describe Chef Jean-Phillipe's cassoulet."

I am not alone, I suspect, in preferring interesting, flawed novels to seamless pieces of hackwork. One of these days, Whitehead, who was born in 1969, will perform an experiment that succeeds in full—perhaps when he applies to the human psyche his penchant for dissection. When that day comes, he will produce a novel for the ages.

★   ★   ★   ★   ★

2009 addendum, from tellcliff.com:
Sag Harbor is not that novel (neither is the very fine *Apex Hides the Hurt*), but it represents a step toward it. The book is set in 1985 in the Hamptons vacation spot of the title, a summer oasis for several generations of middle-

and upper-middle-class blacks. *Sag Harbor* has the feel of Whitehead's most autobiographical novel to date, and not just because it is his first to be written in first person: the narrator, fifteen-year-old Benji, spends his school year in a predominantly white setting and his summers among "the folk," a cultural balancing act that Whitehead writes about with the humor and insight of the experienced.

As for the psyche, he depicts—rather, suggests—the psychological damage inflicted on Benji's family by his father, who is abusive when he's drunk and sometimes when he's not. Like Hemingway, Whitehead makes you feel the pain more by not describing it; it's the literary equivalent of stubbing your toe without being able to yell and hop around afterward.

But mostly the novel is about the events of a summer, or of summers. About halfway through, just when I had concluded that *Sag Harbor* was Whitehead's most ill-constructed novel to date, with nary a plot in sight, it hit me: that's the point. Whose childhood summers ever had plots? They were simply one event or non-event after another—with that overlay, that interweaving of pleasant purposelessness and subtle magic, that defines summer in our memories. With *Sag Harbor* Whitehead gives us a summer in miniature. No mean feat.

RETURN OF THE MARKSMAN

Ralph Ellison's *Juneteenth*

The Threepenny Review, 2000

THERE IS A possibility that had Ralph Ellison lived to see the publication of his second novel, had the decisions about its contents been his alone, the present sense of letdown would have been averted. The possibility is remote, though. Ellison created in *Invisible Man* (1952) a superbly written, well-paced, penetrating commentary on American society as a whole and the nation's racial situation in particular. The nearly five decades that passed between the publication dates of Ellison's first and second novels created delirious expectations among his fans, many of whom (myself included) were born after 1952. Ellison's two, brilliant essay collections, *Shadow and Act* (1964) and *Going to the Territory* (1986), did not fulfill the longing of this crowd, nor did *Flying Home* (1996), the book of apprentice stories published two years after the author's death. It was a novel they wanted; their hunger was unabated, and probably unsatisfiable.

Ellison's slim chances of overcoming the burden of expectation were nullified not only by his death, but by the fact that the work he left behind was, for all its mass, unfinished. Perhaps, as has been speculated, it was simple fear of sophomore slump that kept him at work on the second book so long. (Surely the fire that consumed much of the manuscript in the 1960s was not the whole explanation.) Whatever the reason, Ellison's literary executor, John F. Callahan, was left with a manuscript that, if he is to be believed (and why not?), was both more and less than a novel—ambitious but amorphous, thrown off balance by long, long tangents that ultimately added little to the heart of the story. Callahan faced a tough choice: publish what was not really a novel, or whittle it down and rearrange it until it *was* a novel, albeit one less than half its original length, and not necessarily the book Ellison himself would have wanted to publish. Callahan took the controversial second route. If he faced a no-win situation, then so do Ellison's fans. It is maddening to pick up *Juneteenth* without the certainty that its title and contents are what Ellison had in mind. And yet can we, in the end, not pick it up? Even if we cannot be one hundred percent sure of the point at which Ellison the novelist ultimately arrived, can we resist having as educated an opinion as possible (at least until the scholar's edition comes out)?*

As the narrator of *Invisible Man* discovered, there is a certain liberation that comes with a no-win situation; with no path before us that is decidedly better, we are free to evaluate *Juneteenth*, both on its own merits and as a companion to *Invisible Man*.

To do so, it is helpful to take another look at the first novel. The unnamed narrator of *Invisible Man* is a young black male who makes a journey from South to North, from being a follower of others' beliefs to being an existentialist loner, from a normal if naïve state to a state of arguable madness, the result of being stripped of the illusions that most normal people need just to make it through the day. The novel is largely concerned with race and racism, but while other books tackling this theme tend more often to accent the cruelty and degradation involved in racial oppression, *Invisible Man* evokes the quality that is less obvious but equally abundant in, perhaps central to, racist societies: absurdity. Ellison's narrator finds himself

*Three Days Before the Shooting . . . , 2011

performing actions that are outdone in their craziness only by the situations that have made them necessary. Thus does The Invisible Man (let's call him Tim), as a college-bound youth, participate blindfolded with other black males in a free-for-all, for the entertainment of his segregated town's white businessmen; shortly afterward, for the same crowd, he recites his high-school graduation speech, which he can barely deliver for all the blood in his mouth. The reader, while appalled, feels at a comfortable distance from this poor boy, who must blind himself—literally and otherwise—to the insanity infecting his own life, in order to make it through that life without going mad himself. But the reader feels this distance between herself and Tim only as long as it takes her to ask, "What am I willfully blind to?" At this moment, Ellison's joke is sprung, the timelessness of his themes revealed.

Tim is compensated for his degradation with a scholarship to a southern black college, unnamed but clearly modeled on Booker T. Washington's Tuskegee Institute, where Ellison himself spent three years. Here, Tim's teachers stress the philosophy of "Negro" advancement via hard work, humility, and lack of (overt) antagonism toward whites. These are notions that Tim already held, beliefs that allowed him, for example, to participate in the free-for-all. The course of action this philosophy calls for, though not the philosophy itself, was advocated in Tim's childhood by his grandfather, who confused the boy by advising him to "overcome 'em [whites] with yeses, undermine 'em with grins, agree 'em to death and destruction, let 'em swoller you till they vomit or bust wide open."

Tim is happy at the college, whose values he has swallowed whole, until the day he is entrusted with the job of chauffeuring one of the college's aging white trustees around the town. The trustee, Norton, insists on seeing unfamiliar sights, and so it is that Tim and Norton stumble onto the farm of Jim Trueblood, a black man who proceeds to tell Norton the ludicrous story of how he impregnated both his wife and his daughter. The story proves too much for Norton's delicate constitution, and in his state of wavering consciousness he asks for an alcoholic drink to help buck him up. The only way Tim knows to get one is to go to the Golden Day, a bar/ brothel that, on the days when it is visited by a group of shellshocked black war veterans, doubles as a loony bin. It is on one such day that Tim and Norton arrive there; the events in which they get caught up are outrageous even by the Golden Day's standards, and it is all Tim can do to get Norton out of there alive.

While Norton does not blame Tim for their bizarre afternoon, the college president, Dr. Bledsoe, certainly does. For in the view of Bledsoe—who can be as cruel to other blacks as he is obsequious around whites—Tim has violated a rule so crucial and obvious as to be unspoken, which is that you never, *ever* show the "bad" face of the race to a white person, particularly a kind and influential one. The images of Jim Trueblood and the Golden Day must not be allowed to linger uncountered in Norton's subconscious; corrective action must be taken. Tim, who aspires to Bledsoe's career path, receives as punishment the thing he fears most in the world: expulsion. But Bledsoe offers a ray of hope, in the form of sealed letters of "recommendation" for jobs in New York City. If Tim lands one of the jobs and earns enough money for his last year of college, maybe, just maybe, he will be allowed to return. Only after the irrepressibly optimistic Tim has arrived in Harlem does he discover that the letters are meant to do anything but help him, that his college career is over for good.

In New York, when he stumbles upon an old black couple who are being evicted from their apartment, Tim makes a spontaneous, semi-coherent but impassioned speech that stirs the gathering crowd. He is overheard by, and recruited as a spokesman for, the Brotherhood—a Communist-flavored, white-run but ostensibly color-blind organization whose views Tim comes to internalize as completely as he once accepted Bledsoe's. He discovers, much too late, that the Brotherhood views him not as a person but as a pawn in its reprehensible plan. His humanity and that of other blacks is as "invisible" to them as it has been to the rest of America, where people encountering him see primarily what they need, or have been conditioned, to see.

ELLISON STRESSED REPEATEDLY, in his essays and speeches, the idea that black Americans are inextricably tied to the larger American society (and vice versa) by a common culture, no matter how little either group wants to acknowledge it. (If that seems an innocuous position, it was taken at no small cost to Ellison's reputation among black radicals of the 1960s and 1970s.) For Ellison, America was composed of many separate but interwoven strands, which helped to define each other as well as the nation. "American culture is of a whole," Ellison once wrote in a letter, and he advanced this notion with sly touches in *Invisible Man*. In the underground lair to which Tim is finally driven, and from which he narrates the story, he installs more than a thousand lights—because "Light [read 'whiteness'] confirms my reality, gives birth to my form." After he arrives in New York, but before he is recruited by the Brotherhood, he works for a brief time at a plant that makes paint "as white as George Washington's Sunday-go-to-meetin' wig"—using a black substance that makes the paint appear gleaming white to everyone else in the factory but gray to Tim. For Ellison, the intersection of separate strands in America was a dynamic process, one that made manifest the nearly limitless nature of human possibility; and he believed that the system of American democracy, for all our failure to put it fully into practice, was particularly well equipped to realize this possibility, in all its horror and wonder. In the Epilogue to *Invisible Man*, the narrator, sadder but wiser, having largely spent his anger by telling his story, is ready to embrace this idea. He recalls the advice of his grandfather to "overcome 'em with yeses," and he wonders,

> Did he mean say "yes" because he knew that the principle was greater than the men, greater than the numbers and the vicious power and all the methods used to corrupt its name? Did he mean to affirm the principle, which they themselves had dreamed into being out of the chaos and darkness of the feudal past, and which they had violated and compromised to the point of absurdity even in their own corrupt minds? Or did he mean that we had to take the responsibility for all of it, for the men as well as the principle, because we were the heirs who must use the principle because no other fitted our needs?

Rereading *Invisible Man* recently, I thought of a sequence in the 1987 film *The Untouchables*, in which the sharpshooter-cop played by Andy Garcia trades gunfire with a criminal who uses an innocent bystander as a shield.

In the heat of a seemingly impossible situation, the Garcia character takes careful aim and fires—leaving the innocent man shaken but alive, while the criminal, with a bullet in his head, sinks slowly to the floor. This is part of the feat that Ellison pulled off with *Invisible Man*: the preserving of the American ideal along with the blasting of bigots and other small-minded and unseeing people who have corrupted it.

FAST-FORWARD FORTY-SEVEN years, to the publication of *Juneteenth*, a novel in some ways less successful and in others more so than *Invisible Man*. The earlier book, for all its power and wit, has as its protagonist a cipher, a character defined primarily by the injustices visited upon him; neither weak nor stupid, he stands up for himself quite capably when he fully understands the forces operating against him, but those occasions are few. That is, of course, part of the design of the book. But one result is that Tim is in a way as invisible to the reader as he is to the Brotherhood. He is less a fully rounded character than a device, albeit one with an engaging voice and a fascinating story to tell. When he sits down with a newspaper, which section does he turn to first? If he had a pet, would it be a cat or a dog? Hard to say. But *Juneteenth* has at least one three-dimensional character, in Reverend Alonzo Hickman.

It is the 1950s, and Hickman, a black man getting on in years, "tall and broad and of an easy dignity," has come to Washington, DC, with members of his congregation to deliver an urgent message to US Senator Adam Sunraider. The group is not allowed to see the senator, however, and so Hickman watches helplessly as Sunraider—after having made one of his characteristic racial slurs—is shot on the floor of the Senate. During the events that follow, Hickman is able to establish his connection to Sunraider and is allowed to sit by him in his hospital room. Here, the two men's on-again, off-again conversation and separate inner monologues reveal their pasts and their relationship to each other.

It turns out that Hickman adopted and raised the senator back when he was known as Bliss, a boy of uncertain racial lineage light enough to pass for white. Unlike *Invisible Man*, with its straight chronological narrative, *Juneteenth* moves back and forth in time, circling but never explicitly identifying what turned Bliss—the boy preacher reared in the bosom of a southern black community—into the racist demagogue Sunraider. Unless it has to do with what transpired during one Juneteenth celebration when Bliss was a boy. (The celebration is in honor of the day in 1865 when Union troops walked into Galveston, Texas, and told the blacks there, over two years after the Emancipation, that they were free.) In the middle of the celebration/prayer meeting, a crazed white woman tries to snatch Bliss away, claiming that he is her child. ("Son raider.") She does not succeed, but her act plants in Bliss the seed of longing for his real mother, of whom he knows nothing. His longing is increased when Hickman exposes him to the new medium of film—taking him to the movies so that he can get a taste of the worldly devilment against which he will one day preach; on the screen is an actress Bliss mistakes for the crazed woman, whose claim he is not emotionally able to dismiss. (These events apparently inspire Bliss's pre-Senate career as a filmmaker.) As Ellison was no doubt aware, Bliss's yearning mirrors many black Americans' longing for connectedness to "Mother" Africa. His eventual rejection of blacks is akin to some blacks' rejection of all things white in their quest for a link to their past.

Christian motifs abound in *Juneteenth*. Bliss is Christlike in that he is the product of no sexual union that anyone (except Hickman) knows anything about; he is also looked to initially as a kind of savior: Hickman speaks of "the hope that a little gifted child would speak for our condition from inside the only acceptable mask. That he would embody our spirit in the councils of our enemies—but, oh, what a foolish miscalculation!" For, as Hickman is forced to conclude, in a passage that would not have been out of place in *Invisible Man*: "We just couldn't get around the hard fact that for a hope or an idea to become real it has to be embodied in a man, and men change and have wills and wear masks."

Through all of this, from the days of Bliss's boyhood to his years of demagoguery to the shooting, Hickman emerges as a powerfully human figure. His pain and bewilderment over Bliss's betrayal are palpable; his capacity for forgiveness and truth-seeking—the result not of weakness but of enormous strength—are genuinely moving. And so Hickman's distress over the moral fall of the supposed upholders of the American ideal seems more firmly grounded in human feeling than does The Invisible Man's lament over "the vicious power and all the methods used to corrupt" the idea of democracy.

Finally, the prose in *Juneteenth* is by and large marked by a greater lyricism than that in *Invisible Man*, as in this passage:

> But what a feeling can come over a man just from seeing the things he believes in and hopes for symbolized in the concrete form of a man. In something that gives a focus to all the other things he knows to be real. Something that makes unseen things manifest and allows him to come to his hopes and dreams through his outer eye and through the touch and feel of his natural hand. That's the dangerous shape, the graven image we were warned about, the one that makes it possible for him to hear his inner hopes sound and sing and see them soar up and take wing before his half-believing eyes. Faith in the Lord and Master is easy compared to having faith in the goodness of man.

The specificity of *Juneteenth* is its virtue, but it is also what makes it fall far short of *Invisible Man* in its scope and in its power to define our times—to capture for our current era, as the earlier book did for its own time, both the moral crisis at the heart of, and the beauty inherent in, America. Maybe, coming in at a full two hundred pages shorter than its predecessor, *Juneteenth* is simply not a big enough book for that; maybe the gargantuan novel Ellison might've finally pulled together, had he lived, would have done the job. Maybe. The frustrating thing is that we will never know. But the anticlimax that the publication of *Juneteenth* represents is actually the kind of joke that Ellison appreciated; like the cruel trick played on The Invisible Man by Dr. Bledsoe, it is a disappointment that may ultimately be edifying. The longing for a second Ellison novel was in part a desire for him to make sense for us of the current state of the American experiment, just as he did in the 1950s. The great Ellison's ultimate failure to do so, to fit between the covers of a book all that we are, is indicative of at least two things: the monumental nature of the task; and the possibility that at the dawn of the twenty-first century, the defining of America is not, if it ever was, a job one writer can do alone.

DOUBLE AGENT

Two Novels by Paul Beatty

THE CELEBRATION OF America as a multicultural nation, a "gorgeous mosaic," can come across as a butt in search of a joke. This is because of the denial it can suggest, a perceived sunniness in the face of the fact that opportunity is spread unevenly among the various peoples making up the United States of America. A novelist who celebrates American multiculturalism must therefore do so under cover of darkness ("darkness" in more than one sense) if he or she is to avoid accusations of earnestness or naïveté. Paul Beatty, in his comic novels *The White Boy Shuffle* (1996) and *Tuff* (2000), has shown the necessary spy credentials to do the job; indeed, he operates as a double agent, so skillfully that it is at times difficult to tell which side he is on.

The White Boy Shuffle is narrated by Gunnar Kaufman, who grows up with his sisters in Santa Monica, California, where they are just about the only blacks they know. Life there is good, as far as they are concerned; any racism on the part of their peers or teachers is either covert or unintended and is, in either case, subtle. The only hardship of which Gunnar is aware has to do with his father, Rölf Kaufman, a policeman, who is separated from Gunnar's mother and sees the boy only occasionally. Rölf Kaufman manages to be both black people's and white people's nightmare version of a black man: deferential to the point of obsequiousness around whites (in other words, an "Uncle Tom"—for some, just his being a policeman would prove this), he has also been a drunken molester of his son. This difficulty of which Gunnar is aware no doubt contributes to one of which he is not, at least not entirely: his belief in black people's inferiority. Recalling a night spent at the home of his friend David, for example, he says on the subject of brushing his teeth: "I, like most folks, wet my brush, then put on the toothpaste, but I copied [David] because he was white and I figured maybe I was doing it wrong." In thinking this way, Gunnar follows in the footsteps of his paternal ancestors, "a long cowardly queue of coons, Uncle Toms, and faithful boogedy-boogedy retainers," whose exploits are related to Gunnar and his sisters with peculiar relish by their formidable mother, Brenda. ("There is nothing worse than a loud griot," Gunnar tells us, "and my mother was the loudest.") Whether or not Brenda Kaufman has worsened her children's already dim view of their race, she is shocked when that view makes itself heard: on the day she raises the possibility of their going to an all-black summer day camp, Gunnar and his sisters reject the idea, "because they're different from us." Mortified, deciding that her children need to be around and appreciate people who look like them, Brenda moves the family to the poor, black-and-Hispanic L.A. community of Hillside.

There, Gunnar falls prey to neighborhood bullies, including a pair of pre-adolescent girls named, hilariously, Betty and Veronica; unintentionally befriends Psycho Loco, the leader of the Gun Totin' Hooligans, and finds himself—literally—along for the ride during the Hooligans' nights of gang-banging; discovers a soul mate, Nick Scoby, a jazz fan and basketball player who never misses a shot; and also discovers, through his friendship with Scoby, his own talent for basketball (especially after he grows to six-foot-three). In other words, Gunnar settles into much of what society expects from a young black male. The difference is that in an environment that does not encourage learning, where, in the schools, "many kids, no matter how well dressed, didn't have notebooks," Gunnar—whose most impressionable years were spent in a very different place—not only reads: he devours the likes of Kant, Hegel, and Homer. Finally, Gunnar begins to write poetry, and the title of his first poem, "Negro Misappropriations of Greek Poetry, or, I Know Niggers That'll Kick Hercules' Ass," tips Beatty's hand.

In Gunnar Kaufman, that is, Beatty has created a multicultural Superman, a strange being from another world who blends in with his adopted community, does what they do (in this case, basketball) better than they do it, and also brings with him the unusual powers of the other world. Better yet, he is the ideal immigrant, fitting into the new country while adding something uniquely his own—the old river-fed-by-many-streams model. As a diversity of cultures supposedly makes a stronger nation, so do the various influences on Gunnar make him into a cultural superhero. (By novel's end he has fathered a half-Japanese baby. And what kind of black man's name is Gunnar Kaufman, anyway?) As the novel progresses, it begins to seem that there is little that SuperGunnar cannot do. His volume of poetry, *Watermelanin*, is published to much excitement; he gains fame as a basketball player. He goes east to college, where his renown precedes him and where, with the race consciousness he has developed, he becomes a political force. As for the aforementioned cover of darkness under which Beatty celebrates the idea of a multicultural America: while giving a speech at a political rally, Gunnar ad-libs his way into advocating the suicide of black people. When the media seizes on his words, he stands behind them, adopting the line that racial equality is an unreachable goal, that the attempts to attain it are sad and futile, and that the best way for blacks to preserve their dignity and avoid insanity is to end it all.

The White Boy Shuffle is a very funny novel; it had better be, given the suicide element, or reading it would be the literary equivalent of drinking cod liver oil. In the end, though, the humor either fails to save the novel, or turns out to be the thing from which it needs saving. Scoby takes Gunnar up on the suicide challenge; Gunnar in no way indicates that he feels re-

sponsible for, or even particularly sad over, his friend's death. If this is supposed to be funny—and even dark humor must be humorous—it isn't. But
if we are to take it seriously, then we must conclude that we are reading
about a jerk; and while some of us don't necessarily object to reading
about jerks or flat-out reprobates, we tend to want to know why.

So where is the evidence that Beatty is using a dark plot to disguise his
celebration of multiculturalism, rather than the reverse—putting a multicultural hero in the service of telling a dark story? True, a novel in which
the narrator calls for the suicide of twelve percent of the population might
not seem, on its surface, to be a hymn to the idea of the melting pot. But
sometimes the thing being said is less important than *how* it is said. Gunnar
peppers his narrative with one- and two-liners whose speed in referring to
one culture and then to another, seemingly distant one—or in moving
from a point in "high" culture to what Dwight Macdonald called "Mass-
cult"—can cause the head to spin, the pulse to quicken, and laughter to
ensue: "I raised the back of my left hand to my chin and wiggled my
fingers, giving him the high sign popularized by Stymie and Alfalfa in the
Our Gang comedies. I felt I was speaking a sort of gangland Esperanto. . . .";
"To me *Star Trek* was little more than the *Federalist Papers* with warp drives
and phasers"; "Then there were the bands of bored Bedouins who roamed
Hillside, silently testing my resolve by lifting their T-shirts, revealing a bel-
lybutton and a handgun tucked in their waistband. 'S'up, nigger?' In response I'd lift my T-shirt and flash my weapons: a paperback copy of Audre
Lorde or Sterling Brown and a checkerboard set of abdominal muscles.
'You niggers ain't hard—calculus is hard'"; "Listening to teens who've been
no closer to England than the Monty Python show saying, 'Blimey, Oy-ive
gowht a blooming 'edache' will bring any Negro with a shred of self-respect
to tears."

Perhaps the most convincing evidence of all is found not in *The White
Boy Shuffle* but in the continuation of its themes in Beatty's more-success-
ful follow-up novel. *Tuff*, told in the third person, has as its main character
Winston "Tuffy" Foshay. Like Gunnar, Tuffy represents a very American

idea of self-reinvention, with one major difference: while Gunnar hails from mainstream America and moves to the black ghetto before transcending both scenes, Tuffy attempts the opposite, seeking to rise above the limitations placed on him by life in East Harlem. Tuffy is a physically imposing young man, an enforcer for drug dealers who, when we are introduced to him, has just narrowly escaped being shot to death along with his confreres. Deciding to follow a new path, but uncertain about what it will be, Tuffy—already a husband and the father of a year-old son—seeks a Big Brother, an "educated motherfucker who'll provide me with some focus and guidance and shit," as he explains. This person turns out to be a black rabbi, Spencer Throckmorton, who, as drawn rather contemptuously by Beatty, is indistinguishable from Dick Clark in terms of his cultural sensibilities—who, in other words, does not seem to have taken notice of his own skin color—and who has ulterior motives for hooking up with Tuffy: he wants to write about him. (Spencer suggests a Gunnar who never made it out of Santa Monica.) Also in Tuffy's corner are Inez Nomura, a middle-aged, Japanese-born community activist, and (nominally, at least) Tuffy's father, Clifford, a blowhard poet and former 1960s radical. Spencer, Inez, and Clifford give varying levels of support to Tuffy's quixotic new career plan: running for city council.

If Gunnar Kaufman is Superman, then Tuffy is a Marvel Comics hero, powerful but vulnerable, too. There is no one in his neighborhood Tuffy cannot beat up when the mood hits, which it rather frequently does—but never without a reason; Tuffy is essentially good-natured. He also has, in spite of his having dropped out of high school, decidedly intellectual leanings, attending showings of foreign films ranging from the classic to the obscure, sometimes dragging reluctant friends along. His blind stabs at the life of the mind are endearing, his efforts to transcend the severe limits of his environment touching. Those limits help reveal two things: as we watch Tuffy move through the East Harlem community where he has long been trapped, where he knows *everyone*, we see that his common touch is more believable—because it is more palpable—than Gunnar's, and that his city council campaign may not be so misguided after all. Indeed, he comes closer to succeeding than many would have expected, and his ultimately falling short in his cultural journey—his attempted trip from the ghetto to City Hall—paradoxically makes him more convincing as a multicultural hero than Gunnar is. What is multiculturalism, rather, what should it be, but an attempt to represent all of the people? And what is more universal than failure?

As for the cover of darkness under which *Tuff* celebrates multiculturalism, the novel conveys, as does *The White Boy Shuffle*, the sense that while success is possible for blacks as individuals (the ending of *Tuff* suggests a second escape hatch for its protagonist), the large black underclass seems doomed to remain exactly that. But this message is not Beatty's chief purpose, or more accurately, his chief motivation. If Tuffy's having as mentors a black rabbi and a Japanese woman are not sufficient proof of this, if his discussions of *The 400 Blows* and *The Battleship Potemkin* are not enough, then a line-by-line reading reveals not only the talent and comic imagination of the poet-turned-novelist Beatty, but also where his heart truly lies. As in:

> Two of the more regular worshipers weren't even Jewish: Oscar and Rosa Alvarez, a Puerto Rican couple who loved to listen to the cantor, Samuel Levine, sing his solos ("Dios mío, he sounds like Caruso"). Sometimes in the midst of Levine's chanting "Shema! Adonai elohenu, Adonai echad!" Oscar, moved to the depths of his soul, would wail "Changooo!"—his invocation of the Yoruba god— momentarily bringing the solemn services to a halt. "Lo siento! Lo siento! It won't happen again."

or:

> [H]is girlfriend, Natalie, wasn't exactly what the T-shirted boys outside would call a "real nigga." She chewed gum like an understudy for a college production of *Grease*, and ended every sentence with the exclamation "Fuck, yeah!," "Cool!," or "Excellent!"

or:

The foreign tongues, drawls, and dialects of the tourists buzzed in Winston's ears like mosquitoes. Their gaiety almost fooled him into believing that he too was a foreigner to the urban chaos down below. . . . A German tour guide and his group surrounded him. *"Im Norden liegt Harlem,"* the tour guide said, his hand raised for attention, *". . . die Heimat des schwarzen Amerikas."* The German language made his epiglottis itch, but Winston distinctly heard "Harlem" and wondered what the tour guide was saying. He knew the man wasn't saying anything about Harlem, *Ost* Harlem.

or:

Winston knew exactly who the weepy kid looked like: an extra from John Ford's *Grapes of Wrath*. A Brooklyn Joad. . . .

Beatty's writing might be called inverted sarcasm: "sarcasm" because its tone belies, and trumps, what is being said, "inverted" because, differently from most sarcasm, the real message is less cynical than the one on the surface. Whether or not he acknowledges or even knows it, Beatty is a lover of the interplay of worlds that is, justifiably or not, the American pride and joy.

RUDOLPH FISHER

Forgotten Renaissance Man

Ask the average person of some education—African-American or not—to name the great black male literary figures of the twentieth century, and you are likely to hear: Langston Hughes, Richard Wright, James Baldwin, Ralph Ellison. . . . followed by a perplexed look and a long pause. There are a number of names that should fill the silence. Of those, none is more important than Rudolph Fisher's.

Fisher was part of a famous movement—the Harlem Renaissance—whose participants are now, paradoxically, unknown to large segments of the general public. Hughes, Zora Neale Hurston, Arna Bontemps, Countee Cullen, Claude McKay, Fisher. . . of those people, many have heard of only Hughes and Hurston, who both lived for decades beyond the 1920s, the movement's heyday. The dimming of Fisher's reputation may be attributable in part to his death from a stomach ailment at age thirty-seven in 1934, before the Harlem Renaissance had truly ended and not long after Fisher's literary career—some would say his life itself—had begun.

On a personal level, Fisher was remarkable in that he enjoyed success in two areas that generally don't have much to do with each other: literature and medicine. After graduating Phi Beta Kappa from Brown University, in his native Providence, Rhode Island, Fisher completed medical school at Howard University, then went to New York; there, among other things, he published papers in medical journals, performed research on the effects of ultraviolet rays on viruses, headed a department in Manhattan's International Hospital, and opened a private practice. (This, while starting to publish short stories in such prestigious magazines as *The Atlantic Monthly* and hobnobbing with the likes of Langston Hughes and Paul Robeson.)

It is for his literary works, though, that Fisher deserves to be remembered. While he left behind only two novels and fifteen short stories, every one of those sharply observant, often satirical, sometimes sad works has the same setting, indeed, the same subject—Harlem—making Fisher to that storied neighborhood what Dickens was to London. You will find in Fisher's Harlem black people representing every occupation, from street hustler to police sergeant to physician; sporting every complexion, from almost literally black to light-enough-to-pass; and engaging in every activity, from playing jazz to playing the numbers, from cutting hair to cutting one another. Fisher brings these characters to life in part through his unfailing ear for dialogue. And his prose is never sharper than when he describes the lay of Harlem itself: "It must be explained that of Manhattan's two most famous streets, neither Broadway nor Fifth Avenue reaches Harlem in proper guise. Fifth Avenue reverts to a jungle trail, trod almost exclusively by primitive man; while Broadway, seeing its fellow's fate, veers off to the west as it travels north, avoiding the dark kingdom from afar. A futile dodge, since the continued westward spread of the kingdom threatens to force the side-stepping Broadway any moment into the Hudson; but, for the present, a successful escape," he writes in his first book, *The Walls of Jericho* (1928).

That novel, Fisher's masterpiece, follows two parallel, ultimately converging story lines. One concerns Joshua Jones, nicknamed Shine, a professional piano mover whose very tough exterior conceals a tender heart—which he proceeds to lose to Linda Young, a pretty domestic worker. The other is about Ralph Merrit, a single character embodying several layers of irony: he plans to integrate a Manhattan neighborhood that has until now been the domain of whites, a group he hates with his whole being and yet resembles, except for his kinky hair. In *The Walls of Jericho*, Fisher comically, but convincingly, evokes the worlds of three strata of Harlemite: the educated elite, as personified here by Merrit and others; the small-business-owning class, represented by the unscrupulous barman Henry Patmore and, at novel's end, Shine; and the rank and file, a category occupied by Shine's two assistants, Bubber and Jinx.

Those two characters return in *The Conjure-Man Dies* (1932), reputedly the first mystery novel published by a black American. In the book Fisher functions as both an inheritor and an establisher of tradition. The solving of the mystery—the apparent murder and resurrection of a fortune-teller—is undertaken by Detective Sergeant Perry Dart and a physician, John Archer; the wonderful banter between the tough, urbane detective and the erudite doctor calls to mind the rapport between Arthur Conan Doyle's Holmes and Watson, except that in *The Conjure-Man Dies* it is the detective who struggles to keep up with the mental leaps of the doctor. And in extensively following the Harlem escapades of a secondary character (in this case, Bubber), Fisher anticipated by nearly three decades the work of Chester Himes, author of the celebrated detective novels featuring Grave Digger Jones and Coffin Ed Johnson (among them *A Rage in Harlem* and *Cotton Comes to Harlem*).

Fisher's short stories have been collected in various volumes, including that edited by John McCluskey Jr. and published by the University of Missouri Press as *The City of Refuge*. The stories contain both the most lighthearted and the darkest of Fisher's writing. Those such as "The City of Refuge" and "The Promised Land," which follow characters who have come from the South seeking fortune, escape, or both, depict the cold reality beneath Harlem's surface charm; these sad tales recall the accounts of hardship in America experienced by immigrants, which these characters of Fisher's practically are. "Reg'lar promis' lan,'" an old woman says to another character, describing Harlem. "Well, dat's jes' whut 't is—a promis' lan'. All hit do is promise. Promise money lak growin' on trees—ain' even got d' trees. Promise wuk fo' dem whut want wuk. . . . promise freedom fum d' whi' folks—white man be hyeh to-day, take d' las' penny fo' rent." Published for the most part before Fisher's novels, the stories in *The City of Refuge* show the evolution of his style: while "The City of Refuge" and "The Promised Land" are among his most transparently heartfelt works, others, including "Ringtail" and "John Archer's Nose" (in which Dr. Archer and Sergeant Dart make their second appearance), show glimmers of the ironic detachment that informs *The Walls of Jericho*.

That detachment is the source of Fisher's greatest strength as a satirist—as well as his occasional lapses as a stylist. At its most effective, his writing style might be described as professorial with a wink; at its weakest, the wink is replaced by words, words, words, growing like weeds over and around the thing they're trying to express. Joking, at least partly, John Archer tells Perry Dart, "Never use a word of one syllable, sergeant, when you can find one of six"; at times Fisher seems to take that advice to heart. "There came to her perceptions a decided, if intangible, animation somewhere beyond, a definite impression of subdued excitement in one of the rooms further along . . . ," he writes in "Guardian of the Law," from *The City of Refuge*. (Do you by any chance mean, Dr. Fisher, that she sensed muted excitement in a room further along?) But then there are the sparkling passages in which Fisher applies his stately tone to descriptions of low-down, petty, or pretentious behavior; the contrast between style and subject then becomes, as Fisher might have written, sufficient to move one to mirth. As in these lines from the story "Ringtail":

> The entrance of the Rosina wears an expression of unmistakable hauteur and you know it immediately to be one of the most arrogant of apartment houses. You need not stand on the opposite side of the Avenue and observe the disdain with which the Rosina looks down upon her neighbors. You have only to pass between her distinguishing gray-granite pillars with their protective, flanking grille-work and pause for a

hesitant moment in the spacious hall beyond: the overimmaculate tiled floors, the stiff, paneled mahogany walls, the frigid lights in their crystalline fixtures, the supercilious palms, all ask you at once who you are and what you want here. To reach the elevator you must make between two lordly, contemptuous wall-mirrors, which silently deride you and show you how out of place you are. If you are sufficiently courageous or obtuse, you gain the elevator and with growing discomfiture await the pleasure of the operator, who is just now occupied at the switchboard, listening in on some conversation that does not concern him. If you are sufficiently unimpressed or imprudent, you grumble or call aloud, and in that case you always eventually take to the stairs. Puff, blow, rage, and be damned. This is the Rosina. Who are you?

Dickens, transplanted to Harlem at a tender age, might have come up with that.

In his introduction to *The City of Refuge*, McCluskey relates the following anecdote. One windy, rainy night in the early 1920s, a cabdriver drove from Brooklyn to Manhattan with four young black passengers: Paul Robeson, the educators Edwin Coates and Frank Turner, and Fisher. Several times during the drive the cab skidded to a stop. At one point Robeson, in his resonant voice, leaned forward and said to the driver, "Do be careful. If anything happens to us, you will set the race back three generations," then settled back in his seat with a laugh. Many a truth, they say, is spoken in jest.

ON, ZADIE

The Threepenny Review, 2006

WHEN ZADIE STRODE onto the literary stage in 2000, at all of twenty four years old, she made short work of a problem whose solution, in retrospect, seems as simple as the wheel. The problem had been how to reconcile the traditional concerns of literature—character development and the beautiful illumination of the human condition, however unbeautiful the condition might be—with the attempt to be representative of the best of all humanity, i.e., multicultural. To the multicultural movement in publishing and academia, whose extraliterary mission of inclusion could make reading feel like taking your vitamins, Smith brought her hilarious first novel, *White Teeth,* which seemed by comparison like candy—but here was candy with nutritional value: Smith's characters were well drawn and were, whatever their skin colors or religious beliefs, human beings first and foremost, their racial/social/cultural/political concerns, when they had them, in the service of character definition and story, not the other way around. Rather than putting positive faces on underrepresented groups, Smith achieved the democratizing effect that is the real aim of multiculturalism by revealing the not-always-pretty mugs of *everybody,* and in place of the solemnity and earnestness of so much literature given the multicultural label, she brought her much-noted exuberance. A number of people—including Smith herself—have said that *White Teeth* could have stood more editing (that is, shortening), and yet the novel's chattiness seems an all but inevitable by-product of that exuberance, the words themselves a kind of residue—natural, almost incidental—of the sheer force at work. Smith once compared *White Teeth* to a "hyperactive . . . ten-year-old," but the novel seems to me more of an adult whose sensuality and zest for life have added a few extra pounds to her frame. Such a spirit seems a prerequisite for what Smith seems to be about: a celebration of the glorious untameability of life. Not since Thomas Wolfe has there been a writer so determined to get his/her arms around life in all its fullness and variety; but whereas we can almost feel Wolfe's muscles quiver with the effort, as in this passage from *You Can't Go Home Again* —

> [The truck drivers] came in, flung themselves upon the row of stools, and gave their orders. And as they waited, their hunger drawn into sharp focus by the male smells of boiling coffee, frying eggs and onions, and sizzling hamburgers, they took the pungent, priceless, and uncostly solace of a cigarette, lit between cupped hand and strong-seamed mouth, drawn deep and then exhaled in slow fumes from the nostrils. They poured great gobs and gluts of thick tomato ketchup on their hamburgers, tore with blackened fingers at the slabs of fragrant bread, and ate with jungle lust, thrusting at plate and cup with quick and savage gulpings.
>
> Oh, [George Webber] was with them, of them, for them, blood brother of their joy and hunger to the last hard swallow, the last deep ease of sated bellies, the last slow coil of blue expiring from their grateful lungs.

—Smith pulls off a similar though less purple feat, with energy left over to laugh with us, maybe even to light up one of those uncostly cigarettes:

O'Connell's [Poolroom] is the kind of place family men come to for a different kind of family. Unlike blood relations, it is necessary here to *earn* one's position in the community; it takes years of devoted fucking around, time-wasting, lying-about, shooting the breeze, watching paint dry—far more dedication than men invest in the careless moment of procreation. You need to *know* the place. For example, there are reasons why O'Connell's is an Irish poolroom run by Arabs with no pool tables. And there are reasons why the pustule-covered Mickey will cook you chips, eggs, and beans, or egg, chips, and beans, or beans, chips, eggs, and mushrooms but not, under any circumstances, chips, beans, eggs, and bacon. But you need to hang around for that kind of information.

And yet, for all that, there is something at work beneath her first novel's celebration of wildness that runs counter to it. *White Teeth*'s major characters, all living in London, are the white, likeable, dull, constitutionally indecisive Archie Jones; Archie's much younger, black second wife, Clara, the casually rebellious daughter of a Jamaican-born Christian zealot; Archie and Clara's daughter, Irie; Archie's best friend, the Bengali Muslim Samad Iqbal; Samad's no-nonsense wife, Alsana, and their twin sons, Millat and Magid. The importance of character over naturalism in the novel is underscored when one of the Iqbal twins becomes a scientist while the other embraces radical Islam; the dominance of the human over the ideological is perhaps best illustrated by Samad, who acts against his own beliefs—by, among other ways, sleeping with the young white teacher of one of his sons—while deploring his sons' Westernization; and the triumph of humor over earnestness is evident from page three through page four hundred forty-eight. In one passage Millat and Magid watch their parents slug it out in the backyard, an experience that might scar and haunt characters in another novel; these boys place bets on who will win. The young teacher is dumped by Samad, which might lead her, in another novel, to suicide or long-term depression; in this one, she tells her ex-lover, "Fuck you, you fucking *fuck*." The book's absorbing climax has the major characters and their concerns—science, religion, animal rights—focused on one event, an experiment involving a mouse. Then things get even smaller: by the end of the novel Irie has seduced, within half an hour of each other, both Millat and Magid, one of whom impregnates her; thus two families, with their black, white, and Asian bloodlines, are narrowed like a pencil point to one microscopic, fertilized egg. The matter is safely in hand. *You're all very interesting*, Smith, the ringmaster, might be shouting at her multicultural creatures. *Now, back in your cages!* The world of *White Teeth* only seems wild; it turns out to be a well-run circus.

It is an unsettling business, after all, to follow the idea of life's wildness past its fun parts to its conclusion: the chaos that exists beneath the veneer of order we try to impose on it, that can swallow us at any time if we're not careful, and even if we are, that will get us one day, no matter what. Worse, to focus too long and too clearly on this is to grasp the seeming meaninglessness behind it all, an experience that is profoundly depressing when it is not actually fatal. The novels and stories that successfully take on that theme, directly or indirectly, are celebrated as great works, from *Anna Karenina* to *The Maltese Falcon*, from "A Clean, Well-Lighted Place" to *Invisible Man*.

With her second novel Smith seemed to have become aware of all this, which suggests that *The Autograph Man*, which is shorter and was less well-received than *White Teeth*, was in a way more ambitious. In the prologue to *The Autograph Man*, Li-Jin Tandem takes his twelve-year-old son, Alex-Li, and two of Alex-Li's friends to a wrestling match. Unbeknownst to Alex-Li, his father has a brain tumor that is about to kill him. In contrast to the rest of the novel, the prologue is written in present tense, to highlight the eternal nature of our doomed struggle to impose order—perfectly symbolized by that most carefully planned and predictable of all activities, professional wrestling—on chaos, which is about to take Alex-Li's father from him. The rest of the novel follows the grown-up Alex-Li, who makes his living as a seller of autographs and other items connected, however fleetingly, to movie stars; he finds customers in people who, like him, consciously or (probably) not, seek connections to the movies' ordered world, whose inhabitants need not grow old and die. The theme of meaninglessness, of existential despair, is present in *The Autograph Man*—including the form of despair that (I'm told) can come with great personal success; it is hard not to speculate that Smith, an instant celebrity with the publication of *White Teeth*, is drawing on personal experience when she writes about Alex-Li's professional triumph:

> Feeling the suggestion of a new type of loneliness, one harder to shake than its predecessor, Alex made his way to the bar. Everyone he passed congratulated him; there was suddenly no other subject than his success, no form of conversation but those formal felicitations one overhears at bar mitzvahs and weddings, the ones that sound like bells. But they're just valedictions, thought Alex with horror. Valedictions wearing a different garment! These people are saying good-bye to me. I am no longer of them. I am dead to them. I have passed on.

The Autograph Man ultimately misses, the body of its story failing to achieve the emotional resonance of its prologue; but as with other scarily talented writers, the beauty of Smith's swing is such that we almost don't mind that she strikes out. Apart from a couple of tics, such as the continual references to "the International Gesture for [fill in the blank]," the humor is sharp, and funny observations that might have taken up paragraphs in *White Teeth* are delivered here with concise jabs that contain whole sociological treatises, as in, "Her face was a brazen challenge, the kind no woman in England ever wears unless drunk and talking to her mother." And while *The Autograph Man* has more going on thematically than it can resolve or, in some cases, even acknowledge—Judaism, biracialism (a staple in Smith's novels), infidelity (another staple)—those themes' open-endedness is perhaps a tacit comment on, concession to, true wildness.

In her third novel, *On Beauty*, reexamining the theme of life's frightening lack of order—this time, the lack that exists even within individuals—Smith has turned for inspiration to E. M. Forster's *Howards End*. If *White Teeth* was like a person carrying extra weight, then in *On Beauty* the person has seen her weight harden into muscle: the parts exist not for themselves but to strengthen the larger body, which has, paradoxically, learned about its own and others' vulnerability. Humor is not lacking in *On Beauty*, nor is human folly, but the latter now has its costs: when one member of a family strikes another, we feel it, as it were, and the adultery dismissed with a triple expletive in *White Teeth* results, in *On Beauty*, in possibly irrevocable harm to a marriage and to the heartbreaking image of a large, grown woman weeping loudly and uncontrollably. (From *White Teeth* to *On Beauty* Smith seems to have undertaken a journey similar to that of Clint Eastwood, who shot up bad guys without blinking for two decades before declaring, in his incarnation as William Munny in the 1992 film *Unforgiven*, "Hell of a thing, killin' a man. You take away all he's got and all he's ever gonna have.")

On Beauty shares its title with a poem, more or less an ode to elitism and amorality, written by one of the characters, a female celebrity poet/ professor whose progressivism disguises a dangerous self-absorption. In *Howards End* the characters see the pursuit of beauty as particularly German behavior, and the valuing of friendship as a more British trait; *On Beauty* sees these behaviors as belonging, respectively, to two groups equally foreign to each other: men and women. The failure—on the part of one character in particular—to reconcile these inclinations, to "only connect," in Forster's famous phrase, is what threatens to wreck the New England family of the white, British-born art-history professor Howard Belsey; his African-American wife, Kiki, a nurse; and their three grown or nearly grown children. Still, the battles of *On Beauty* take place within and between individuals, not groups—as, once again in Smith's work, the human trumps the sociological. When one character tells another toward the end of the book, "You people aren't even black anymore," the line has an ironic ring, spoken in a novel in which blacks represent every political persuasion, economic class, and temperament under the sun.

On Beauty is a rich, funny, moving, satisfying novel, but to understand just how many plot elements it draws from *Howards End*—if my experience is representative—is to feel one's awe at Smith's achievement lessened. The coming years, with luck, will bring us a true Zadie original with the zest of *White Teeth* and the qualities on display in *On Beauty* and even *The Autograph Man*: the lessons learned about what faces us all; the knowledge that each word counts, as does each character the words evoke; and the ability to laugh at our condition while sympathizing with us, too.

THEY WENT THATAWAY, TOM

from tellcliff.com, 2011

IN THE 1985 Western film *Silverado*, in an unusual bit of casting, the British comic actor John Cleese played a small-town sheriff who takes a philosophical approach to his job. The townspeople value him, the sheriff tells the movie's good guys, because he maintains peace and order, even if that means placing them above fairness and justice. And so when the good guys threaten that peace, the sheriff and his men move to apprehend them. During the chase, one of the pursued, played by the black actor Danny Glover, opens fire, not hitting anyone but leaving no doubt about his ability to do so; when the sheriff shows signs of abandoning pursuit, his deputy reminds him that Glover is still in their jurisdiction. "Today," the sheriff replies, his hat having just been shot off, "my jurisdiction ends here."

That line came to mind as I read Tom Wolfe's 2004 work *I Am Charlotte Simmons*, the third and most recent of his novels. Like the sheriff, Wolfe has a mission and a philosophy. He has urged others to take them on as well, most famously in his 1989 *Harper's* essay, "Stalking the Billion-Footed Beast," in which he chided his fellow American storytellers for spinning anemic tales from the comfort of the study rather than facing the challenge of capturing, and stuffing between covers, the spirit and vastness of their great nation, of seeing American life up-close and personal in all its dizzying diversity and sending reports from the front. And like the sheriff, Wolfe has abandoned the task he set for himself, after coming face-to-face with a black character. In *I Am Charlotte Simmons*, Wolfe—having successfully taken on the challenge of getting inside a black man's head in his second novel, *A Man in Full*—falls back on the evasive maneuvers he got away with in his maiden voyage, *The Bonfire of the Vanities*, creating two-dimensional black cut-outs in place of flesh-and-blood people and staying as far from their thoughts and feelings as Cleese did from Glover's sharpshooting. Wolfe is, of course, free to write about whatever and whomever he pleases, but his evasion is puzzling given his apparent fondness for covering the areas in which black and white worlds intersect in uncomfortable ways, and it is disappointing given the thoroughness and fearlessness that characterizes his larger body of work.

What a body of work. It started back in 1963, when Wolfe was sent by *Esquire* to California to cover the Hot Rod & Custom Car show. There, finding what he later described as "all these . . . weird . . . nutty-looking, crazy baroque custom cars, sitting in little nests of pink angora angel's hair for the purpose of 'glamorous' display," he knew he had stumbled onto something significant. Try as he might, though, back in New York with his deadline staring him in the face and *Esquire* editors demanding an article, he couldn't seem to write the thing. Finally, Wolfe agreed to type his notes and send them to the magazine so someone else could write the actual story. From eight in the evening until shortly after six the next morning, typing "like a madman" with his radio tuned to an all-night rock-and-roll station, Wolfe recorded what he had seen; when he was done he had forty-nine pages, which were not only published as he had written them but served as the spark—and the title essay—of his first collection, *The Kandy-Kolored Tangerine-Flake Streamline Baby*. As he recalls in the introduction to that book, what he realized partway through his "manic" writing session was that in California he had had a clear view—however odd the angle—of a new societal order, according to which a more and more pervasive culture was being created not in the usual top-down fashion but by a decidedly non-aristocratic class that suddenly, in the prosperous postwar era, had the money and time to devote to its interests. This was one of many instances in Wolfe's career of what he would come to call "Aha!" moments, lightning flashes that illuminated for him some aspect of how America operates.

In those terms, the "Kandy-Kolored" essay is as representative as any of Wolfe's work, but other pieces in his first collection better illustrate the uniqueness of Wolfe's contribution to American letters. In the "Kandy-Kolored" essay Wolfe views his subjects, however skillfully, from the outside. But in "The Fifth Beatle," about the deejay Murray the K; in "The Secret Vice," about hotshot professional men quietly obsessed with the finer points of tailored clothing; in "Purveyor of the Public Life," about the scandal-sheet publisher Robert Harrison, Wolfe nearly *becomes* the people he is writing about, signaling with exclamation points his "Aha!" moments of insight into other's viewpoints, expanding journalism to include elements of two other professions: acting and fiction writing.

Actors inhabit characters, of course. Fiction writers do, too. Fiction writers also paint the scenery through which the characters move—description and imagery, to resort to the usual terms. Consider a line from the *Kandy-Kolored* essay "Las Vegas (What?) Las Vegas (Can't hear you! Too noisy) Las Vegas!!!!" (A number of Wolfe's titles perform the trick of being both memorable and hard to remember.) In his description of a St. Louis gambler, Wolfe does not come off as a frustrated novelist so much as a fiction writer in journalist's clothes: "Big Sid Wyman . . . is there, with his eyes looking like two poached eggs engraved with a road map of West Virginia after all night at the poker table."

Wolfe's acting and fiction writing continued in his two nonfiction books of 1968, the essay collection *The Pump House Gang* and the full-length work *The Electric Kool-Aid Acid Test*. In the *Pump House* piece "The Mid-Atlantic Man," for example, he describes a faux-English men's club as "a wonderful dark world of dark wood, dark rugs, candy-box covings, moldings, flutings, pilasters, all red as table wine, brown as boots, made to look like it has been steeped a hundred years in expensive tobacco, roast beef, horse-radish sauce and dim puddings." In "What If He Is Right?", about Marshall McLuhan, he describes an advertising executive's laugh as coming "in waves, from far back in the throat, like echoes from Lane 27 of a bowling alley, rolling, booming far beyond the immediate situation." Wolfe inhabits one character, or character type, per essay in *The Pump House Gang*; for *Acid Test* he applied that approach to a whole movement, the outlaw LSD squad whose public face was that of Ken Kesey.

By now Wolfe had fully established his style, one that was symbolized by and even enhanced by—but did not depend on knowledge of—the way his physical appearance contrasted with the nature of his work. This was a man who, in his ever-present white suit, looked as if he belonged to the British-wannabe club he portrayed so vividly in "The Mid-Atlantic Man"— but who wrote about an encounter between Kesey's Merry Pranksters and the Hell's Angels. That juxtaposition found a counterpart in his writing: into grammatically sound sentences of exquisitely chosen words and almost musical flow, Wolfe tossed ellipses, exclamation points, sound effects, repeated words and nonwords (see *Acid Test* for the coinage, so far as I know, of "molly fock")—managing the kind of poetic incongruity achieved in the past by Juilliard-trained jazzmen playing their beautiful sounds amid the shouts and laughter of bucket-of-blood joints in the small hours of the morning. Wolfe brought that high-low style to the documentation of a changing culture, one that he felt was the natural territory of a generation of novelists. Then, in 1973, declaring the novelists to have abdicated that role, Wolfe claimed it for himself and his fellow nonfiction writers, whose works he and E. W. Johnson excerpted in *The New Journalism*.

In the meantime, he had written the two pieces published together in his 1970 book, *Radical Chic & Mau-Mauing the Flak Catchers*, whose one-hundred-thirty-odd pages signaled three new dimensions of the Wolfe oeuvre. He still inhabited characters, adopting their viewpoints, but in the long essay "Radical Chic"—about a fund-raiser held by wealthy New Yorkers to benefit the Black Panther Party—he laced the viewpoint with irony, which is as good a definition as any of satire; the actor was also an impressionist.

(He found something fascinating, he would say later, in the notion of New York's upper crust donating money to a Marxist group dedicated to taking away all they had.) In his satiric role as the collective consciousness of the condescending rich encountering the Panthers, Wolfe writes,

> These are no civil rights Negroes *wearing gray suits three times too big*—
> —no more interminable Urban League banquets in hotel ballrooms where they try to alternate the blacks and whites around the table as if they were stringing Arapaho beads—
> *these are* real men! [Italics Wolfe's]

That passage and others like it set the tone for two subsequent Wolfe books: *The Painted Word* (1975), his evisceration of the art world, and *From Bauhaus to Our House* (1981), which performed a similar service for architecture.

The above passage also signaled a second new element. If American race relations were a human body, then such lines as "these are real men!" would be sharp pokes to that body's rib cage. Hearing the heroes of the civil rights movement dismissed as being less than men stirs up anger (in me, anyway), the more so because the anger cannot rightly be directed back at Wolfe; he is not saying *he* feels this way, but that others do, and there you can't argue with him. He leaves himself open to attack in *Radical Chic*, though, with the prototype of a stock Wolfean figure, the third new element: the black character described so vividly from the outside that one nearly forgets Wolfe's usual practice of going *inside*, inhabiting, adopting a point of view (even a satirical one), a service he does not extend to the Black Panther we meet in these pages.

More nonfiction followed: the essays in *Mauve Gloves & Madmen, Clutter & Vine* (1976); *The Right Stuff* (1979), Wolfe's magnificent full-length work about the space program; and the collection *In Our Time* (1980), which weighed in at all of one hundred forty-four pages, half of them filled with the author's drawings. The most significant thing about *In Our Time* may be its title, which it shares with a volume of Hemingway stories. This was vintage contrarian Wolfe: alluding to Papa, with his manly codes of behavior, right at the peak of the Alan Alda–led "sensitive male" heyday. History seems to have sided with Wolfe this time, since reverence for manly behavior has never truly gone away (see *Silverado*, from the same decade), while the notion of the sensitive male has a place in the time capsule between the Pet Rock and Rubik's Cube. (Rightly so, perhaps—not because there is anything wrong with touchy-feely men, but because, as a female friend of mine, the short-story writer L. E. Miller, once said to me, a lot of your so-called sensitive males are sensitive mainly to their own needs and wants.) *Mauve Gloves & Madmen* is notable for being the first book to contain Wolfe's fiction. Nestled among the essays are the title story (a misfire—I had finished reading it before I realized it was fiction) and "The Commercial," in which Wolfe, for the first time and fairly credibly, inhabits a black character. That character's encounter with an Irish-American has rib-poking, blood-pressure-raising powers that make *Radical Chic*'s look mild by comparison.

And then came . . . drum roll, please . . . *brrrrrrrrrrrrrr* . . . the novels. In this trio (so far) of seven-hundred-page works, Wolfe the fiction writer has thrown off his disguise, while Wolfe the actor has made the declaration that everyone in the profession makes sooner or later: *What I really want to do is direct.* That is, rather than concentrating on a single performance, Wolfe the novelist oversees whole casts, rotating among their points of view. His first novel, *The Bonfire of the Vanities* (1987), is on one level about what happens when a successful Wall Street trader tries to escape the consequences of his actions; on another level it concerns the ambiguity at the heart of much if not most human interaction, and the dangers of building notions of absolute truth on such shaky foundations. The trader, Sherman McCoy, a husband and father, is having an affair with Maria, a woman as long on sex appeal as she is short on morals. After picking her up from the airport one night, Sherman gets lost in the Bronx and encounters two black males whose intentions are unclear; with Maria at the wheel of his car, Sherman escapes the scene—if indeed there is anything to escape—but not before Maria slams into one of the black males, leaving him in a coma. Thanks to pressure to pursue the case—including televised demonstrations —spearheaded by a black activist, the Reverend Bacon, the net tightens around the not-exactly-innocent, not-entirely-to-blame McCoy, who sweats dimes while a high-minded DA, an opportunistic assistant district attorney, and an alcoholic journalist ignore any facts standing between them and their prey. McCoy is sacrificed at the altar of preconceived ideas, just like the boy in the coma (Henry Lamb, ha ha). Facts may be inconvenient or hard to determine, Wolfe is saying here, but when ideology, be it that of racism or political correctness, tries to ignore or do without those facts, people suffer—usually the wrong people.

Ambiguity, then, is a necessary element of *The Bonfire of the Vanities*, which may explain Wolfe's reluctance to reveal too much by exploring the consciousness of Henry Lamb or his companion. But what about Reverend Bacon? He is the character, after all, who sets in motion the events that lead to McCoy's undoing, and is thus an important force in the story; it would seem worth the reader's time to know what he is thinking. At the same time, that knowledge would not compromise the ambiguity, since Bacon knows less than McCoy—or even the reader—about what happened on the night Henry Lamb was hit by a car. Is the charismatic Bacon a Man of the People, a ruthless, cynical con artist, or both? The question is, pleasingly, left unanswered, but it might well remain unanswered if Wolfe revealed his thoughts, which he declines to do. We spend a considerable portion of the book inside McCoy's head, after all, yet in the end we could give any number of answers to this simple question: Is he the victim or the culprit?

In the 1998 work *A Man in Full*, though, Wolfe gives us a fully realized black character—perhaps mindful of the omission in *Bonfire*, or perhaps in an attempt to compensate for the effect of the second novel's central character, for whom Wolfe has obvious sympathy: the unreconstructed white southerner Charlie Croker. Charlie is the last man's man, a sixtyish, gregarious, balding but strapping former college football star, a financially overstretched plantation owner and real-estate developer who catches snakes and says "lat bub" for *light bulb*. Charlie is the kind of guy who says "niggers" not out of anger, and not out of racism (at least as he would define it), but because—unless you are talking to a prissy New York liberal or happen to be one yourself—that's just what you call black people, much as you might call your Volkswagen Beetle a Bug, with something approaching affection. It is through a case of alleged rape, involving the (white) college-age daughter of one of Charlie's best friends and a (black) college football star, that Charlie comes in contact with the novel's major black character, the lawyer Roger White II—referred to in most of the book by his college nickname, Roger Too White.

It must be said that in *A Man in Full*, the seams—the areas where Wolfe the journalist/essayist meets Wolfe the novelist—show in a way they don't in *Bonfire*. In his essays Wolfe can supply nuggets of scrupulously dug-up information, or his own opinions, in a straightforward way, but in his novels he must (or so he seems to feel) delegate the task to his character-surrogates, often by having one explain a term or concept to another. Wolfe is still directing here, but with his surrogate approach, the movie becomes sort of like a scene in *Being John Malkovich*, the one in which the title character enters the portal leading inside his own mind and thus sees himself in every person around him. He manages to transcend that effect, though, with three characters: Charlie Croker; Conrad Hensley, an unemployed laborer turned prison inmate turned Stoic philosopher; and Roger White. Roger is a complex individual: a fortyish, culturally conservative man, he is torn between a nagging if ill-defined sense of loyalty to his own and an aristocratic individualism, between defiance of mainstream society and conformity with it; as he looks at the uninhibitedness of blacks half his age, one part of him wants to set them straight, another to join the fun. Roger is, in other words, a human being, the central figure of what John Updike was moved to call (in an otherwise largely negative assessment) a "strange but honorable" attempt at "a Great Black Novel."

Maybe that makes *I Am Charlotte Simmons* a Great White Novel. Roger White, after all, is a black man negotiating his way professionally and psychologically in a white world; his opposite number in *Charlotte Simmons* is Joseph J. "JoJo" Johanssen, the only white starting player on the basketball team at an Ivy League university. JoJo is one of three male students (the others are a dweeby Jewish intellectual and a blond, handsome, monstrously self-absorbed frat boy) who vie for the affection of the title character, an upright high-school valedictorian from the hills of North Carolina struggling to maintain her selfhood in college. If the seams show in *A Man in Full*, they positively rip in *Charlotte Simmons*, nowhere more loudly than the passage in which JoJo delivers a soliloquy to a fellow white team member on the discrimination faced by nonblack players. We are not privy to the black players' thoughts on this issue, or on anything else, though we are given to understand—repeatedly—that in a place otherwise devoted to the life of the mind, the (nearly all-black) basketball players are scornful of academic achievement when not just plain mentally deficient. No doubt aware of what he is opening himself up to, Wolfe gives us an exception to this rule in the form of Charles Bousquet, a black player who manages to excel in the classroom as well as on the court. Surely this would be rich literary territory: the mental balancing act of a young man who finds acceptance in two worlds—one black, one white—that are not only separate, as in the case of Roger White, but antithetical to each other. But Wolfe leaves it unexplored. Charles's thoughts are unknown to us; he is just part of the background.

In this background the *Being John Malkovich* effect is again present, though this time one of the Wolfe-faces that flash by in the author's sweeping gaze may really be his, at least as he views it. Charlotte Simmons has a philosophy professor, Mr. Starling, whom she thinks of as a "slender and surprisingly debonair figure . . . who must have been close to fifty." It is given to Starling—a minor character—to articulate the novel's central idea, which is that what we think of as the self may be nothing more than a marriage of biology and environment. (Just ask poor Charlotte, a deflowered "C" student by the end of the book.) Consider this passage from Professor Starling's lecture: "The new generation of neuroscientists—and I enjoy staying in communication with them— . . . laugh at the notion of free will." Now compare it with this passage from "Sorry, but Your Soul Just Died," an essay in Wolfe's 2000 collection, *Hooking Up*: "The new generation of neuroscientists are not cautious for a second. In private conversations, the bull sessions, as it were, that create the mental atmosphere of any hot new science—and I love talking to these people—they express an uncompromising determinism."

Determinism: So, maybe Wolfe just can't help himself. I prefer to think, though, that the man who gave us *The Electric Kool-Aid Acid Test*, *The Right Stuff*, Roger White, and all those dazzling essays could turn out better, more fully realized novels if he tried hard enough, if he kept up the chase.

PART THREE

ON THE SCREEN

PARIS BLUES, VISITED

The Iowa Review, 1996

FOUR FACTS DETERMINE the kind of escapism I often seek: (1) I love cities; (2) I love films; (3) I often fantasize—and probably that is the right word—about living in an America less characterized by violent crime, a thing so common that it has come to seem less an outrage than a fine exacted for being too naïve or careless; and (4) being black and, more important, possessing a grain or two of social awareness, I am sensitive to the ways in which different groups of people are portrayed in the media. The combination of these four apparently disconnected and possibly even contradictory phenomena sometimes leads me to watch certain films made circa 1960, particularly those set in large cities. For diversion-hunters of my persuasion, such films, among them *Breakfast at Tiffany's*, *La Dolce Vita*, and *Sweet Smell of Success*, have it all. They serve almost as strainers for the city in which I live, getting rid of the stray bullets and carjackings but leaving intact the cosmopolitan flavor; I feel that if I could just step past the screen and into one of these films, I would inhabit a world where it's possible to find a cup of coffee or listen to a jazz quartet at any hour of the night and then walk home, in the pleasantly cool night air of these films' eternal late spring, in safety. Forget a home where the buffalo roam: give me an apartment like the one in *The Apartment*, where Jack Lemmon paid $87 a month to live alone (on Manhattan's Upper West Side!) in a space big enough for a family of three. Better still, give me a city where the Jimmy Stewart character in *Rope* (okay, so it came out in '48) could attract the attention of the police by stepping onto the balcony and firing two or three shots into the air from a *revolver*. The civil rights movement had gained momentum by 1960 and was leaving its mark on everything, so that the black actors who (with admitted infrequency) appeared in these films were not called upon to shuffle, wear headrags, or grin until their cheeks hurt. And the beginnings of a modern sensibility were evident in another way: male/female relationships on the screen had come to resemble, at least somewhat, those in my own life. By 1960—three years, incidentally, before I was born, which may help explain my romantic view of that year—by 1960, a kiss was just a kiss, not a signpost on a one-lane road to either marriage (a la *It's a Wonderful Life*) or murder (see *Double Indemnity*). When Piper Laurie used the words "make love" in *The Hustler* (1961), she meant precisely what we mean by them today. At the same time, there was a restraint in that and other films of the period that has been largely—and purposely—absent in more recent decades. Back then, one could see two people in bed together without having to watch every act they performed there. Films from around 1960 represent, for me, a happy overlapping of old and new, the best of a number of worlds.

No surprise, then, that I was excited to discover in my neighborhood video store Martin Ritt's *Paris Blues* (1961), a story of two expatriate American jazz musicians set in the City of Light, filmed in black and white, and starring Paul Newman and the tall-walking, groundbreaking black actor Sidney Poitier. But I found that the escape which the film provided was not pure: my visit to the world of *Paris Blues* was like a visit to a real place in that what I encountered left me entertained but also glad I had a home to come back to. I have called the film a story of two jazz musicians; more precisely, it is the story of their relationships with a pair of vacationing American women, played by the white actress Joanne Woodward and the black actress Diahann Carroll. The women meet Newman and Poitier for the first time after stepping off a train in Paris, where they intend to spend a carefree week. The way in which the inevitable romantic pairings play out can be viewed, depending on a number of things, as either emblematic of the changing attitudes of the time or as the same old stuff dressed in new clothes.

What could tip one toward the more cynical view is the presence in the film of the jazz giant Louis Armstrong—in two scenes that at first appear to be merely superfluous but, on reflection, seem intended to lend the film some sort of legitimacy. And in some people's minds it needs just that, since, to the extent that it is the story of jazz musicians, it is the white actor Newman's movie: his composer/trombonist is the leader of the band in which Sidney Poitier's tenor saxophonist is a sideman. That much is okay with me. If a white musician has the skill, knowledge, and heart to do justice to the African-American art form in question, then my only response is, Play on. But the makers of *Paris Blues* didn't see it that way, or, more likely, weren't confident that we would. Why bring in Armstrong otherwise? Not to sell tickets—Newman and, for that matter, Poitier were established leading men by then. No, Armstrong is on hand, grinning and blowing, for purposes of legitimacy. The result is an interesting bit of layering: on the bottom there is Poitier's black jazzman; above him, both in terms of the film's focus and the hierarchy that exists within the story, and therefore negating whatever authenticity Poitier's blackness brings to this movie about jazz, is Newman's character; above *him* (at least in the hierarchy within the story), vouching for this white guy and so restoring authenticity, is the world-famous black trumpeter portrayed by Armstrong, the world-famous black trumpeter. The question then becomes: Who will vouch for Armstrong, a man who by 1961 had come to be perceived, wrongly or not, as Uncle Tom himself? (And in film, is perception not everything?) To the black nationalists who would burst onto the scene a few years later, Louis Armstrong would be no more appropriate a focus for a movie about black people's art than would Paul Newman.

The filmmakers' little game, unsuccessfully played, reveals itself to be a game, and puts us on our guard for others. And so we come back to the aforementioned romantic pairings. Although, as we expect, the black man ends up with the black woman and the white woman with the white man, the film goes out of its way to let us know—or think—that it ain't *necessarily* so: Newman initially tries to pick up Diahann Carroll, because it is she whom he meets first, but the upright Carroll prefers Poitier's even temper to Newman's surliness. Having thus given the appearance of breaking the color barrier without actually having done so, *Paris Blues* then has two characters, Joanne Woodward's and Poitier's, discuss two new, nonracial categories of humanity: "day" people, or the world's practical, sensible nine-to-fivers (represented here by Carroll and Woodward), and "night" people—hip, fast-living jazz musicians and their hangers-on (Newman and Poitier). (This allows Poitier to deliver the irresistible line about how he wouldn't mind living next door to a day person but wouldn't want one to marry his sister.) These new categories don't hold, however, and since the old, race-based ones have not been truly done away with, they continue to assert themselves. As soon as the film has established which guy goes with which gal, *bam*, we see Joanne Woodward, compliments of the new 1960s cinematic frankness, in Paul Newman's bed. Where does that leave Poitier and Carroll? Literally out on the street: their romance seems to be carried on entirely outdoors, where they are at all times fully clothed and surrounded by Parisians. Alas, it may be nineteen sixty-one in Newman's bedroom, but for these dark-feathered lovebirds it is about nineteen *forty*-one, and, as a movie actually made around that time informs us, a kiss is still a kiss. Whether because Ritt and company didn't consider these characters to be real human beings, complete with sex drives, or because they thought white viewers wouldn't want to watch two half-naked blacks prancing around, the film is half over before Poitier and Carroll—out in public and dressed from neck to toe—get to *kiss*, and not only is this bit of high-school business the only physical affection in which they are allowed to indulge, it is followed immediately by their declarations of love for one another. If this is the life of a night person, Lord have mercy on the day shift!

Ritt and his collaborators on *Paris Blues* could have dealt with their apparent insecurities in far better ways—for example, by *honestly* taking on the issue of a white man playing jazz, instead of pulling in Armstrong, whose famously wide grin is not quite wide enough to obscure the issue. Or they could've simplified things by making a different movie—one focusing on a black musician—and shown courage by investing him (or her) with some complexity, as happens, for instance, in Clint Eastwood's movie *Bird* (1988) or Spike Lee's *Mo' Better Blues* (1990). *Bird* is not a great film, and *Mo' Better Blues* is not even a particularly good one, but they are signs of their time: stories in which fully human blacks are the main characters in stories about black people's art. As such, they form part of the landscape to which I was happy to return after my visit to the world of *Paris Blues*.

All that said, I'm glad I went there. *Paris Blues* at least attempts, however naively, to say some positive things, and in that way it is as representative as anything else of the tragic, glorious period of the 1960s. Would that I could bring that aspect of the film back to my world. From the perspective of the faction-obsessed mid-1990s, it is heartbreaking to hear Diahann Carroll trying to persuade Poitier to go with her back to the United States by telling him that things are changing there, that *blacks and whites are working together* to change things. And the film evokes another quaint notion from the period in which it was made—the idea that our all coming together not only was the right thing to do, but might even be *fun*. One of the opening shots says it all: a pan of Newman's jazz club, showing the patrons, black and white alike, grooving to the cool Duke Ellington score, not appearing to think about much, just relaxing and having some serious fun. Those people, the film seems to be saying, are us, the viewers, if we will only do as they do. And in truth, theirs is probably the best way to enjoy *Paris Blues*.

REVENGE OF THE NERD

A Look at Black Exploitation Films

The Iowa Review Web site, 2002

WHEN THE FILMS in the so-called black exploitation or "blaxploitation" genre had their original run, in the early 1970s, I was a boy of eight, nine, ten, living in northeast Washington, DC—an all-black section of a mostly black city. This put me in the group most likely to see these movies. Most of them were rated R, but that did not stop many of my fellow fourth-graders from getting in to see them, either accompanied by older relatives or abetted by lax ticket sellers. I never went myself. My own parents and older siblings did not particularly want me to see such films, and even if they had, I probably wouldn't have gone; I was easily upset by TV and movie images in those days, and I knew the R rating meant blood. So I did homework and other things while the kids who were "bad" (black early-70s-speak for "cool") went to see the likes of *Super Fly* and *Coffy*.

The "exploitation" aspect of those films has to do with the fact that Hollywood, several years late as usual, witnessed the passions stirred up in the African-American community by the Black Power movement (and by 350 years of oppression before that)—and saw money to be made. The punchline to the joke is that most of the dollars black moviegoers spent for the thrill of seeing one of their own stick it to The Man ended up in the pockets of white movie industry executives. The exploitation label also refers to those executives' cashing in on the stereotype of the African-American male as criminal. If people in my neighborhood thought about any of this back then, though, they didn't seem to care.

Time has a way of lending a veneer of respectability to many things, and in the case of blaxploitation films, time had some help from the hottest filmmaker of the 1990s, Quentin Tarantino. Owing much to the genre, Tarantino's films helped bring about something of a blaxploitation revival. When *Hell Up in Harlem* and the rest began to be displayed prominently in my local video store, I realized that I still associated them, all these years later, with the things I just wasn't cool enough to do at one point in my life. I realized, secondly, that as a grown-up man with an adult's tolerance for movie gore and my very own VCR, I was perfectly free to see what I hadn't seen as a kid. And lastly, I realized that I secretly hoped I would find the movies laughable, thereby making it okay that I had missed them. Call it Revenge of the Nerd.

In some cases I got my wish. To begin with, there is Larry Cohen's *Black Caesar* (1973), starring the former football star Fred Williamson, and its sequel, *Hell Up in Harlem*, made in the same year by the same director and lead actor. Williamson plays Tommy Gibbs, who has performed small tasks for the mob in New York since his boyhood and now, as an adult, makes his move into the big time, initially as a hit man; his real power comes after he kills three white men to obtain a ledger that lists payoffs made to New York City officials. *Black Caesar* is adequately—sometimes nicely—filmed, and Williamson is not without screen presence; but he is up against an inept script, and he is badly overmatched. Scenes meant to be powerful receive no build-up, so that by the time we understand the significance of one sequence, another is already being bungled. An example is when Gibbs shows up at the luxury apartment of his white lawyer and his wife; Gibbs presents them with a check for a large amount of money, in exchange for the apartment and everything in it, plus their immediate departure. Not until the next morning, when the lawyer's maid discovers Gibbs in the bed, do we learn that the maid is Gibbs's mother, that she has worked for the lawyer's family since Gibbs was a boy, and that Gibbs has bought the apartment to give to her. She initially balks at the idea, but does she eventually change her mind? Hard to say: when next we hear of her, she has died, as we learn from the soundtrack (a whole source of hilarity unto itself, particularly in *Hell Up in Harlem*). *Black Caesar* leaves us hanging in other ways, large and small. Scenes trail off with nebulous bits of dialogue ("I travel a lot"; "I want my clothes back"); plot lines are unresolved, such as those involving Gibbs's father, who abandoned him when he was a boy, and Gibbs's minister-friend, whose preaching is a con until he undergoes a real religious conversion. These two threads are picked up again in *Hell Up in Harlem*, which would suggest that the films are two parts of a coherent whole, except that the movies make even less sense together than they do separately. *Hell Up in Harlem* begins with one of the more ludicrous sequences from *Black Caesar*, one in which Gibbs is gunned down in the street and then climbs, bleeding, into a nearby taxi (so *that's* what a black man has to do to catch a cab!). But this time, instead of pushing on—bullet wound and all—to kill his nemesis, then wandering, God knows why, to his old neighborhood, where he is beaten and left for dead by a gang of young punks (here endeth *Black Caesar*), Gibbs contacts his father, who saves him with the help of Gibbs's associates—never mind that they were all killed in *Black Caesar*!

One could go on about the shortcomings of these two movies, but there wouldn't be much point; to a great extent, one bad movie is like another. Still, bad movies are sometimes interesting for reasons that have nothing to do with aesthetics. What's notable about *Black Caesar* and *Hell Up in Harlem* is the picture they paint of a society in which mobsters, cops, and elected officials are all part of the same corrupt, dog-eat-dog system, a society in which any attempt to do right is, at best, a waste of time. Given this, it makes sense that Williamson's lines about helping the people of Harlem and driving away drug pushers come off as lip service. No, the passion of *Caesar/Hell* lies elsewhere, and to find out where, one need only fast-forward to the climax of each movie—and see Gibbs kill a corrupt, vicious white man in a manner whose significance one is not allowed to miss. In *Caesar*, he beats a police captain to a pulp with a shoeshine box, after smearing his face with black polish; in *Hell*, he lynches a district attorney (with a necktie!). This is eye-for-an-eye stuff, nothing more or less; maybe this is what was called for, once.

But there is something more going on, something for the ages, in Barry Shear's *Across 110th Street* (1972), based on the novel by Wally Ferris. The title, a reference to Harlem's downtown border, neatly sums up one of the aims of the movie—acknowledging boundaries (between black and white, cop and criminal) while demonstrating where those boundaries lose their meaning. The story begins as two struggling, workaday black friends, a building superintendent (Paul Benjamin) and a dry-cleaning employee (Ed Bernard), with a third friend (Antonio Fargas) waiting in the getaway car, set out to rob members of the white-controlled mob operating in Harlem. In this volatile situation, the robbery turns into a massacre, with cops among the dead; the friends make off with a large sum of money. The crime sets two parallel processes in motion. On one side of the law, a white, not-getting-any-younger cop (Anthony Quinn), under whose jurisdiction the killings would normally fall, is ordered for public-relations reasons to work alongside a younger, black detective (Yaphet Kotto). On the other side, an Italian-American mobster (Tony Franciosa) is instructed to make an example of the killers and show the blacks in Harlem who really runs the place. So far, so what: the characters all seem poised to carry out the roles they have been assigned by their jobs and by racial stereotypes. But then something odd happens—the characters turn human on us. As we watch Quinn's detective operate among the residents of Harlem, it becomes clear that it is he, not Kotto, who understands these people's ways—his experience being more important than his skin color. A conflict emerges between Quinn's street-smart, rule-bending methods and Kotto's by-the-book approach. Meanwhile, Franciosa tries—without much success—to look tough in front of the black, heckling mob underbosses in Harlem (led by Richard Ward, an actor with a voice like two hunks of granite making love); as if in compensation for this, Franciosa's pursuit of the killers takes on a particularly nasty edge. *Across 110th Street* distinguishes itself from the *Caesar / Hell* movies, in which bad guys do evil things simply because they're bad guys. We learn eventually that Quinn is on the take; his reasons are not so far removed from the motivations of the killers (who finally become sympathetic characters): in a time and place that is tough on *everybody*, people do what they can to get along. The movie is shot in such a way that the colors are positively lurid, threatening to explode beyond the forms they occupy, just as the story's tensions—racial and otherwise—constantly threaten to do. (The only camp value in *Across 110th Street* is provided by Fargas, who plays straight the kind of character he would spoof sixteen years later in Keenen Ivory Wayans's devastatingly funny *I'm Gonna Git You, Sucka!*)

Almost as good as *Across 110th Street* is the movie probably mentioned most often in discussions of the genre, Gordon Parks Jr.'s *Super Fly* (1972); almost as bad as *Black Caesar* and its sequel is Jack Hill's *Coffy* (1973). Almost: what makes *Coffy* arguably better than the *Black Caesar* movies is that it is at least sincere about the subject of stopping drug pushers. Man, is it sincere. The title character (Pam Grier), a young nurse, wages a one-woman campaign against dealers after her eleven-year-old sister gets hooked on smack. Some sequences, in which Coffy pumps her policeman-friend or an addict for information about where the drugs come from, take on the feel of a *60 Minutes* segment, but Mike Wallace never went after his prey quite like this: by the movie's last frame, the body count Coffy has racked up beats Joe Pesci's total in *Goodfellas*.

Like *Black Caesar* and *Hell Up in Harlem*, *Coffy* is interesting for reasons all its own. Make no mistake—this movie is an example of substandard filmmaking, in terms of acting, writing, and other areas too numerous to list here. (One more does bear mentioning: particularly clumsy and obvious use of stunt doubles, which, again, makes Wayans's *I'm Gonna Git You, Sucka!* seem less like parody than reportage.) But what's intriguing about *Coffy* is the war that seems to take place over the film's very soul. On the one hand, the strong, vengeful, taking-matters-into-her-own-hands Coffy comes across as a feminist crusader; on the other, the filmmakers—in a bald-faced attempt to sell tickets—put in the movie what is possibly the most misogynistic sequence this writer has ever seen. Several men look on eagerly as Coffy, who has gone "undercover" as a call girl, gets into a fight with a group of jealous fellow prostitutes, every one of whom gets her dress ripped just so—leaving her breasts to bask in the light of day.

In *Super Fly*, Ron O'Neal plays Priest, a successful, Harlem-based cocaine pusher who wants to make one last, million-dollar deal so he can retire from the business, "before I have to kill somebody or before somebody ices me." But his (black) partner and the (white) guys higher up in the illegal narcotics food chain have other ideas. *Super Fly*, unlike the other movies, acknowledges the appeal that the dangerous but lucrative drug trade ("the only game the Man left us to play") can have for blacks with few other options. But mostly it is a well-paced, involving film that builds tension and tells a good story; and the question of whether and how Priest will make it out of the business takes on added dimension, as the film asks—but does not answer—another question: what else will Priest do, in a world he has occupied up to now only as a criminal? (*Super Fly* is notable for two other things: a great soundtrack by Curtis Mayfield, who appears in the film; and the fact that this hard-edged tale is told without a single gun going off.)

Many other films could be discussed here—*Sweet Sweetback's Baadasssss Song*, *Shaft*, *Friday Foster*, and *The Mack* are just a few—but the point has been made: movies in the so-called blaxploitation genre, like science-fiction movies, war movies, horror flicks, or romantic comedies, vary widely in quality. That leaves the question of whether these often profitable films really amount to condemnable exploitation or just to good old American supply and demand. Yes, a space alien watching these movies would probably conclude that all American blacks are violent criminals; yes, studios' and distributors' interest in these movies obviously had more to do with dollars and cents than with a desire to promote black consciousness. On the other hand, it could be argued that watching Fred Williamson or Ron O'Neal get even with The Man satisfied a genuine desire, however base,

and that the fact that these images actually made it to the screen represented, at one time, a form of progress, however crude. But in the end all
of this is probably beside the point. The fact is that for whatever reason, for
better or worse, black people flocked to these movies. And in the end, the
greatest gesture of respect toward any group is to give them credit—and
responsibility—for knowing what they need and want.

GOOD MOMENTS IN A TOUGH WORLD

Films by Charles Burnett

Cineaste, 2008

For DECADES, Charles Burnett's film *Killer of Sheep* was nearly as short on luck as one of the African-American Watts residents it portrays. Made for less than ten thousand dollars, shot over a number of years (because one member of Burnett's nonprofessional cast was in prison for much of that time), the film was completed in 1973 but not shown until five years later, and even then not in wide release—since Burnett had not secured rights to the music in it. *Killer of Sheep* did take home the Critics' Prize at the Berlin International Film Festival, become one of the first fifty films chosen for the National Film Registry of the Library of Congress, and help Burnett win a MacArthur Foundation "genius" grant; its honors, in fact, seemed to outnumber its viewers. That changed this year, when the film, seen since the 1970s mainly at film festivals in 16-mm prints or on clunky machines in libraries (which is how I first saw it), was restored in a gorgeous 35-mm print by UCLA and released in theaters at the end of March. Burnett may disagree, but I'll say it anyway: it was worth the wait.

Shot in black and white, *Killer of Sheep* focuses on Stan (played by Henry Gayle Saunders), a resident of a lower-class neighborhood in Watts, married father of two, worker at a sheep slaughterhouse—and insomniac. Stan is never shown lying wide-awake in bed, because he has given up even trying to sleep; he drags himself through his off-hours as he does through his work shifts. He has similarly backed away from any effort to communicate in a meaningful way with his family, particularly his long-suffering wife (Kaycee Moore), from whom he seems cut off emotionally and sexually; the most heart-rending scene in the film shows the two slow-dancing to a Dinah Washington song, she kissing his bare chest, he remaining impassive before simply walking away, leaving her in an agony of frustration and yearning.

A decade ago, in a piece for *Cineaste* about Burnett's films, I wrote, "Stan's true problem is not that he can't get to sleep but that he seems to be in one long, tiresome dream from which he can't rouse himself; episodes in the film, as in a dream, don't conclude so much as blend into different episodes." True, as far as it goes—but it now seems to me that the foray into the world of dreams in *Killer of Sheep* is deeper and more deliberate than that passage suggests; deeper, even, than that in such surrealist films as Buñuel's *Un chien andalou* or *L'age d'or*, whose raison d'etre seems to have been limited to shocking and teasing. *Killer of Sheep*, by contrast, uses dreamlike sequences to show some eternal and unsettling truths. Show them—not tell them. Indeed, one of the triumphs of *Killer of Sheep* is that it does not interpret for us; as in the world of dreams the film so beautifully emulates, things happen for no spelled-out reasons and in no apparent order—they simply happen, and, like the characters, we make of them what we can.

Stan's emotional detachment seems to be a defense against the bleakness and hopelessness of his surroundings. His environment is one in which people have little and must struggle and fight even for that; the primary focus is on survival. In the pretitle sequence, a boy (young Stan?) is berated by his father and slapped by his mother for not jumping in to help his brother in a fight—never mind that the brother started it. The boy and his brother, the father says, will have only each other if their parents are not around, and so they must stick together. For these characters, morality is synonymous with staying alive, and whatever it takes to do that; as another character later puts it, "Animal's got its teeth, man's got his fists." That line reinforces the connection between the people with whom Stan lives and the animals (sheep) around which he works—an obvious connection, maybe, but one Burnett underscores in subtle and even brilliant ways. (One is a shot, straight up, from ground level, of boys leaping from one rooftop to another. It suggests the jumping of the sheep Stan would be forced to count if he tried to go to sleep, while demonstrating the dangerous nature of even the leisure-time pursuits of these characters.) The sheep in the slaughterhouse, of course, have no clue about who is responsible for their condition and little perspective on the condition itself. They're just in it. The same is true of Stan's peers, who give no thought to the forces dictating the way they live—only to their occasional, doomed efforts to change it.

Which brings us back to the dream world. Two characteristics of dreams are that their logic frequently leads to a dead end, with bizarre details along the way connected to nothing at all, and that, for all the disorder of dreams, they sometimes cut to the heart of what we think, feel, or fear. Those two things would seem to contradict each other, but *Killer of Sheep* goes a long way toward reconciling them. Stan and his friends make two attempts to improve their lives just a little. The first takes Stan and a buddy to the house of a man with a car engine to sell. The scene in the man's home, though it is not technically a dream sequence, does as good a job as anything ever filmed of capturing the subtly askew nature of the things we see as we sleep. The owner of the engine, seated at a table next to his wife but playing cards by himself, wears a suit whose unremarked-upon design would turn heads on a New York City street; lying on the floor is his nephew, nursing wounds from a beating by a man who "didn't have nothing else to do with his hands and feet." The nephew gets into an argument with the wife, who begins beating him herself. Stan and his friend remark on this to the owner of the engine, who, pulling at his very full head of hair, responds, "Can't you see I don't give a damn? My hair's falling out." Why was the nephew beaten up the first time? Why does the man think his hair is falling out, and why has the subject come up at all? Just as well to ask: Why do the characters have to live this way? The answer, in a world—our world—devoid of reason and morality and defined by evil and randomness, is the same in each case: Because. Any other questions?

Once they have the engine, Stan and his friend maneuver it laboriously down several flights of stairs, then place it in the backless bed of a pickup truck parked on a hill. We know what will happen as soon as they try to drive away—and so do they, on some level, as one of them makes clear with his very assurance that everything will be all right. The moment they start up the truck, of course, the engine is thrown to the street and broken beyond repair. As in many dreams, the men see their path heading toward disaster, yet they follow it anyway. The second attempt by Stan and his friends to get ahead involves a drive to a race track to put money on a promising horse; on the way they get a flat tire and realize they don't have a spare. Both the engine and race-track sequences involve cars and aborted attempts at forward motion. Who hasn't had the dream in which you try to run but your legs either won't get into a proper rhythm or weigh half a ton each?

If the world of *Killer of Sheep* is a dream, the characters are the sleepers, a party—through their obliviousness—to their own wretchedness. In this world, Stan, who does not sleep, is a hero. He even manages to get small moments of enjoyment out of his life, comparing the feel of a mug of coffee on his cheek to that of the forehead of a woman with whom one is making love, or exchanging a rare smile with his daughter over a southern expression: the rain is caused by "the devil beating his wife." In the closing shots of the film, when Stan shouts noiselessly at the sheep, is he performing a routine part of his job, or is he—as I like to think—exhorting the sheep, and by extension his fellow humans, to wake up and pay attention?

Hard to know. Better, perhaps, to simply focus on the movie's beautiful shots. One of them, one of a number of shots of children playing that intersperse the film, shows boys running to throw rocks at a passing train—from the train's point of view. Some of the shots of the sheep are lovely, one of them particularly so, showing them in an almost ghostly light. They look beautiful, these dumb creatures, making all the more heartbreaking what is not far in their future.

From dreams to reality: in the fall of 2007, Milestone released a two-disc DVD set, *The Charles Burnett Collection*, containing *Killer of Sheep*, four of Burnett's short films, and his full-length work *My Brother's Wedding*, first shown in theaters in 1983. If *Killer of Sheep* represented a one-upping of surrealist filmmakers' treatment of the dream world, then *My Brother's Wedding* might be said to be Italian neorealism brought to black urban America. Luchino Visconti's *La Terra Trema*, for example, depicted life in a poor Sicilian fishing village, using nonprofessional actors from the village itself to tell the story. Burnett did much the same thing with *My Brother's Wedding* (and *Killer of Sheep*, for that matter), using locals to portray conditions in an impoverished black Los Angeles neighborhood. There, Pierce (Everett Silas), a thirty-year-old employee of his parents' dry-cleaning store, is torn between the upward mobility of his brother and soon-to-be-sister-in-law (which he views as selling out) and the wild ways of his best friend, Soldier (Ronnie Bell), who has just gotten out of prison. Burnett even manages a subtlety missing from *La Terra Trema*, which relied on a voice-over to explain what was before our eyes (to be fair, the Sicilian dialect was reportedly hard to make out even in Italy). *My Brother's Wedding* evokes, without comment, the contrast between the older neighborhood residents' religious values and the danger of the environment where they find themselves; hence the behavior of Pierce's elderly relatives, who interrupt their Bible reading to pick up a gun so they can answer the door.

The bad news is that *My Brother's Wedding* is KO'd by a one-two combination of clumsy dialogue and wretched acting. (Somehow bad performances work better in unintelligible Sicilian.) The worse news is that those shortcomings do not detract from an otherwise solid story—rather, they distract us from the film's failure to answer a basic question: why is the seemingly normal, generally easygoing Pierce friends with an apparent sociopath whom everybody else would like to see back in the joint?

As for the shorts, *The Horse*, a moody, mysterious work from 1973, is the best from a visual perspective; some shots of the doomed animal of the title, in particular, rival the photography in *Killer of Sheep*. Speaking of that film, another of the shorts—*Several Friends* (1969)—could pass, I do not exaggerate, for a series of *Sheep*'s outtakes. In *Quiet As Kept* (2007), a family of displaced Hurricane Katrina victims muses about the lessons the disaster has taught them about America. In my earlier piece on Burnett, discussing another of his films, I wrote, "Drama and political message can dance well together, provided drama leads. Here, it struggles in vain to keep up." That assessment applies word for word to *Quiet As Kept*.

In terms of storytelling, the best of the shorts is *When It Rains*, from 1995. In it, a woman with a young daughter is threatened with eviction for nonpayment of rent. Desperate, she hurries to a nearby outdoor mall, where, amidst a music festival, she finds her friend Babu (playing himself). With his graying dreadlocks and African-style clothing, Babu looks like a kind of wise village elder; the truth, as we gradually discover, is slightly different. As Babu circulates among his acquaintances, trying with mixed success to raise the money for his friend's rent, he comes to seem less like an all-knowing figure and more like an ordinary but large-hearted guy willing to drop what he's doing to help the good people around him. At one point, money fresh in hand from a sympathetic acquaintance, he is set upon—before he can take a step—by another fellow, who calls in a previous loan. In the end, Babu succeeds in helping his friend not through wisdom, but, as he acknowledges with good humor in the voice-over narration, through pure dumb luck—but hey, he'll take it. A funny, sweet little film, *When It Rains* contains the message found in some of Burnett's best work: that in a tough world, the wise enjoy what they can, and are grateful for that.

THE BROTHER FROM ANOTHER RACE

Black Characters in the Films of John Sayles

Cineaste, 1996

"YOU AFRAID OF ME? Don't be," a minor black character says in John Sayles's 1992 film, *Passion Fish*. The character is addressing the crippled former soap-opera star played by the white actress Mary McDonnell, but he might be talking to the American moviegoing public. Virtually alone among black movie characters, who are largely either walking history lessons (*Glory* or *Malcolm X*), second-banana types whose jobs are to marvel at the daring of the white heroes (*Die Hard with a Vengeance* or the *Lethal Weapon* series), or nameless, small-time criminals (you name it), blacks in John Sayles's movies are what real blacks know themselves to be: flesh-and-blood people. That Sayles is a white writer-director constitutes nothing less, in my mind, than a ray of hope not only for the future of American films but also for black-white relations in that Hollywood suburb called Real Life.

Sayles has shown a progression in this regard. The first of his movies to feature a major black character—and the only one to date in which a black heads the cast—was *The Brother from Another Planet* (1984), starring the woefully underappreciated Joe Morton. The Brother, a fugitive slave who crash-lands on Earth, is not a fully realized human being, in part for the very good reason that he really does come from another planet, but also because Sayles has idealized him. Morally, the silent Brother can do no wrong, and, given his situation, he is extraordinarily good-natured. Even the frustration he experiences while trying to fit in on Earth is not interpreted by Sayles as being simply the outgrowth of a cultural gap or as a sign of limited patience on the Brother's part. When the Brother tries to enter a nightclub, for example, and is told by the sympathetic doorman that the money he has put down is not enough, he walks away in disgust. His gesture is a comment on human materialism, his anger that of Jesus chasing the money-changers from the temple.

But subtler elements are also at work in the film. In Harlem, the community where the central character finds acceptance, if not exactly understanding, much of the action takes place in a bar, where the black owner, his wife, and their customers present a wonderful mix of humor, foibles, and essential decency—the stuff, in other words, of humanity. (The bar owner, on being asked by his wife what he wants for dinner: "You mean what do I want, or what do I want that you can cook?" The wife, after her husband has suggested that they go out to dinner and asked her where she wants to go: "You mean where do I want to go, or where do I want to go that you can afford?")

In terms of his development of African-American characters, Sayles took a step up with his sprawling, multiplotted urban tale, *City of Hope* (1991). His point man again is Joe Morton, in the role of a city councilman seen as too liberal by his colleagues and as too ineffectual and too tied to the "system" by his mostly black constituency.* Morton's councilman learns that leadership involves more than good intentions and moral correctness. Just as importantly, he proves to be more than a type, a political opinion wearing a suit; he is instead a complex man whose troubles stem in part from his ability to see more than one side of an issue. "Half of everything you say is true," he tells a committed, Afrocentric community activist who has just spouted a line of propaganda. "The other half is *shit!*"

* a kind of proto-Obama

Sayles topped himself again with *Passion Fish*. In that movie, Mary McDonnell's soap-opera actress suffers a car accident that leaves her unable to walk. She subsequently retires to her large southern home, where she wallows in bitterness and drives away one home-care person after another. Enter the latest applicant for the job, a black woman played by Alfre Woodard. It is easy to imagine this story in the hands of another writer-director: instead of Woodard, Whoopi Goldberg shows up, to do another version of the insufferably all-knowing figure she has perfected in other movies and TV shows, and by film's end she has led the self-pitying McDonnell to accept—nay, to be grateful for the personal growth that has resulted from—her disability. But Sayles knew better. A single parent struggling to overcome a drug habit, Woodard's character is at least as screwed up as her employer, and these two wounded women work slowly, together and separately, to overcome some of their difficulties.

The movie runs counter to our worst fears in other ways, too. When Woodard's father shows up at McDonnell's house, we find that he is not the hard-drinking, unemployed child molester who all along was The Cause of this poor black woman's problems (are you watching, Alice Walker? Sapphire?). Instead, he is a dignified, even stuffy, physician disappointed in his daughter's low station. Woodard's own daughter turns out to be not one of those preternaturally cute, sassy miniadults with one eye on the camera, à la *The Cosby Show*, but a plain, bespectacled, touchingly shy little girl, one you would never expect to see in a movie precisely because she reminds you of someone you know. "There are twenty million African-American stories," Sayles as much as says. "This has been one of them."

The most amazing sequence in *Passion Fish*, for my money, is the one in which McDonnell is visited by a group of her successful actor friends, one of them a black woman played by Angela Bassett (Joe Morton's wife in *City of Hope*). During one scene, Woodard is working alone in the kitchen when Bassett wanders in. Again, one cannot help but envision their exchange as written by some Hollywood hack. (Woodard: "I don't care how many limos you done rode in. You might think you just like them, but you a black woman, just like me!" A chastened Bassett: "I guess no matter where we go, this"—pointing to some area of her skin—"never changes.") But with the firm support of Sayles's writing and direction, these two great actresses convey through the hesitancy in their faces and gestures what words could not convincingly get across: the oddness of their relation to each other, the fact that they are separated by social standing but made similar by skin color and, if you like, heritage. We wait with them to see which of these factors will set the tone of their discourse; we share their (unspoken) relief when they hit on a topic of conversation that reflects neither their class difference nor their racial solidarity but their common humanity.

To point to Sayles's uniqueness is to take nothing away from gifted black filmmakers like Charles Burnett or Julie Dash. Burnett and Dash have provided the invaluable service of showing black people among themselves, at home in their culture, in situations that do not call for them to react—at least directly—to the actions of whites. But the truth is that black Americans are *not* by themselves, and the trick is to show them within the larger society without having the contrast reduce them (or those around them, for that matter) to one of a number of stereotypes. Sayles has done this repeatedly in the past, and he does so again with his most recent move, *Lone Star*. Chris Cooper, as the sheriff of a small Texas town, investigates the death, forty years earlier, of one of his predecessors—an equal-opportunity shakedown artist and killer played by Kris Kristofferson. One of those on whom Kristofferson preys is a black barman, played in his youth by Gabriel Casseus. In a testament to the power of both Casseus's acting and Sayles's writing, the barman manages to acknowledge that he is up against a force greater than himself while still maintaining his dignity. (Also on hand is Old Faithful himself, Joe Morton, as the barman's son, an army colonel with a compassionate heart beneath his spit and polish.)

For a black writer-director to have pulled this off would be a cause for celebration; that a white one—Sayles—has done it is something of a miracle. He has shown, through his films, that it is not necessary to actually *become* a person of another race in order to sympathize with him or her, to understand something of the other person's situation. In these racially troubled times, for even one person to display such sympathy and insight is a justification for hope; and hope, nothing less, is what John Sayles has offered us.

DOUG STREET BLUES

Cineaste, 2008

WENDELL B. HARRIS JR. based *Chameleon Street*, his 1989 masterpiece and the only film he has directed to date, on the true story of the serial impostor William Douglas Street. In the bitingly funny 94-minute comedy, newly released on DVD by Gethsemane 84 and Image Entertainment, Harris plays the title character, who over the course of the story passes himself off as a *Time* magazine journalist, a surgical intern, a French-speaking Yale student, and a civil rights attorney. On paper, certainly, Doug Street does not come across as someone who would inspire many of us to say, "Now there's a guy I can identify with!" But it is Harris's singular achievement in *Chameleon Street*, which beat out some formidable competition to capture the Sundance Grand Jury Prize in 1990, to make us see—with this portrait of a professional liar—a bit of the truth of our own lives.

The film, set in the late 1970s and early 1980s, opens with a conversation between the African-American Street and a white man, apparently a prison psychiatrist, who expresses doubt that Street will reform and offers a theory about his condition: that Street intuits what a given person wants and then becomes that thing. That theory, parroted later in the story by Street himself, hits two wrong notes. (The desires of the movie's gall-bladder patient presumably do not include being operated on by a man who never spent a day in medical school.) What Street does is intuit small aspects of what the mass of humanity *experience*, at least some of the time—namely, boredom, discontent, and the feeling that they're not suited to the roles they're playing —and then embody those things to a monstrous degree. The early part of the story finds him working for the senior Doug Street, an installer of bur- glar alarms; Junior's duties seem to consist mainly of waiting around in the passenger's seat of the parked company van. Who has not, at some point in his or her working life, uttered a cry like the one Street lets out one day on the job: "This is *BOR-ING!*" The thing that sets him apart, of course, is how far he is willing to go to address that particular problem.

Another motivating factor for Street—the one that drives his doomed efforts at extortion and sports journalism, among other activities—is money, or, rather, the lack of it. Street wants more money; he and his friends sit around and talk, in a very funny scene, about ways to get it; his wife, Gabrielle (Angela Leslie), embraces him while urging him to make more of it. Money, necessary for living, is a motif in *Chameleon Street*, as is the symbol and substance of life itself, i.e., blood. At the beginning of the film, Street's burglar-alarm co-worker suggests he make money by selling his blood, and Street replies that he would never sink so low; later, we see him in the act of having his blood extracted, the technician unable to find a good vein. Street is being drained, in other words, of his life force—by the usual culprits: the rat race, the demands of fatherhood, the need to keep his wife happy. (He doesn't help himself, on the last score, by temporarily running off with another woman.)

Boredom at work . . . lack of money . . . marital stress . . . any of it sound familiar? To make art out of life's common troubles is to sing the blues, which is, at bottom, what Harris does with *Chameleon Street*. And, baby, does he have the voice for it. Harris/Street provides comic voiceover narration, and anyone thinking of doing the same for his or her own movie needs to check this one out first, because the ante has definitely been upped. Harris's baritone, which slides down into a bass as he gets more sardonic, is like music; he sings just by talking, navigating the episodes of his picaresque tale like a vocalist gliding over chord changes, elevating his witticisms to the level of melody and even making the odd banality sound good.

In addition to having a sexy voice, Harris is a strikingly handsome man. It's no wonder everyone wants to believe that Street is what he says he is on any given day. But deep down, beneath the show we present to the world, don't most of us yearn to reveal our worst (or dumbest, or weakest) selves and be accepted, loved, anyway? When you give another film a prominent place in your own film, you'd better have a point to make, and the human need to be loved in spite of our ugliness seems to be at the heart of having Street see a revival of his favorite movie, Cocteau's *Beauty and the Beast*. Later, at a costume ball (which he attends, naturally, in the hope of winning the prize money), Street dresses as the Beast, while his mistress, Tatiana (Amina Fakir), goes as Belle. At one point, lying back while Tatiana strokes him and holds a champagne glass to his lips, his handsome features covered by his monster's disguise—an inverted reflection of his true self— Street says, with wonder in his voice, "I'm happy." That state, needless to say, does not last.

Where *Chameleon Street* deviates from the universal is in the area of race. What Harris has to say here is interesting, if scattershot. One sequence could stand alone as a short titled "This Is Not a Blaxploitation Flick." In it, Street and his wife are having a meal in a bar/restaurant when a white man approaches Gabrielle and makes the crudest advance imaginable; Street's response, and the other man's counter-response, reverse almost every stereotype associated with black males and white males. In another scene, Street sits down to lunch with a group of "fellow" lawyers, all of them white and male; treating the lawyers as representatives of the white race, Streets takes them to task for going to tanning salons and embracing African-American culture while hating black people. When he goes on to call them "wily Caucasians," Street tips his hand. It is not whites' oppression and hatred that anger Street; it is that in making their skin darker and listening to black music—i.e., in trying to act like what they are not—they provide an unflattering reflection of Street himself.

The DVD's bonus features include an essay on the film by the critic Armond White; an extensive trailer for Harris's long-gestating film "Arbiter Roswell," with real and dramatized interviews of people present during the rumored discovery of extraterrestrials; and "The Process," a short documentary on the making of *Chameleon Street*. The most amusing feature is "Colette Vignette" (itself a Grand Jury Prize winner at the 1986 Sony U.S. Visions Contest), Colette Haywood's one-woman performance based on her audition for *Chameleon Street*. (She won the part of Melissa, a hilariously talent-free poet who serves as assistant to the basketball star Paula McGhee, who plays herself.) "The Process" adds little to the package, showing exchanges between cast and crewmembers and outtakes from *Chameleon Street* but offering no real insight into the motivation behind it.

But who cares? A great film with an unilluminating bonus feature beats deep thoughts about a piece of hackwork every time. And *Chameleon Street*, unlike its subject, is the real thing.

MONSTER'S BALL

Cineaste, 2002

THREE TIMES IN Marc Forster's *Monster's Ball*, Billy Bob Thornton's character is shown wiping blood off various surfaces—a shopping bag, a carseat, the back of a leather chair—in a literal and symbolic attempt to hide the marks of the cruelty and carelessness that people demonstrate to one another. This is a brilliant touch, but also an ironic one, given that the film itself tries to do much the same thing. Whereas the Thornton character quite realistically fails at his task, *Monster's Ball* negates that honesty by wiping him clean in a very short time of a life's worth of racist indoctrination. It is no doubt a good sign that *Monster's Ball*, which makes a serious attempt to address the problem of racism, has received such thunderous praise. The praise is not wholly unjustified, and the film's heart is certainly in the right place. Its head is another matter.

But let's start with the things that *Monster's Ball* gets right. One is its look. The action takes place in a small town in Georgia; the film shows us the South not of wide, tree-shaded porches, rolling hills and sparkling streams, but of bleak stretches of highway dotted with cheap motels and dingy diners—shot in a way that accentuates shadows, so that whatever color there is seems to have fought its way through some kind of murk. In this dark atmosphere, a dark act is committed: the electrocution of a black man, Lawrence Musgrove, played by Sean Combs. (His crime is unknown to us; more on that in a bit.) The movie comments on this act with an understatement that is quite effective. During a dry run for the execution, the stand-in for Musgrove is a black police officer, a fact that doesn't seem to strike any of the characters as telling. The witnesses to the execution are separated from the condemned man by a pane of glass; his reflection in the glass is superimposed on the images of the witnesses, as a reminder that he is as human as they. Reflections are a subtle motif in the film—several times, for example, characters peer into mirrors that give them distorted or severely limited views of themselves.

But the characters are distorted in other ways, too, not all of them intentional. Thornton plays Hank Grotowski, a white corrections officer overseeing the execution; Halle Berry gives an Oscar-winning interpretation of Leticia Musgrove, the wife of the condemned man and mother of their young son. Which of these two turns in the better performance depends on one's definition of acting. Berry succeeds at getting her mouth around such southernisms as "shoulda had gave me" and stretching out the word "red" like a piece of taffy, but on several occasions these flourishes seem to be exactly that; we become aware of watching not a southerner but Berry doing an admirable job of playing one. Thornton, on the other hand, manages to disappear inside Hank, but maybe that's because the screenplay leaves him plenty of empty space to fill.

Hank, in other words, is a mystery, a series of contradictions in human form. The question becomes whether the contradictions make him a complex character or an unrealistic one; there is a good case for the latter view, which is a large part of what's wrong with *Monster's Ball*.

We know that Hank can be cold, because early in the film he fires a rifle into the air to scare two innocent black boys off the family property; the boys are friends of Hank's son, known as Sonny (Heath Ledger). This scene establishes Sonny's humanity while throwing Hank's into doubt. Hank mercilessly berates Sonny, who is also an officer, for falling out of line and vomiting as the condemned man is being walked to the electric chair; later, Hank tells Sonny, who has a pistol pointed at him, "I always hated you," to which Sonny replies, "I always loved you"—before shooting himself in the heart. It is not clear why Hank hates Sonny, if indeed he does. Maybe it's because Sonny is the kind of man who drinks and has occasional, thoroughly meaningless sex with a local prostitute—except that we later see Hank with the same woman, who is obviously not meeting him for the first time. (To the filmmakers' credit, they do not use the old Hollywood trick of turning us on with acts we all supposedly look down on. Rarely has consensual sex seemed as joyless as it does here.) More likely, Hank hates his son because Sonny is weak enough, or strong enough, to do what Hank won't, or can't: show compassion for black people in a setting where racial attitudes date back to the nineteenth century.

Hank, by contrast, does what is expected of him. When he fires the rifle to frighten the boys, he is spurred to do so by his father, Buck (Peter Boyle, who looks distractingly like a decrepit version of Marlon Brando in *Apocalypse Now*). But there is a glimmer of compassion in Hank: as he slaps and yells at Sonny for falling out of line, he asks him, "How would you like it if somebody fucked up *your* last walk?" To take this question at face value, and not simply as a weapon with which Hank can batter Sonny, is to conclude that there is a heart somewhere inside Hank. So is he a hard-hearted bigot, or a compassionate soul? The answer given by *Monster's Ball* seems to be that he is the second disguised as the first, and that he comes to shed his disguise like an old, moth-eaten coat.

If only it worked that way. It is possible to believe that Hank acts as he does before he falls in love with Leticia, and it is possible to believe that he acts as he does afterward, but to believe both requires an enormous leap of faith. For a grown man to scare two boys in the manner Hank does, and for the reason he does—even if he is led to do so by external realities—suggests some level of complicity with those realities, some internalization of the thinking behind them. Such internalization cannot be shed on cue or simply wiped away, but this, so *Monster's Ball* would have us believe, is what

Hank does once he falls in love. Hank's transformation appears to cost him nothing—he feels no conflicts between his new insights and anything he truly holds dear, has no apparent regrets of any kind. The burden and pain of dealing with Hank's past is instead shifted to Leticia, who thus has the same job as her ancestors: doing the white folks' work for them.

To back up a moment: Leticia meets Hank after her son (Coronji Calhoun) is struck fatally by a hit-and-run driver; Hanks happens by the scene of the crime and drives mother and son to the hospital. In the wake of the boy's death, Hank checks in on the grief- and poverty-stricken Leticia, empathizing with her because of his own son's death. (This is the first hint of remorse we see Hank experience in connection with his son; indeed, Sonny seems to have existed—for Hank and for the film—mainly as a way for Hank to get next to Leticia, and much the same can be said for Leticia's own boy. On the other hand, in the sequence leading up to the couple's first lovemaking scene, when Leticia laments her lost son, Berry is heartbreakingly convincing, fully evoking the mix of love and exasperation known to every parent.) After Leticia becomes involved with Hank, her affection for him takes two hits. The first is when she looks for Hank at his house and instead finds his father. If Hank is a complicated character, the elder Grotowski is a simple one—an out-and-out racist, and crass, to boot. And yet, for all that, he is probably the more realistically drawn of the two men. This is not a man whose views will be changed by love; when he grasps that Leticia is Hank's lover, he recalls that he, too, as a younger man, liked "nigger juice." There are two things wrong here. The first is that no black woman born and raised in the Deep South would be shocked by a racist remark, no matter how hideous. The second is that this conflict, which drives Leticia away from Hank for a time, is too easy, focusing on an external problem—Hank's father—and thus making racism itself appear to be an external factor, an annoying detail, like a cold sore. How much more complex matters would be if Leticia had to deal with a racist aspect of Hank himself, instead of just his family.

Later, the film attempts just such a scenario—but fails. Unbeknownst to Hank, Leticia discovers that Hank was one of her husband's executioners.

Earlier, Hank himself makes the connection between Leticia and her husband, but says nothing about it; his only visible reaction—make that audible reaction—is to throw up. (It must be said that *Monster's Ball* makes expert use of vomiting.) Leticia's learning the truth makes for an ending to the film that is rare and laudable in its ambiguity. But again, as with her encounter with Hank's father, Leticia has stumbled upon Hank's external reality. As a participant in Lawrence Musgrove's execution, Hank was only doing his job. He is an understandable target for Leticia's rage, but not, ultimately, the right one.

Of course, given what is left out of the story, it is impossible to know what—in this case—*is* the right target. Because we do not know what Lawrence Musgrove has been accused of, or whether or not he is guilty, we do not know to what extent injustice is being done, or if it is. Are we to assume that Musgrove has been found guilty of whatever the crime is because he is black (or, come to think of it, that he *is* guilty because he's black)? That he is guilty, but that society drove him to do what he did? That capital punishment is an inappropriate response even if Musgrove is guilty and responsible for his own actions? The movie provides no answers. *Monster's Ball* says to us, "Check *this* out"—then walks away as we are asking, "Check *what* out?"

Hank Grotowski, however, remains the film's biggest shortcoming. This character makes sense only as a man who accommodates the racism around him until he has a reason not to. That accommodation suggests a weakness that not even love could make disappear overnight. After quitting his job as a corrections officer, Hank buys a filling station and names it for Leticia; when Leticia is evicted from her home, he brings her into the house he shared with his father (who is conveniently moved into a nursing home). He does all this with no apparent regard for what the community thinks. Are these the acts of a man who would frighten boys with a rifle in order to keep up appearances? Maybe, but more than likely not—and to think that they are is to underestimate the power of racism in our society. We shall overcome, but not this easily.

ALI

Film Quarterly, 2002

THE FIRST MINUTES of Michael Mann's *Ali* are beautifully shot and, in retrospect, representative of the film's twin weaknesses. Set in 1964, they show the great heavyweight champion, then a twenty-two-year-old named Cassius Clay (played by Will Smith), in training for his historic first fight with Sonny Liston. Interwoven with those shots are scenes of Ali's friend, the soul singer Sam Cooke, performing for a crowd composed mostly of hysterical women. The Ali/Cooke comparison subtly points to Ali's status as the first truly sexy heavyweight champ. But shortly afterward, once that has been accomplished, Cooke takes a quick stroll through the champ's hotel room—and out of the movie, which does not show or refer to him again. (He was killed late in the same year.) The singer is thus a harbinger of factual elements that are dealt with haphazardly, or just plain ignored, in the rest of the movie. But it is in the shots of young Clay/Ali that we find a metaphor for the film's worst flaw. In the training scenes, we see a frontal close-up of the boxer as he hits a punching bag; the bag flies back and forth in front of him, making that famously pretty face appear as it would on the rapidly moving images of an old-fashioned film reel. The point, no doubt, is to emphasize the larger-than-life, ready-for-the movies nature of Ali as both a person and a fighter. But this choice is perhaps more apt than Mann realizes: the Ali he proceeds to give us is the one-dimensional version we already know from TV and magazines, and even that isn't intact. Instead of adding depth to this image, Mann's *Ali* takes a scalpel to it. Here is a case in which less is less.

What circumstances helped to form the man who became possibly the greatest boxer of all time, the fighter whose name and face are known—decades after his last fight—by people who can't name the current heavyweight champ? The answers provided by *Ali* are so sketchy as to be meaningless. This is because Mann, in trying to squeeze into one film what might have filled a trilogy, not only leaves out important aspects of Ali's story—he has no time to explain what he does present. Over and over, we are given the what of Ali's life but not the why, with the result that key events appear to take place in a vacuum. One example is Ali's joining the Nation of Islam. His receptivity to its strict, separatist philosophy was the result of the racism to which he had been exposed early in his life, but the examples of such racism in *Ali* are reduced to headlines: we see the boy Cassius on a bus, stealing a glimpse of a newspaper account of the murder of Emmett Till. His personal encounters with racism, as depicted in the movie, are limited to a cop's asking him as he does his road work, "What you running from, boy?" Later, when Ali explains his refusal to fight in Vietnam with the celebrated line, "No Viet Cong ever called me nigger," the response of the uninitiated might be, "So what? Nobody else did, either."

But back to the Nation of Islam: its teachings are represented for Ali, so the film would make one think, almost wholly by Malcolm X, played here adequately if not excitingly by Mario Van Peebles. Confusion thus results when, after Malcolm's well-documented differences with Elijah Muhammad and the Nation have begun, Ali takes the side of the Nation. When next we see Malcolm, he is gunned down; cut to Will Smith, a tear rolling down his cheek as the wistful "A Change Is Gonna Come" plays on the soundtrack. (Which raises an interesting question. If you feature a Sam

Cooke song in a movie in which Cooke is a character, why use the Al Green version?)

Mann's handling of Ali's boxing career brings to mind what Spencer Tracy said about Katharine Hepburn's figure: What's there is choice. The fights depicted here—particularly those against Sonny Liston (Michael Bent) and George Foreman (Charles Shufford)—come as close as anything since *Raging Bull* to conveying a sense of what it's like to be in the ring. The spinning camera shots allow us to experience a boxer's disorientation, and one can almost *feel* the punches Ali absorbs on the ropes as he lets Foreman wear himself out. But the problems with the fights in *Ali* are (1) that they point up, by contrast, the static nature of what takes place in between them, and (2) that they, like nearly everything else in the movie, are presented without the buildup necessary to make their significance clear. Take the Joe Frazier fight. Ali's first bout with Frazier (James N. Toney), in 1970, occurred after a three-year gap in his career, during which he was stripped of his heavyweight title and denied the chance to fight because of his refusal to be inducted into the army. Ali thus faced Frazier after having spent the prime of his ring life outside the ring. But since the movie downplays the passage of time, Ali's loss to Frazier comes across not as the struggle of a fighter robbed of the best years of his career, but as a simple case of losing to a better fighter.

It is getting late in the movie at this point; and so *Ali*, like a boxer who knows he is behind on the judges' scorecards, begins to move faster as its aim becomes less sure. The story now jumps ahead four years, to the Foreman fight—completely missing the second Ali/Frazier match (won by Ali, as was the third) and likewise making no mention of a very muscular thorn in Ali's side by the name of Ken Norton.

But let's focus on the Ali/Foreman fight. Held in Zaire in the fall of 1974 and billed as "The Rumble in the Jungle," the fight was nearly incidental to the story that was taking place around it; Mann could have made a whole film about those events, except that it might have been superfluous, in light of Leon Gast's excellent 1996 documentary on the same subject, *When We Were Kings*. (Come to think of it, a viewer would do well at this point in

Mann's movie to switch over to Gast's.) The Rumble was promoted in grand fashion by the hyper-loquacious, preternaturally shrewd, hard-as-bricks former convict Don King, who would have been a fitting subject for Shakespeare (one of the many writers and thinkers King likes to quote). Hosting the events was Zaire's leader, Mobutu Sese Seko, the brutal dictator and plunderer of his nation's mineral wealth whose own contribution to the events tells all one needs to know about the quality of his leadership. According to Norman Mailer's book *The Fight*, Mobutu, in order to clean up the city of Kinshasa in time for the Rumble, ordered police to round up three hundred known criminals, a random fifty of whom were then shot to death underneath the very stadium in which Ali would face Foreman. How is all of this dealt with in *Ali*? Mobutu is portrayed very briefly, shown sitting at a table and looking like the villain in a Bugs Bunny cartoon; most of what we learn about him and King from *Ali* is tossed off in a few lines of dialogue during an argument between Ali and his wife (Nona Gaye). Mykelti Williamson gives a quick, entertaining turn as King, in all his long-finger-nailed, high-voltage-haired glory, but for the most part these rich story ingredients are served uncooked—or not at all. No mention is made of the prisoners' execution, or of the widely publicized story that when Foreman got a cut over his eye prior to the fight, which then had to be postponed, Mobutu protected his investment by trapping the fighters in Zaire. As with many other aspects of *Ali*, prior knowledge of events is needed to make sense of what is going on; but such knowledge guarantees frustration over what is left out.

Adding to the frustration is that *Ali* features fine performances. The pumped-up Will Smith succeeds in capturing not only Ali's cadence and cocksureness but the simple—in the best sense—soul they adorn. Jamie Foxx, looking sort of like Denzel Washington's ne'er-do-well brother, does a good job as Ali's sweet loser of a cornerman, Drew "Bundini" Brown. One area in which the film does actually explore below the surface of events is its depiction of the behind-the-scenes affection between Ali and the men with whom he publicly traded insults and punches. Jon Voight makes a fine Howard Cosell, Ali's nemesis and friend. And one of the sweetest moments in the film finds the now title-less Ali riding in a car with Joe Frazier—who has become champ in his absence—and pleading with Frazier to fight him. Frazier tells Ali he will do so, promises to defeat him resoundingly (or words to that effect), and then asks him if he needs any money in the meantime.

Would that these performances had been given in a movie that made them matter. Smith's Ali is a good characterization, all dressed up with nowhere to go. The script attempts much too late to reveal different sides of the man; when the married Ali falls for another woman in Zaire and makes no secret of it, his wife objects to being publicly humiliated, explaining that this is worse than his previous, "casual" affairs—the first we have heard of such things. Ali then confides to the Other Woman (later his third wife) that he should have found Islam at age fifty, because his youthful weakness for women conflicts with its tenets. An interesting idea, subsequently abandoned.

Michael Mann has directed a number of handsome, high-profile, action-driven films and TV shows, such as the movie *Heat* and the series *Miami Vice*. Like that show, *Ali* has some showy effects whose purposes are not clear. Perhaps film, a visual medium after all, does not have to justify looking pretty, but it's fair to ask why *Ali* periodically shifts from color to sepia. The answer may be that Mann makes certain shots look like old photos in order to stress the historic nature of what he is representing; but if so, this backfires for the same reasons that the opening shots of Clay/Ali in training do.

The movie ends with the Ali/Foreman fight—fittingly, since Ali's victory over the angry young giant was the last great, and arguably least expected, win of his career. (There were many who feared that Ali would not survive the match, much less stand over the horizontal Foreman at the end of it.) The very last shot is a freeze-frame of Ali with his hands raised in triumph. But having this pose cap the entire film, and not simply the fight, begs the question, Triumph over what? What is this movie about? Perhaps the answer is: the man we already know. But *Ali* fails to give us even him.

FAITH AND FAITHLESSNESS

Films of Alexander Payne

The American Shot, 2011

A FACT ABOUT RELIGION—monotheism, at least—is that it places at the center of one's life a figure who cannot be communicated with, at least not in the usual way. All-important but unknowable, the figure leaves one to guess at his/her/its wishes and intentions, with a faith that may fulfill the believer or lead him to frustration, bewilderment, bitterness, and rage. The films of Alexander Payne might be said to examine what happens in secular society when that faith is aimed not at a god but at equally un-knowable figures—men and women, one another and ourselves.

In *Election* (1999), Tracy Flick (Reese Witherspoon) is the high-school version of that person we've all had the misfortune to meet: one with a hardwired, unblinking, means-justifying belief in her own inevitable and self-evident rightness, one who can't be bothered to look back at the de-struction and ruined lives in her wake. Paul Giamatti as Miles in *Sideways* (2004) is a study in similar self-belief as it begins to flag for lack of evidence to support it: a forty-something, unpublished writer with a manuscript nearly the size of his unrealized ambition, Miles begins to face the possibility that his faith in his own abilities will not pay off.

About Schmidt (2002), meanwhile, found that misplaced faith aimed not at the self but at the chief Other—the spouse. Playing very much (and very refreshingly) against type, Jack Nicholson is the utterly unremarkable title character, a mild, widowed, newly retired insurance executive who discovers—now that he has time to go through his wife's letters and other belongings—that she had an affair with a friend of theirs. Schmidt takes that knowledge with him on a road trip to his daughter's wedding, bridging the geographical but not the emotional gap between himself and his only child, the other unknowable figure in his life. During his trip, sitting outside under the stars, in a setting that many seek to talk to God, the heartbroken Schmidt instead asks another unresponsive party, his dead wife, "Was I the one you wanted?"

And speaking of unfaithful and unresponsive wives, we now have Payne's *The Descendants*. Elizabeth (Patricia Hastie), the wife of Matt (George Clooney), is worse than dead, a state in which she could at least be remembered at her best and best-looking by her family and other survivors; because of a head injury sustained while water-skiing, she is *near*-dead, lying unconscious in a hospital bed, hooked up to life support, and appearing ghastly and helpless. That helplessness does not stop Matt, his older daughter, Alexandra (Shailene Woodley), and a wronged wife, Julie (Judy Greer), from venting their rage at Elizabeth as she lies still, unable to defend herself or even hear what's being said. *The Descendants* is in part a catalogue of inappropriate, unfortunately timed human feelings and poses: at certain moments Matt looks comic if not ridiculous in circumstances that are anything but funny, running in flapping house shoes to the home of neighbors to confront them about his wife's adultery or poking his head above shrubs to get a peek at his wife's lover; Matt's senile mother-in-law, told that she is being taken to the hospital to see Elizabeth, thinks she's going to visit the queen (the one character who sees humor in this gets punched in the head); and Elizabeth's lover (Matthew Lillard), confronted by Matt and Alexandra, flashes them a ridiculous grin for the benefit of his unsuspecting wife—the only one who can't see it—when she rejoins them on the porch. Poor Matt can't even get satisfaction from his righteous indignation toward his wife, since he hears from more than one party that her cheating was his own fault.

Matt, a lawyer, lives with his family in Hawaii—which, like married life, can appear to be uninterrupted bliss until you've been in it a while. In the 1800s Matt's ancestors came into possession of a huge area of Hawaiian land, which has been passed down through the generations, an act of faith in the unborn descendants. The trustee of the property, Matt must decide whether or not to sell it to developers, as most of his relatives—who stand to make oodles of money—want him to do. Meanwhile, sitting on great wealth, Matt nonetheless lives on what he earns, wanting, like his father before him, to give his children "enough to do something, but not enough to do nothing." Matt's withholding of wealth is a metaphor for his withholding of emotional intimacy from his wife.

To backtrack a minute: *Sideways* was a fresh, thought-provoking film with a central flaw—the implausible nature of the road trip that the shy, inward-looking, cerebral Miles takes with his old college roommate, Jack (Thomas Haden Church), an extrovert who will never be accused of overthinking anything and can't seem to remember that he's engaged to be married. Miles and Jack would be perfectly believable as roommates thrown together at eighteen, but their friendship twenty-odd years later strains credulity. The flaw in *The Descendants* is not so much the implausible as the unexplained. Matt is presented as a man so preoccupied with work (or something) that he can't show his love for his wife, but we see no evidence of that preoccupation, and the only sign of the love is his rage at being betrayed. When at last he calls Elizabeth "my love, my friend, my pain, my joy," the words seem to come out of nowhere.

On the plus side: the acting in *The Descendants* is uniformly good, and the portrayal of the relationship between Matt and Alexandra hits the bull's-eye. When Matt tells Alexandra that she and her sister "have no respect for authority," she gives him a look familiar to any father of a teenaged girl: *If I told you what I'm thinking,* that look says, *you couldn't go on living.* Still, Alexandra defends her father at a crucial moment, as Matt finally does for his wife. Once in a while, it seems, our faith in one another is well-placed.

PART FOUR

IN YOUR EAR

ON JAZZ

Notes of an Enthusiast

The Threepenny Review, 1999

A major difference between the trumpet and sax has to do with adaptability. In the right hands, the saxophone—baritone, tenor, alto, or soprano—becomes an extension of the person playing it; the trumpet remains the trumpet.* As I have learned in conversations with musicians, the trumpet is just a hard, hard thing to play, an instrument you don't so much master as come to an understanding with: if I do *this,* you'll sound like *this.* That said, the trumpet has some versatility in terms of the sounds it will allow a musician to produce. A trumpeter can play a ballad dreamily; but then so can a saxophonist. The trumpet, like the sax, can be—often is—the vehicle for a high-speed rollercoaster of a solo, but such labyrinthine passages sound just a hair more *natural* emanating from the bell of a sax. Listening to an uptempo trumpet solo, one is put in mind of a four-footed animal moving quickly, darting this way and that, but a sax (down to its actual

---

*I still find this to be true, though not to the extent I once did. The wonderfully reckless style of the trumpeter Lee Morgan, for example, does not sound like the muscular tone of Bill Hardman.

physical shape) is more like a snake—it doesn't have to dart this way or that, because some part of its body is already *there*, in each place. In other words, the sound of a sax is, if sometimes almost imperceptibly, more fluid. What the trumpet is uniquely capable of is a function of its very rigidity: a declaration, a marking-off of territory, a clear, sharp sound that says, *This is how it is.*

Louis Armstrong (1900–71), the inventor of the jazz solo, explored these various functions of the trumpet and created the mold for the modern trumpet player. He had a sound whose sheer power is perhaps unmatched to this day. (During one recording date, the rest of the band gathered in the studio while Armstrong stood with his trumpet out in the hall, so as not to drown out the combined sounds of the other musicians.) His solos contain declarations, as can be heard on such early tunes as "Wild Man Blues" and "Potato Head Blues," both recorded in 1927 with his Hot Seven band. He could play rapidly, and he could play dreamily, and he could even do both at the same time, as he demonstrates in the 1925 recording of "Cold in Hand Blues," on which he is paired with the blues diva Bessie Smith. (Here he actually plays the cornet, very similar to the trumpet but smaller in size and sound). Armstrong comes in behind each of Smith's lines about her no-good lover, echoing her, registering this bad news with a musical shake of the head, pouring out notes whose vocal equivalent would be, *Ump, ump, ump.* Armstrong is the prototype of the twentieth-century jazz musician, and especially the trumpeter.

Yet in *A Great Day in Harlem* (1995), a wonderful jazz documentary, Dizzy Gillespie (1917–93)—himself one of a handful of jazz trumpeter-giants of the twentieth century—is heard saying that it was not Armstrong but another major figure, Roy Eldridge (1911–89), whom he wanted to sound like. Which makes sense. The diminutive Eldridge, nicknamed "Little Jazz," was in some ways the link between Armstrong and the bebop pioneer Gillespie: like Armstrong, he made declarations with his instrument, some of which I will discuss later, but his solos were faster; Gillespie took this rapidity and did new things with it. Gillespie's solos were often based on harmony rather than melody, so that where Eldridge's lines seemed to move forward, parallel to the rest of the band's sound, Gillespie's moved outward, floating somewhere above it, in extended asides. Also, Gillespie was one of a few jazz musicians who came close to achieving total fluidity on the trumpet. (A few others are Clifford Brown, 1930–56, Booker Little, 1938–61, and Freddie Hubbard, 1938–2008.) Listen to the tunes on *Bird and Diz* (Verve), recorded in 1950, and you will hear Gillespie matching the solos of his bebop compatriot, the sax great Charlie "Bird" Parker, note for note, nowhere more demonstrably than on the four takes of "Leapfrog." And yet, for all that, the sound remains as much that of the trumpet as of Gillespie himself.

Which brings me to Miles Davis (1926–91). Davis, to my mind, was the exception to the trumpet rule. Gillespie wanted to play like Eldridge; Davis wanted to play like Gillespie. He couldn't. He rarely matched Diz's agility or range on the trumpet. But what he somehow accomplished in spite of that was the complete channeling of himself into the instrument, which suggests that Davis, who could be one mean, nasty sumbitch, was deep down a very sad man: his playing was beautifully, heartbreakingly mournful, to the point where he sometimes seemed to be weeping through his horn. He plays many such passages on the Columbia recordings *Miles Ahead* (1957) and *Porgy and Bess* (1958), both with orchestras under the direction of Gil Evans. And Davis could make declarations, too, as on the wonderful *Sketches of Spain* (Columbia, 1960), another collaboration with Evans, which at the same time exhibits his mournfulness.

★   ★   ★   ★   ★

THREE OF the twentieth century's half-dozen or so saxophone titans were almost exact contemporaries: Ben Webster (1909–73), master of the tenor sax, and that instrument's Founding Fathers, Coleman Hawkins (1904–69) and Lester Young (1909–59). Each played with orchestras before freelancing or leading groups of his own. Webster matured under Duke Ellington; Young achieved fame with Count Basie; all three performed for a time with Fletcher Henderson. The sounds of these three saxmen were as distinct from one another as were their faces.

Hawkins demonstrated what the tenor sax was capable of in terms of harmonic inventiveness and manful authority. Webster always strikes me as being Hawkins's darker twin: the Rolling Stones to Hawkins's Beatles, the Malcolm X to Hawkins's Martin Luther King, any number of analogies will do—Webster's sound coming off as darker, earthier, but in the end possessed of "Body and Soul" (a signature Hawkins tune) no greater than Hawkins's. Talking to a friend, I once compared the experience of listening to Webster to that of drinking a dark beer, which would make Hawkins's sound like the taste of very expensive champagne. I have the feeling of being able to reach out and grab a Webster solo, to feel its weight and texture like chunks of earth in my hands. Hawkins's sound is showier, marked by vibrato, or reverberations. But anyone who questions its substance should listen to "Picasso," the magnificent piece he recorded without accompaniment in 1948. (It is the last cut on the Verve label's *Jazz Masters 34—Coleman Hawkins*.) Hawkins and Webster often played together, and these collaborations are showcased well on *Ben Webster & Associates* and on *Ben Webster and Coleman Hawkins* (both Verve).

Lester Young was something else again. If Miles Davis was the jazzman who made his trumpet sound like himself, then Young is the one who made the saxophone sound like *itself*. There is a purity of tone, an almost ethereal quality, to a Lester Young line. In the magazine *Américas* (vol. 43, no. 1, 1991), David Lyon wrote about the Mexican photographer Manuel Alvarez Bravo that the "most significant part" of one of his photographs "is often what is missing from the frame and, therefore, must be imagined by the viewer." The musical equivalent of this can be found in Young's solos—one almost feels there is more there than meets the ear, which can make listening to Young a fascinating as well as frustrating experience. But Young could sometimes dig in and deliver the goods, as he does on *Master Takes with Count Basie: Lester Young* (Savoy) and on some cuts from *Charlie Parker Plays the Blues* (Verve).

Which provides an opening for a discussion of Parker. As the soul of the bebop movement of the 1940s and early 1950s, the alto player Bird was unlike any saxophonist before him. Bebop and the cult that grew up around it went beyond a style of music to encompass an approach to life, which was thought to be experienced best on the edge; it is no accident that Bird's name often comes up in Jack Kerouac novels. But for all the tales of Bird's perilously fast living (he died at the age of thirty-four), he has always seemed to me the original nerd. Here was a man who, in his youth, was chased off a bandstand by the drummer "Papa" Jo Jones because he could not play his horn. (Rejected by the other boys!) He then retreated to his home, where he spent hours alone, day in and day out (today's computer geeks come to mind), perfecting his playing. Eventually he surrounded himself with a group of like-minded men, and a musical revolution was born, led by people for whom showmanship and crowd-pleasing were far down on the list of priorities, if they were there at all. (Miles Davis would not talk to his audiences, and eventually took to playing with his back to them; the pianist Thelonious Monk couldn't even be bothered with playing the right notes, although he made the wrong ones sound awfully good).

A perfect example of this, and of the contrast between Parker's sound and that of older saxophonists, was his 1950 duet with Coleman Hawkins on "Ballade" (available on *Charlie Parker: 'Round Midnight*, on Verve). Backed by the rhythm section of Hank Jones, Ray Brown, and Buddy Rich, Hawkins takes it first, offering a lilting sixteen bars. Enter Parker. His first note is a bleat, which he blows with entertainment seemingly the last thing on his mind. Soon he is off on a lightning-fast flight of harmonic fancy, an exhibition of his vibratoless tone, as thin and hard as a needle—and we have left the conventional beauty of Hawkins's solo behind. But it works. By the time Parker turns our ear back over to Hawkins, we feel as if we've heard not a different story from the one Hawkins was telling, but some bizarre and interesting twists in the same one.

★ ★ ★ ★ ★

ON A VERSION of "Embraceable You" recorded on September 18, 1949 and available on *Charlie Parker: 'Round Midnight* and *Charlie Parker: 1949 Jazz at the Philharmonic* (Verve), several of the musicians mentioned above can be heard in top form. A pretty piano intro by Hank Jones is followed by solos—

each about two minutes long—by Roy Eldridge, Lester Young, the trombonist Tommy Turk, Charlie Parker, and the tenor saxophonist Flip Phillips. Eldridge intersperses wistful tones from his trumpet with gentle declarations; Young steps up next, at his gossamer best; a good, modest turn by Turk is followed by Parker's nerdy beauty; and then Phillips brings it home, with the others playing quietly behind him. In the end, all reactions to art are subjective, and here is how I think of the last two minutes of this piece: Phillips, a lesser light than the others (with the exception of Turk), talented and determined but unable to finish this job alone, is guided back to shore by his fellow horn players. At the end of the piece, the live audience erupts into applause, and one voice—a woman's—rises above the others in an extended, "Yaaay!" It is as lovely a thing as I have ever heard.

WHAT IS THIS THING CALLED LOVE?

The Threepenny Review, 2007

A BOY IS BORN, and after a period of several years that see his personality form yet leave no mental trace, vague impressions and isolated memories at most, he begins the first phase of his true, conscious personhood. In it, tenderness and thoughtfulness have an overlay of roughness, which exists both for its own sake and for the boy's protection. Years pass, and for this boy, now a young man, the roughness finds an outlet in the convictions he forms, some of them his own, some reflecting the influence of others. He is fierce, this young man, and knows his purpose—until, without warning, that purpose changes, because he has found love. Following that emotional storm, the young man becomes more thoughtful; he finds that changes, accommodations must be made, because life is not all or even principally about himself now, and perhaps a certain conformity ensues, more so than before, at any rate; but is that so bad? It doesn't seem so, until the man—no longer quite so young—becomes thoughtful again, this time about different things. Suddenly it seems to him that the usual background noise of life has stopped, and all he can hear is the steady, up-to-now quiet sound of the Timekeeper, setting the pace at which the man is passing into oblivion. With a new sense of urgency, to meet the challenge of doing all he can in the time he has left, the man marshals the forces of his personhood—his roughness and conviction, his tenderness and thoughtfulness, the lessons he has learned from others—exhibiting them by turns as he moves, full-bore, toward the end of his time.

Who is this man? No one, and everyone.

★ ★ ★ ★ ★

IN JULY 1952, ten jazz musicians—three alto saxophonists, two tenor men, a trumpeter, a guitarist, a bassist, a pianist, and a drummer—assembled in a Los Angeles studio at the behest of the producer Norman Granz to record several tracks. One of the tracks, one among hundreds of jazz versions of Cole Porter's "What Is This Thing Called Love?", can be found on the compact discs *Charlie Parker: The Cole Porter Songbook* and *Charlie Parker: Jam Session*—ironically, since Parker may have the least playing time of all the musicians heard on that fifteen-minute cut, and since Parker, while the most famous today among those men, was not necessarily so at the time. The other two alto saxophonists present that day were the most influential players of the instrument in the first half of the twentieth century. Temperamentally, Johnny Hodges and Benny Carter were similar, both reserved in nature; physically, Hodges was on the small side, while Carter's stature has been called "imposing"; and in terms of their musical styles, the two could not have been more different. Hodges gained his greatest fame as a member of the Duke Ellington Orchestra, where, like other Ellington stalwarts, he played music that had been written specifically to showcase his unique sound—in his case, a nakedly emotional and sensual appeal that happened to be delivered through the bell of a sax. Hodges's latter-day equivalents are the soul crooners who seem none the less manly for having a direct line to the innermost feelings of their female fans.

Hodges's playing could be called "dreamy," and so could Carter's—but whereas a Hodges solo might evoke the dreaminess of romantic or emotional yearning, Carter's stylings are closer to the dreaminess of a man absorbed in arranging his books according to subject. Carter was one of jazz's renaissance men, proficient on the trumpet, trombone, clarinet, and piano as well as the saxophone; he began working as an arranger early in his career. He was a musician with an overview, a sense of grand design, and he conveyed that sense in his solos—which are so meticulously thought out, so evocative of structure, that it is easy, on listening to them, to forget that you are hearing one note at a time. (One note from a Hodges solo, by contrast, can seem while it lasts to be the only note there is or ever will be.) For all that, Carter, with his lovely, lilting tone, could *swing*.

Hodges and Carter wrote the book on the alto sax—the edition of it, anyway, that existed before Parker's arrival. The bebop pioneer Parker, nicknamed Bird, can almost be seen as Hodges and Carter's stylistic offspring, exhibiting by turns the intricacy and intellectual bent of Carter's work and the sheer feeling of Hodges. He did not have the older men's personalities; Bird was a clown, a user of ten-dollar words for comic effect ("my worthy constituent Dizzy Gillespie"), an often charming user of people, a compulsive embracer of life—the last-named quality one that oozed from his music: Bird's tinny, warp-speed solos communicate a desire to take in all of life at once, to squeeze in as many experiences—as many notes—as possible, an impulse that perhaps accounts for his death at age thirty-four. (It might also account for one of the most vivid passages in Miles Davis's autobiography, a book with no shortage of vivid passages. Davis recalls being in the back seat of a car with Bird, who ate chicken while a woman performed a sexual act on him.) But the complex, cerebral nature of Parker's work needs stressing, too: his playing on fast numbers was not simply a mad scramble for notes but a careful arranging of them, even if some of the arranging, as is the jazz way, occurred only seconds before the notes were played. Hearing his melodic tap dance over rapidly shifting chordal foundations can be like listening to someone talk quickly and excitedly about a subject you *almost* understand, that you want to grasp because he makes it sound so important, so *cool*.

One of the tenor saxophonists present that day in 1952 was Ben Webster. He was not one of the men who occupied positions on tenor that Hodges and Carter claimed on alto; those spots went to Coleman Hawkins and Lester Young. But there was no more distinctive sound than Webster's on tenor. Webster, a large man, was no stranger to alcohol, leading many who knew him to make comments along the lines of what his friend Jimmie Rowles, a pianist, told Whitney Balliett: "When Ben was sober, he was the sweetest, gentlest, nicest man in the world. When he was juiced, he was out of his head." Both sides of Webster's nature can be heard in his tone, a breathy, deeply human sound: it is rough even as it suggests vulnerability, and it seems to be rough *because* of the vulnerability, as if it hurts to say what he is telling you. He could emphasize one or the other aspect of that sound, playing with an outright snarl in uptempo tunes and with heart-piercing tenderness on ballads.

The other tenor man on the scene was Flip Phillips. An August 5, 1975 *New York Times* article noted that while "Ben Webster is often cited as the basic influence on Mr. Phillips's playing," there is "now also a strong feeling of Lester Young." As they say in New York these days, *Ya think?* The casual listener might have thought Phillips *was* Young, even back in '52, given their similar lightness of tone and Phillips's tendency to copy Young's techniques, if not his inventiveness; in one passage in "What Is This Thing Called Love?", he uses Young's trick of repeating one note in staggered fashion, giving a sense of simultaneous forward and backward motion, the audio equivalent of log-rolling. . . The trumpeter Charlie Shavers was on hand—Shavers, who described himself as "a wanderer, you know, a rebel," who performed high-flying acrobatics on the instrument he called "the iron master" . . . On percussion was J. C. Heard, who once said that he and the eminent drummer Papa Jo Jones "played so much alike—personality, everything," leading one to wonder if, on that day in July 1952, Heard reminded Parker of Jones, the man who had ended a teenage Bird's incompetent solo by tossing a cymbal at his feet . . . The guitarist Barney Kessel was there. Kessel once played in a trio with the dean of bassists, Ray Brown, and the piano luminary Oscar Peterson—the other two men present for "What Is This Thing Called Love?"—and said about that experience, "It was as if I joined the trio at a time when I was just about capable of driving a sports car at 60 miles per hour, but straight away Ray and Oscar kept pushing that pedal down and I found I was trying to control a car at eighty!"

★   ★   ★   ★   ★

THE LYRICS to "What Is This Thing Called Love?" are your standard I-loved-you-but-you-done-me-wrong fare: "I saw you there one wonderful day / You took my heart and threw it away . . ." What gives the song lasting power is the wistful tone created by its bent, or blue, notes. But the whole of the sung portion of the tune, as recorded by, say, Frank Sinatra, lasts a mere sixteen bars in four-four time, barely enough space for a jazz ensemble to clear its collective throat. A jazz version of a pop tune is about expanding, exploring, digging like oilmen for the dark treasure beneath the surface, and, sometimes, discarding: one could strain one's ears—as I did—to identify a semblance of Porter's original melody in the version played by Parker et al before realizing that it simply isn't there, that what Parker and the boys did was to create a new tune by burrowing down to the song's chord structure, where, you might say, they hit a gusher.

A period that sees his personality form . . . Oscar Peterson begins it all, laying out the basic chordal pattern, each left-handed chord followed by a four-note melody from the right. Then the rest of the rhythm section kicks in: J. C. Heard keeps a steady beat, not the dominating rumble of Art Blakey or the impossible dexterity of Tony Williams but a *ticking*, like that of a souped-up second hand on a watch, the beat that gives the tune its great beauty and power, its sense of musicians working, blowing, plucking, living against time.

Tenderness and thoughtfulness have an overlay of roughness . . . Now comes Ben Webster, his first two notes seeming to say, "I'm here," his tone both rough and easy until, about a minute into his solo, he turns more fierce. Charlie Shavers follows—*the roughness finds an outlet in the convictions he forms*—making the clear, sharp declarations that only a trumpeter can, nailing notes in the high register, until Johnny Hodges takes over, laying out buttery tones at the beginning, alternating between ardor and tenderness, different modes of love, as his solo progresses. Barney Kessel's mellow, introspective turn comes next, with its gentle, pearl-like individual notes, followed by Benny Carter, thinking, building a structure through sound and seeming to ascend, over the course of several measures, to its peak. Now there is Flip Phillips, *conforming,* his light tone containing just a hint of the Ben Webster crust as he plays longer than anyone else, sliding here and there into a Lester Young–like maneuver. Bird takes over, as thoughtful as Carter, *this time about different things,* starting phrases in a high register and tumbling downward, descending where Carter had ascended; until—

The horns stop. For half a minute there is just piano, bass, and the ticking of Heard's drums. Peterson prompts Ray Brown, whose bass supplies round tones that seem to come from deep, deep down, like a heartbeat; like a heartbeat, they will not continue forever.

The trading of fours begins. Hodges, Webster, Carter, Parker, Phillips, Shavers—all but the guitarist Kessel, that mellow element missing now—take turns for the last twenty-four bars; urgency is the only constant as the sounds of intellect and ardor alternate, at one point seeming to clash: for one space of less than a beat, Phillips either cuts off another horn (whose?) or starts in one direction and turns sharply in another. Now Shavers, now Bird, now Carter . . . At just short of sixteen minutes, the end comes, the melody, the beat, the chords all cease. Are the musicians content? Did they achieve what they were aiming for? Did they have enough time? Does anyone?

FOR BEAN

The Threepenny Review, 2004

I GREW UP in the 1960s and 1970s in a semi-detached brick house in Washington, DC. The house from which it was not detached belonged to my aunt and uncle; my great-aunt and great-uncle lived in the house on the other side of them; and still another aunt and uncle were up the street. People seldom appreciate what they have when it's there, and it is only now, living in a New York apartment surrounded by neighbors I sometimes have trouble even recognizing, that I understand what I had as a boy. In those days my neighbors were family members, transplanted country folk, who often dropped by unannounced—a rarity today—and stayed to chat for half an hour, an hour, or more. These chats were not the polite, antiseptic exchanges of neighbors who understand that they will probably never be friends; it was full of the shared humor and allusions, the warmth—sometimes the heat—that grew among adults who had known each other all their lives. For a child there is nothing like such talk among adults, even if the child is not listening or consciously aware of hearing it. What are important are not so much the words as the tide of sound on which they reach the ear: the low, whiskey- and tobacco-tinged voices of the men, the knowing tones of the women—sounds that tell a small boy, as he plays on the floor with plastic soldiers, that while he may not understand the workings of the world, he is in the care of people who do.

There are many definitions of adulthood. One of mine is: a period spent alternately running from, and trying to recapture, childhood. Sometimes, when I am nostalgic for the adult voices of my youth—most of which can no longer be heard—I imagine I can hear something similar to them in the recordings of a number of jazz musicians, themselves gone, who often played together. The group includes the trumpeter Roy Eldridge, the tenor saxophonist Ben Webster, the drummer Papa Jo Jones, and others. At its center stands the towering figure of Coleman Hawkins.

Hawkins—nicknamed Bean—was the first important tenor saxophonist, the man who turned a horn previously relegated to circuses into the quintessential jazz instrument. His sound was mighty, its vibrato pronounced, like the tremblings of the ground as a giant makes its way across it; he awed, inspired, intimidated other sax players for forty years, from the era of the flapper to the sweltering days of the civil rights movement. If I fancy I can hear something like my relatives' voices in his playing, maybe it is partly because he was colorful and eccentric enough to have been one of them. On stage, in contrast to Louis Armstrong, he was all business (a forerunner, in this way, of Miles Davis). In person, though, he was a practical joker, who would set friends at odds by telling each he had been slandered by the other; one who could talk knowledgeably about art, flowers, or automobile assembly; a sharp dresser; a frighteningly fast driver; a man whose distrust of banks was so complete that he would walk around with thousands of dollars in his pockets; a big, sturdy man who could drink staggering quantities of alcohol and then play flawless solos.

Hawkins was born on November 21, 1904, in St. Joseph, Missouri. (He was fond of telling interviewers that he had been born at sea as his parents were returning from a vacation in Europe.) At his request, on his ninth birthday he received a tenor saxophone, and by the time he was twelve he was playing it professionally at school dances. Before his eighteenth birth-

142

day he had made it to New York, where he performed with Mamie Smith's Jazz Hounds. In early 1924 he began his decade-long stint with Fletcher Henderson's group, the first important swing band, with which he made many recordings and won worldwide fame.

The crowning achievement of the first half of his career was his three-minute 1939 recording of "Body and Soul," which would become his signature tune, one he recorded on a number of occasions. The original version of "Body and Soul," with music by Johnny Green and lyrics credited to no fewer than three others, is a rather simple affair ("My heart is sad and lonely / For you I sigh, for you dear only"). Listening to what Hawkins did with it brings to mind the scene in *Amadeus* in which Mozart announces that he has written some variations on one of Salieri's compositions: "Funny little piece, but it yielded some good things." For the first eight bars, Hawkins is faithful to the original song, or as faithful as a great jazz musician knows how to be; after that, he abandons melody for harmony and for chord changes that were radical at the time, exploring interstices of the piece never suggested by Johnny Green. And while retaining the gentleness, the bittersweetness of the original, he also conveys a sense of relaxed might; this is not the thin, sentimental sound of one who can play no other way (Kenny G comes to mind), but the music of a colossus captured in a reflective mood.

As a young man, even while he made his name in Henderson's band, Hawkins often found himself playing not only with other musicians but against them. His reputation preceded him in after-hours clubs across the East Coast, the South, and the Midwest, where saxophonists lay in wait, eager to test themselves against Hawkins in "cutting" contests, like Wild West gunslingers using horns instead of pistols; most of the time Hawkins literally blew them away. (I will come, in a bit, to the exception.)

Not all of Hawkins's encounters with younger musicians were antagonistic. He recorded with young players until the end of his career; he championed the odd-playing and odder-acting Thelonious Monk, for example, decades before *Time* magazine put the pianist and composer on its cover. But my favorites of Hawkins's recordings are those he made with his contemporaries, when all had reached maturity as men (for they were all men) and as musicians—when, seasoned by cutting contests, by world tours, by the trappings and traps of fame, by the indignities of traveling as blacks in segregated America, by simply having lived five decades and more, they sat down to play together as friends. The Verve label album *Coleman Hawkins and Ben Webster*, whose tracks were recorded from 1953 to 1959, showcases the two tenor players' stylistic similarities and differences, their mingled toughness and beauty, their artistic kinship; indeed, it is easy to image these big men as cousins—Webster's full, raw sound contrasting with Hawkins's equally full but more refined tone, the two together swapping tales like a country boy and his citified counterpart, on such tunes as "Blues for Yolanda," "You'd Be So Nice to Come Home To," and the sublime "La Rosita."

For the tunes on Verve's *Ben Webster and Associates*, all recorded on April 9, 1959, Hawkins drops by Webster's house, you might say, where he also finds Roy Eldridge, Papa Jo Jones, Budd Johnson, Leslie Spann, Jimmy Jones, and Ray Brown. The first track, a twenty-minute version of Duke Ellington's "In a Mellow Tone," is a masterpiece—and a consummate example of jazz-as-conversation. A call-and-response between Jimmy Jones's coy piano and Brown's game, I'll-play-along bass serves as the intro; the head is a second call-and-response, with the horns of Hawkins, Eldridge, and Johnson supplying the theme in unison (this might be, "Hey, Ben!") and Webster answering back ("Come on in, y'all!"). After these greetings comes the real talk—the solos. Each man has a tale to tell. Some are thoughtful, reflective; a couple begin that way, then become more insistent: Jimmy Jones plays single piano notes, gentle raindrops, before laying down chords, warming to what he is saying—a point echoed later by Eldridge, who begins his muted trumpet solo with low tones, progressing through his trademark long, fluid-filled notes toward the higher register. He is followed by Hawkins, who alone plays insistently from beginning to end, building on, furthering the more fiery statements made by Jones and Eldridge; I see him sitting with the others at a table, where he is the biggest man present, holding forth, telling a story that expresses anger, though not at those present (perhaps it is shared by them). A brief comment from Papa Jo's drums brings it back to Webster, who must acknowledge all that has been said, all the feelings conveyed—and in his solo the fire from Hawkins, the fellowship from all, dovetail before the final call-and-response, a reflection on the long, good evening that has passed, the shared respite from the world's dangers.

For there *were* dangers, and in the case of Hawkins, many took the form of the tenor saxophonist Lester Young. Born in 1909, nicknamed "the President" (soon shortened to "Pres") by his soul mate Billie Holiday, Young was Hawkins's archrival; he couldn't top the sheer force of Bean's playing—nobody could—but he developed a very different style that some came to prefer to it. While Hawkins approached chords like an athlete training on stadium steps, going up, going down, hitting every note, Young—in his light tone—spun out haunting passages that were based on harmonies yet linear, merely *suggesting* the chords. So that whereas Hawkins was descended from the Thomas Hardy of *The Mayor of Casterbridge*, telling not only what happened but how it felt and what it meant, Young claimed as kin the Hemingway of *The Sun Also Rises*, giving spare accounts and letting you imagine the rest for yourself. Which brings us to the cutting contest Bean didn't win: in a Kansas City club called the Cherry Blossom in 1934, while on the road with Fletcher Henderson, he encountered a number of horn players, Pres among them. According to some, Bean—underestimating the competition—tried in vain to top Young, until, with day breaking and Henderson's band having already left for a gig in St. Louis, he hurried to catch them, frying his new Cadillac in the process. In Puss Johnson's basement club in Harlem five years later, as some remembered it, Bean evened the score; others claimed that Pres repeated his victory. But if Hawkins was not able to "beat" Young, then neither was Young ultimately able to beat Hawkins—as proven, for me, even by those who say today that they prefer Young's sound; for the finality of some statements is undermined by the speaker's need to make them. (Who, today, feels the need to state a preference for Mozart's music over Salieri's?)

And if Hawkins was not victorious that night in 1934, then maybe it is because his friends, rather than his adversaries, brought out the best in him.

I think my favorite of the recordings he made with his peers is *Coleman Hawkins and Roy Eldridge at the Opera House* (on Verve), taped for the most part at the Civic Opera House in Chicago in the fall of 1957. The record *swings*, and though no authoritative definition of that word exists ("If you have to ask, you'll never understand," as Louis Armstrong is supposed to have said when asked to define jazz), one could do worse than to explain "swing" in terms of what *Opera House* possesses: an infectious forward thrust. More than that, the album evokes the feel of two friends getting together for a good time. "Bean Stalkin'," a tune that appears on *Opera House* in two versions, typifies this spirit. Its theme, which Hawkins and Eldridge play together, is joyful, almost comic; next, backed by an able rhythm section, particularly the delicate, nimble drum work of Connie Kay, each man takes a long solo—tells a tale—and then the conversing begins, the raucous trading of fours and then twos, leading to the chorus that ends the tune, one of the finest Hawkins ever played.

It was only in the last several years of his life that Hawkins's playing declined, as the years, and drink, took their toll. He died in New York City on May 19, 1969. His records, of course, live on. Most often I listen to them simply because they contain great music; sometimes, though, relaxing at night with a glass of bourbon, listening to Bean's collaborations with peers, I think of the conversations of my older relatives. Jazz is not about words, but then neither, for me, were those conversations; they, like Bean's music, had less to do with what was told than with voice, tone—sound, pure sound.

MINGUS, MARCUS, AND US

The Threepenny Review, 2008

THE WORLD IS a screwed-up place. That has always been more or less true, if more true lately. For statesmen, military leaders, and political activists, the question is how to make the world less screwed-up; for most others, given the negligible extent of our ability to affect world events—beyond the occasional and very limited exercise of power known as voting—the question is not how to improve the world but how to live in it as it is, in the least painful way possible. Much of that amounts to how we think about the world and ourselves. Some of us, though we may be tempted by the seeming comfort of believing that there is a reason for everything that happens, determined by a higher, benevolent power, are unable to make the intellectual leap away from what we can see and touch (or at least read about in *The New York Times*); instead of an other-centered (that is, God-centered) approach to life, we take one that is, in the most positive sense, self-centered. We may say to ourselves, if not quite consciously: I will lead the best—most principled, most successful, or most enjoyable—life I can and not worry about the rest.

Sometimes it works. And yet surely, for even the happiest, most enviable, and most upstanding among us in the self-centered camp, there come those dark moments when, even if we don't ask What It's All About, we tremble in acknowledgment of the great, seemingly random, and non-benevolent forces outside our control. Even if the world were at peace—which it never will be—there is the stuff of ordinary human life to contend with. We can be struck down early, or we may live to be very old and weak; either way, we will die, an outcome that is closer every day. With luck no tragedy will befall our children; they will simply grow up and leave us, move on from our deaths with a mix of sadness and relief, then grow old and die themselves. In the moments when we consider these things, we may seek solace—one not based on faith in the unseen but incorporating, perhaps in a sense even stemming from, a clear-eyed look at life's bitter truths.

WHEN I think of the jazz bassist and composer Charles Mingus (1922–79), the word "canvas" comes to mind, for a couple of reasons. Non-visual artists who create works broad in scope are often said to work "on a large canvas," a phrase that certainly applies to Mingus's compositions. And his works bring to my mind's eye—I have just realized this—an image that *is* very much like a painted canvas, a wide, Jackson Pollock–like work: abstract, full of energy and simultaneous happenings, dark here, humorous there, turbulent, explosive. The strapping Mingus was no stranger to fistfights, sometimes drawn in by racial slights, real or imagined, that no doubt recalled for him the abuse he suffered at the hands of benighted teachers in his youth. His humor is evident in his works as well as many of their titles, notably "Bemoanable Lady," "The Shoes of the Fisherman's Wife Are Some Jive-Ass Slippers," and the prize winner—a riff on the title of the jazz standard "All the Things You Are"—"All the Things You Could Be By Now If Sigmund Freud's Wife Was Your Mother." He dealt with his feelings about racism in intellectual/compositional as well as physical ways, titling one of his works "Fables of Faubus," after the segregationist Arkansas governor Orval E. Faubus, and another "Meditations on Integration," also known simply as "Meditations." Several years ago, the bassist's widow, Sue Mingus, discovered tapes containing performances of those two works—each a half-hour in length—along with other tunes recorded at a 1964 concert at Cornell University. In 2007 Blue Note released the recordings as a two-CD set, under the title *Charles Mingus Sextet with Eric Dolphy—Cornell 1964*.

One of my college English professors was fond of saying, "Great writers write greater than they know." I would change "greater" to "with a greater variety of meaning," and expand "writers" to include writers of music. Racism and integration are certainly weighty subjects, but what I hear in listening to "Fables of Faubus" and "Meditations" on *Cornell 1964* are musicians grappling with issues that are weightier still, if only because they are timeless: the path of the self-centered individual, and that same individual buffeted by the much, much larger forces of the world and the universe.

Traditional jazz pieces feature one or more soloists backed by a rhythm section (piano, bass, and drums), which keeps up a more or less steady beat. In "Fables of Faubus," the tempo provided by Mingus, his pianist, Jaki Byard, and drummer, Dannie Richmond, is all over the place, meaning that trumpeter Johnny Coles, tenor saxophonist Clifford Jordan, and multi-instrumentalist Eric Dolphy play against a kind of moving background; that, in turn, lends the piece a journey- or story-like feel that is as much like classical music as jazz. (As Nat Hentoff noted in his 1961 book *The Jazz Life*, Mingus considered "all music as one.") The sextet plays the composition's theme—with Mingus, as was his way during performances, gabbing unintelligibly—and then, not quite two minutes in, Coles takes the first solo. His vibratoless lines suggest the hardness, the durability, of youth. Still, he plays over a bass/piano/drum accompaniment that is alternately frenetic and somber, and his trumpet sounds downright sleepy during one slow phase of the rhythm section, as if the pace and quality of his lines, of his young life, are not up to him. Byard, who has the next solo, encounters much the same difficulty, but as a slightly older, stronger version of the character voiced by Coles, he is able to resist the bass/drum slowdowns a bit more, carrying the melody—that is, taking charge of his life despite external events—by launching playfully (in the jazz way) into tunes including a slightly cracked version of "Yankee Doodle" that morphs into Chopin's funeral march. Jordan continues that progress, establishing his own pace even as the other horns wail like coyotes behind him, setting the stage for the performance of the character as fully mature, in-command individual: Mingus. The bassist, playing either a cappella or with minimal piano or drum accompaniment, holds forth for six minutes, a big man producing deep, round, resonant tones; nimble-fingered, full of fire and humor, *he alone makes the music happen*, sliding here into "It Ain't Necessarily So," there into "When Johnny Comes Marching Home Again." The last solo is from Dolphy, here on bass clarinet; he interlaces his deep, hard tone with squeaks and honks, the eccentricities of the aged, before his lines give way to the composition's theme. (The date of the recording was March 18, 1964. Three months later, on June 20, Dolphy turned thirty-six, and nine days after that, he died, of a diabetes-related heart attack.)

I FIND no evidence that Mingus had Marcus Aurelius (A.D. 121–180) in mind when he composed "Meditations," which shares its title with the classic text by that Roman emperor and Stoic philosopher. In my own mind, though, there is a connection. Marcus was one who believed that there is an order to the universe, established by a good higher power, which he referred to variously as "Nature," "the gods," or even "Zeus." His philosophy, however, seems grounded at least as much in an assumption of hardship as in a belief in the goodness of Nature. (Marcus, who wrote his great work while at war with the barbarians, knew a thing or two about hardship.) For him, Nature and hardship were not conflicting things, or even different things. Just as a medical consultant "has prescribed horseback exercises, or cold baths, or going barefoot . . . so in the same way does the World-Nature prescribe disease, mutilation, loss, or some other disability," he wrote. How should one deal with hardship, whose forces have one outgunned? Largely through attitude: "Here is a rule to remember in future, when anything tempts you to feel bitter: not, 'This is a misfortune,' but 'To bear this worthily is a good fortune.'" For, in Marcus's view, what is important is not pleasure but how we conduct ourselves, how successful we are at bringing forth the best that is in us, in times of happiness or its opposite—especially its opposite. "Either the world is a mere hotch-potch of random cohesions and dispersions, or else it is a unity of order and providence," he wrote. "If the former, why wish to survive in such a purposeless and chaotic confusion; why care about anything, save the manner of the ultimate return to dust; why trouble my head at all; since, do what I will, dispersion must overtake me sooner or later? But if the contrary be true, then I do reverence, I stand firmly, and I put my trust in the directing Power." Here, some of us would disagree with Marcus, feeling that our conduct should not depend on an order to the universe or its lack. We just might, though, see wisdom in what he wrote in another passage: "Be master of yourself, and view life as a man, as a human being, as a citizen, and as a mortal. Among the truths you will do well to contemplate most frequently are these two: first, that things can never touch the soul, but stand inert outside it, so that disquiet can arise only from fancies within; and secondly, that all visible objects change in a moment, and will be no more. Think of the countless changes in which you yourself have had a part. The whole universe is change, and life itself is but what you deem it."

Marcus also wrote that "oneness of feeling exists between all parts of nature, in spite of their divergence and dispersion"—not a bad description of Mingus's compositions. In the beginning of Mingus's "Meditations," the horns and bowed bass intersperse an ethereal melody with a repeated three-note phrase, the near-formlessness of the one bringing to mind primordial mist, the hardness, relentlessness, and unfeelingness of the other suggesting prehistory's great cataclysms—the forming and breaking of continents and other nonhuman events. Later, in wonderful, delicate passages, Dolphy, on flute, and Byard explore the ethereal mode further. Not until nine-plus minutes into "Meditations" do traditional-style solos, with piano/bass/drum backing, begin. In other words, the solos—individuals and their achievements and statements—are not the point here, at least not the whole point. That is true even *during* the solos: here, the rhythm section does not so much accompany/support each soloist as spar with him—Dolphy first (on bass clarinet), then Byard, Coles, Mingus, and Jordan; of them, only Mingus plays without such adversity. (Do we hear this as rare human triumph, or, since Mingus is otherwise part of the rhythm section, as total domination by external events?) Coles faces a particularly fierce piano/bass/drum onslaught, and Jordan's solo is subjected to the return of the harsh, insistent phrase from the beginning of the piece. How do the trumpeter and saxophonist hold up? It is difficult to say if they triumph, or even what that would mean; but they are beautiful in the attempt. Not a bad thing to have said of us, when all is finished. Marcus Aurelius, of course, would scoff at our striving for even that modest tribute. "This mortal life is a little thing, lived in a little corner of the earth," he wrote in his own *Meditations*; "and little, too, is the longest fame to come—dependent as it is on a succession of fast-perishing little men who have no knowledge even of their own selves, much less of one long dead and gone."

JAZZ GODS AND MONSTERS

The Threepenny Review, 2006

"[O]ne by one the various keys were touched which formed the
mechanism of my being; chord after chord was sounded, and soon
my mind was filled with one thought, one conception, one purpose.
So much has been done, exclaimed [my] soul . . . more, far more,
will I achieve; treading in the steps already marked, I will pioneer
a new way, explore unknown powers, and unfold to the world the
deepest mysteries of creation."

—Mary Shelley, *Frankenstein*

THE FIGURE OF the mad scientist has long been an object of fascina-
tion, largely because his creations appeal to the often unacknowledged but
powerful human attraction to the odd, the misshapen, the seemingly un-
natural. The mad scientist has incarnations in a broad array of fields; in
jazz, he has elicited the "You call that music?" response in his guises as
Ornette Coleman, Albert Ayler, and Cecil Taylor, among others. He first
did so in the person of the pianist and composer Thelonious Monk.

Monk (1917–82) established himself on the music scene in the bebop era of the 1940s and '50s, in the company of Charlie Parker, the young Dizzy Gillespie, and the younger Miles Davis; before he was done, he would emerge as the most distinctive of that group of revolutionaries, through the oddness of his performance style and compositions. His works are not *just* odd, but oddness is a full partner with artistry in accounting for the appeal of those immortal tunes. "Straight No Chaser," "Brilliant Corners," "Epistrophy," and others of Monk's best-known melodies are full of the unexpected, both in their rhythmic shifts and jerks and in the way passages are accented; it was Monk's genius to give such curiosities not only coherence but—to borrow the title of one of them—an ugly beauty. One of his less-cited works, "Skippy," available on *Thelonious Monk—Genius of Modern Music, Volume 2*, surprises me every time I hear it: its opening is a rapid burst of piano notes that begins in a high register before tumbling downward, righting itself, and scurrying forward; the effect is a startling immediacy, as if an invited guest had bypassed the doorbell and dived in through your window.

Dance music, this isn't—unless you imitate the singular dances Monk broke into when his sidemen took their solos. In that and other ways, Monk not only was the mad scientist but acted the part. Charlotte Zwerin's excellent 1988 documentary, *Straight, No Chaser*, shows Monk wearing a scruffy goatee and a wide, wild variety of hats and—in idle moments—spinning in place. In his 1961 book *The Jazz Life*, Nat Hentoff recalled going to see Monk play in Coleman Hawkins's band at the Savoy one night in the mid-1940s. Hentoff stayed until the club's owner closed up for the night; out on the sidewalk, the owner, remembering that he hadn't seen Monk leave, sent the bouncer back inside. The bouncer couldn't find him. Then, sometime later, Monk emerged from the club's cellar. When the owner asked where he'd been, "Monk looked at him as if from a great distance and answered with slow, calm dignity. 'I was walking on the ceiling.'"

Then there is his piano playing. The *New York Times* columnist Frank Rich used possibly the best single adjective to describe it: "splintery." Monk often seemed, in playing the notes he intended, to snag parts of others as well, making for a dissonant, spiky sound—arguably the most recognizable in all of jazz. Even so, Monk is probably best remembered for his creations, most of which were musical compositions. One of his creations, like that of Shelley's Victor Frankenstein, literature's prototypical mad scientist, was a person—to the extent that one can create a person who already breathes and walks.

Before 1957 John Coltrane (1926–67) was known in jazz circles as a good but not world-changing tenor saxophonist. He had played in bands led by Dizzy Gillespie and others, and he had become famous as part of the group now remembered as Miles Davis's first great quintet; among other albums, that group had recorded four for the Prestige label in one long session in 1956—*Walkin,' Relaxin,' Steamin,'* and *Cookin.'* Coltrane's work on those beautiful records is still recognizably his, owing to his signature, raw-boned tone; but those lyrical solos give no hint of what was to come. Between performances, and sometimes during them, Coltrane—hardly alone among jazz musicians, or even among Davis's band members—was letting heroin and alcohol get the better of him. Backstage one night in October 1956, the same month that *Walkin'* and the rest were recorded, Davis got fed up and fired Coltrane, slapping and punching him in the process. A third man had wandered innocently into this scene: Thelonious Monk. Monk berated Davis and told Coltrane, as Davis recalled in his autobiography, "Man, as much as you play on saxophone, you don't have to take nothing like that; you can come and play with me anytime."

In 1957 Coltrane did just that. He spent a great deal of time in Monk's home, discussing musical ideas, and played in a quartet with the pianist in now-storied dates at the Five Spot, in New York City. "Working with Monk brought me close to a musical architect of the highest order," Coltrane wrote in *Down Beat,* as quoted in Carl Woideck's 1998 book *The John Coltrane Companion: Five Decades of Commentary.* "I felt I learned from him in every way—through the senses, theoretically, technically. I would talk to Monk about musical problems, and he would sit at the piano and show me the answers just by playing them. I could watch him play and find out the things I wanted to know. Also, I could see a lot of things that I didn't know

155

about at all." Monk planted the seeds of the Coltrane we know today. In doing so, Monk allowed more of himself to be discovered.

In a literature course I took in college, a question arose as to whether the narrator of a novel we were reading was "really" the author. The professor responded that the narrator is a creation of the author, and the author cannot create himself. Maybe not. But what is the self? For the average individual, it is a quivering point between the extremes of the person she would like to be and the one she fears becoming—with occasional excursions in either direction. Fiction writers may not be able to create themselves, but they can create figures that shed light on previously hidden sides of themselves. In the case of Shelley's 1816 novel, it is not the author but the protagonist who creates such a being. Victor Frankenstein is a brooding, obsessive figure born and raised among good, loving, cheerful people; he feels love for them, which he professes, as well as other emotions, which he does not. When he is very young, his parents adopt a girl, Elizabeth, whom they raise along with him and whom they hope he will one day marry. As a young man Victor befriends the irrepressibly cheery Henry Clerval. And then Victor creates his monster. Revolted when his creation comes to life, he flees. At first, touchingly, the monster seeks a loving relationship with humankind, but after fearful humans reject and attack him, he turns bitter and murderous. He finds Victor and, in order to inflict upon his creator the suffering he has felt, strangles to death those closest to the young scientist. Victor is consumed by guilt—which, though he does not say so, is the guilt of having one's most terrible desires realized. Might not a man as dark-natured as Frankenstein want inwardly to silence a friend as relentlessly sunny as Clerval? Might not a man rebel at the prospect of marrying a woman who is more or less his sister—and might he not, if only briefly and secretly, entertain the idea of killing her on their wedding night, before the marriage can be consummated? The one thing about which Victor feels no guilt is the pain he has caused his rejected creation to suffer; but then, a person usually does not feel guilty about evils he commits against himself. For the monster *is* Victor: his repressed self come to life.

As Frankenstein's monster doggedly taught himself written and spoken language until his eloquence exceeded that of most humans, Coltrane—beginning in 1957, the year of his collaboration with Monk—worked to master the tenor saxophone in a way no one ever had; and just as Frankenstein's monster towered physically over men, Coltrane came to stand head and shoulders above other saxophonists (with the possible exception of Sonny Rollins), creating music that other horn players are still trying, and failing, to match. Finally, Coltrane—like the monster—exposed new facets of the man who might be called his creator. Take "Nutty," available on *Thelonious Monk with John Coltrane*, from 1957. Its roughly sixteen-bar theme is, for a Monk tune, straightforward, even upbeat. Following the break, Coltrane avoids the melody while following it harmonically, ranging far afield, improvising, exploring the possibilities contained in Monk's theme—checking back in periodically to change chords according to the tune's pattern before heading off again. (Similarly, one passage in *Frankenstein* has the monster following his creator yet staying out of sight.)

"Monk was one of the first to show me how to make two or three notes at a time on tenor . . . ," Coltrane wrote in *Down Beat*. "If everything goes right, you can get triads." (Shelley herself achieved a triad: in an extended section in the middle of *Frankenstein*, the monster tells his story to his creator, a story contained in the one Frankenstein himself tells Robert Walton, the novel's frame narrator—a layering of three, the literary equivalent of harmony.) There are demonstrations of this technique, and an early taste of what Coltrane would achieve in the remaining decade of his life, in his solo on Monk's "Trinkle, Tinkle." Ira Gitler famously described as "sheets of sound" what Coltrane manages to achieve here and elsewhere, but that description, to me, misses the three-dimensionality of Coltrane's solos. A small handful of older tenor men, including Coleman Hawkins and Ben Webster, achieved such solidity of sound through the strength of their tones, but Coltrane, whose tone was actually thinner, created extra dimensions through his sheer multitude of seemingly simultaneous notes, a sound that was everywhere at once. Close your eyes during his solo on

"Trinkle, Tinkle," and you can imagine that a tornado has suddenly grown up amid Monk's piano, Wilbur Ware's bass, and Shadow Wilson's drums. That power would carry Coltrane through his reunion with Miles Davis and through the work he did in the 1960s in his own quartet, with the pianist McCoy Tyner, the drummer Elvin Jones, and the bassist Jimmy Garrison.

Recordings of the Monk-Coltrane collaborations are few, and some insist that what there is doesn't capture the magic of the live performances at the Five Spot. And so the 2005 discovery of a tape of November 1957 Monk-Coltrane shows at Carnegie Hall was met with particular enthusiasm. *Thelonious Monk Quartet with John Coltrane at Carnegie Hall* does not, to my ear, represent an achievement superior to the Monk-Coltrane records that existed before; but since those records are great and too few, more of the same is a good thing. The nine tracks are classic Monk compositions, including "Evidence," "Crepuscule with Nellie," and "Blue Monk." Backed by Shadow Wilson on drums and Ahmed Abdul-Malik on bass, Monk contributes his trademark key-banging, providing the framework for Coltrane's solos. The saxophonist alternately sprints and wails, exploring the territory Monk has claimed, the geography of that fertile mind; not, like the monster, demonstrating the worst of his creator, but shining a light on Monk's eccentric, beautiful best.

BRIGHT MISSISSIPPI

Oxford American magazine, 2011

On November 1, 1962, in a studio in New York City, Thelonious Monk—together with three sidemen—recorded several takes of a tune that had an unusual history. Its original title was "Sweet Georgia Brown"; if that sounds familiar, it's because Monk's composition began life as his version of that 1925 favorite by Ben Bernie, Kenneth Casey, and Maceo Pinkard. So extensive were Monk's changes to the melody that in the end his creation needed its own name. He called the tune, which he dedicated to the civil rights struggle, "Bright Mississippi."

1962: a black man named James Meredith, after serving his country in the U.S. Air Force for nine years, showed up as a student at the University of Mississippi at Oxford—in what would be an innocuous act today but at the time resulted in riots on campus and led President John F. Kennedy to dispatch federal troops. The following year, in the same state, the civil rights worker Medgar Evers would be murdered outside his home; the previous year, a group of young, intrepid blacks and whites had boarded buses in the nation's capital bound for Jackson, Mississippi, to exercise their right—

on behalf of all Americans—to integrated travel facilities. As thanks, many of them were beaten and jailed.

Those Freedom Riders, as they became known, did not necessarily have among them the best minds, the most charismatic figures, the greatest visionaries the American liberation struggle had ever seen. Frederick Douglass had been dead for sixty-six years, Harriet Tubman for forty-eight; W.E.B. DuBois was in his nineties; Malcolm X regarded civil rights struggles as misguided attempts to embrace a sick society; and the great Martin Luther King Jr. himself backed away from the bus campaign. But the Freedom Riders had belief and resolve, they had guts and each other, and they performed that one act ever crucial to success: they showed up.

They had a counterpart in one of the sidemen who showed up for Monk's 1962 session. Charlie Rouse, who played with Monk from 1959 to 1970, did not have the big sound of some of the other tenor saxophonists of the era, men like Gene Ammons, Sonny Rollins, Dexter Gordon, or the dean, Coleman Hawkins; he didn't play light-speed solos the way Johnny Griffin, Eddie "Lockjaw" Davis, Sonny Stitt, or the incomparable John Coltrane could. His tone was a touch ragged, the threat of a squeak or a honk always near, making for tension and volatility, the don't-know-what-might-happen feel of a march or a sit-in on a hot day with emotions running high . . .

Then there was Monk's tune, beginning where the first two bars of "Sweet Georgia Brown" ended, with three notes descending the scale. This was a cut to the chase, a reduction to essentials, mirroring the brilliant simplicity of the civil rights message: no by-your-leave, no "cast down your bucket where you are," but *We've come for what's ours!*

So: Monk lays out the theme on piano, maybe the sparest one he ever played, the usual kinks and spikes flattened out, the trademark dissonance remaining; John Ore on bass and Frankie Dunlop on drums start in, setting the relentless pace; and Charlie Rouse is off. Over many, many bars, bars like the miles covered on foot in a march or by a bus heading south, Rouse carves out a fine solo—melodic in the main, but with harmonic musings here and there, comments on the unfolding action.

Four and a half minutes into the eight-and-a-half-minute piece, it's Monk's turn. Monk, the goateed, the chapeauxed, the inscrutable master of the keyboard, playing as much or as little as he wants . . . his solo, like Rouse's, is not especially note-heavy, but the notes are placed just so, dancing over the bass and drums like points of sunlight sparkling on moving waters. It is deep into his solo that he creates the in-the-thick-of-it feel of a civil rights action: playing single, high notes near the edge of the keyboard, evoking the extremes of human experience, improvising a melody that must relate to his theme, as the marchers and Freedom Riders must—far from home, facing down fire hoses and police dogs—remember what they've been taught and why they've come.

"ONCE YOU play it the first time, that's where the feeling and everything is. And after that, it starts going *down*hill. So it's more like a challenge when you do that, you know. You know that you've got to play it correctly the first or second take, or that's it, [Monk] would take it anyhow. If you mess up, well that's it, that's your problem. You have to hear that all the rest of your life. Heh. Ha ha ha . . ." So speaks Rouse, as heard on the soundtrack of Zwerin's documentary *Straight, No Chaser.* Sure enough, the version of "Bright Mississippi" included on the original release of *Monk's Dream* (1962), the one I tried to describe above, was the first take. Interestingly, then, the alternate version included as a bonus track on the CD of *Monk's Dream*, issued in 2002—twenty years after Monk's death, at sixty-five—was not the second take but the third.

It's not quite true that "the feeling and everything" is missing from this take of "Bright Mississippi." The feeling, rather, has changed, from heat-of-the-moment to something like reminiscence. In the third take, which is nearly two minutes longer than the first, there is an allusive quality in both Rouse's and Monk's solos, as if no one present needs to hear the tale because they were there when it happened; Rouse, in particular, has largely switched from playing the melody to riffing on it. There is a more relaxed feel, as among veterans who have seen it all together and whose main job now—shared with the listener—is not to forget.

SAY IT LOUD

The Threepenny Review, 2005

IN WASHINGTON, DC, in 1974, I ran for political office—vice president of the student council at Richardson Elementary School. My opponents were three other fifth-graders, a boy and two girls. We campaigned for all of one day, reading our speeches in the school auditorium to kids in the first, second, and third grades in the morning and to fourth-, fifth-, and sixth-graders in the afternoon. We did our best to capture the tone of talks by real politicians; our speeches, in other words, were as bland as could be, all but indistinguishable from one another. The whole thing might have ended in a four-way tie, had it not been for one passage in my speech. "Maybe I'm not the baddest dude that ever crossed your path," I said. "Maybe I can't sing and dance like James Brown. But I possess leadership ability . . ." I don't remember what I said after that, but it doesn't matter, because none of the students in the audience heard it. Those kids, all of them black, like me, retained exactly two words from my speech, and I found out which two as I walked out of the auditorium and heard someone yell in my direction, "Hey! James Brown!" On Election Day I fell half a dozen votes short of beating all three of my opponents combined.

For me that episode demonstrated, as well as any lip-synched tribute at an awards ceremony ever could, what a cherished figure James Brown is—in the black community and beyond. No singer in American history has been more effective than Brown was, in his prime, at conveying the sheer feeling of being alive, with all the joy and pain—but especially the joy—that suggests. As Marc Eliot writes in one of the few illuminating passages in his introduction to Brown's superfluous, unfortunate 2005 memoir, *I Feel Good*: "[Brown's] scream was the collective measure of our scream, the one that still lurks inside all of us but that we don't always know how to release."

I, *feel*, and *good* are the second, third, and fourth syllables of one of Brown's biggest hits, the 1965 song "I Got You." The first syllable, *Owwww*, is arguably not even a word, which is appropriate, because it reflects an emotion that defies language—one that comes from the barest possible victory of joy over pain, a triumph whose slimness makes it that much sweeter, makes the scream that much louder. (For a little bit, the words following *Owwww* could be, "I've been shot.") The unspoken message in Brown's best-known work is that the two emotions are not that far apart, and that joy is felt most—perhaps exclusively—by those who have known something else.

If that is true, then Brown, almost from birth, had the makings of a world-class joy aficionado. He was born in 1933 in South Carolina, to dirt-poor parents; his mother left him and his father when Brown was four years old. His father then had an aunt come live with them, and the three soon moved across the river to Georgia, where the father, too, became largely absent from the boy's life. Brown and his aunt next went to live with another relative, known as Aunt Honey, who sheltered and fed more than a dozen other people in her home. She also ran a whorehouse there, and Brown, from the age of about six, brought home customers. He lived with a brutal, pistol-packing crowd; one of his housemates, Aunt Honey's brother, once hung him naked in a burlap sack and beat him with a belt until he was nearly unconscious. Brown didn't attend school past the age of ten, and even during his student days the rag-clad boy, to his intense embarrassment, was often called into the principal's office for wearing "insufficient clothes." And then, of course, there was his being black in the South in the 1930s and 1940s.

Small wonder, then, that despite his athletic skill and the musical ability he demonstrated at a very young age (he danced for pocket change and taught himself to play the organ one day when he was about seven), Brown landed in juvenile detention at age sixteen, convicted of petty theft. Even there he earned a reputation for his singing, and it was partly on the strength of a recommendation from Bobby Byrd, a local gospel singer who had heard the young man perform, that Brown was released at age eighteen. At the urging of none other than Little Richard, Brown and Byrd formed a secular R&B group, the Famous Flames, of which Brown soon became the main attraction. The Flames' first recording, the 1956 single "Please Please Please," was one of Brown's biggest hits.

I Feel Good suggests that "Please Please Please" forever divorced black music from "desexualized," smooth, grunt-free pop. After its release, "nothing about the sound, the look, the emotion, and the culture of modern American Black music would ever be the same," Eliot writes. That assessment fails to take into account an obscure little development of the 1960s; let's call it—oh, I don't know—Motown. Still, Eliot has a point, even if it relates more to Brown's music than to black music in general. Brown is most famous for his shouts, dance moves, and generally unbridled stage persona, and while listening to a collection of his 1950s songs reveals that he began his career as a crooner, he was a crooner with a difference. On ballads including "Please Please Please," the late 1950s hits "Try Me" and "Bewildered," and such lesser-known songs as "Just Won't Do Right" and "Begging, Begging," Brown's voice is on-pitch but rough; you get the feeling that the man unable to get what he needs by repeating "please please please" has recourse to other measures.

Then there were his stage antics. As a boy Brown had enjoyed watching preachers who "would really get down," as he revealed in his earlier and much, much better autobiography, *James Brown: The Godfather of Soul* (1986), written with Bruce Tucker. "I liked that even more than the music. I had been to a revival service and had seen a preacher who really had a lot of fire. He was just screaming and yelling and stomping his foot and then he dropped to his knees. The people got into it with him, answering him and shouting and clapping time. After that, when I went to church . . . I watched the preachers real close. Then I'd go home and imitate them. . . ." (Brown's use of a cape in his stage act, too, was inspired by a preacher—Daddy Grace.) Just as Brown screamed in a way that revealed the close relationship of joy to pain, he moved in a way that combined the religious and the not-so-religious, doing his church-derived dance while singing his classic "Sex Machine."

"'Try Me' initiated an incredible run of seventeen James Brown chart toppers," Eliot writes in *I Feel Good*—misleadingly, since that makes it sound as if Brown recorded seventeen songs in a row that reached number one, whereas the (R&B) chart toppers were spread over a sixteen-year period, from 1958 to 1974. That clarification in no way downplays Brown's achievement. Those years saw the release of, among others, "Out of Sight," "I Got the Feelin'," "Licking Stick," and "Papa's Got a Brand New Bag," some of his best songs and some of the greatest soul recordings of all time.

Greatness, once achieved, can never be taken away, but that is not true of popularity. Disco and rap were the one-two punch from which Brown's career never quite recovered, even if appearances in the movies *The Blues Brothers* (1980) and *Rocky IV* (1985) offered him brief returns to the spotlight. (That is ironic in the case of *The Blues Brothers*, which grew out of the *Saturday Night Live* routine in which the white performers John Belushi and Dan Aykroyd played musicians dressed in fedoras, dark glasses, cheap black suits, and black ties; the movie was widely criticized for exploiting the work of African-American musicians, but in *I Feel Good* Brown credits it with reviving his career. In it he played, appropriately enough, a preacher.) Only three years after the release of *Rocky IV* and "Living in America," the single that Brown performed in the film, the singer hit bottom: the drug addiction fueled by his fall from the record charts led directly to his imprisonment for aggravated assault and resisting arrest. After his release, in 1991, much was made of his return to touring and recording, but the outpouring of love that greeted him was inspired more by his past achievements, and his having survived his recent experiences, than by his diminished abilities as a performer.

Given that one Brown autobiography already existed, *I Feel Good: A Memoir of a Life of Soul* seems intended for two purposes: to give us Brown's side of the story of the 1988 arrest, which occurred after the publication of *The Godfather of Soul*, and to make the case for the singer's contributions to, and thus relevance in the era of, hip-hop. The case has considerable merit; I wish I had a dollar for every time I've started singing along with a James Brown hit, only to discover a few beats later, to my considerable disappointment, that I've been listening to a sample from some fly-by-night hip-hop "song." But the larger truth is that fans of Brown's music don't care about its relation to hip-hop, just as we don't care about who did what at the time of his arrest. (Suffice it to say that in his encounter with the police, there was enough blame to go around.) *I Feel Good* does not call itself an as-told-to memoir, but that's what it is, as Brown reveals in a strange passage near the end of the book: "I've often wondered if I would someday be able to tell my story the way it should be told, with all the important stuff put in and all the unimportant stuff left out. When I met the right person to help me, Mr. Marc Eliot, I knew I had found the right one." The "unimportant stuff" would seem to include an index and detailed discography (which Tucker's book has and Eliot's doesn't), as well as the many details that make *The Godfather of Soul* such a pleasure to read—for example, that the five-foot six-inch Brown had to stand on a Coca-Cola crate to sing into the microphone while recording a demo tape with others in the 1950s; or that the children rounded up at the last minute to shout "I'm black and I'm proud" on the 1968 hit "Say It Loud" were mostly white and Asian. Part of an as-told-to writer's job, presumably, is to capture a subject's voice at its most natural and forceful. In *The Godfather of Soul*, Brown/Tucker writes, "If you push me, you got a problem." That simple statement, which I can perfectly imagine coming from Brown's mouth, is a warning we ignore at our peril, and it resonates a good deal more than the platitudes and other bland pronouncements in *I Feel Good*. To declare one's knowledge of what another human being would or would not say is to flirt with presumptuousness; that said, one suspects that such phrases as "media-imposed cloak of invisibility," from the section of *I Feel Good* ostensibly written by Brown, comes from Eliot rather than his subject. In his introduction to that book, where he is not hiding (badly) behind Brown, Eliot makes a full display of his own talent, as in this bit of wounded English: "Even as he learned how to buck and smile for Redneck Whitey, the Black chip on his shoulder turned into a hot boulder, and soon rebellion won out over compliance and the young would-be tough-kid thug found himself in serious trouble."

The person seeking an introduction to James Brown would do much better to track down a copy of *The Godfather of Soul* than to open *I Feel Good*. She would do better still to put "Licking Stick" or "Sex Machine" on her stereo. I know a group of former elementary-school students who continue to do so, and there are many more where they came from.

PART FIVE

dispatches from

TELLCLIFF.COM

THE OTHER ME

A True Story

It seems one doesn't have to be Superman, Batman, or Captain Marvel to have an alter ego. A book/film/jazz über-nerd like me can have one, too, as the following story proves:

It is ten years ago, give or take, and I'm standing in Last Exit, a second-hand bookshop, one of three in Park Slope during that era—this one run by Alan, a bearded white guy whose voice shouts, along with whatever else he happens to be saying at a given moment, *I'm from Brooklyn!* There is one other customer: black like myself, though of a different shade and build. We get to talking; he's looking for a book related to a scholarly piece he's writing on Ralph Ellison. Around this same time I have written an essay that appears in *The Threepenny Review*—a piece about Ellison. Two black guys in a bookshop, both writing about the author of *Invisible Man*; no big deal. But then . . .

It is a year later, maybe two. I am in Holy Cow!, a second-hand record shop, one of two music stores in Park Slope at the time—this one run by Steve, an easy-going, olive-skinned fellow with short black hair. I have picked out a CD by Lennie Tristano, a pianist well-known in the jazz world but very far from being a household name. There is one other customer near the register: the Ellison scholar. He looks at my CD and says matter-of-factly, "Lee Konitz plays on that."

Okay: so this guy, who is black, hangs out in places where I alone (of the people I know) hang out, he writes about things I write about, he listens to music that I alone (of the people I know) listen to. So what? Ralph Ellison—very popular writer; a lot of people read him, and some of them write down their thoughts. The music of Lennie Tristano—yes, that's a little specialized, but hey, a niche has room for two people. No cause for alarm; the *Twilight Zone* theme music is premature.

After all, if you really want to talk obscure, we should talk about another magazine I've done a lot of writing for: *Cineaste*. This is a publication for serious film geeks. Two or three years after the Holy Cow! episode, I am invited to a party at the *Cineaste* offices, hosted by the magazine's friendly, grizzled veteran hard-core movie-guy editors. Standing among those good souls when I show up, calmly holding his drink, as if he expects to see me, is . . . the Ellison scholar/Tristano fan.

This is too much. I walk up to him and say, "What are *you* doing here?"

He says with what I consider to be, given the circumstances, outrageous calm: "I write for *Cineaste*."

And so he does. His name turns out to be Geoffrey Jacques; he is an accomplished essayist, poet, and college teacher.

Every so often, in the years that follow, I run into Geoff on the street in Park Slope. We say hi, chat a minute or two, keep going. I write a novel, *Signifying Nothing*, and publish it myself. To publicize it, I produce a You-Tube video of its first scene; I need someone to play the father in the story, someone with the look and bearing of . . . Geoff. I ask him. He graciously agrees. We're both in the two-minute video (though not together—just as Clark Kent is never around when Superman shows up . . .).

This summer Geoff moves to the West Coast (keep that geographical designation in your mind) to be with the woman he loves. I am invited to his goodbye party. He invites the guests to go through the boxes of CDs he can't take with him. I come away with good stuff, all, of course, jazz: Charlie Christian, Antonio Hart, Phineas Newborn . . .

. . . and Stan Getz. Now we're up to yesterday: I listen to one of the Getz records, a lovely work, and find myself transported to the world shaped by his warm, mellow but sinuous tone. I pick up the CD case to remind myself of the name of the world where I have been taken: *Stan Getz – Best of the West Coast Sessions* . . .

THERE ARE MANY, many films I admire for their acting, cinematography, writing, direction, etc., but the ten below—presented in no particular order—are the ones I find most memorable. I love them for many reasons, but as I looked over the list, I realized that each one is a powerful evocation of something:

Matewan. The necessity of struggle, and its cost. The great Chris Cooper, as a labor-union organizer, meets miners and cold-blooded Pinkertons in 1920s West Virginia. An explosive and heart-tearing climax. And the underappreciated David Strathairn is the coolest sheriff ever filmed.

Raising Arizona. Pure hilarity.

Lawrence of Arabia. Pure spectacle. This movie is also the definition of an epic. And, riding his youthful earnestness and enthusiasm quickly to a position of great power, Lawrence is like . . . a proto-Obama.

The Maltese Falcon. A Kantian devotion to duty. As the private eye Sam Spade, Humphrey Bogart does right by his trade and his dead partner, even though "all of [him] wants to" chuck it all and run off with Mary Astor. Spade is worldly to the point of cynicism, but he does what he's supposed to do—making him, as he calls the Maltese Falcon, "the stuff dreams are made of."

To Sleep with Anger. A primal fear: an evil force at work against your family. Not a horror flick, but an exquisite drama, with the great Danny Glover as evil itself.

The Graduate. That youthful mix of passion and confusion.

Miller's Crossing. The individual taking on the world. Gabriel Byrne gets beaten up by *everybody* in this movie—including his girlfriend—but wins the day.

Raiders of the Lost Ark. Pure adventure—and the key element of the adventurer: a jazzman's ability to improvise. Says Indy, "I'm making this up as I go along."

Annie Hall. The absurdity of romance. "Most of us just need the eggs." Who has said it better?

The Godfather. What is there to say about perfection?

FOREIGN FILM FRAGMENTS

W EEKS AGO, after I posted "Cliff's 10 Best Movies of All Time," an appalled colleague of mine asked if I had purposely omitted foreign films from my list. The answer was no. I stand by the list, but the question got me thinking about why there are only American films on it. I concluded that while film is, of course, a visual medium, and while many people (including my colleague) prefer to think of film primarily if not solely in those terms, the other elements—sound, story, character—cannot be divorced, singly or together, from the overall movie-viewing experience. The fact that I am fluent in exactly one language can't help but affect my response to a film; subtitles are available, of course, but many are (or so I'm told) crude approximations of what characters are saying in their own languages, and, anyway, an understanding of tone and inflection is essential to grasping the full meaning of a line delivered by an actor. No subtitle could capture, for example, the way Humphrey Bogart's tone informs his words when he asks Ingrid Bergman in *Casablanca*, ". . . Or aren't you the kind to tell?" English-language movies resonate most deeply with me simply because they're the ones I understand best. Sue me.

This is not to say that I don't watch or enjoy foreign films. I've even been known to become mildly obsessed with them. (Talk to my wife.) And I have often found their story lines and characters to be moving. But, sort of like a blind person whose hearing becomes more acute, I've found that the language barrier present with foreign films often leads me to concentrate more heavily on the visual element. (Also, directors of classic foreign films—which are the ones I gravitate toward—tend to pay more attention to visuals than their American counterparts.) When I think of foreign movies I've found memorable, single images are often what come to mind. Here are some, all in black and white:

Cleo from 5 to 7. A gorgeous view from a car as it winds along the streets of Paris.

L'avventura. Three images here. In one, Gabriele Ferzetti sees a bottle of ink and a set of architectural drawings and, unable to control even his most childish impulses, dumps the black ink on the white paper. Then an opposite image, at film's end: the white hand of Monica Vitti coming to rest on Ferzetti's black hair; ironically, she comforts him after he cheats on her, because, of the two of them, he is the more pathetic. Earlier: the camera tilts back and forth, mimicking the motion of the boat on which Vitti is a passenger—because her world has just been rocked.

La Strada. A side view of a young man who has just received what turns out to be a fatal pummeling from Anthony Quinn. Stumbling forward, about to collapse, he looks in panic at his wrist, worrying aloud that his watch is broken. I don't think there is a more heart-rending image in all of cinema, unless it's the one from

Rocco and His Brothers in which a woman staggers away, mustering all the steadiness and dignity she can, after her ex-boyfriend has forced himself on her—while the man's brother, who is the woman's current lover, was forced to watch. Less upsetting, but just as sad, is the final image of

Late Spring, in which an old man gives way to silent tears while peeling a piece of fruit.

I just realized what downers these are . . .

There is no decade easier to make fun of than the 1960s, unless it's the 1970s. And yet the period of roughly ten years beginning in the late 1960s saw the releases of some of the most interesting American films ever made. This was the brief, great era when major studios put movies in theaters without first market-testing them to the point where you could say the dialogue along with the actors, to the point where the endings were visible from a distance of ninety minutes. Of course, the films of that period —*Midnight Cowboy, The King of Marvin Gardens, Carnal Knowledge, Scarecrow,* and many others—were predictable in their own way: things were going to turn out badly, it was just a matter of how, and how badly. But their characters' antiheroic march toward defeat usually represented an honest search for some human truth on the director's part, and along the way there were many memorable scenes. Think of Dustin Hoffman's Ratzo Rizzo crossing the street in *Midnight Cowboy* ("I'm *wawlkin"* here!") or Jack Nicholson's diner scene in *Five Easy Pieces.*

Nicholson did his best work during that era (in *Pieces, Carnal Knowledge, One Flew Over the Cuckoo's Nest, The Last Detail,* and other films), and his reputation survived it: by the time the 1970s were over there was no bigger star in Hollywood. Without taking anything away from Nicholson, though, I wonder if his prominence owes as much to luck and chance as to talent. I wonder this because of an actor who, to my mind, gave equally compelling performances in the 1970s and who today turns up in bit parts, while Nicholson gets millions for suspicious-looking projects like *The Bucket List* (which I admit I didn't see).

I'm thinking of Elliott Gould. In a string of films in the 1970s, he was a magnetic presence, conveying a combination of laid-back cool and rebelliousness topped only by Marlon Brando's work in the 1950s. (He lacked

Brando's physical grace, but he lacked it to *such* an extent that that became another part of his charm.) In Peter Hyams's *Busting,* with Robert Blake, Gould managed to look like a rebel while playing just about the squarest thing you could be at the time: a vice cop. Maybe nothing better exemplifies what Gould did than his role as the private eye Philip Marlowe, a '70s update of the Raymond Chandler character, in Robert Altman's *The Long Goodbye.* He spends half the movie repeating his (and the 1970s') motto, "Okay by me." Then, at film's end, he commits an act that feels both outrageously wrong and exactly right. Gould was great in *MASH,* even greater in *California Split* . . . Why doesn't he have the status that Nicholson has?

THE TWO ALS

THE OTHER DAY, bleary-eyed but happy, my eleven-year-old returned home from a sleepover—a misnomer if ever there was one—and announced that she had a new favorite movie: Alfred Hitchcock's *Rear Window*. She pronounced Grace Kelly to be "awesome," and she said that at the truly frightening moment when the killer played by Raymond Burr looks straight into the camera—i.e., when he realizes that the crippled Jimmy Stewart has been watching him—she and her friends "screamed bloody murder."

Her excitement got me thinking about other Hitchcock movies she might like. And that got me thinking about the master's movies in general, and which I find the most memorable. I came up with two.

When most people think of the scariest Hitchcock, they think of *Psycho,* but the Cliff Prize in this category goes to *The Birds.* This is not to take anything away from *Psycho*, a brilliantly shot film that plays with equal brilliance on everyone's fear of meeting the wrong person under the wrong circumstances. *The Birds*, though, evokes something ultimately even more terrifying. Avoid the Bates Motel and you avoid the psychotic Norman, but there is no getting away from the birds, which makes them a stand-in for any number of things, or all of them together: illness, the ravages of old age, terrorism, economic disaster, or the hundred other elements of chaos waiting to break through the thin surface of everyday life.

Then there is *North by Northwest.* Here, Cary Grant, James Mason, and Eva Marie Saint are wonderful, and the political intrigue is fun. But what I love most about this movie, what strikes me as its essence, is how it channels the spirit of life's unpredictability. One minute Grant is going about his business like everybody else; a short time later—in one of my favorite movie sequences of all time—he is being chased through a cornfield by an airplane.

Grant does a good job as that Hitchcock-style hero, the decent, ordinary man who gets caught up in dangerous, crazy-seeming events. (Jimmy Stewart was no slouch in this department, either.) But what a pity that Hitchcock never worked with the all-time champion: Alan Arkin. Arkin is best-known lately for his role as the kind, lecherous grandfather in *Little Miss Sunshine.* In his leading-man heyday, though, there was nobody better at playing a guy waging a subtly comic struggle to keep a level head when he appears to be the last sane human being around. He did it very well in *The In-Laws,* and he did it brilliantly in *Catch-22,* in which he delivered one of the best lines in all moviedom: "He died. You don't get older than that."

I KNOW black people who read only books by other blacks. In part they want to support the work of black writers—a laudable goal. Partly they enjoy seeing themselves, their experiences and concerns, reflected in what they read. (Who doesn't?) And the choice is also partly about self-protection. There are enough casual displays of white racism, privilege, and entitlement in the real world, the thinking goes, so why risk encountering them while relaxing with a novel? These readers cast a wary eye on works by contemporary nonblack writers. Books by dead white authors? Forget it.

As a black reader, I understand that attitude. I just don't share it. This statement will make me sound like—perhaps reveal me to be—the world's original sap, but I look on books as representatives of the best that the world of human thought has to offer. Greedy fellow that I am, I want unfettered access to that thought. I wouldn't want to live in a world where I couldn't read Virginia Woolf or John Cheever, just as I wouldn't want to live in one that was missing Zora Neale Hurston or Ishmael Reed.

Over the years my openness has been richly rewarded. From time to time, of course, my reward is to read a sentence like this one, from *Decline and Fall*, by Evelyn Waugh: "With or without her nigger, Mrs Beste-Chewynde was a woman of vital importance."

What am I supposed to do when I come across a passage like that? Do I rip the book in half at the spine and throw the pieces across the room, feeling that to continue reading would be an act of self-hatred? Do I sigh heavily and plod on, seeing the need to accept the book for what it is— a product of a different time? Do I recognize the separation between author and narrator and give the author the benefit of the (wafer-thin) doubt? Or do I remember my rule about separating any work of art from the artist? I love, for example, the music of Miles Davis, a man not exactly on the cutting edge of feminism. (Of course, his misogyny didn't come through in his records.)

Whatever justification I give it, I am not likely to change the way I read. I look on the world of books as an adventure; adventure suggests unpredictability—and a certain amount of risk.

WHAT DOES it mean to be black in an era that has brought us both the presidency of Barack Obama and the tragedy of Trayvon Martin? At a time when the possibilities for blacks have never seemed greater, while the prison population has never been darker? Touré's *Who's Afraid of Post-Blackness?: What It Means to Be Black Now* is an attempt to address these questions, and if his book feels a tad disjointed, his answers at times contradictory, it's less a reflection of his approach than of the nature of the subject matter. Touré is just trying to stay on top of this Taurus, not tell it where to go.

"Post-black," here, means neither nonblack nor post-racial. Instead, it represents a decision to acknowledge the burdens of being black while refusing to add to those burdens by placing limits on ourselves. Post-blackness means that instead of disdaining the fencing team as the kind of group white boys join, you pick up a sword, discover you're good with it, and show the world what you can do. Post-blackness means that you don't revoke a person's membership in the black race because of his or her proper speech or white spouse. It means that there are as many ways to be black, to celebrate the culture, as there are black people.

Having ably defined post-blackness, Touré proceeds not only to shift gears, slipping back into plain old blackness, but to forget what he has already written. After agreeing with one of the 105 prominent blacks he interviewed that the term "oreo" should be abolished, he carefully assures us in a later chapter that during his freshman year of college, "I was no oreo, I got along with my Black classmates," even if he "spent way more time with my white friends." When he refers to the "social mistakes" he made as a freshman, it's not clear whether or not he is being ironic, but my sinking feeling is that the answer is no.

The part of the book I personally found the most strange was the chapter "The Most Racist Thing That Ever Happened . . ." Airing his own feelings, sharing the thoughts of his interviewees, he essentially equates contemporary blackness with a state of perpetual self-consciousness, fear, and suspicion, with being stuck in the Harrison Ford/David Janssen role in a version of *The Fugitive* that has no ending. From wondering what plum job racism may have cost you without your knowledge, to worrying that you'll confirm stereotypes if you eat fried chicken or watermelon in front of white people, blackness is presented here as one blood-pressure-raising moment after another, from the time of waking until your head hits the pillow. I read this chapter with rising discomfort, feeling as if I were having dinner with someone who kept turning to address a third person I couldn't see. I know, everyone knows, that racism has not gone away. Like every black person, I am forced to think about it; sometimes I think about it a lot. Does the subject make me angry? Damn right it does. But it is not the center of my life, which means, to my mind, that it has not defeated me. So who is the fool—me, or my dinner companion?

That is not a rhetorical question; I honestly wondered what the answer was, until I had an epiphany. Touré writes that when he was a boy in just about the only black family in his neighborhood, his parents constantly warned him against confirming white people's worst ideas about blacks. My parents, in my all-black neighborhood, did nothing of the kind. I was not, in other words, mentally hampered from the word "go," and I realize that I have one more thing to thank my late parents for. I can't say I haven't run into problems as a black man; but with regard to that job I was surely if theoretically denied because of racism, I ask: Why would I want to work for racists? What would my blood pressure be like then? I love fried chicken, and I can take or leave watermelon, but I would eat both in front of whites as quickly as I would in the company of blacks. A person who sees me enjoying a drumstick and concludes "Yep, black people really *do* love chicken" is an idiot, plain and simple, and I don't give a rusty goddamn *what* he thinks.

So I give Touré credit for this: he has written a work that led me to look at myself and the world and draw conclusions I might not have otherwise. A book that makes someone do that cannot be said to have failed.

Touré concludes his book with a description of the tightrope that Barack Obama, Deval Patrick, and other successful black politicians have walked on the way to power. As he urges other blacks to take the same tortuous, torturous path, one that no white politician would have to follow, his message is both inspiring and, by its very nature, sad—an apt description of the state of black America.

PAINTING IS the branch of the arts in which I feel the sharpest division between what I admire and what I respond to emotionally. For example: I admire the mastery, the skillful re-creation of reality of the painting *Ivy Bridge* by J. M. W. Turner, and God knows I could never duplicate it. But, honestly, it leaves me cold.

Likewise: Francisco Goya, Caravaggio, John Constable—I admire them all, and for the same reasons, but I wouldn't make a special trip to see their paintings. No, the works that stir me tend to combine simple forms with vivid color, to eschew photograph-like realism—the trompe l'oeil style—in favor of bolder statements. At the same time, I generally require *some* element of representation—exceptions to this rule being the work of Kandinsky and Pollock. (I feel about abstract and, particularly, conceptual art the way Robert Frost felt about free verse, I guess—that it's like tennis without a net.)

The painters I respond to, then, tend to be Impressionists and—especially—post-Impressionists: Picasso, Matisse. And check out a 1919 painting by Kees Van Dongen, titled *The Corn Poppy.* Or Matisse's *Nono Lebasque,* from 1908, and *Laurette in a Green Robe,* from 1916.

Maybe what I like—this is just a theory—is that these works allow me to form a partnership with the artists, in a way that conceptual art is supposed to but never does. With conceptual art I feel I am doing *all* the work (there are some pieces that truly make me feel as if the artists have done none). With a work by Turner or Caravaggio, there is nothing for me to do but marvel. But viewing a work like *Laurette,* armed with Matisse's bold impressions of this woman, I can imagine her in full myself—I feel on my own that I know her, or at least know something about her.

RECENTLY MY wife and I went to see the Monet exhibit at the Gagosian Gallery, on 21st Street in Manhattan. There are around three dozen paintings done by the great Impressionist of scenes in his own garden: trees, flowers, ponds, lily pads. The paintings are, of course, very very beautiful, and they become more so the longer you look at them (and the farther away you stand).

Looking at the objects represented, I found that they often fell into two broad categories: those in front of the painter, and those (tree limbs and leaves, clouds) reflected on the surfaces of ponds. So on many of the canvases, there are two realities going on—one fully present, the other seen but existing elsewhere.

And it occurred to me that in this way, Monet's paintings find either a parallel or an opposite in the modernist novels of Virginia Woolf. Consider these lines from *To the Lighthouse* (1927), in which Mrs. Ramsay reads to her young son James. Mrs. Ramsay, we learn, is "reading and thinking, quite easily, both at the same time; for the story of the Fisherman and his Wife was like *the bass gently accompanying a tune, which now and then ran up unexpectedly into the melody* [italics mine]. . . . Oh, but she never wanted James to grow a day older! or Cam either. These two she would have liked to keep for ever just as they were, demons of wickedness, angels of delight, never to see them grow up into long-legged monsters. Nothing made up for the loss. When she read just now to James, 'and there were numbers of soldiers with kettledrums and trumpets,' and his eyes darkened, she thought, why should they grow up, and lose all that?"

Monet's paintings and *To the Lighthouse* are opposite in this way: in the scenes depicted on the canvases, where clouds seem to be part of the garden but aren't, we see more than is really there, whereas in the passages from Woolf's novel, we see less: we witness one reality—a woman reading to her son—through which passes another, in which past experience informs present fears. But of course the two works are also parallel. Are the clouds less real than the lily pads, if both are before our eyes? Are Mrs. Ramsay's thoughts and memories not, in a way, even more real than the act of reading to her son, since they consume more of her attention and energy?

I feel myself veering close to areas—existential philosophy and all that —I'm not equipped to discuss. Better stop here.

A CONFESSION ABOUT JAZZ

YEARS AGO, as a young(er) man, I struggled to define my identity as both black and American. In the end I turned to jazz ,whose sound I loved, as a symbol of black Americans' inventiveness and as a basis for a sense of cultural identity. That decision both helped me to relax and launched a music-buying addiction that hasn't gone away.

To know anything about me is to know that I'm not a racist. But I do have to confess to something. Sometimes, when I put on a record by a white jazz artist, even if it's one I love, I sigh inwardly. For me, after all, listening to jazz is not just a pleasurable experience, but an act of cultural communion. So what does it mean when I listen to a record by a white jazz musician? That is not a rhetorical question; I really want to know.

Maybe one clue is that, even if I sigh, I go ahead and put on the record. And maybe I do it because I sense that if there is an irony and contradiction in what I'm doing, it is merely the irony and contradiction inherent in any American identity. But this is especially true of African-Americans. One fact epitomizes this for me: jazz was started in New Orleans with brass instruments left over from the Civil War. And so, from the debris of the Confederate States of America—that institution founded on and devoted to black slavery—grew black Americans' greatest contribution to U.S. culture.

While I continue to ponder all this, I offer—in good faith and good will—recommendations of jazz records by some of our "white brothers," as Cornel West might call them.

The Bill Evans Trio: Sunday at the Village Vanguard, 1961. The music of the pianist Bill Evans is a little like baseball. Some find it boring and wonder what all the fuss is about. Others see—rather, hear—its beauty. I address this to potential members of the latter camp. Evans had a lilting sound and a beautiful, distinctive way with block chords. And to listen closely to this record is to realize that the bassist Scott LaFaro was, in his own way, every bit the monster-in-our-midst that Coltrane was in Miles Davis's first great quintet.

The Best of Django Reinhardt, **1996.** This illiterate Belgian (1910–53) who lost the use of two fingers in a fire was somehow able to rival Charlie Christian as the most influential jazz guitarist of all time.

Mulligan Meets Monk, **1957.** The great baritone saxophonist Gerry Mulligan brings his gorgeous, raw-boned sound to Thelonious Monk's tunes, accompanied by the genius pianist/composer himself.

The Teddy Charles Tentet, **1956.** Charles is a white guy and a vibraphonist —strike one and strike two, right? Wrong. These tunes are gems, some of them moody in that '50s jazz way, some of them hard-driving. In the second category is "The Emperor," an eight-minute mini-adventure.

EAST MEETS WEST

or, Sonny and Trane

EVERY PERSON or thing with a claim to being the greatest of his/her/its kind has a rival nearly as great. The question with each pairing is: which is the greatest, and which is the rival? There are Tolstoy and Dostoyevsky . . . Coke and Pepsi . . . The Beatles and The Rolling Stones . . Martin Luther King and Malcolm X . . . Ella Fitzgerald and Billie Holiday . . . and, speaking of jazz: The tenor sax greats John Coltrane and Sonny Rollins.

As with The Beatles (who broke up in 1970) and The Stones (who are still with us), there is no comparison in terms of longevity between the two saxmen: Coltrane died in 1967, at age 40, and Rollins is somewhere blowing right now. That has not stopped fans from comparing them. Sonny and Trane are the greatest tenor saxmen of their—some would say any—generation. Of the two, I have a preference. It's just that my preference depends on what day it is.

I find a pair of metaphors helpful for describing their styles and the different moods they create, the different sensibilities they convey: the big, bad city vs. the wide-open West. Trane is the city: *intense*, a million notes like the million people on any street, and vertical, leaving a harmonic audio trace whose visual equivalent might be the Manhattan skyline. As for Sonny, is it an accident that one of his best records is called *Way Out West*? With just a bassist (Ray Brown) and drummer (Shelly Manne) as accompaniment, Sonny is free to let his great big tone roam, spread out horizontally like a herd of something wild. Sonny is cool. Trane is hot. What's your pleasure?

THE MUSIC OF FALL

THE DAYS are shorter; the air outside has gone from sweltering to pleasant, sometimes even cool; and now the official date has arrived. Fall is here. And so I pull out the fall music.

I discovered it this way: Years ago I was very fond of a TV commercial for a bank. Citibank? Chase? I don't know. To tell the truth, I don't even remember much of the ad itself. My vague sense is that it portrayed a city—not with views of the Empire State Building and the like, but with shots of people waiting at street corners or other, similarly innocuous scenes, representing the kinds of unrushed moments in which a city dweller's thoughts might be anywhere. What I do remember clearly is the music in the ad, which fit perfectly: a lilting clarinet solo, capturing the feel of a person's wistful, private musing. (You can write me off as a stooge manipulated by marketing, but if I am, why can't I remember the name of the bank?)

One day, in a bookstore, I heard the music from the ad. I asked the store clerk about it and learned that it was track number three, "How Am I To Know?", from the CD *The Benny Goodman Sextet*. I went to a nearby music store and bought it immediately.

And I play it still, often at this time of year. The euphoria of summer is over; the rush and requisite cheer of the holidays are still a ways off. It is a good time for reflecting on where we've been, where we might go. *The Benny Goodman Sextet* is good music for such reflection.

My only advice is to skip the track "Four or Five Times," on which Goodman proves that prodigious skill on the clarinet does not make one a singer. It reminds me of the great, smoking record *Sonny Side Up*, with Dizzy Gillespie and two tenor saxmen, Sonny Rollins and the underappreciated Sonny Stitt—which includes Dizzy's endearingly bad vocals on "Sunny Side of the Street."

But back to my main point: What music reminds you of particular seasons? Ponder that and other matters sometime soon, round about dusk, as you pour yourself a drink and listen to "How Am I To Know?" . . .

The Autumn House Nonfiction Series

Michael Simms, General Editor

DESIGN AND PRODUCTION

Cover and text design: Chiquita Babb
Cover art: Clifford Thompson
Author photograph: Kate Slininger

Text set in Monotype Dante, a mid-20th century font designed by Giovanni Mardersteig, influenced by types cut by Francesco Griffo between 1449 and 1516. Dante was first cut by Charles Malin between 1946 and 1954, then redrawn for digital use by Ron Carpenter in 1993. Display text set in Futura, a geometric sans-serif typeface designed by Paul Renner in 1927.

Printed by McNaughton & Gunn on 55# Glatfelter Natural

CONTENTS

FOREWORD

When I began my career at the Hearing and Speech Clinic in Halifax, Nova Scotia, in 1972, I quickly learned that I preferred working with young children and their families and, in time, I became the pediatric audiologist at this center. Unlike the adults who often chose not to use hearing aids, the hard-of-hearing children and their families with whom I worked were positive and optimistic about hearing instrument technology, such as it was, in those years.

Relative to the knowledge and vast array of instrument technology we have today, we had very little to work with in the early 1970s: there were no electrophysiological systems to test the hearing of young infants, no devices to measure the performance of hearing aids, and no systematic way to prescribe hearing aids for children.

Our limitations became especially apparent in the mid-1970s, when a major rubella epidemic broke out in the Canadian Maritime provinces. At that time, the Nova Scotia Hearing and Speech Clinic provided audiology services for three provinces: Nova Scotia, New

Brunswick, and Prince Edward Island. Within a month or two of the epidemic, close to 40 babies were referred to our clinic. To this date, I remember the names of many of those babies and the faces of those young mothers and fathers. Because our knowledge of pediatric hearing loss was limited, there was a lot of "guesstimating" but mostly there was a lot of hoping. The young parents kept bringing their babies back and in the process, together, we all learned a great deal.

I made a few observations during this experience. First, I observed that when I was lucky and somehow provided the baby with "appropriate" hearing aids, for which there were only very crude criteria, things began to happen. Most but not all of the babies seemed to be hearing. In fact, some seemed to be hearing very well. Through these experiences, I came to understand how powerful and helpful this work could be.

I also observed that the progress these babies made did not seem to depend entirely on the degree of their hearing loss or the appropriateness of the hearing aid fitting. Certainly there were babies who appeared to derive little or no real benefit from the hearing aids. A number of them had profound hearing losses and, unfortunately, it would be some 15 or more years before cochlear implants would become available for young children. We worked with families to help them to choose the communication option that was best for them and their children.

At the same time, though, I saw that there were some babies with quite severe hearing losses who were making remarkable progress with amplification. In time I concluded that one of the most important factors appeared to be the extent to which the parents (and in many cases, the grandparents) were engaged in the process. Some parents came to our sessions with a seemingly endless list of questions and important observations about their child. In contrast, other parents spent the first year or more flying to Montreal, Toronto, and the United States to get second, third, and fourth opinions about their child's hearing. There was something very important and interesting going on here—something worth learning more about. If we could understand this process better from the parents' perspective we might then design our services to be more helpful to them.

In 1976 I decided to take my clinical experiences and my many questions back to school. At the University of Connecticut, working with pediatric audiology pioneer Dr. Mark Ross, I learned more about the process of hearing aid fitting in pre-verbal children. I also studied counseling with Dr. Thomas Giolas, who was one of very few audiologists to recognize the enormous importance of the counseling process in our work with clients and their families.

Since then, my research program has focused on developing a pediatric hearing instrument selection and fitting method so that audiologists and families have a scientific approach to hearing instrument fitting that I did not have in 1972. Along the way, I have learned a great deal from many children, parents, and grandparents. I thank them deeply for this. My life has been enriched greatly through these experiences and, hopefully, I have been of some help to them.

The book Debby Waldman has written with Jackson Roush is a great gift to us all. It is a book beautifully written *for* parents. With great skill, these authors provide the reader with important technical details about hearing loss in children, interwoven with powerful stories from the heart. I only wish that I had had a book like this to read when I began my career. While the book has been written for parents, it is my fervent hope that it will also be read by audiologists, physicians, early interventionists, speech-language pathologists, educators, and by the many students who want to be helpful to children with hearing loss and their families. Thank you, Debby and Jack, for this precious gift.

Richard C. Seewald, Ph.D.
Professor and Canada Research Chair in Childhood Hearing
National Centre for Audiology
The University of Western Ontario
London, Ontario, Canada

AUTHORS' NOTE

Having a child diagnosed with hearing loss is a new and unfamiliar experience for most families. Our goal for this book is to provide information at a level that is informative to parents without being unnecessarily detailed or technical. It is written in first person, but we worked together to combine accuracy with personal experience in hopes of making it useful and interesting to parents looking for an alternative to what is typically offered in booklets and handouts. The book will be of interest primarily to families who choose to communicate with their child using an oral language method in conjunction with hearing aids or cochlear implantation. We respect the right of families to choose a non-oral method such as American Sign Language (ASL) or one of the sign systems that provide a visual representation of English. Information regarding those methods is provided in the Resources section. The section also provides resources for additional information on all topics presented in this text, as well as a list of recommended readings and websites.

We do not want to mislead parents into thinking that hearing aids or cochlear implants benefit all children equally or that they alone will solve every problem. Some children, especially those with disabilities in addition to hearing loss, may not benefit from either technology. Still, it has been our experience that nearly all children with hearing loss benefit from hearing aids, cochlear implants or, in some cases, a combination of the two. Our goal is to help parents understand the processes involved in the assessment of hearing, the selection of hearing instruments, and the various communication options. We also provide information to assist with the process of acquiring and, when necessary, advocating for special services when needed.

Finally, we want to acknowledge that this book is aimed primarily at the practical issues associated with hearing loss in children. You will read some interesting and heartfelt testimonials from parents who share interpersonal aspects of parenting a deaf or hard-of-hearing child, but we make no attempt to present in depth the psycho-emotional aspects of hearing loss for parents or children. Readers interested in a more detailed exploration of these important issues are referred to several excellent books listed in the Recommended Reading section.

The authors welcome comments and suggestions from parents and professionals. Please feel free to contact us via email at childshearing@shaw.ca or jroush@med.unc.edu.

PREFACE

When my first child, Elizabeth, was diagnosed with a permanent hearing loss two weeks after her third birthday, I was shattered. Although her dad and I had suspected something was wrong with her hearing, neither of us was remotely prepared for the news that she would have to wear hearing aids, we would probably never know what caused the loss, and no operation could fix her ears.

"I'm a surgeon," said the pediatric ear, nose, and throat specialist we were sent to after her diagnosis. "If I could operate, I would."

Instead of the hospital, we headed to a "dispensing" clinic about ten minutes from our house, where an audiologist injected blobs of blue putty-like silicone into Elizabeth's ears to make impressions for her first set of earmolds, to go with her first pair of hearing aids.

By this time, my husband, Dave, and I had had a few weeks to adjust to the idea that our daughter really had a hearing problem. We talked out loud about what we'd each realized privately: that Elizabeth could hear when we pressed our lips to one of her ears and spoke into it, but she couldn't hear her one-year-old brother crying from the other side of the room, and if we called to her from a distance, unless she could see us, she wouldn't know where to find us.

At the clinic that day, we collected more pamphlets about hearing loss and hearing aids, which we added to the pile that included brochures from an audiologist in North Dakota (the older sister of one of Elizabeth's babysitters) and from the social worker at the rehabilitation hospital where Elizabeth had undergone the tests that confirmed her hearing loss and where she would eventually attend preschool for hard-of-hearing children.

The brochures were informative, but limited. There was nothing from other parents, nothing to prepare us for how this new reality would affect our daily lives. At the rehab hospital library, I searched the shelves in the hearing impairment section and found a wide variety of books for parents of deaf children, but only one for parents of a child who needed the assistance of hearing aids. It was by the mother of a boy who had been diagnosed with a mild-to-moderate hearing loss back in the early 1980s, a period I had already come to consider the dark ages of hearing aids for children. The story was interesting, but not exactly relevant to what I was experiencing at the dawn of the twenty-first century.

In September 1999, about half a year after Elizabeth began wearing hearing aids, she started preschool at the rehab hospital. She had four classmates, all of whom wore hearing aids. I couldn't stop myself from peppering their parents with questions: How did you find out about your child's loss? How did you deal with it? How often do you change batteries? Have you found a more useful hearing aid cleaning tool than that flimsy little toothpick-with-a-wire contraption that costs $2 at the clinic and breaks after one use? How often do you have to get new earmolds? Does your child put in his own aids, or do you have to do it? How can you tell the difference between when your child can't hear because the equipment isn't working properly and when she just doesn't want to listen to you?

The conversations we had were lively and nonstop; we all had questions our audiologists couldn't answer, and our children weren't in elementary school yet. From sessions with the parent liaison at the preschool program, we learned that once elementary school began, we could expect to deal with even more issues.

The germ of the idea for *Your Child's Hearing Loss* was born during the year Elizabeth spent in preschool. While the professionals who worked with her could and did provide me with technical information about her equipment and educational needs, only other parents helped me understand what I needed to help Elizabeth and the rest of my family on a daily basis.

One of the first things Jack Roush and I did after agreeing to co-author this book was put together a questionnaire for parents of children who were hard of hearing and wore hearing aids, or who were deaf and used cochlear implants. Our goal was to get enough responses to provide a broad range of experiences. Between the questionnaires and interviews I conducted, including contacts with hard-of-hearing adults and teenagers, we collected more than 40 stories.

No two families had identical experiences, although there were recurring themes. About one-third had no trouble getting a diagnosis: their children were tested at birth, through newborn hearing screening programs or as part of testing for a genetic syndrome. Others were tested after an illness, usually meningitis, and so the hearing loss came as no surprise. Another third had no trouble getting a diagnosis after telling their physician they were concerned about their child's behavior. The remaining third, however, had their concerns dismissed by doctors. The implication seemed to be that mom and dad were too inexperienced to know the difference between real and imagined problems, and that they were simply worrying too much.

"Doctors said, 'He's a boy, he's a boy, they talk later, blah blah blah,' " recalled Cheri, who began worrying about her middle child, Carter, when he was an infant. Unlike her outgoing and chatty oldest, "Carter just seemed different to me," she said. "He would sit in his car seat and gaze out the window. He wasn't engaged unless he was looking at you. There was a part of me that kept saying, 'Oh, no, it couldn't be anything,' but I knew something was wrong."

Carter developed the first of many ear infections when he was two weeks old. At nine months, he got his first set of tympanostomy tubes to prevent the accumulation of fluid in his middle ear. The doctor assured Cheri that Carter would be hearing well within a couple of days. A couple of days went by, and Carter still wasn't responding to sounds, so Cheri brought him back to the doctor, who clapped his hands behind the baby's back. When Carter felt the breeze and turned to the source, the doctor said he was fine.

Cheri never went back to that doctor. Instead, she took Carter to an audiologist who was convinced he had some hearing. Still certain there was a problem, Cheri then brought her son to a larger clinic at the University of North Carolina, where he was tested more extensively. That's when she learned her son was profoundly deaf. "I was devastated," she said. "My husband was out of town and I felt like my child had just died. You think, oh my God, he's never going to say my name, he's never going to talk. The only experience I had with a deaf person was in seventh grade, where I had a phys ed teacher who was deaf. I remember kids making fun of him behind his back, and I thought, this is what my son's going to have. It was really life altering."

Jennifer, too, was an experienced mother when she began wondering if something was wrong with her infant, Danny, though she didn't suspect deafness. An occupational therapist, she wondered if something was wrong with his sensorimotor skills.

"I started asking my pediatrician when Danny was four months old if something unusual was going on," she said. "The doctor told me that nothing was wrong and that I, being an occupational therapist, knew too much and was in a sense looking too hard for something to be wrong."

By the time Danny was nine months old, the pediatrician agreed with Jennifer and ordered blood tests to determine if he had muscle disorders. At one year old, Danny was diagnosed with a profound hearing loss.

"It was difficult news to get," Jennifer said. "But having worked with deaf children and children with disabilities, I knew that we—and he—would be okay, and that we would do what was necessary to give him a full life."

When my neighbor Kathy read an early draft of this book, one of her first comments was to caution me against scaring parents. Kathy has six daughters. Her youngest, Becky, has a hearing loss similar to Elizabeth's. Her second oldest, Elfi, has spina bifida. One of the first books Kathy read after Elfi was born came with the following caveat: "Marriages rarely last in the case of a child with a disability."

It never occurred to Jack and me to ask parents in the questionnaire whether their marriages had survived their child's diagnosis of hearing loss. One parent, herself hard of hearing since birth, said she felt guilty about her child's loss and her husband didn't really understand. But no one said anything about their marriage having broken up as a result. Still, the diagnosis of hearing loss is stressful for any family. Uncertainties and conflicting advice can add to the tension. Mothers often take on the additional burden of "family expert" on matters related to the child's special needs.

A diagnosis of hearing loss can be devastating and most families need time to grieve. Fortunately, there is much that can be done through technology and intervention, and most families eventually cope well. That's not to say that hearing loss is without its recurring frustrations and tensions. I can guarantee it will sometimes eat up more time and energy than you have to spare, that your child will lose or damage his hearing aids, and that a battery will die on the day you've forgotten to bring the bag with fresh ones.

In the grand scheme of things, however, it's something most of us learn to live with. As hard as it is to believe, you may even find things to appreciate about hearing loss. And as Kathy pointed out to me, eventually the child, not you, will take responsibility for the hearing loss.

Elizabeth began taking responsibility for her hearing aids when she was around seven. She knows how to change batteries, and she no longer asks me to take out her aids at night or put them in in the morning. When she was three and newly aided, I honestly assumed I'd be doing those tasks until she graduated from high school and left home. But they're her aids, and she wants to care for them, as she is making increasingly clear.

"You don't own it; the child does," Kathy reminded me. "Essentially, you are teaching the management skills right from the beginning, and she'll teach you."

It's my hope, and Jack's, that this book will help make that process a smoother one for you and your child, and for everyone involved in your child's life.

Chapter One

IN THE BEGINNING

One of the first things I did after bringing my newborn daughter, Elizabeth, home from the hospital was take her on a tour of the house. Holding her close, I walked from room to room, explaining the origin of each piece of furniture and introducing her to the people in the photos that lined the walls and bookcases.

My husband, Dave, welcomed her home by ringing a bell next to her ear. She didn't seem to notice. "I don't think she can hear," he said.

"You worry too much," I told him. "She's an infant. She can't even turn her head."

When Elizabeth was 14 months old and a proficient walker, Dave wondered why she didn't come to the door to greet him when he arrived home after work.

"She's busy focusing on something else," I said. "She's not like one of the dogs you grew up with; she's not going to fetch your slippers in her teeth and run to the door."

On a business trip when Elizabeth was 17 months old, Dave sat on the plane next to a mother and her 13-month-old daughter. This baby girl could make animal noises. When Dave returned home, he talked more about her than he did about his trip.

This time, instead of feeling bad that he was worrying unnecessarily, I was insulted. "The reason Elizabeth can't make animal noises is that I have better things to do all day than sit around and teach her to bark and moo and oink on command."

Thinking back about those moments, I am overwhelmed with two feelings: One is guilt. The other is that there's a lot of merit to the old adage, "Hindsight is 20/20."

It was easy for me to dismiss Dave's concerns. After all, I was with Elizabeth all day, every day, and she didn't seem to have any hearing problems as far as I could tell. When I did worry was when she failed to express any interest in sharing books. During my pregnancy, I'd fantasized about holding my baby on my lap and reading my favorite stories out loud. But as soon as Elizabeth was mobile, she'd crawl off my lap after about the second page and find something that interested her more.

It never occurred to me to call a doctor, much less an audiologist. Instead, I did what came naturally: I asked friends whether their babies liked being read to. Inevitably, when someone told me their child loved books, I felt like a failure. When someone told me their child reacted like Elizabeth, I felt we were both failures.

Elizabeth had no interest in television, either, but far from worrying, I considered that a point of pride, a sign of her discriminating taste; she had more important things to do than spend her time with Barney or Bert and Ernie.

I had no doubt she could hear me and everyone else who talked to her. People often commented on how intently she looked at them when they spoke. "She really makes eye contact!" they would say, and I, the new and naive mommy, proudly agreed. Now, of course, I know she was staring at them not because she had good manners—

she was a toddler, for goodness' sake!—but because she was watching their lips.

Perhaps if she'd had trouble talking, I might have taken Dave's concerns more seriously. But she cooed and babbled on schedule, and said her first word, *doggy*, when she was ten months old, pointing to a friend's bouncy English springer spaniel.

By the time she was 15 months, her vocabulary was growing steadily. She didn't talk nearly as much as her friend Joseph had when he was her age, but Joseph's toddler vocabulary was more sophisticated than that of many adults I'd encountered. (When he was about 18 months old, he looked up at me one day and said, "How do you like my trousers?") As far as I was concerned, he was the anomaly, not Elizabeth.

The summer that Elizabeth was two and a half and her brother, Noah, eight months old, Dave and I packed the kids into our Toyota Corolla and drove the nearly 3,000 miles from Edmonton, Alberta to Cape Cod, Massachusetts, stopping along the way to visit family and friends. Compared to some of our friends' children, Elizabeth seemed quiet—quieter than I remembered her being at home—but Dave and I figured she was shy.

When we got back to Edmonton, though, Elizabeth began having temper tantrums. Up until then, she'd been quite mild mannered. I'd considered myself blessed to have given birth to a child with such a lovely disposition. Maybe, I thought to myself, she was going through the Terrible Twos.

Joseph was 11 months older than Elizabeth, so one day when we were at his house and Elizabeth was throwing a fit, I asked his mother, "Did Joseph have a lot of tantrums last year at this time?"

She thought for a minute. "No," she said. "He'd pretty well outgrown them by then."

What's wrong with my kid, I wondered, but I had no answer, nor did I have any idea where to look for one.

That fall, I signed Elizabeth up for gymnastics, music, and

playschool. She missed the first week of playschool because we'd been out of town, but on her first day, she quickly joined a group of girls dressing themselves from a trunk of clothes and pretending to mother a collection of dolls in a playhouse.

After a while, the teacher announced it was time to clean up and get ready for a story. The kids began pitching in to put the toys away. The playhouse girls began tidying up, tossing clothes back into the trunk just outside the door. Elizabeth stayed in the house, oblivious to what was going on around her.

Playschool was held in our neighborhood community hall, an expansive high-ceilinged room with a half-dozen oversized windows, shiny linoleum floors, and nothing to absorb the sound of 14 busy preschoolers. But I didn't stop to consider that noise might be the problem. I figured Elizabeth wasn't familiar with the routine, so I stuck my head through the little doorway and called to her, repeating the teacher's words. Then the teacher, who hadn't moved from her spot in the front of the room, made the announcement again. Elizabeth remained in the house, playing. I called to her again. No response.

Eventually Elizabeth left the playhouse. Tired of being alone, she decided to see where her new playmates had gone. The first person to catch her attention was the teacher. Upon seeing the look of impatience and irritation on her face, which matched the tone of her voice, Elizabeth burst into tears and didn't stop crying for what seemed to me like ages.

I took her aside and comforted her, explaining that the teacher wanted her to clean up, that it was time to go listen to a story. By the time I calmed her down, the children were sitting in a circle around the teacher.

Elizabeth took the only available space, directly across the circle from the teacher; she was at 6 o'clock to the teacher's 12. She sat attentively for about two minutes. Then she stood up and padded softly away. Nearby was a shelf of toys. She sat quietly in front of it, playing. I didn't urge her back to the circle; she didn't seem to be disturbing anyone, and I didn't want to upset her again. After a minute or two, one of the boys joined her. That's when the teacher told her—and the boy—to come back. I held her on my lap and cuddled her and she remained quiet and well behaved for the rest of the morning.

I took Elizabeth to playschool one more time. This time I stayed for only a short while before kissing her goodbye and telling her I was leaving. In the five minutes between when I left the school and arrived home, the teacher called and left a message. "Elizabeth is in tears," she said. "She didn't know where you were. You'd better come back." So went our first preschool experience. She was too young, I figured. I was neither surprised nor upset. We'd sign her up again in January, after she turned three. In the meantime, we still had music and gymnastics.

The music teacher held classes in her basement, in a warm and cozy low-ceilinged carpeted room she'd designed especially for that purpose. There were about ten parents and almost twice as many kids in the room, but it never seemed too noisy, even when the children were hitting drums with sticks, or shaking maracas, or banging on tambourines. Elizabeth seemed to enjoy it immensely; she paid attention and participated along with everyone else.

Gymnastics was another story. The room was huge, cavernous. The teacher made the most of the space; she used it all, which meant she was usually calling to her students and their parents in a loud voice that got lost in the vast distance between her lips and our ears. I got used to repeating her instructions, but I wasn't always happy about it.

"If you're not going to pay attention, we're going to have to quit this class," became my mantra, but it made no difference. More often than not, Elizabeth went one way while everyone else went another, and I had to remind her of what the teacher had just said. In this case, I couldn't dismiss her behavior as a function of her age; in a class for children 18 months to three years, she was one of the oldest. There was another little girl in the class who was only a month older, and she did everything exactly when and as the teacher ordered.

I couldn't figure it out. At home and in music class, Elizabeth was obedient, well behaved, chatty, and happy to participate in anything. At playschool and gymnastics, she was either quiet and confused or dissolving into tears. Once again I found myself wondering what was wrong with my daughter, but this time I had an answer. Maybe Dave had been right. Maybe she did have a hearing problem.

What made me finally take his concerns seriously was remembering a story that my mother had told me years ago. It seems that at the end of my kindergarten year, the teacher called my mother and informed her that I was going to have to repeat the class.

"I was going to flunk kindergarten?" I asked my mother.

"You were going to be held back," she said.

Semantics, I thought to myself.

My mother wasn't about to let the teacher go ahead with her plan. "Why are you holding her back?" she wanted to know.

"She's immature," the teacher said. "She doesn't pay attention. She doesn't listen. She doesn't know how to follow directions."

My mother, who was also a kindergarten teacher, was aware that there were reasons other than immaturity that children might not pay attention in a classroom. "Have you had her hearing tested?" she asked.

"No," the teacher said.

"You don't hold her back until you have her hearing tested," my mother said.

My mother's instincts were right. I had a hearing loss, one that was corrected that summer when I underwent surgery to have my adenoids removed and tubes inserted in my eardrums to keep fluid from accumulating there and making it impossible for me to hear clearly. Instead of repeating kindergarten, I entered first grade that fall.

What surprised me more than the news that I was almost held back in kindergarten was that my own mother, who lived with me, hadn't detected my hearing loss sooner.

"We thought you weren't paying attention," she said.

At school, with near constant background noise, I wouldn't have heard much of anything, so my inattentiveness would have been consistent. At home, where it was quieter, I probably did hear much of what was going on, especially when whoever was addressing me was close by. When I didn't pay attention, my mother automatically assumed it was because I didn't want to listen.

How many times, I wondered, had I gotten scolded because I couldn't hear and my mother had misinterpreted it as defiance? How many times had I scolded Elizabeth and lost my temper with her because I thought she wasn't paying attention when, in fact, perhaps she couldn't hear?

I had no idea where to take Elizabeth for a hearing test, so I called one of my family doctors—the less busy one—for a recommendation. He insisted on examining Elizabeth first. As it turned out, so much wax was clogging her ear canals, he couldn't see through to her eardrums.

"Would impacted wax make it hard for her to hear?" I asked.

He nodded.

I couldn't believe how relieved I felt. Once the wax came out, Elizabeth would be able to hear again! The temper tantrums would end! She'd be able to hear her gymnastics instructor!

"I'll make an appointment for you to see an audiologist," the doctor said, "but first we have to get this wax out."

I figured it would take a few minutes. Instead it took three weeks, during which Elizabeth had to have her ears flushed out four times and Dave and I had to put mineral oil in them every night to soften up the remaining wax.

During that time, she had her first hearing test. The clinic was close to our house, run by a husband-and-wife team. The wife had been an audiologist for a long time; the husband, a former school-teacher, had only been practicing for a few years. For the purposes of this story, I'll call him Mike. He was a very nice man, and quite sweet to Elizabeth, but his inexperience showed, and it made me nervous.

Mike looked into Elizabeth's ears and then projected the enlarged image onto a screen so I could see. Her ear canal was now the diameter of an empty paper towel roll, and what it contained was neither pretty nor reassuring. Although her ears had been flushed out three times in the past two-and-a-half weeks, gobs of wax remained, blocking any view of her eardrum.

"Will you be able to test her hearing?" I asked.

"We'll try," Mike said, although I could tell he wasn't confident.

He put a probe into Elizabeth's ear. The probe was connected to a wire that was connected to a little computer screen that displayed an empty graph. As we watched, a line stretched and squiggled across the graph. I had no idea what kind of test this was and what purpose it served, but I was so consumed with worry about Elizabeth's wax-filled ears that it didn't occur to me to ask. Also, it seemed as if Mike was having problems. He kept adjusting the probe and rerunning the test, but clearly he wasn't getting the results he expected. After trying nearly a half-dozen times, he summoned his wife into the room for help.

Months later, after umpteen trips to different audiologists, I learned that the test was called a tympanogram, and it's used to evaluate middle-ear function. If the eardrum and middle ear are moving properly, the line will form a peak in the middle of the screen. If the middle ear contains fluid, which makes it difficult if not impossible for the eardrum to vibrate normally, the line will be flat.

Elizabeth's middle ears were filled with fluid, but I didn't know that at the time and, because the wax was blocking the view, neither did Mike. With his wife nearby, he tried the test once more. Then, with her blessing, he gave up and took Elizabeth into the sound booth for a hearing test. I stayed in the waiting area with Noah, who was awake and fidgety. After a short time, Mike brought Elizabeth back to the waiting room. The wax in her ears was making it impossible to get any usable results.

"Why don't you bring her back after her ears clear up?" he suggested. "We'll be able to do a thorough job then."

I figured that would be in another week. I was wrong. The next day, the doctor was able to flush the remaining wax out of Elizabeth's ears, but then he discovered she had otitis media in both ears.

I was shocked. Ear infections? My daughter? In the 33 months since she'd entered the world, Elizabeth had never, to my knowledge, had an ear infection. I'd always considered that an accomplishment of sorts. Besides, didn't kids who had ear infections scream, pull at their ears, and develop raging fevers to match the raging infections?

"Not all kids react the same way," the doctor said. "I'm going to give you some eardrops and a prescription for penicillin. Come back in ten days, after the antibiotic's run its course, and we'll look at her ears again."

"Would an ear infection make it hard for her to hear?" I asked the doctor.

"The fluid in her ears certainly would," he said. "And it would make her uncomfortable, which could explain the tantrums."

Filled with hope that Elizabeth would soon be back to normal, I went off to the pharmacy to fill the prescription. Elizabeth took her medication dutifully. Her mood seemed slightly improved. Then, a little over a week later, on a Saturday morning, she woke up with pinprick red dots covering her torso.

"Is that chicken pox?" I asked Dave.

He had no idea, so we called our neighbor, Joan, a pediatrician. She wasn't our doctor— we'd never felt the need to have a pediatrician—but she was a friend, and she came over and inspected Elizabeth.

The verdict: either a virus or a reaction to the penicillin. We decided to go with the reaction-to-the-penicillin assessment and stopped giving it to her. The dots disappeared. The infection, on the other hand, lasted another two weeks.

The Monday after Joan examined Elizabeth, I tried to make an appointment with our regular doctor, to get a new prescription for Elizabeth. The doctor was sick and I didn't want to wait until he got better, so I was sent for the first time to a Dr. M, a pediatrician whose practice was nearby.

Dr. M's office was tiny and crammed full of children. The walls were covered with pictures of his patients, an inordinate number of whom, it seemed to me, were in wheelchairs or had Down's syndrome or other unusual conditions. There were grateful letters from parents of children who had died, but had apparently benefited from Dr. M's loving care when they were alive.

Dr. M asked me to explain Elizabeth's situation. I told him the whole story, stopping occasionally to make sure he really needed all the details. He encouraged me to go on. When I finished, he asked me to get him a copy of the report from the audiologist.

"I don't think there is one," I said. Mike hadn't gotten any results worth recording; that's why he hadn't charged me and why he'd told me to come back when Elizabeth's ears were in better shape.

Two weeks later, Elizabeth's ear infection was gone, but Dr. M told me not to schedule a hearing test. "Let's wait until her ears are cleared up," he said.

At the time, I didn't understand what he meant, nor did I feel the need or have the comfort level to ask for an explanation. Now I know that fluid that accumulates in a child's ears because of a cold or an infection can linger for months. I also know that it's possible to have middle-ear fluid without an infection.

At the end of December, about ten weeks after the ear infection was diagnosed, Dr. M examined Elizabeth and pronounced her healthy.

"Her ears are beautiful," he said.

Depending on my mood, I now consider his assessment bizarre, arrogant, ignorant, or amusing. At the time, I found it comforting.

"Should I take her back to the audiologist now?" I asked.

"Is she talking more?" he asked. "How's her behavior?"

"Great," I said. "She's doing really well."

"I wouldn't bother," he said.

"But she still isn't talking much," I pointed out. "And she's not always speaking clearly."

Speech therapy is available through our local public health clinic here in Edmonton, but according to Dr. M, there was a six-month wait. "You could make an appointment," he said, "but most likely by the time she gets in, her speech will have cleared up."

To this day, I'm not entirely sure why I didn't just take Elizabeth back to the audiology clinic right away. I didn't need Dr. M's referral; I already had an invitation to come back and finish what I'd started. But I didn't want to be a worrywart and take up the audiologist's precious time with my apparently baseless concerns when there were clearly other people with more serious needs.

True, Elizabeth had had a hearing problem—she'd had two, actually—but we'd cleared up both of them. There was no doubt she could hear better, and that her behavior had improved. Dave and I agreed there was no need to pursue this further; if the doctor said she was fine, she was fine.

But I couldn't get rid of the nagging, gnawing feeling that I had to see this thing through to its logical conclusion. I'd taken Elizabeth to the family doctor because I wanted her hearing tested by a professional. I still wanted that. But if the pediatrician, who clearly had far more experience with children than I, wasn't worrying, why should I?

At choir practice less than a week after Elizabeth had been pronounced cured, I shared my concerns with a friend, a neonatal intensive care nurse who had worked with Dr. M in the past.

"Take Elizabeth to the audiologist, for your own peace of mind," she said.

I called Mike's office the next morning. It was the end of December. The next opening was February 1. Dave was going to be out of town, but that didn't worry me. I was going to bring Elizabeth to Mike, he was going test her and tell me her hearing was perfect, and I would go home knowing I'd followed through as planned.

Noah was asleep when we arrived at the clinic, and I was grateful, thinking I'd be able to watch the test undisturbed. Elizabeth and I followed Mike into the sound booth. I took a chair against the back wall and rested Noah on my lap. Elizabeth sat in front of me, her back to us. It was clear almost from the start that her hearing wasn't normal. When Noah woke up after a few minutes, it was even harder for me to ignore the truth. Noah consistently turned his head in whatever direction the sounds were coming from; Elizabeth stared straight ahead until the volume went up discernibly.

Say something! I wanted to yell at her. *Respond! Tell the nice man you can hear the beeps! How could you not hear that beep? Why can't you hear that? I can hear it! Noah can hear it! Why can't you?*

I took Noah out of the room not long after. I told myself he was bored, squirming, and becoming a distraction, but deep down I know it's because I couldn't bear to see that my daughter couldn't hear sounds that were so obviously audible to the rest of the world.

Yet when Mike and his wife summoned me to an office after Elizabeth's test, I was stunned when they told me the news: "Your daughter has a permanent hearing loss and will have to wear hearing aids for the rest of her life."

I felt as if I'd been told she had a terminal disease, not a correctable problem. Months later, when she had her first pair of hearing aids and her behavior and speech were noticeably improved, I wondered if my reaction might have been different if the news had been broken to me more gently, more positively. Perhaps if Mike and his wife had said, "Your daughter has a permanent hearing loss, and we know this because of how she reacted to all the tests we gave her, but she'll do great with hearing aids and we're going to find the best ones for her," I might not have felt so devastated. But all I could grasp was that my beautiful, lovely, healthy, perfect little girl was suddenly not so perfect. She was going to have to wear hearing aids for the rest of her life, and who knew if that would help? What did I know about hearing aids, anyway? How could Mike and his wife be so sure they were right? They weren't doctors. Surely there was some operation that could fix her ears. They were wrong that the problem was permanent. I was certain they had made a mistake.

I couldn't bear to hear anymore. I tried, unsuccessfully, to hold back the tears as Mike and his wife talked kindly to me about ear, nose, and throat specialists and having Elizabeth fitted for earmolds before the end of the week. I had no idea what an earmold was. I changed my mind a half dozen times in two minutes over whether to have Elizabeth fitted—whatever that meant—immediately, or to bring her back when Dave returned from his trip.

Mike and his wife were unfailingly patient. While I dithered about the earmold fitting, they tried to figure out which ear, nose, and throat doctor Elizabeth should see. Mike suggested one, and his wife said he'd retired. She suggested another one, and he reminded her that the doctor was on vacation. I wasn't encouraged. By the time I left, they still hadn't given me a name, but that seemed the least of my worries.

I was literally halfway out the door with Elizabeth and Noah when I realized that almost nothing that Mike and his wife had said had sunk in. The sun had set and the office was closed; the receptionist had gone home for the day. I made my way back through the darkened waiting area to where Mike and his wife were doing their end-of-the-day chores. They didn't seem surprised to see me again so quickly, nor did my request strike them as unusual.

"I don't remember anything you just told me," I said. "I need a piece of paper, and I need you to tell me everything again, please, so I can write it down, so I won't forget."

Chapter Two

WHAT IS A HEARING LOSS?

On the way home from the clinic, I tried to conjure up the image of a child with hearing aids. I couldn't. I'd never seen one. Hearing aids were for old people, not children. Especially not little children. Especially not my perfect beautiful little daughter. I had a distant cousin who was deaf, the result of birth trauma. When I was growing up, my father had a colleague whose daughter lost her hearing after a childhood bout with meningitis. When she spoke, her voice was deep, flat, and nasal. The cousin didn't speak at all; she signed, beautifully. Her hands moved with a grace and lightness that made me think of butterflies.

But Elizabeth wasn't deaf. The audiologists had insisted on that, even when I tried to protest. "If she can't hear, she's deaf, isn't she?" I'd asked.

"She's hard of hearing," Mike and his wife had said gently. "A mild-to-moderate sensorineural hearing loss means she has some hearing."

It wasn't until months later, after Elizabeth began speech therapy at a local rehabilitation hospital, that I began to have a better understanding of how hearing loss works. Rachel, Elizabeth's speech pathologist, played a tape for Dave and me to give us an idea of how and what a child with a loss such as Elizabeth's would hear. The words sounded muffled and chopped up. (You can hear similar recordings at www.babyhearing.org.)

Rachel also gave us a picture from the Canadian Hearing Society, which provided an illustration of the difference between how sounds are perceived by people with normal hearing and how they are perceived by those with hearing loss. People with normal hearing hear everything clearly. People with hearing loss hear fragments of sounds, or, in some cases, no sound at all. Exactly what and how much they hear depends on the severity of the loss and how it affects the ability to perceive sound at various frequencies. What is consistent, despite the degree of loss, is that people with hearing loss don't hear as clearly as those with normal hearing. For example, without her hearing aids, Elizabeth might hear the word *some* as *thumb*.

What I didn't understand was how she could have developed any sort of a working vocabulary given that her loss apparently prevented her from hearing many of the individual sounds comprising speech, never mind sound blends such as "fl" and "sm."

"You have a loud, clear voice," Rachel reminded me. "That's a good thing. She was able to hear you. Your house is quiet, so that helped. And she has a mild-to-moderate loss, not one that's severe or profound."

At least if her loss were more serious, Dave and I would have been quicker to have had her tested, I thought, but there was no point continuing to torment myself about that. We'd figured out the problem; now we needed to understand and treat it.

Until I did some work as a broadcast journalist a few years before Elizabeth was born, I didn't give much thought to the technicalities of sound transmission. I knew the term dB, short for decibels, but only because it was the name of a rock band that was popular on the college circuit during the 1980s. I'd heard about sound waves and frequencies, but there was far too much physics involved for me to bother delving into either subject.

During my brief career at a radio station, I had no choice but to gain a greater insight into decibel levels and frequencies. That, combined with the audiogram, the graph used to show what a person can and can't hear, allowed me a basic understanding of Elizabeth's hearing loss. Especially helpful was an audiogram that showed the intensity and frequency level of various speech and environmental sounds. (See Figure 2–1.)

There are two sets of numbers on the audiogram. The numbers on the left side of the chart denote decibel levels. The numbers across the top denote specific frequency levels.

Decibels are the units used to measure sound. Audiologists and others who work with these units use different decibel scales depending on how and for what purpose the units are used. The decibel scale depicted on an audiogram is dB hearing level (or dB HL) which is used to represent the sound levels required to reach audibility. Nonprofessionals tend to use the familiar term *loudness,* but loudness actually refers to the listener's subjective interpretation of intensity—that is, the greater the intensity of the sound, the louder it seems to the listener.

On an audiogram, the decibel hearing level ranges from 0 dB HL, a reference for the lowest (softest) sound level a young normal-hearing person can detect, to 120 dB HL, a very high-intensity sound. Imagine sitting near the speakers at a rock concert and you'll have a sense of what 120 dB HL sounds like.

Frequency on an audiogram is measured in Hertz (for the nineteenth-century German physicist Heinrich Hertz). It is abbreviated Hz and represents the rate of vibration (cycles per second) comprising the individual components of a given sound. We nonprofessionals like to use the more familiar term *pitch*. Like loudness, pitch corresponds with the listener's subjective experience. High-pitched sounds are

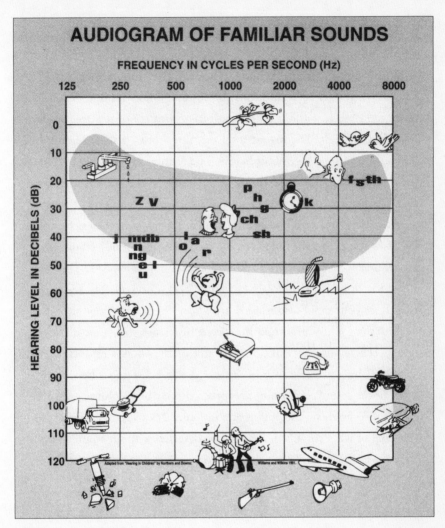

FIGURE 2-1 • Audiogram of familiar sounds. Courtesy of the American Academy of Audiology.

created when vibrations occur at a rapid rate. Low-pitched sounds occur when vibrations occur at a relatively slow rate. The higher the frequency, the higher in pitch it sounds to the listener.

For example, the key at the far left on a piano keyboard (it's an A, by the way) sends to your brain a signal that vibrates at approximately 28 cycles per second, or 28 Hz. It is the lowest note on the piano, and for the normal-hearing listener, would be perceived as a

AUDIOGRAM INTERPRETATION

The audiogram is used to record the softest sounds (pure tones) a listener can detect, without amplification, at a range of test frequencies from low to high. The lowest level or "threshold" is recorded on the audiogram using the symbols below. The normal range is at the top of the audiogram between 0 dB HL (the softest level a person with normal hearing can detect) up to about 20 dB HL. People with normal hearing have thresholds within this range for all frequencies. Hearing losses in the 20-40 dB range are often described as mild, 40-60 dB as moderate, 60-90 dB as severe, and 90 and over as profound. The banana-shaped region in the middle (see Figure 2-1) represents the sounds of speech. If your child's thresholds are *above* the speech region, he will hear all the sounds important for speech. If his thresholds are all *below* the speech region, he will not hear any of the sounds important for speech. If his thresholds are *in or near* the speech region, he will hear some of the sounds important for speech. It may be helpful to plot your child's thresholds on the audiogram in figure 2-1 to get a better understanding of what sounds (if any) can be detected without amplification. Your audiologist can help you with this.

very low-pitched sound. At the other end of the keyboard, on the far right, the key (a C) sends to your brain a signal that vibrates at approximately 4,200 cycles per second, or 4,200 Hz. It is the highest note on the keyboard and would be perceived by the listener as a very high-pitched sound. On most audiograms, frequencies range from a low of 250 Hz to a high of 8,000 Hz.

Every person has hearing thresholds, which are the lowest decibel levels their ear can detect. The threshold levels may differ across frequencies. For children, the normal range of hearing sensitivity is usually considered to be between 0 and 15 dB HL. For young adults, the normal range of hearing sensitivity is from 0 to 20 dB HL.

Children tend to have more sensitive hearing than adults because most have been spared the effects of exposure to high-intensity noise. Also, loss of hearing sensitivity, especially in the high frequencies, is a normal part of the aging process, so most older adults have some degree of hearing impairment.

However, the implications of a hearing loss present at birth are greater than they are in later years. Children need to hear the widest range of sounds necessary to develop proper speech and language skills. In contrast, an adult who has already acquired normal speech and language can better fill in the missing information. Of course, many adults require amplification too, but their problems are more specific to receptive communication—in other words, hearing aids help them to better hear what people are saying. For children still acquiring language, hearing aids are essential tools not only for hearing speech and language, but for developing and using speech.

When I was pregnant with Elizabeth, friends and magazine articles suggested I talk to my fetus. Apparently the more monologues I directed to my belly, the more comfortable the fetus would become with my voice. Once it was born, it would be that much more comfortable with me.

I couldn't bring myself to do it. Assuming it had normal hearing—and at that point I had no reason to assume otherwise—the fetus was going to hear me whether I talked directly to it or to my neighbor across the fence.

By the nineteenth or twentieth week of gestation, a normally developing fetus can detect sound. But what's filtered through the womb is very different from what a baby will hear once it's out in the world. In the womb, sounds must pass through tissue and amniotic fluid. The normal tempo of speech is retained, but the higher pitches are reduced, making them sound lower in pitch.

If you want a sense of how a fetus hears, ask someone to talk to you with their face buried in a pillow. You'll hear sounds, but they will be low pitched and muffled. If you try really hard, you might be able to pick up a rhythm to what you're hearing. Interestingly, these rhythmic characteristics of speech, called timing cues, are important to a hard-of-hearing child once they enter the world, and can be vital to acquiring speech and language.

However, although the unborn child can discern sounds, there is little hope of acquiring speech comprehension in the womb. The ability to make sense of language doesn't begin until after birth, when the brain has had weeks and months of exposure to sounds.

How the Ear Works

The ear is divided into three parts: the outer ear, the middle ear, and the inner ear (see Figure 2–2). The outer ear consists of the pinna, the visible part of the outer ear, and the ear canal, also known as the external auditory meatus, which leads to the eardrum (also known as the tympanic membrane). The ear canal contains hairs, as well as glands that produce wax, which is also known as cerumen. Both the hair and cerumen help keep debris away from the eardrum. The pinna and ear canal direct sound waves to the eardrum and the middle ear.

The eardrum is the dividing line between the outer ear and the middle ear. Inside the middle ear are three tiny bones—the smallest bones in the body—the malleus, the incus, and stapes. One of the few facts I retained from junior high school biology is that those bones are also known as the hammer, the anvil, and the stirrup, which they closely resemble. The three comprise what is called the ossicular chain.

The stapes, which is closest to the inner ear, is attached to the oval window (also known as the vestibule), the membrane at the opening of the inner ear. Vibrations from the ossicular chain are transmitted

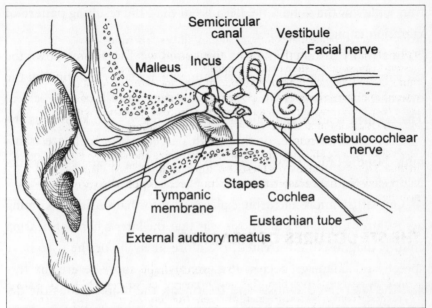

FIGURE 2-2 • Anatomy of the ear. (from *Anatomy and Physiology for Speech, Language, and Hearing,* Second edition, p. 566, by J.A. Seikel, D.W. King, and D.G. Drumright, 2000, San Diego: CA, Singular Publishing Group. Copyright © 2000. Reprinted with permission.)

to the fluids of the inner ear by movements of the stapes in and out of the oval window.

The fluid-filled inner ear consists of two parts: the semicircular canals, which are essential for balance, and the cochlea, which is the sensory organ for hearing. It is through the cochlea that nerve signals travel from the ear to the brain.

Cochlea is Latin for snail. Contained within a bony chamber smaller than a pea, the cochlea is coiled two-and-a-half times into the shape of a snail shell. Along the length of the fluid-filled cochlea is a membrane lined with microscopic hair cells that react to movements of the stapes in the oval window.

High frequencies stimulate the hair cells nearest the oval window. Low frequencies stimulate the hair cells at the far end of the cochlea, deep inside the coil. Most sounds we hear consist of many different frequencies at the same time. Because of that, the resulting pattern of vibration is highly complex.

In an ear that functions normally, sound waves traveling down the ear canal cause the eardrum to vibrate, which makes the bones of the ossicular chain vibrate, which stimulates the hair cells of the cochlea. The cochlea sends signals to the auditory nerve (also known as the vestibulocochleer nerve, or the VIIIth nerve). The signals are transmitted to the brain, which interprets the sounds. These pathways develop early in life, after the brain has been exposed to sound.

One of the more disturbing pieces of information I kept coming across after Elizabeth's diagnosis was that the later a hard-of-hearing child is diagnosed and treated, the more likely he or she is to have speech and language delays. Presumably, the more severe the loss and the later the diagnosis and treatment, the more serious the delays. Studies have shown that some late-diagnosed children never catch up to their normal-hearing peers, although the effects of early identification and intervention are still under investigation.

Nowadays, late is described as anywhere from six to 18 months. In other words, a baby with a hearing loss that goes undetected for 18 months is considered late diagnosed. The reason is that technology has advanced to the point where babies can be diagnosed at birth and fitted with hearing aids within the first weeks of life. By those standards, Elizabeth was ancient by the time she was diagnosed at age three.

Initially I considered such literature yet another example of groundless fear-mongering designed to shake my already fragile faith in my parenting ability. But what was either missing or what I failed to glean is that there is an optimal period of time for children to learn speech and language, and the door is opened widest during the first three years of life. That's when most of the neural development occurs and language understanding begins.

I found it easiest to understand this phenomenon when it was explained in the context of someone learning a foreign language in high school; reading and understanding will come relatively easily, but that person will probably never speak like a native because they didn't learn the language at the most optimal time.

Similarly, children who have missed out on speech and language development because they couldn't hear properly may never learn to speak as well as those who have had that advantage. The less severe the hearing loss, the greater the chance the child will be able to successfully compensate. But the degree of loss is only one factor that will affect a child's speech and language development. Other factors that can and do make a difference are family support, speech and language stimulation, appropriateness of the hearing aid fitting, maintenance of the hearing aids, and the child's learning style.

Seven months after Elizabeth was diagnosed, she entered a preschool program for children with hearing loss. She had four classmates. The only other girl was a three-year-old named Nikki, whom I'd heard about from Rachel, the speech pathologist. Nikki was born with a severe-to-profound high-frequency hearing loss in both ears.

Rachel was unabashedly impressed with Nikki's speech, vocabulary, and comprehension. "Her grandmother spends hours with her, reading, speaking, and practicing," she said. "It's unusual to find a three-year-old with that degree of hearing loss who speaks as well as she does."

When I met Nikki and her grandmother, Gwen, and saw how they interacted, it became even more clear that Dave and I would play a significant role in helping Elizabeth make up for what she'd missed the past three years. With another toddler to care for, I didn't think I could spend the time Gwen did, making and laminating flash cards, reviewing worksheets, and playing endless vocabulary games. What I could do was talk more. I began pointing out things I'd always considered obvious—"See how hard that doggie is panting! Look at all that sweat on his owner's face!"—and asking Elizabeth questions—"Why do you think they're so hot? I think they must have gone jogging. What do you think?"

"Children pick up a lot of language incidentally—not necessarily from conversation, but from what they hear around them," Rachel explained to me early on when I discovered, much to my shock, that Elizabeth didn't understand concepts as basic as *fast* and *high*.

Like all children with hearing loss, she'd never had the advantage of being able to overhear. For her, simply hearing what was happening immediately in front of her was a challenge. As I've discovered during the past few years, when she's presented with the opportunity to learn, she will. But where her younger brother seems to increase his vocabulary simply by soaking up what he hears or overhears, with Elizabeth we have to be more active, pointing out words, providing definitions, and reinforcing what we've just taught her.

Hearing Loss: We've All Experienced It to Some Degree

Anyone who has ever had a head cold or impacted wax has no doubt experienced what's known as a conductive hearing loss, which is temporary and occurs when something prevents sound waves from being passed along to the inner ear. Causes can include otitis media, an inflammation with fluid in the middle ear, which keeps the eardrum from vibrating properly, or an obstruction in the ear canal from a buildup of wax, for example.

In either case, the inner ear is not affected. Sounds from the environment—music, other people's voices, traffic noises, rain falling on the roof—which must travel to the inner ear via the outer- and middle-ear pathway, are reduced in intensity, but as long as your cochlea is intact, you can still hear your own voice clearly.

This is because some sounds can be conveyed directly to the inner ear fluids via bone conduction. The most common mode of bone conduction stimulation is a speaker's own voice. During speech, the movements of the larynx (voice box) send vibrations through the intervening bones and tissue, directly stimulating the fluids of the inner ear. As a result, people with conductive hearing loss have no problem hearing their own voice. However, outside sounds are reduced by the outer- or middle-ear disorder, resulting in a conductive hearing loss. Later in this book, I will discuss bone conduction testing performed by the audiologist as part of the hearing assessment.

In contrast to conductive hearing losses, which are usually temporary, sensorineural hearing losses are almost always permanent. Until Elizabeth was diagnosed, I'd never heard the word *sensorineural*. At the time, I was so overwhelmed by the idea that she had a permanent hearing loss that I didn't stop to think about how sensible a term it is. Sensory refers to inner-ear function, and neural refers to the auditory nerve.

Most permanent losses are due to sensory (inner ear) dysfunction—for example, a malformation in the cochlea, hair cells that never developed, or hair cells that developed but were then destroyed. Neural hearing loss occurs when there is a disturbance in the auditory nerve or the higher auditory pathway. A rare condition known as auditory neuropathy or auditory dysynchrony is thought to be the result of poor neural timing in the auditory nerve or higher auditory pathway while sensory (inner ear) function remains intact.

AUDITORY NEUROPATHY

Children with auditory neuropathy have difficulty understanding speech and other sounds because of a disturbance in the transmission of signals from the inner ear to the brain. The condition is also known as "auditory dysynchrony." It usually affects both ears.

Some children may benefit from amplification; others do not. It now appears that many children benefit from a cochlear implant, perhaps because electrical stimulation helps to synchronize the auditory system.

Young children with auditory neuropathy usually have a team of specialists including an otologist, audiologist, and early intervention providers. See Resources for further reading and web-based resources.

(See box, below.) The condition affects only a small proportion of children with congenital hearing impairment.

Elizabeth didn't seem to fit into any of the known categories, and for the first two years after she was diagnosed, I spent a lot of time—too much, probably—trying to come up with an explanation.

The audiology clinic where we eventually went for her hearing aids had a lot of pediatric patients. On any given visit, we were likely to see at least one other child. One morning I got into a discussion with the parents of a girl who was a little younger than Elizabeth and had been wearing hearing aids since around her first birthday. Her parents had to watch her constantly to make sure she didn't drop them into their coffee or the toilet bowl. She had a much more severe loss than Elizabeth; her speech was incomprehensible to me.

"Did you go for genetic testing?" I asked them.

They looked at me as if I were nuts. "No," they said, the unspoken message being, "Our child can't hear. Her situation can't get much worse. We have more important things to think about."

Searching for the Cause

For the first time, I wondered if my search for an explanation was a trivial luxury that was keeping me from dealing with the real problem. Maybe it was, but it didn't stop me. Other people had explanations. Didn't we deserve one?

Nikki, Elizabeth's preschool classmate, experienced meconium aspiration at birth, which severely compromised her oxygen levels. The hair cells of the inner ear crave oxygen. When Nikki was born, her hair cells, deprived of oxygen, stopped working. To date, no one has come up with a way to regenerate hair cells in humans, although scientists have discovered evidence of hair cell regeneration in chickens. At least for the time being, however, the loss of cochlear hair cells in humans means a permanent loss of hearing.

Could Elizabeth's hearing loss have been caused by birth trauma? I posed the question to Dr. Elliott, the ear, nose, and throat specialist we saw a week after her initial diagnosis. I was induced two-and-a-half weeks before my due date because of high blood pressure, and Elizabeth's heart rate plunged even before I went into labor, necessitating an emergency C-section. But she was fine when she eventually emerged; she did so well that my doctor granted both of us permission to leave the hospital a day early.

No, Dr. Elliott said, he doubted her hearing loss had anything to do with the circumstances of her birth.

Becky, who lives across the street from us and is a year younger than Elizabeth, also has a high-frequency loss, though not as severe as Nikki's. Becky's parents initially thought her loss may have been caused by Gentamycin, an antibiotic she received intravenously, first when she was born with a collapsed lung, which the doctors initially diagnosed as pneumonia, and then three months later when she developed a high fever from a bladder infection.

Kathy, Becky's mom, didn't know that Gentamycin can be harmful to the ear. Even if she had, she might not have protested. "If you're staring at a child who you're being told could have pneumonia, would you withhold that drug?" she asked.

Tests eventually showed the Gentamycin hadn't caused Becky's hearing loss. Her parents still don't have an explanation. I, meanwhile, pressed on. Was it the antibiotic ear drops Elizabeth had been prescribed to fight the ear infection we discovered when she was two and a half, I asked Dr. Elliott? No, he said. Those drops wouldn't have gotten past her eardrum; they'd been nowhere near her inner ear or her bloodstream.

Dr. Elliott sent Dave, Elizabeth, and me to our local university's genetic clinic for testing, which also turned up nothing. He sent Elizabeth for a CT scan, which he said had a 20 percent chance of showing an abnormality of the inner ear. All it showed was that she had fluid in her middle ears. No surprise there; at the time of the CT scan, she was recovering from a cold and we had known she had fluid in her ears. On the other hand, the test also showed that her bone structure was normal. In one sense, it was a relief; at least there was nothing wrong with her bone structure. But it was yet another source of frustration. How were we ever going to figure out what *had* caused the problem?

"For most children who have permanent hearing loss, there is no explanation," Dr. Elliott stated during our first visit, but every time I came up with another possibility, I brought it to him.

Dr. Elliott had a six-month waiting list and no partner with whom to share the patient load. His small office once seemed so crowded that Elizabeth and I opted to wait in a nearby donut shop. Yet he seemed to have endless patience for what another physician might have considered mindless, irritating questions.

It was after I wondered, for perhaps the tenth or eleventh time, if Elizabeth might have lost her hearing because of a high fever that I quit asking. Maybe it was his answer, that an audiogram such as Elizabeth's was usually a sign of a malformation deep in the cochlea, one that can't be detected. Or maybe I'd just come to the same conclusion as that family of the little girl in the audiology clinic: my daughter can't hear very well, but lucky for us, it looks as if her hearing isn't getting any worse.

Scientists have begun to identify a number of recessive genes that may be associated with hearing loss. Recessive genetic inheritance occurs when two normal-hearing parents have the same abnormal gene for hearing. The parents are unaffected because they also have a dominant gene for normal hearing. But when two people match up the same abnormal-hearing gene, they have a one-in-four chance of having a child with hearing loss. Screening is now performed only for the more common genetic abnormalities, among them a mutation called Connexin 26, which is responsible for one-third of all cases of genetic hearing loss.

The summer after Elizabeth turned six, when I had completed a draft of this chapter that concluded with, "Even as I write this, I am confident that in a lab somewhere, someone is trying to figure out what causes losses like Elizabeth's," we got a call from the genetics clinic we'd visited when she was first diagnosed.

"We've started testing for Connexin 26," the genetics counselor Karin said to me. "Would you like to have Elizabeth tested?"

Dave, who will do anything to avoid contact with a needle, didn't think we should bother. The chances that Elizabeth would test positive were slim, and besides, hadn't we already accepted that we would never know the cause of her hearing loss, that what was important wasn't finding a cause but dealing with the problem?

CAUSES OF SENSORINEURAL HEARING LOSS IN CHILDREN

The causes of permanent hearing loss in young children include both genetic (inherited) and acquired conditions. Genetic causes are now believed to account for about half of all hearing loss present at birth. Non-genetic causes account for about one-fourth. The cause of the remaining one-fourth is unknown.

Within the half known to be genetically linked, nearly three-fourths are due to a form of inheritance called "autosomal recessive," which occurs when each parent has an abnormal gene for hearing loss. This results in a one-in-four chance of the child being born with hearing loss. Other types of genetic inheritance can occur when only one parent has an abnormal gene.

There are many causes of non-genetic (acquired) hearing loss in young children. Sensorineural hearing loss has been associated with medications that damage the ear or infections and illnesses that occur at birth or later, including meningitis, measles, mumps, and some neurological diseases.

"She likes hospitals," I reminded him. "Besides, they've offered, and it's free. We might as well do it. Maybe we'll learn something."

Elizabeth had an appointment at the genetics clinic in early fall. She missed half a morning at school, answering the geneticists' questions, standing and sitting patiently, and finally heading down to the blood lab where she impressed the technician with her ability to sit still while her blood was drawn into little vials. Nearly two months later, in mid-November, Karin called to tell me Elizabeth had tested positive for two mutations on the Connexin 26 gene.

To this day, I can't believe my reaction. I was elated. I felt as if I'd won a lottery. I could barely keep my feet on the ground or my voice from shouting for joy. Apparently learning the root cause had been more important to me than I'd wanted to admit. Yet with the exception of the rare instances when someone asks how Elizabeth lost her hearing, the test results have had no discernable effect on our daily lives.

Research has shown that most Connexin 26 hearing losses tend to be stable, but we'd already suspected Elizabeth's hearing loss isn't progressive. None of our relatives have been tested, although they've been offered the opportunity. As for Noah, we don't know if he is a carrier; the genetics clinic won't test him until he's old enough to decide for himself.

After the initial excitement of the news wore off, I felt guilty all over again. Elizabeth had been hard of hearing at birth, and we had missed it. But those feelings diminished quickly. The time for tormenting myself was long past. It was better to use my energy for more important things, like helping Elizabeth get the most out of the hearing she has, and out of life in general.

Chapter Three

ASSESSMENT AND INTERVENTION

When Elizabeth was a baby, I would take her to our local health clinic for immunizations. That's standard practice here in Edmonton, the Canadian city where I live. It was also standard practice for the public health nurse to ring a bell at some time during these visits, presumably to see if Elizabeth could hear. Elizabeth always turned to look at the bell. In other words, she passed the test, something I'd completely forgotten until I brought Noah in for his last immunization when he was five and Elizabeth almost seven. I didn't see a bell anywhere.

"Do you still ring a bell to test hearing?" I asked the nurse.

She shook her head. "We were told to stop," she said. "It didn't work. Now we ask the parent questions, and if there's any sign of a hearing loss, we recommend following up with an audiologist."

To be fair, our public health nurses aren't the only ones who once thought the best way to test hearing was to make a loud noise and observe the child's reaction. I've heard from countless parents whose pediatricians and even ear, nose, and throat specialists have employed this crude method.

The reason it's so popular is that it's simple, and the results appear indisputable. But no matter how effective it may look, it's never going to be accurate because people are sensitive to motion. If we sense movement, we'll turn in that direction regardless of what we hear. People with hearing loss are especially attuned to visual cues in the environment. Another reason crude noise tests can be misleading is that a child with a high-frequency hearing loss, with normal or near normal low-frequency hearing, may respond consistently to speech and other sounds while much of the high-frequency information is missing.

Whenever there is any question about hearing, an audiologist should conduct a thorough assessment of hearing, especially in a young child. I'll say more about audiology and audiologists later in this chapter.

Identification of Hearing Loss and Middle-Ear Problems

Hearing screening tests are designed to identify children who are at risk for hearing loss—that is, children who should be referred for diagnostic assessment by an audiologist. Diagnostic tests are used to determine the type and extent of the hearing problem—whether it's permanent or a disorder that can be corrected such as impacted wax (cerumen) or fluid (effusion) behind the eardrum. With young kids, there can be a combination of permanent and temporary causes. The nature of the problem will determine what referrals and intervention are needed.

Newborn hearing screening requires physiologic tests, which are tests that can be administered without the baby's active participation. In contrast, behavioral tests require the child to respond in some repeatable way to sounds presented from a loudspeaker or earphone. Because behavioral tests are not reliable until babies reach a developmental age of about six months, newborn hearing screening is conducted using physiologic tests. Although physiologic tests do not provide a direct measure of hearing, they can be used to identify hearing loss in an infant or young child.

Newborn Hearing Screening

In several Canadian provinces and most states in the United States, newborns are screened for hearing loss at birth, before being discharged from the hospital. At the time of this writing, in Canada the provinces with universal screening were Prince Edward Island, New Brunswick, and Ontario. Newfoundland was starting a program, Quebec was in the planning stage, and in British Columbia, only babies in Victoria were screened. For information about screening programs in the United States, see www.ncham.org, which provides a summary of policies and procedures for each state.

There are two technologies used for newborn screening: otoacoustic emissions (OAE) and the auditory brainstem response (ABR). For either test, the ideal scenario is a sleeping baby. Newborns can be screened in natural sleep, but older infants or toddlers often require sedation.

OAEs are low-intensity sounds produced by the inner ear—specifically, the outer hair cells of the cochlea. They are detected by a sensitive microphone placed in the ear canal. Successful recording of OAEs means there is both a healthy inner ear (cochlea) and normal or near normal middle-ear function. OAEs are said to be preneural because they occur only at the level of the cochlea. This makes it possible to evaluate the cochlea without involving higher levels of the auditory system. The sounds used to produce an OAE may be clicks or tones. When OAEs can be measured, it usually means normal hearing sensitivity or no more than a mild hearing loss. But absent OAEs can be due to a variety of conditions ranging from middle-ear fluid to profound cochlear hearing loss. Other tests are needed to determine why OAEs are absent. OAE screening may be conducted by a variety of professionals including nurses and pediatricians. Diagnostic OAE testing is usually conducted by an audiologist as part of a diagnostic test battery.

As with OAEs, ABR is produced by presenting clicks or tones through a probe in the ear canal. What's different is that responses are recorded from small electrodes attached to the head. The responses provide information about the function of the auditory nerve and the auditory pathway through the brainstem. No electricity is delivered to the child. Rather, the ABR equipment detects and amplifies the tiny electrical (neural) events that occur in response to the test sounds. Unlike OAEs, which are usually present or absent, the ABR test can be used to estimate the amount of hearing loss across a range of frequencies. As noted earlier, ABR can be used for screening in the newborn nursery. Audiologists use more advanced ABR tests and auditory steady state responses to obtain the information needed to diagnose hearing loss and begin the process of hearing-aid selection and fitting.

Hearing and Middle-Ear Screening for Older Children

For older children, routine hearing screening is often done by a nurse or other health care professional. It usually begins with a visual inspection of the outer ear for noticeable signs of disease, malformation, or other abnormality. This is followed by an otoscopic inspection, which involves examining the ear canal and eardrum (also known as the tympanic membrane). This requires an otoscope, an instrument that functions as both a flashlight and a magnifying glass.

It's not unusual for a child to balk at the idea of having the oto-scope tip inserted into the ear canal. If that happens, the person performing the exam may be willing to take some time to explain what the instrument is and how it's used. You can hold your child on your lap if it makes him feel safer and helps to keep him still. If he's brought along a stuffed animal or doll, you can ask the cli-nician to provide a demonstration. Taking a little extra time to make your child comfortable can save time and frustration over the long haul.

Once the otoscopic exam is complete, the clinician will often screen for otitis media (fluid behind the eardrum) using a machine called a tympanometer. A soft probe tip, similar in size and appear-ance to the OAE probe, is inserted into the ear canal and pressure changes are made to determine how the eardrum and middle ear re-spond. The test doesn't hurt and takes less than a minute, but your child must be still so your lap may be needed again.

The tympanometer prints out a graph illustrating how the eardrum and middle ear are working. There is supposed to be a small air-filled chamber behind the eardrum. When there is air in the middle-ear space—that is, when the middle ear is functioning prop-erly— the tracing on the graph will form a peak, like a hill that nar-rows at the top. If the Eustachian tube, which provides an airway from the middle ear to the throat, isn't functioning well because of allergies, cold, or an upper respiratory infection, the test may indi-cate negative pressure in the middle-ear space. The most likely out-come when there is fluid behind the eardrum is a flat tracing. While this is usually a temporary condition, the fluid adds additional con-ductive hearing loss to the underlying permanent hearing loss. Need-less to say, the last thing a hard-of-hearing child needs is additional loss due to otitis media. That's why it's important to have regular middle-ear monitoring. For example, your pediatrician will probably use the otoscope to check the ears at each visit. Your audiologist is

OTITIS MEDIA

Otitis media, an inflammation of the middle ear, is one of the most common diseases of early childhood. It is often incorrectly referred to as an ear infection, but an ear infection, which usually results in an earache and fever, occurs when there is infected fluid in the middle ear. Pediatricians call this "acute otitis media" and they often choose to treat it with antibiotics. It is possible to have middle-ear fluid without infection. This is called "otitis media with effusion" (OME). When a child has OME there are no symptoms other than hearing loss due to the blockage created by the middle-ear fluid. This hearing loss is temporary and goes away once the fluid has drained, which can take up to six weeks. To insure good health and optimal hearing, children with permanent hearing loss should be routinely screened for otitis media.

When there is a history of chronic or frequent OME, the pediatrician may recommend "pressure equalization tubes," referred to by most lay people as "tubes." Tube placement is a routine medical procedure performed by an ENT specialist when the child is under general anaesthetic. Most children need a tube in each ear, some may need only one ear treated. Tubes provide a consistent airway from the ear canal to the middle-ear space, allowing equal air pressure on both sides of the eardrum. Tubes rarely need to be removed; they usually fall out within months or, in rare instances, a year or more.

likely to obtain a tympanogram with each assessment. You should seek a medical opinion and hearing assessment any time you feel there may be a change in hearing or other symptoms of otitis media. It's important to keep in mind that otitis media can occur even in the absence of ear pain or other symptoms.

Behavioral Hearing Assessment

As noted earlier, behavioral testing requires the listener's participation. Almost all of us have had some experience with behavioral hearing screening. When I was in elementary school in the 1960s, the school district's audiologist set up shop in our gym a couple of times a year. Armed with a portable audiometer—a machine designed to emit sounds at varying frequency and decibel levels—he would fit a cumbersome pair of headphones over my ears and deliver a series of beeps. My job was to tell him in which ear I heard the sounds.

Based on my antiquated experience. I thought I knew what Elizabeth would go through when she had her hearing tested. But technology has come a long way in the more than 30 years between our tests. The sleek sound booths in the Edmonton audiology clinics I have visited during the past few years are considerably more sophisticated than what the Utica public schools had at their disposal back in the 1960s and early 1970s.

Elizabeth's first hearing tests fell into the category of pure tone audiometry. She had to identify which ear was hearing a high-, medium-, or low-pitched beep presented through earphones at varying decibel levels. Elizabeth was always cooperative at her hearing tests; she was an ideal, agreeable patient. Not all children are. In fact, I've heard about behavioral assessments taking weeks or even months to complete. It took my neighbor's daughter, Becky, six months to get a diagnosis.

"Becky was really scared," her mom, Kathy, said. That's because before she even made it to the audiologist, she'd had a handful of other traumatic medical experiences. She'd had huge amounts of wax flushed out of her ears with a large metal syringe. She'd had visits with other specialists at the same hospital where the audiologist was located. In the course of testing her for a syndrome similar to muscular dystrophy, one doctor, a physiatrist, "came at her with a huge foot-long reflex hammer, and that just sent her around the bend," Kathy recalled. "These things were not helping. They were taking place at the same site as the hearing test. Every time we pulled up to the parking lot, she'd refuse to get out of the car."

Kathy began scheduling the audiology appointments further and further apart. "Each time, Becky would be completely noncompliant and lay on the floor in a ball," Kathy said. "I thought we were wasting our time, and I was damaging our child emotionally. I didn't want it to be a traumatic experience, so we kept on lengthening the time between the visits."

At each visit, Kathy and the audiologist tried something new—toys, stickers, games. What finally made a difference was bringing in another child—Becky's six-year-old cousin—to model the correct testing behavior. When Becky saw her cousin sitting through the hearing test, apparently experiencing no pain, she was willing to try too. "She saw it was safe, it was okay, and she could do it," Kathy said. "We finally got some testing completed, and she was more and more compliant as we went along."

Nowadays it's not necessary to delay the intervention process when children are difficult to test. Although older infants and toddlers require sedation for ABR and other diagnostic tests, in the long run it is much more efficient—and easier on both the child and parents—to complete the testing as soon as possible.

While OAE and ABR provide important information regarding the auditory system, behavioral tests provide additional information regarding the type and degree of hearing loss. The first behavioral test, visual reinforcement audiometry (VRA), can be administered when the child reaches a developmental age of about six months. For this test, the infant is seated in a high chair or, more commonly, on a parent's lap while the audiologist presents tones at different frequencies and intensities. When the baby turns toward the sound, he is rewarded with a flashing light and moving toy (the visual reinforcement). Eventually, most children will allow small insert earphones to be placed in their ears, making it possible to observe responses from each ear. Until then, VRA can be done with the tones presented from a loudspeaker. Since testing with tones from a loud-speaker does not allow delivery of the sound to each ear separately, it provides a measure of the ear more sensitive to sound at that test frequency.

Eventually most children are able to be tested using play audiometry, a method of testing that allows a child to respond by dropping a block or performing some other play activity. Sometimes the audiologist will use a combination of VRA and play audiometry. The goal is to determine a threshold at each frequency—that is, the softest level a child can detect at each frequency.

VRA and play audiometry, as described here, involve presenting air conduction sounds, those that travel through the air before they arrive at the eardrum. The audiologist is also interested in how the inner ear responds—that is, a response without the participation of the middle ear. This is accomplished by stimulating the inner ear directly with a bone vibrator.

A comparison of responses to air-and bone-conducted sounds allows the audiologist to determine not only how much hearing loss there is at each frequency, but whether part of the loss is due to a middle-ear problem such as otitis media. Eventually a complete picture will emerge, making it possible to construct an audiogram, the graph that shows hearing sensitivity for each frequency.

Your child will undergo many behavioral tests. In the early years, the purpose of this will be to accurately define the type and degree of hearing loss. Later it will be important to provide monitoring to determine whether the loss is stable or changing.

How Much Information Is Needed?

The goal of the hearing test is to obtain a detailed assessment of hearing sensitivity for each ear. It is important to emphasize that a complete diagnostic picture is not needed in order to proceed with hearing aid selection and fitting. I have heard from parents whose referral to the audiologist was delayed for weeks or even months. A diagnostic ABR test performed by a pediatric audiologist will provide sufficient information—accurate predictions of low-and high-frequency hearing sensitivity—to proceed with hearing aid selection and fitting. Over time, additional information will be added making it possible to refine the hearing aid fitting. It should be noted that the hearing aid fitting is usually the first step even for children who will later receive cochlear implants.

Specialists in Your Life

In most families, the child's primary health care provider is a pediatrician. Once a child is diagnosed with permanent hearing loss, the pediatrician becomes one member of a team of health care and educational professionals. If your family decides to use an oral-language approach, you and your child may work with a speech-language pathologist (SLP), an auditory-verbal (AV) therapist, a teacher of deaf and hard-of-hearing children (TOD), or a combination of specialists. Depending on the degree of hearing loss, your child may also need an interpreter, a translator, or a transliterator. If your child has other disabilities or health problems (and many do), there will be even more professionals involved.

Your priorities and your child's needs will determine the members of the team, and there may be personnel changes along the way. If your health insurance provider or school district is resistant to covering necessary services, or if you feel their services are insufficient, you will need to advocate for your child (see Chapter Eight).

Pediatrician or Primary Care Physician.
The pediatrician or primary care physician will continue to address your child's primary medical needs, but after the diagnosis of hearing

WHEN HEARING LOSS OCCURS WITH OTHER DISABILITIES

Studies have shown that nearly 40 percent of children with permanent hearing loss have one or more disabilities in addition to hearing loss. These conditions range from mild learning problems to severe disabilities. According to a recent survey by the Gallaudet Research Institute, the most common conditions that occur with hearing loss include learning disabilities, intellectual disabilities, attention disorders, visual impairment, and cerebral palsy.

If you feel your child has an undiagnosed disability in addition to hearing loss it is important to share your concerns with your pediatrician and other service providers. Referral to a specialist or evaluation by a multidisciplinary team may be needed to determine if the condition is present and, if so, the best treatment or course of action.

loss, his or her responsibilities will include referral to appropriate specialists, including an otolaryngologist and, if you wish, a geneticist or genetic counselor. Keep in mind that even pediatricians who have been practicing for years may have limited experience with permanent hearing loss. Make sure the other professionals keep your pediatrician informed and up to date regarding your child's hearing loss and its management, and make sure *you* are on everyone's mailing lists as well.

Pediatric Audiologist.
An audiologist is a hearing health care professional with a master's degree or doctoral degree (Au.D.) from an accredited university program. Audiologists are educated in the functions of the ear, how to determine if there's a hearing loss, and what to do when there is. Although other professionals may conduct hearing screening and other

tests, when there is any doubt about a child's hearing, the test should be conducted by a pediatric audiologist.

It is important to understand that not all audiologists have experience with infants and young children. I strongly recommend that you try to find one who does, and who enjoys working with them. The websites of the American Academy of Audiology (www.audiology.org), the American Speech-Hearing Association (www.asha.org), and the Canadian Association of Speech-Language Pathologists and Audiologists (www.caslpa.ca) include directories of member audiologists (see the Resources section). CASLPA lists only private practitioners who wish to be listed. If members have specified that they work with pediatric patients, that information is included. Your pediatrician, primary care physician, or other professionals may also be able to help you find an audiologist who works with young children. As you meet other parents, they too will be helpful. Finding a well-qualified and experienced pediatric audiologist, even if it means traveling some distance, is well worth the effort.

Otolaryngologist.
Any child suspected of having a permanent hearing loss should be examined by an otolaryngologist. An otolaryngologist specializes in diagnosing and treating the ear, nose, throat, and related disorders of the head and neck. An otolaryngologist is also known as an ENT. Those who specialize in ears only are called otologists.

The ENT examination is essential to ensure that your child receives a comprehensive diagnosis. In addition to checking for middle-ear disorders, the ENT will check for other medical problems. This is important because, as noted earlier, some children with congenital hearing loss have one or more other conditions that may be associated with illness or other disabilities.

If your child suffers from chronic otitis media with effusion (OME), which further degrades his hearing, the ENT may perform minor surgery to insert pressure equalization tubes (PE-tubes) in the eardrum. If your child needs a cochlear implant, an otologist will provide the surgery. As with any professional who will work with your child, it's best if you can find an ENT who specializes in pediatrics. An ENT can also make a referral to a genetic counselor for families who want that information.

Geneticist or Genetic Counselor.

A geneticist is a health care professional (M.D. or Ph.D.) with special training in genetics, which is the study of heredity. Most permanent childhood hearing loss is hereditary. Sometimes it is part of a syndrome, which means that other medical abnormalities are present. If your pediatrician, primary care physician, or ENT physician cannot determine a cause for your child's hearing loss, you will probably want to consult with a geneticist. If a genetic cause is found, it can spare you and your child from other diagnostic procedures. You can also find a geneticist on the National Society of Genetic Counselors website (see the Resources section).

The geneticist may work with a genetic counselor (a certified professional who usually has a master's degree or Ph.D.) who can explain the genetic reasons for hearing loss, take a family history, and help you decide whether you or your child should be tested. If a test is done, the counselor can explain the results and put you in touch with other resources.

The geneticist will review your child's medical records and your family history, examine your child for signs of a syndrome, suggest appropriate medical tests, and explain the results of genetic testing.

Genetic testing usually requires a blood test, although some doctors will test a piece of skin. The sample is sent to a lab, which runs tests to determine if there are changes or mutations that can cause a hearing loss. It may take several weeks to complete the test.

If testing reveals the cause of your child's hearing loss, the geneticist or genetics counselor may also be able to tell you whether your child is likely to have or develop additional health problems, and whether the loss is likely to be progressive or remain stable. You and your spouse may also be tested. If you are planning to have more children, the geneticist may be able to tell you the likelihood of those children being born with a hearing loss. If your child's hearing loss is part of a syndrome, the geneticist may be able to refer you to a support group or provide additional information.

Genetics is an evolving science. The most common cause for childhood hearing loss not related to a syndrome is a mutation in a gene called Connexin 26. Tests for that mutation didn't exist until the 1990s. If your child has genetic testing and the test results are inconclusive, don't despair. Eventually there may be a test that will provide an answer. In the meantime, remember that genetic tests provide information, not a cure. A geneticist cannot fix your child's hearing. But having a better understanding of the underlying cause can be helpful, and also useful for planning purposes. Some day your child may also be interested in this information.

Ophthalmologist.

An ophthalmologist is a physician and surgeon who specializes in treating diseases and disorders of the eye and optic nerve. A child with a hearing loss obviously needs optimal vision. The Joint Committee on Infant Hearing in the United States recommends that every child with hearing loss have an ophthalmology exam. Regular monitoring should be provided to rule out late-onset vision disorders that might be associated with hearing loss. The ophthalmologist will tell you how often a reexamination should be provided based on your child's history. Of course, an eye examination should be scheduled any time you have concerns about your child's vision.

Communication Options

For the parents of a child newly identified with hearing loss, choosing a communication system can be frustrating and bewildering. Professionals are understandably devoted to their preferred methods of communication so getting unbiased information is not always easy. In reality, the choices may be limited, especially in a small town or rural area. Still, it's important to know about the various communication options and to choose the method best suited for your family. It's also important to remember that you can change your mind. What may seem optimal at one point in time may change as you learn more and as your child develops. Following is a brief description of each. Additional information on each of these methods can be obtained from the organizations and websites listed in the Resources section.

Auditory/Oral.

Auditory/oral methods emphasize maximum use of residual hearing through hearing aids or cochlear implants. Hearing is supplemented by visual cues—lipreading, facial expressions—but without the use of sign language.

Auditory/Verbal.

Auditory/verbal methods emphasize the use of hearing but without using lipreading and other visual cues. Auditory stimulation is often provided in individual teaching sessions with the goal of preparing the child to function well in mainstream environments.

Cued Speech.

Cued speech incorporates eight hand shapes, or cues, representing different sounds of speech. Cuing provides a supplement to lipreading by making it easier for the child to differentiate sounds that look alike on the lips, such as "m" and "p."

Total Communication.

Total communication uses a combination of methods that include sign language, fingerspelling, and speechreading, in addition to hearing. Signing used with total communication follows English word order and grammar. Sign systems such as Signing Exact English take their core vocabulary from American Sign Language (ASL) in combination with signs created to represent the grammatical features of English.

American Sign Language (Bilingual/Bicultural).
American Sign Language (ASL) is a manual language with its own grammatical rules, different from English and from sign systems that represent English. Those who advocate ASL as a first language for deaf children recommend that English be acquired as a second language, once a primary language base via ASL has been established.

Communication Specialists

Speech-Language Pathologist (SLP).
If your family chooses an oral-language approach, an SLP is likely to play an important role in helping your child learn to communicate orally with the outside world. A qualified SLP will have a master's or doctoral degree from an accredited university program. In the United States, an SLP will also be certified by the American Speech-Language-Hearing Association. In Canada, certification is optional for SLPs; however, certification is required to work at any institution certified by the Canadian Association of Speech-Language Pathologists and Audiologists. In most states and provinces, the SLP must also have a license to practice.

Your child's SLP is someone with whom your family may well have a long relationship, so you'll want to make sure it's a healthy and happy one. One way to ensure that you're starting off right is to ensure that the SLP is qualified.

I knew even before Elizabeth saw a speech pathologist for the first time that she had trouble pronouncing certain sounds—her "s" sounded like "th" and she mixed up her "p" and "f" sounds so that "put" came out as "foot." Children with severe-to-profound hearing loss may not be producing any speech sounds clearly. Even for kids with normal hearing, certain speech sounds develop later than others—for example, "r," "l," and "s"—but in Elizabeth's case, the problems may have been exacerbated by her hearing loss. Like most children who aren't diagnosed and fitted with hearing aids until relatively late, she hadn't heard all the sounds she needed to develop proper speech skills.

Generally speaking, the more severe the hearing loss, the more severe the speech and language problems. An SLP experienced at working with hard-of-hearing children can be helpful regardless of the degree of hearing loss. In addition to evaluating how a child produces speech sounds, the SLP will evaluate the receptive language ability—what the child understands. The SLP can also help your child develop auditory processing skills, including learning to listen, learning to recognize words, and learning to make sense of what he's hearing. In normal-hearing children, this ability develops automatically.

If your child needs speech therapy, the SLP will develop a program to teach him to speak clearly and audibly. Among the tools in the speech pathologist's arsenal will be a mirror, which allows your child to see how to shape his mouth or tongue; and games to make learning more fun. With children who have profound hearing loss, the SLP may use a computerized program that allows the child to see the speech signal and get a better understanding of how soft or loud his voice is.

Developing age-appropriate speech and language skills takes time and work. Children with more severe hearing losses may have more than one session a week. A child with a milder loss may have only a few sessions a month. Either way, the SLP will give your child exercises to practice. Do them together. If the exercises don't appear to be interesting to your child, ask the speech pathologist for something different if she isn't connecting with your child either because of inexperience or a personality conflict, do your best to find a more suitable match. Other parents are often your best resource.

Auditory-Verbal (AV) Therapist.

As noted earlier, auditory-verbal therapy emphasizes listening to develop spoken language and improve communication and social skills. It works well for children with severe losses who benefit from hearing aids or children with profound hearing losses who benefit from cochlear implantation.

According to the Auditory-Verbal International website (www.auditory-verbal.org), children who use auditory-verbal therapy learn to monitor their own voices and the voices of others "to enhance the intelligibility of their spoken language." An AV therapist, whose background may be in special education or speech pathology, often works one on one with a child. The therapist also works with the child's parents and caregivers, who take on the responsibility of implementing AV practice throughout the day. AV therapy is an ongoing process that may continue for months or even years.

Signing Instructor.

If you choose a manual system of communication, your child and your family will need to learn it. There are a number of manual systems, but the most common in North America are American Sign Language (ASL) and Signing Exact English (SEE). As noted earlier, ASL is a visual-spatial language separate from English. It has its own unique grammar, structure, and vocabulary. As with any new language, learning takes time and effort. ASL is used primarily by deaf people who do not use hearing aids or cochlear implants. SEE is a system that borrows its core signs from ASL, but adds signs so that English can be accurately represented on the hands. It, too, is primarily a manual form of communication. Because it follows the word order and rule features of English, it is easier for parents to learn. Some experts feel that the use of an English rule–based sign system facilitates the acquisition of English, while others feel that deaf children are better off acquiring a language such as ASL, and then acquiring English as a second language. Families who favor the use of sign language and sign systems will find the National Association of the Deaf a valuable resource (see the Resources section).

Interpreter/Translator.

If you choose to use sign language or a sign system, an interpreter, translator, or transliterator will translate a speaker's words into either American Sign Language (ASL) or a signing system such as Signing Exact English (SEE). Some hard-of-hearing children may need an oral interpreter or translator in school or group activities.

The interpreter, translator, or transliterator must be fluent both in the spoken language being used and in the sign language or sign system your child uses. Otherwise, your child will not have access to all that is being said. The interpreter or translator will also translate what your child says into spoken English, so that your child can actively participate in discussions. An interpreter or translator should be well qualified and should not change the information or apply her own interpretation to what is being said or signed.

As with any profession, some interpreters and translators are better than others. If you choose to use a sign system, it's important to check your interpreter's or translator's credentials and references to make sure she is qualified for the job. As you'll see later in this book, it's also important to check with your child and his teachers to make sure the interpreter or translator is performing her duties appropriately.

Teacher of the Deaf and Hard of Hearing.

In the past, most children with hearing loss were educated in special schools for the deaf. Nowadays most children with hearing loss are integrated into mainstream classrooms. Even those who require special instructions are likely to be served in regular schools. An itinerant teacher of the deaf and hard of hearing may work with your child outside the classroom and may also serve as a consultant to you and to school personnel. This person is likely to have a bachelor's or master's degree in special education and/or education of the deaf. Her responsibilities include making sure your child's educational needs are being met, which can mean working with teachers to help them understand your child's needs and equipment, helping with the transition between schools and with graduation from high school, making sure equipment is functioning and possibly making minor adjustments, monitoring your child's speech and language development, and providing one-on-one tutoring. Most itinerant teacher specialists are responsible for many students, so they travel from school to school and may work with your child for only an hour or two a week.

As parents, we don't expect to develop close friendships with the medical and audiology professionals who treat our children, though after years of checkups, exams, fitting, and repairs, it's not unusual for that to happen. The same may not hold true with the specialists who help guide our children through their school years, in part because we're not with our children throughout the school day. Still, I can't stress enough how important it is to develop a good working relationship with them, even once your children are out of elementary school. They may play a significant role in your child's education. For some parents, they will be a primary contact during the school years. As you'll discover while reading Chapters Eight and Nine, working together with these nonmedical specialists is one of the best ways to help your child, and maximize the chances of making the school years enjoyable and productive.

Chapter Four

HEARING AIDS, FM SYSTEMS, AND COCHLEAR IMPLANTS

The Modern Hearing Aid:
Good Things Come in Small Packages

The first time I saw a child-sized hearing aid, I wanted to cry. It was about the size of one knuckle, yet it seemed enormous. I thought hearing aids were for senior citizens, not for a lively little girl with her whole life ahead of her.

When Elizabeth's audiologist Paulette said, "They're really quite small. Years ago they were much bigger," I was convinced she was in deeper denial than I. "They look like the Empire State Building," I blurted out.

"Well, at least she has long hair," Paulette said in an unsuccessful attempt to make me feel better.

Nothing could have made me feel better. I hadn't yet reached the point where I was focusing on the reality that, unappealing though they were, hearing aids were going to make things better for Elizabeth.

I'm not alone. It's hard enough for parents to accept that their child has a hearing loss, but at least until the child is aided, we can continue to fool ourselves into believing nothing has changed and nothing is wrong. Once hearing aids become part of the picture, especially when they seem so massive and visible, denial becomes more difficult. However, for the vast majority of hard-of-hearing children, hearing aids improve everything from communication to behavior.

Many parents have asked their audiologist why their child can't have those nice little hearing aids that fit right inside the ears. They're called in-the-ear (ITE) instruments. The tinier ones that are completely in the ear canal are called, not surprisingly, completely-in-the-canal (CIC) instruments. It's important to remember that the needs of a child differ from those of an adult, and that some features that may be helpful for adults may not be for children.

Neither ITE nor CIC instruments have the advantages behind-the-ears (BTE) aids provide for children. BTE aids are more versatile, they're compatible with other devices that will help your child, and they offer better control of whistling, which the experts refer to as acoustic feedback. Their size will also prove to be an advantage on those occasions, and let's hope they're rare, when your child loses them on the soccer field or the beach or the playroom floor.

Picking up Elizabeth at a birthday party not long ago, I met a mom named Paige who has worn hearing aids for 37 years, since she was three. Paige noticed Elizabeth's aids almost immediately, perhaps because she wears one blue one and one red one, and at the time her earmolds had colored sparkles in them. (She's since gotten bigger earmolds. One is purple and pink, and the other is green and yellow.) "She's lucky," Paige said to me. "Hearing aids are so much better now than when I was a kid."

Indeed, hearing aids are a lot better now than they were as recently as the 1980s, and hearing aids from that era were a huge leap forward from the earliest versions. Hearing aids, in one form or another, have been around for centuries. The first attempts to amplify sound used animal horns and other devices fashioned into ear trumpets. Early experiments with electricity resulted in the development of amplifiers that provided a greater increase in sound than nonelectric devices. In fact, Alexander Graham Bell, inventor of the telephone, was first a teacher of the deaf whose goal was to develop an electric hearing aid. But it wasn't until the second half of the twentieth century, when hearing aids moved from vacuum tubes to transistors, that hearing aids were capable of delivering clear, amplified sounds.

How Hearing Aids (Are Supposed to) Work

The hearing aids of today are technological marvels employing tiny, sophisticated components and circuitry. For parents, they can be puzzling and even a bit overwhelming, at least in the beginning. The main purpose of a hearing aid is to make speech and environmental sounds audible without exceeding levels of comfortable listening. Your child's audiologist will refer to the latter phenomenon as loudness discomfort. As noted earlier, the most practical option for infants and young children is a behind-the-ear (BTE) aid, also known as an ear-level aid.

In most cases, the audiologist will recommend a hearing aid for each ear, referred to as a binaural fitting, even if the loss is different in each ear. With both ears working, your child can hear better in a noisy environment and more easily determine where the sound is coming from. This is known as sound localization. Hearing aid microphones can be located at ear level, which makes it possible to achieve stereophonic reception, which provides a more natural listening experience. In a sense, it's the aural equivalent of spatial perception. Another advantage of a binaural fitting is that your child is always likely to have at least one functional hearing aid in the event of a malfunction, although it's always best if your audiologist can provide a loaner hearing aid at those times. Finally, BTE hearing aids can also be coupled to FM systems, which will be discussed later in this chapter.

A hearing aid has several components. The microphone picks up incoming sound waves and converts them to electrical signals. The amplifier increases the intensity and, when necessary, further modifies the incoming sound. The receiver converts electrical signals back to sound waves that are delivered, through the earmold, to the ear of the listener.

Modern hearing aids, most of which include digital features, can do many things to the incoming sound before it is delivered to the user. Conventional hearing aids, the ones that have been around for many years, are analog devices that take incoming sounds and provide amplification across a range of frequencies. A small screwdriver is used to make the adjustments that determine how much amplification is delivered and at what frequencies. The incoming signals are amplified by shaping the sound according to the amount of increases needed across the frequency range, and then delivered through the earmold to the child's ear.

However, most audiologists prefer hearing aids that can be digitally programmed because they allow better control of the amplified signals. The simplest way to understand what digital means is to think about a clock. Clocks traditionally used continuous movement of gears and hands to display information regarding the hour and minute. Digital clocks, instead of providing a continuous stream, divide the hour into segments that are displayed as numbers. Digitally programmable hearing aids are not necessarily fully digital hearing aids. A digitally programmable aid uses analog signals, but a computer chip inside the aid allows it to be attached to a computer and programmed to provide amplification patterns appropriate for a variety of different listening situations. Instead of a screwdriver, the audiologist adjusts the hearing aid using a computer.

The most advanced and expensive hearing aids are fully digital. Digital aids are not only programmable but the incoming sound waves are divided into digitized segments in a way that allows the most sophisticated signal processing. For example, digital hearing aids have special circuitry to reduce noise and acoustic feedback.

There are some important features that can be incorporated into both programmable and digital hearing aids. One is a circuit design called wide dynamic range compression (WDRC). This sounds highly technical and it is. However, the purpose of WDRC and why many audiologists prefer it for children is simple: hearing aids with WDRC are designed to take soft sounds and make them louder, and to take very loud sounds and make them softer. Because children are subjected to listening environments that cover a wide range of sound levels, WDRC helps them hear comfortably as conditions change. Another important feature many audiologists prefer for children is directional microphones. Simply stated, a directional mic amplifies sounds in front of the listener more than sounds at the side of or behind the listener. In noisy conditions, or when the goal is to direct the child's hearing toward the person talking, directional mics can be very helpful. In other listening situations, it is better to have omni-directional sound, which is sound that surrounds the listener in a more natural way—for example, during free play in a preschool. In those situations, the directional mics are simply switched off. Your audiologist will explain how these microphones work and how and when they should be used.

Remote controls for hearing aids can also be helpful, allowing parents to turn a device on or off or to activate or deactivate directional microphones without interrupting the child's activities. By seven or eight years of age, most children can take responsibility for these adjustments.

The Earmold: A Blessing and a Curse

I was still in shock about Elizabeth's diagnosis the first time I heard the term *earmold*. Had I been in a better mood I probably would have laughed out loud. Let's face it, it's a pretty odd-sounding term for something that is critical to your child's hearing. Earmolds for children are made of a soft, compliant material. Some children are allergic to the standard materials, and this will become apparent if your child develops a rash or swelling. Fortunately, special hypoallergenic materials are available when needed.

In any event, the process of making an earmold is the same. The audiologist inserts into your child's ear canal a cotton or foam ball with a string attached. Using a plastic syringe, she will then fill the canal with soft silicone to make a form or impression. This will be sent to a laboratory where it will be made into a custom mold, perfectly fitted (we hope) to your child's ear. Within the earmold is a clear plastic tube that connects the earmold to the behind-the-ear hearing aid.

It sounds simple, but early earmold experiences can be terrifying for your child. I know they were for Elizabeth—and for me. For her, it was the idea of having her ear filled with gunk for what seemed like ages (though in truth it took only a few minutes). For me, it was fear that the string would break and the silicone would be lodged in her ear forever. Both our fears were groundless. In fact, Elizabeth now looks forward to having earmolds made because the audiologist always lets her play with the little bits of extra silicone, which are like modeling clay until they dry, at which point they become smooth and even a bit bouncy.

Elizabeth's first earmolds seemed to fit very snugly into her ears—so snugly, in fact, that I often had a difficult time putting them in. I eventually discovered that swabbing them with a diaper wipe just before inserting them provided the right amount of lubrication. Even better is a product called Otoease (Figure 4–1), which you can get

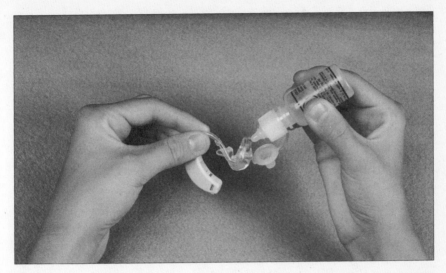

FIGURE 4-1 • Otoease, a lubricant, is applied to an earmold to make insertion easier.

from your audiologist. As Elizabeth grew, her earmolds slipped in more easily. As I became a more experienced mother of a hard-of-hearing child, I learned that when putting in the earmolds was too easy, they were probably too small and it was time for new ones. The greater the hearing loss, the more critical it is for the earmolds to fit snugly.

Selecting and Fitting the Hearing Aid: What Your Audiologist Will Do

Before the hearing aids can be fitted, the audiologist needs to determine how much hearing loss there is and how the hearing sensitivity differs across the frequency range for each ear. For example, a child whose loss is only in the high frequencies needs different amplification than one whose hearing loss is about the same in all frequencies.

Young infants cannot be evaluated using behavioral tests until they reach a developmental age of about six months. Therefore, their hearing levels must be determined using physiologic tests. Recall from Chapter Three that a diagnostic of auditory brainstem response, which can be obtained from a sleeping baby, is needed because it provides an estimate of hearing sensitivity across a range of frequencies.

Once there is sufficient information to determine the degree of hearing loss and shape of the audiogram, your audiologist will decide which type of hearing aid is most appropriate and how they should be adjusted. To do this, she'll use special instruments designed to measure the amplification in each frequency region.

Real ear measures involve placing a microphone in the ear canal to accurately determine the amount of amplification delivered to the ear. Accurate measurements are critical because infants have smaller ears than older children or adults. Even within an age group, there may be differences in the size, shape, and other ear characteristics. The most important difference is the smaller size of the ear canal. Because of the way sound levels are affected by the amount of space between the tip of the earmold and the eardrum, infants get more amplification than older children even when the same hearing aid is adjusted to the same settings. Think of it in terms of noise levels in a room. If you play a stereo at full blast in an auditorium, the volume level may be just right, but play it at full blast in a small room, and the noise will be overwhelming.

In addition to checking the amplification levels for typical sounds such as speech, it's also important to check the hearing aid's maximum output to ensure that the hearing aid does not exceed safe and comfortable listening levels. In fact, excessive amplification can cause a child to reject hearing aids. In extreme cases, overamplification can even damage the cochlea. However, an overly conservative approach results in amplification levels that are too low, providing little or no aided benefit.

In recent years, audiologists have developed a way to adjust hearing aids using a coupler attached to a probe and test box, making it unnecessary to insert a probe into the ear of a child or infant who has neither the ability nor desire to sit still for the amount of time necessary to properly adjust the aids. This calculation results in greater ease of testing and more accurate measurements.

How Much Benefit Should You Expect?

Many people think hearing aids are like eyeglasses; wear them and everything comes in clearly. That's not the case. True, hearing aids have improved technologically in recent years—and some are even becoming fashionable (instead of being limited to flesh-colored ear-pieces and clear earmolds, there is now a rainbow of colors from which to choose). But while ear aids boost the intensity of sound and perform other enhancements, they cannot fully compensate for the lack of clarity that often occurs with a sensorineural hearing loss. Also, it needs to be understood that the greater the hearing loss, the harder the hearing aids have to work. Even when using hearing aids, a person with a severe-to-profound hearing loss is not likely to hear as well as someone with a mild-to-moderate loss.

Parents can play an important role in monitoring and recording their child's progress with amplification. Two assessment tools for parents are the Early Language Function (ELF) and the Child Home Inventory of Listening Difficulties (CHILD), both developed by audiologist Karen Anderson. Information about both can be found in the Resources section. These parent inventories allow family members and caretakers to monitor their child's progress and better understand the implications of hearing loss.

How Long Do Hearing Aids Last?

As with any electronic device, parts eventually break or wear out. Your child's audiologist should be able to help you determine when it's time to purchase new instruments. Hearing aids are expensive, so be sure to discuss with your audiologist options and any available payment assistance programs. Because of technological advances your child will likely hear differently with his new aids, which will probably be more sophisticated than his last pair. It's a good idea to have your audiologist tell your child, in advance, to expect some changes in how he hears. In most cases he will adapt quickly and like his new aids even better than the old ones. If he does have problems, however, be sure to consult your audiologist.

Bone-Conduction Hearing Aids

Most permanent hearing losses in children are due to abnormal inner ear function referred to as sensorineural impairment. There are rare congenital conditions, however, that result in a hearing loss due to middle and/or outer ear abnormalities. These losses are often associated with normal inner ear function. When an outer ear problem makes it impossible to use a standard earmold and hearing aid, a bone-conduction device may be recommended. The sound is delivered using vibrations directly to the inner ear by a bone vibrator worn on the head. Although a bit cumbersome, this arrangement can provide the stimulation necessary to help a child acquire language and develop speech. Some parents cleverly adapt hats or headbands for this purpose. In recent years, a surgically implantable bone-conduction device, coupled to the head by way of magnetic coupling through the skin, has been developed for older children and adults.

FM Systems

A personal FM system is a device used by many children in conjunction with hearing aids. It allows a child to hear a speaker's voice without the distraction of background noise. Its components include a microphone worn by the primary speaker (usually a parent or teacher), a transmitter (with an antenna) connected to the microphone, and an FM receiver (see Figure 4–2). The speaker wears the transmitter and microphone, and the child wears the receiver. The microphone, worn around the neck, on a headband, or clipped to a piece of clothing, is linked to a small transmitter that can be attached to the user with a belt clip.

Most of us are familiar with FM from listening to the radio. With a personal FM system, the transmission range is far less than that of a local FM radio station, but it's more than adequate for most listening situations. The advantage of an FM system is that amplified sounds are delivered to the ear as if the person speaking were only a few inches from the person talking. In other words, regardless of the distance between the speaker and listener, signals arriving at the ear

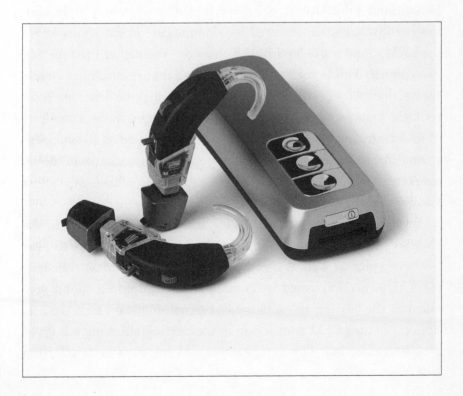

are the same as if the child were close to the person talking. A potential disadvantage is that if anyone else is talking at the same time as the person controlling the microphone, the child will have trouble hearing other voices. This problem is overcome by adjusting the hearing aid to deliver FM only (when appropriate) or FM plus hearing aid (with the hearing aid at a level slightly lower than FM). Other sound sources, such as the audio signal from a TV or video recorder, can also be delivered via FM. The most important advantage of FM is that the listener receives the signal at a level well above the background noise. The outcome is an improvement in the level of the primary signal—your voice, for example—in comparison to competing background noise.

Audiologists sometimes use the term *signal-to-noise ratio* to express the relationship between speech and noise. When the signal-to-noise ratio is zero, it means that the primary signal and the background noise are at equal levels. Unfortunately, people with hearing loss are often required to communicate in situations where the background noise level is as high as or even higher than the primary signal. This is regrettable considering that research has clearly shown that people with hearing loss require a better listening environment than people with normal hearing to achieve the same level of understanding. Although FM cannot create a perfect listening environment, it can greatly reduce the problems of background noise, speaker-listener distance, and reverberations or echos—all factors known to make listening more difficult.

Several options are available for getting the FM signal to the child's ear, but it's important to remember that she needs to hear her own voice as well as the sound delivered by the FM transmitter. This is accomplished by combining the amplified sound provided by the hearing aid with the FM signal. In most cases, the best option is a direct FM connection to the hearing aid using a boot or plug-in connection. This arrangement makes it easy to switch from hearing to FM plus hearing aid, and back again. Another advantage is that the amplification delivered to the ear is similar for FM and hearing aid.

In most listening situations, the hearing aid microphone must be switched on to allow the child to hear her own speech as well as the speech of others in the immediate vicinity. In other situations, where only the input from the FM is important—for example, when listening to an audio recording—the hearing aid microphone can be switched off. Proper location and use of the microphone are critical—that is, the FM microphone and transmitter must be located near the source of the primary input signal, such as the teacher's or parent's mouth, another child or sibling, television, tape player, and so on in order to get the full advantage of FM. It is important for parents, caretakers, and teachers to understand proper use of FM since an inappropriately used system can create a poorer listening situation than hearing aids used alone.

The signals sent by FM systems travel on specific frequencies. The frequency of the transmitter and receiver must be compatible. It is important to be aware of interactions between devices. I once heard about a girl who spent the first half of the academic year convinced she was going crazy because whenever she was in school, she heard voices in French. She was embarrassed to tell her mother what was going on inside her head. What she didn't realize at the time was that she wasn't the only hard-of-hearing child in the school. Unbeknownst to her, a student in the French immersion program was also using an FM, and he was on the same channel. Once the FMs were put on different channels, the problem was solved. Some school districts have access to an educational audiologist to assist in sorting out these issues. If an audiologist is not involved in the management of classroom listening equipment, you may want to ask for this (see Chapter Eight).

Don't be surprised if your child eventually says he doesn't want to use the FM system. Usually around the time they reach junior high school, kids become increasingly determined to blend in with everyone else. The mother of a middle schooler told me her daughter's protest went like this: "When I get married, do you think my husband's going to use the FM during the wedding ceremony?"

Toby wanted to quit using his FM in sixth grade, but his mother wouldn't let him. He's grateful for that. "You don't miss anything the teacher says," he explained. The school owned Toby's FM, so he didn't have it to use at home or for extracurricular activities. Although he has a moderate-to-severe loss, if there was no background noise in class, he could hear well. In eleventh grade, he abandoned the system altogether.

"It was this thing I had to truck around with me all the time and it wasn't benefiting me as much," he said, adding that going without forced him to pay attention. "I just sat at the front of the room and told myself, 'I'm not going to have this when I get out of here, so I might as well get used to it.' "

Fortunately, this scenario is changing. Toby and others who use assistive listening devices will, and in many situations already do, have the benefit of FM, infrared, and other technologies in theaters, auditoriums, and places of worship. In the United States, the Americans with Disabilities Act ensures that communication is accessible to people with hearing loss, just as a building is accessible to people with physical disabilities. Moreover, people with hearing loss are incorporating assistive listening devices into their daily lives to enhance communication with friends, family members, and coworkers. With the popularity of personal stereos and cell phones, hearing aids and assistive listening devices are not as noticeable or stigmatizing as they once were. Eventually our children will become their own advocates. For now, we must encourage them to take advantage of available accommodations to the listening environment through technology and by educating those with normal hearing.

WHAT IF THE HEARING LOSS IS ONLY IN ONE EAR?

A "unilateral" hearing loss is one that affects only one ear. People with unilateral hearing loss often have difficulty determining the location of a sound or understanding speech in a noisy situation, especially when sounds are directed toward the poorer ear.

Diagnosis requires medical assessment, usually by an ear specialist (ENT), to determine if the loss is medically treatable and whether it's associated with other conditions. Assessment by an audiologist is necessary to determine if a hearing aid or other hearing instrument is needed. When a unilateral sensorineural loss is in the mild-to-moderate range, some children may benefit from a "monaural" hearing aid fitting, especially if the loss is detected early. In cases of more severe unilateral hearing loss, amplifying the abnormal ear may be detrimental to the child's overall hearing.

Most children with unilateral hearing loss do well in school but studies have shown that as many as one-third are at risk for educational problems. Careful monitoring of hearing and the listening environment is essential. Limiting background noise whenever possible is especially important. An FM system may be helpful. The child should be aware of the need for extra care around traffic and other hazardous situations.

Sound field FM.

The sound field listening system is an example of FM technology that is sometimes used in a classroom setting with older children who have milder hearing losses. In this arrangement, a teacher wears a transmitter and microphone, and the FM signal is transmitted to a receiver and amplifier. The signal is broadcast through loudspeakers, enabling the teacher to move freely around the room. Because a microphone is worn close to the teacher's mouth, amplified signals are heard at consistent levels throughout the classroom.

Although this arrangement is not as good as direct-input FM, it is a less expensive option that has the advantage of providing a more favorable listening environment, even for normal-hearing classmates.

Cochlear Implants

One of the first questions friends and relatives asked after they learned about Elizabeth's hearing loss was whether she was going to get a cochlear implant. The answer was no. It was never a consideration. Elizabeth has enough of what is called residual hearing—that is, her cochlea and auditory nerve are functional for the use of amplified sound.

Cochlear implants are for people who get minimal benefit from conventional hearing aids. Unlike hearing aids, which amplify what the user can hear, a cochlear implant takes incoming sounds and converts them to an electrical code that allows the deaf person to understand speech and environmental sounds. This is accomplished by several components that include external parts (a microphone, speech processor, and transmitter) and internal parts (a receiver, electrodes, and magnet) that are surgically implanted by an otologist. An additional magnet is used to hold the device on the head. (See Figure 4–3.)

At one time, cochlear implants provided only gross awareness of sound. Using them made it possible to hear, which made lip-reading easier. Actual speech discrimination—that is, clearly understanding specific words and sounds—was still difficult, if not impossible. As the devices have improved, so have the benefits. Research is ongoing, and there is still much to learn about the optimal age of implantation and other variables. Studies, however, have shown that cochlear implants allow many children to make excellent progress with speech and language, although there is a range of performance and it's not always predictable.

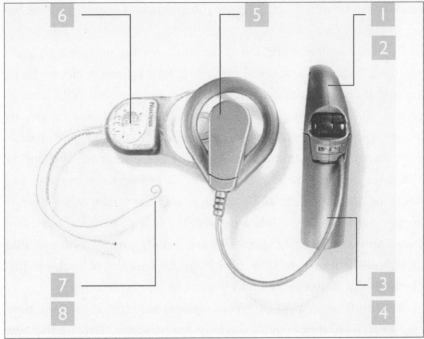

FIGURE 4–3 • The parts of a cochlear implant and what they do.   1. Sound is picked up by a directional microphone.   2. Sound is sent from the microphone to the speech processor.   3. The speech processor analyzes and digitizes the sound into coded signals.   4. Coded signals are sent to the transmitter via radio frequency. 5. The transmitter sends the code across the skin to the internal implant.   6. The internal implant converts the code to electrial signals.   7. The signals are sent to the electrodes to stimulate the remaining nerve fibers.   8. The signals are recognized as sounds by the brain, producing a hearing sensation. Courtesy of Cochlear Corporation.

Unlike hearing aids, cochlear implantation requires surgery followed by an adjustment process called mapping. An otologist does the surgery and an audiologist handles the mapping process, which involves programming the implant's speech processor for optimal hearing. Proper mapping also ensures that speech and environmental sounds will not exceed levels of comfortable listening. The audiologist will select the most beneficial program. The mapping process occurs frequently at the beginning and may continue over a period of months or even years. Changes occur as the child becomes more accustomed to sound and as more information is acquired about his use of the device.

Cochlear implants are considered only for the most severe hearing losses because the surgical procedure for placing the electrodes in the cochlea requires destroying whatever cochlear hair cells remain. That means destroying any chance that the ear will ever be able to receive sound in the usual manner. It's also why the cochlear implant team sometimes recommends implanting the poorer ear if there's a difference between the two. This allows a person to continue to use a hearing aid in one ear and a cochlear implant on the other. Even if the person does not use a hearing aid, because of practical considerations and cost, cochlear implants are usually provided on one side only. Some centers are now exploring the benefits of cochlear implantation in both ears. Results appear to be encouraging.

As with hearing aids, cochlear implants are intended for full-time use. Therefore, they require ongoing maintenance. Despite the best efforts, breakdowns occur. Parents, teachers, and other caretakers play a critical role in checking the external device and its cords, ensuring that controls are at the proper settings and making minor repairs when necessary. Most cochlear implant centers do an excellent job of informing family members and others of their roles.

As much as you may want your child to have a cochlear implant, the choice is not yours alone. Deciding who's a candidate requires a team approach. Along with the parents, team members will include the otologist, audiologist, speech-language pathologist, educators of the deaf, and sometimes a psychologist or social worker.

Cochlear implants are expensive. Hardware and surgical fees cost thousands of dollars. Fortunately, financial assistance is often available. It is important to thoroughly investigate insurance benefits available through your private insurance, or assistance available through state or provincial agencies.

Regardless of whether your child uses hearing aids or a cochlear implant, there will be an initial period of adjustment. For some children, it will go more quickly than for others. Some may discover that the fitting is not optimal, and it may take time to make the necessary changes. Don't lose hope. An experienced and patient pediatric audiologist will find what works best for your child. And once that happens, and you and your child settle in to the wonderful world of better hearing, the inevitable will happen: something will break. In the next chapter, you'll learn more about how to prolong the life of your child's hearing devices and what to do when things fall apart.

Chapter Five

TAKING CARE OF HEARING AIDS

For most hard-of-hearing children, hearing can serve as the primary channel for acquiring speech and language, but only if amplification is appropriately fitted and consistently maintained. The amount of aided benefit is determined by a variety of factors, including the type of hearing loss, amount of hearing loss, and clarity of amplified sounds. The amount of time the aids are worn and consistency of use are also important variables. Family members, teachers, and caretakers play an important role when it comes to keeping things working properly. Needless to say, the best hearing aids are of little value if the batteries are dead, the earmold is clogged, or the child refuses to wear them.

Parts and Maintenance

Batteries.
There's nothing more basic to proper hearing aid use than batteries. Yet discharged or improperly inserted batteries are still a major cause

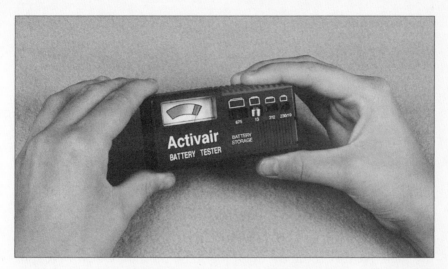

FIGURE 5–1 • Battery tester designed for hearing aid batteries.

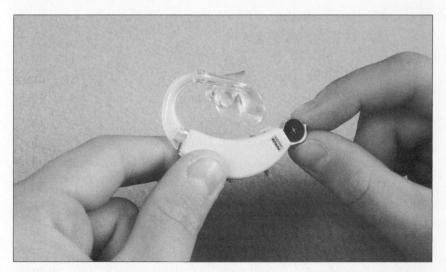

FIGURE 5–2 • The hearing aid battery must be properly inserted. Hearing aids for children should have tamper-resistant battery doors.

of malfunction. Your audiologist will provide a first set of batteries and a battery tester (See Figure 5-1), along with an orientation on how to test and insert the batteries. It is important to make sure the batteries are properly inserted (see Figure 5-2) and that the battery door is fully closed after insertion. Unlike the batteries in your wrist-watch, hearing aid batteries need to be changed frequently. How often depends on the degree of your child's hearing loss and how the hearing aids are used. You're likely to go through batteries more frequently if the weather is cold, if the environment is noisy, and if your child uses an FM system.

When Elizabeth first began wearing hearing aids, I changed the batteries every 13 days. By the time she was in first grade and using an FM every day, I had to change the batteries once a week. But when she got a new FM at the end of second grade, I suddenly had to change the batteries every four days. I couldn't figure out the problem. Neither could the audiologist. So the aids, which were four years old, were sent in for reconditioning.

By then it was summer, and because Elizabeth wasn't using the FM, I could go a week or more without changing batteries. But once school began again, so did the annoyingly frequent changes. I met people in the audiology clinic whose children had far greater hearing losses than Elizabeth, and their batteries lasted over a week. What was wrong with ours? After a thorough question-and-answer session with the audiologist, I learned something: the new FM boots sucked power from the hearing aid batteries even when the FM wasn't being used. After that, I began taking the boots off after school. Soon we were back to having batteries last a week.

Batteries are the lifeline for hearing aids. They're also just the right size and shape to be chewed or swallowed. Hearing aids designed for young children have tamper-proof battery doors. It's important to make sure they are properly closed and that batteries not in use are properly stored.

For some children, however, tamper-proof doors aren't protection enough. Long before his first birthday, Collin, Arthur and Tracy's son, figured out how to pull off his hearing aids and discovered the joy of sucking on them. His saliva short-circuited the on-off switch and leaked into the battery compartment, causing corrosion. It wasn't unusual for the family to go through two sets of batteries a day. His parents cleaned the battery door with a Q-tip dipped in alcohol in an effort to dry the unit, but the damage had been done. The hearing aid had to be sent away for repairs. After that, Collin's audiologist recommended Superseal, a stretchy latex cover that fits over the hearing aid to protect it from moisture.

Listening Checks.

First thing in the morning and as many times as possible throughout the day it's important to attach the hearing aids to a stethoset (See Figure 5–3), a device available from your audiologist, and listen carefully as you repeat various sounds and phrases. Although it seems a little strange at first to be talking to yourself, with practice you'll become proficient at noticing when things go wrong. A hearing aid with no output is not difficult to detect, but it's also important to notice a loss of clarity or loose connections that cause intermittent output.

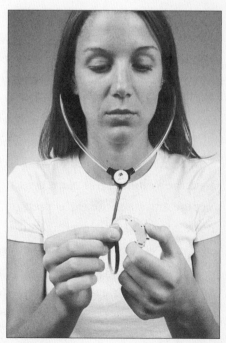

FIGURE 5–3 · "Stehoset" used to perform a listening check on a BTE hearing aid.

Volume Control.

While your child is young, you'll need to make sure the volume control stays at the proper setting. Snap-on volume control covers are available and highly recommended to ensure that the hearing aid is not delivering too much or too little amplification.

Earmolds.

To understand the earmold's purpose and pitfalls, it's important to understand how it is intended to work. A channel within the earmold, known as the sound bore, contains a short length of plastic tubing. Together, the tubing and earmold carry amplified sounds from the hearing aid to the ear canal.

It all sounds pretty straightforward, but several things can and, at some point, will go wrong. The most common problem is acoustic feedback, the annoying whistling sound familiar to parents, hearing aid users, and anyone who has ever attended a school assembly where a PA system is in use. In the latter case, the whistling occurs because the microphone is too close to the speaker, creating a squeal so loud it can be heard in the next county. The cause is overamplification of incoming sound; when the microphone gets too close to the receiver, it causes an amplification loop that overloads the amplifier. The only solution, in the case of the PA system, is to lower the volume, which defeats the purpose of the device, or to move the microphone farther from the speaker, which is the appropriate solution.

In some ways, a hearing aid is like a miniature PA system. Because the volume level cannot be turned down without defeating its purpose and since the ear is pretty much unmovable, hearing aids use another method to prevent acoustic feedback: the earmold. The earmold creates a sound barrier between the microphone and receiver. All is well as long as the earmold fits snugly into the external ear and ear canal. But an earmold that is too small or improperly inserted will create a leak, resulting in acoustic feedback. Feedback can also occur if earwax has accumulated, which will create an obstruction

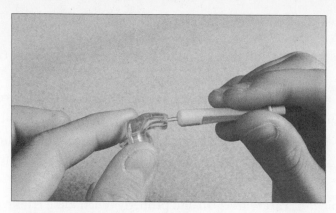

FIGURE 5–4 • A small "wax loop" is used to remove debris from the earmold.

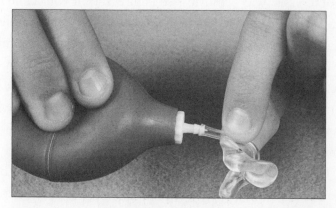

FIGURE 5–5 • A small squeeze ball is used, after cleaning, to clear water and debris from the earmold tubing and sound bore.

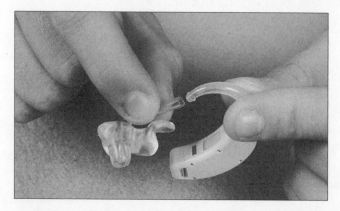

FIGURE 5–6 • Attachment of earmold tubing to tone hook (tubing is glued at the other end where it enters the earmold).

that prevents the amplified sound from passing through the ear canal.

Regardless of the cause, you'll need to take care of the problem. If the mold is loose or not fitting properly, the earmold will likely have to be remade. If the problem is impacted earwax, your child may have to visit the pediatrician, although some audiologists can remove earwax.

Keeping the earmolds clean and properly functioning requires careful inspection and cleaning. Your audiologist may provide you with a small tool to assist wax removal (see Figure 5-4). If your child's ear is like Elizabeth's and secretes enough wax to discolor a new earmold in two weeks, that tool may be too flimsy. You can also use a mild detergent, such as dishwashing soap and a damp—not wet—cloth. However, the tubing must first be separated from the hearing aid. With most earmolds, the tubing is glued into the sound bore. But where it attaches to the tone hook, it is pushed into place (see Figure 5–3). After the earmold has been removed and washed, it should be dried before reusing. Blowing through the tubing or using a small squeeze ball designed for this purpose (see Figure 5-5) will clear water or other debris trapped in the sound bore. When reattaching the earmold to the hearing aid, it's important to make sure you have it pushed securely in place and that it is properly oriented (see Figure 5-6).

Problems You May Encounter

You may be the most careful and conscientious person in the universe, but when your child spends his waking hours wearing small, fragile, expensive, and highly sophisticated electronic devices, problems will arise. The best advice I can offer is this: expect the unexpected, be flexible, and, if possible, have backup aids or loaner instruments. Insurance is well worth considering. It also helps to have a sense of humor.

Acoustic Feedback.

The only good thing about acoustic feedback is that we know it's happening. Correcting the problem is not always as easy. Most feedback problems are due to improper insertion. However, young children quickly outgrow their earmolds, which results in a loose fitting. If feedback persists even when the mold is properly inserted and snug with no blockage or leaks in the earmold tubing, consult your audiologist.

Earmold Remakes.

The earmold is the least technical part of the hearing aid, but it is often the weakest link. If your child's ears are full of wax, even the most expensive and sophisticated hearing aids won't help. Likewise, the most optimal hearing aid is useless if the earmold doesn't fit properly. Either the hearing aids will fall out (and risk being lost or trampled upon) or they will whistle continuously.

Babies often outgrow their earmolds within a few weeks. The replacement cycle usually slows down, but during the early years, you may feel as if you're spending more time with the audiologist than at the playground. Telltale signs that it's time for a new earmold are when they come out or go in too easily, when you can see gaps around the edge of the earmold, when acoustic feedback becomes a regular part of your day, or when the earmold falls out simply because your child has tipped his head to one side or another or rubbed the side of his head against something. When high-power aids are required, however, some feedback is inevitable when hats, hands, or anything else is close to the hearing aid.

Collin was fitted for his first pair of hearing aids when he was two months old. He and his family live in North Carolina and the pediatric audiologist they go to is more than an hour from their home. By the time Collin was 11 months old, he was on his sixth set of earmolds and his parents had put a lot of miles on their car.

"The audiologist explained to us that it would happen quickly because his ears grow so fast," said Arthur, his father.

On the positive side, Collin's parents have an alternative to photography for chronicling Collin's growth. "We have all the earmolds from the first ones all the way up," Arthur said. "It's amazing to look at the size of them!"

Impacted Wax.

Recall from Chapter One that it's normal to have some earwax on the walls of the ear canal. Obstruction from impacted cerumen is often a problem for hearing aid users because the earmold tends to push the wax back in. Make sure you have your child's ear canals inspected any time there is a medical or audiology appointment. When a significant wax buildup does occur, it should be removed by an experienced clinician, usually a physician or nurse. (Some audiologists will clean ears but most do not.) It's best to avoid over-the-counter earwax removal products for children.

Comments and Advice of Strangers (and Friends!).

No matter how well intentioned, the comments of people on the street, in checkout lines, and in other public places are, at times, unwelcome. Collin was diagnosed shortly after birth with a moderate bilateral sensorineural loss. His sister, Hannah, who is almost three years older, took it upon herself to inform the general public. Noticing the stares from an elderly woman with a small child at the grocery store one day, she said, "This is my baby brother, Collin, and he has hearing aids. Your baby doesn't have hearing aids," to which the woman replied, "Thank God."

"I don't think Hannah picked up on it, but it hurt my feelings," explained Collin's mother, Tracy. "I said to Hannah, 'Let's just move on down the aisle. Let's just leave these guys alone.' "

What Goes in Comes Out.

Every parent knows that children love to remove shoes, hats, and other things. The earmold is an easy target because of its convenient location. Fortunately, two factors work in our favor. First of all, most children, once accustomed to their hearing aids, prefer to wear them; in fact, some object strongly when they're taken out. Second, audiologists and suppliers of hearing aid accessories have come up with ingenious ways to retain the devices. Your audiologist can provide a product called Huggie Aids to hold the hearing aids in place, and clip-on retention devices to prevent them from getting lost if they do fall out of the ear.

Elizabeth got her first hearing aids on a Friday. The audiologist warned us that there would be an adjustment period. "It will probably take her the weekend to get used to them," she said. "Don't be surprised if she tries to take them out, but remind her, that's your job."

At three, Elizabeth was too young to be responsible for removing her aids—not that that stopped her. On Friday, she pulled them out repeatedly. To be fair, one episode, during which she yanked them out and fled from the room screaming and crying, occurred immediately after I turned on the vacuum cleaner when she was standing next to it. Important lesson number one: do not turn on the vacuum cleaner or any other loud appliance near your newly aided child. By Saturday, Elizabeth was down to pulling them out a handful of times. By Sunday, she wanted them in all the time and even protested when we took them out at night.

Not all children will react the same way. Babies, especially, are notorious for yanking out their hearing aids. But older children, too, will sometimes refuse to wear them, even after months or years of compliance. When that happens, your goal should be to determine the problem. Resist the urge to remind your child that the aids help and that he must wear them. If he has been willingly wearing them until this point, he undoubtedly knows they help.

"Fighting is not a good solution," said Brad Ingrao, an audiologist in Framingham, Massachusetts. "It sets up a power struggle that you're bound to lose."

Quite often, the reluctance stems from a physical problem. If the output is set too high, the aids will be too loud, which will be uncomfortable. If the output is too low, your child won't hear clearly, which can make the aids seem pointless. In either case, the audiologist needs to be informed of your concerns so settings can be checked.

If your child sweats excessively, the earmolds may be causing discomfort. A cut, sore, or rash can make it painful to wear an earmold. A mild external ear infection or fungus can make the earmold feel itchy. Again, you should consult your audiologist about these problems. In the latter instance, your child may have to leave the aid or aids out until the ear is healed, as having something rubbing against a sore will only prolong the problem.

Kim, who is 37 and has worn hearing aids for her profound sensorineural loss since she was nearly four, said she always found her earmolds uncomfortable. When she sweated—and as an active person, that happens often—the earmolds felt as if they were clogging her ears. When she smiled, which was also often, the aids whistled.

Her problems were solved, she said, when "a smart audiologist" concluded that when she smiled, ate, or chewed gum, her jaw joints might be altering the shape of her ear canals where the ends of the molds rested. The audiologist recommended that she use Comply Canal Tips, which are made of a soft foamlike material and act as a cushion to improve comfort and seal. They also absorb moisture, so sweat is less of a problem. Comply Canal Tips should be available at your audiology clinic.

Moisture Problems.

Some children, especially toddlers, enjoy dropping their hearing aids into the toilet, the bathtub, or whatever other body of water is nearby. A few parents have told me about dropping hearing aids into water by accident, usually because one person is handing them to another just before getting into a pool or the tub.

As a toddler, Toby dropped his "with great ceremony" into his milk, recalled his mother, Vicki. "When I took it in for repair, the receptionist said, 'You really should control him better and not let him do that!' Relations between she and I were tense for a number of years after that, but in the end, we became quite good friends."

Important lesson number two: keep hearing aids as far from bodies of water as possible. Sweat can also damage hearing aids. If your child plays sports or sweats a lot in general, you may want to consider purchasing Superseals, which should be available at your audiology clinic.

You can dry your hearing aids with a towel, but to make sure all the water is gone, you'll need a dehumidifier. One such device, known as a Dri-Aid Kit, is a small container with a small tabletlike device to absorb the moisture. A more expensive option is a Dri and Store unit. Your audiology clinic will have these. In humid environments, they are routinely recommended. In a pinch, you can also make your own by filling a container with rice and placing the aids inside at night or when they need to be dried out.

Lost Hearing Aids.

Despite the best efforts, hearing aids are sometimes lost. You may be lucky and find them, though it might take time and effort.

Ian lost an aid while helping to cut down a Christmas tree. A branch grabbed it, and as he turned, the aid flew off. The family wandered through the snow, hunting, but eventually gave up.

"When we got home, Ian and my husband took off the net wrapping and stood the tree up," recalled Ian's mom, Jill. "As they shook the branches to get the tree to fill out, the hearing aid fell out of the tree."

One mother told me that her son hid one of his aids inside drywall. "What fun we had ripping the wall apart to get the aid," she recalled, with more than a bit of irony. Another child hooked his to the springs underneath the front passenger seat in the family car. Yet another hung his on his bike wheels. When his mother went to look for them on the bike, they were gone. "He shrugged and said, 'Must have fallen off,' and was about to go off and play some more," his mother recalled. "I calmly replied, 'You are going *nowhere* until we find those hearing aids!' " She enlisted the help of her older son and his friend, who immediately found an aid on the front lawn. They spent 45 minutes searching for the second one, which turned up in the neighbor's front yard under the sprinkler.

Not every lost hearing aid story will have a happy ending, and paying for the replacements can take a bite out of any family budget. Ask your audiologist about hearing aid insurance policies or replacement benefits provided by some hearing aid manufacturers. If you have insurance on your home or apartment, you should also check the cost of adding a hearing aid replacement benefit to your existing policy.

Fortunately, most states and provinces have programs to help parents pay for hearing aids. Organizations such as the Lions Club also have programs that may be able to help cover the cost of your hearing aids. Your audiologist should be able to provide you with information. The Resources section also contains a list of agencies and organizations that can help you with more information about how to pay for hearing aids.

More Adventures in Amplification

Before Elizabeth got hearing aids, I used to get really upset about things like lost pacifiers and missing mittens. The hearing aids helped put things into perspective, a process that began in earnest when Elizabeth's first aids were four months old. I was getting her ready for bed when I discovered she was wearing only one. My stomach lurched, my heart began to pound, and I felt weak and ill. The only place the aid could have been was at the playground, and the playground was a vast sand-covered expanse that, at 9:30 p.m., even up here above the fifty-third parallel in mid-July, wasn't going to be well lit. I left Dave with the kids and fled to the playground where I scoured the sand until I forced myself to admit I was wasting my time.

Then I remembered that Elizabeth had been nodding off to sleep in the car earlier that day. I decided, just for the heck of it, to look around the back seat. Sure enough, there was the hearing aid.

I learned an important lesson that night: if a hearing aid falls out just because your child's head has rubbed up against a car seat, chances are the earmold no longer fits properly. Soon after that incident, we went to the audiologist who ordered new earmolds for our rapidly growing daughter.

Our next disaster occurred two summers later, when Elizabeth and Noah went swimming at a friend's pool. Dave, who was watching the kids with the friend's dad, left the hearing aids on a bench in the yard. While the kids were in the pool and the dads were chatting, the friend's puppy ate one of the hearing aids. By the time Dave discovered what had happened, all that remained was the earmold (which was apparently indigestible), a shred of flesh-colored plastic casing, and bits of unidentifiable masticated electronics. The dog was throwing up, which is what I felt like doing when I returned home and got the news.

I was certain that our insurance rider would cover the cost, but how was I going to explain to the audiologist that we'd been so careless?

"Oh, don't worry," the receptionist told me when I called. "This sort of thing happens all the time."

In fact, when we brought what was left of the hearing aid to the clinic the next day, one of the mothers in the waiting room told me the same thing had happened to her son's aid years earlier. I was so relieved to know I wasn't alone that I pulled the shredded plastic out of my pocket to show her.

"Oh my!" she said, her eyes wide with surprise. "Ours wasn't nearly that bad!"

William wears a hearing aid in only his right ear. His left ear has no residual hearing, so there's no point in aiding that ear. As a toddler, he once yanked off his hearing aid in the grocery store, pulled it apart, and threw it under a shelving unit. His mom, Cindy, had to crawl under the unit to retrieve it.

Another time she took William and his older sister to the beach in their home state of North Carolina for a weekend. Her husband was to meet the family there. The night before he arrived, Cindy realized William's aid was missing.

"There was a guy on the beach with a metal detector," she recalled. "I asked him if he had come across a hearing aid. He hadn't. I walked back and forth from the restaurant to the hotel trying to find it. I was in tears the whole time."

The next day, Cindy called the audiologist to report the missing aid and ask for a loaner. "If he had two hearing aids, even if he lost one, it'd be all right, but because that is the only one, if it's gone, it's gone," she said.

Cindy has vivid memories of how anxious she felt. "You're short of breath, you feel like you're going to start crying to the man with the metal detector, you're trying to hold it together with these two children standing there, and afterward, you start to think, I need to start signing with this kid. What if? What if? What if? What if? Is that my only mode of communication with him? Is that my only way to reach him, this piece of technology that may or may not be there?"

Cindy's husband arrived that night. He was the one who found the aid, under her overnight bag in the bathroom. "It was another set of eyes, another perspective," she said. "Why, in all of this, I didn't pick it up and look underneath it, I don't know."

Another time, the aid went missing at a garden center in Seattle, during a visit to Cindy's mother. William had been taking off his hearing aid that day and throwing it around, but it wasn't until they left the center that Cindy realized it was missing.

"We went back but it was already closed," Cindy recalled. "So I climbed the fence. My mother was outside with her two dogs and my two kids. I'm trespassing. I'm breaking the law. I'm going through the garbage. I pictured what would happen if the police came: 'Ma'am, why don't you steal a plant instead of just rifling through the garbage?'

"The next day we found it," Cindy said. "It was one of those 5 o'clock-in-the-morning things. I remembered he'd taken it off on her deck and thrown it through the slats.

"When you do lose it, that's all you can think about, and then you think, phew, another close call. But really, how many close calls can your heart take?"

Toby was two when he got his first pair of hearing aids more than 20 years ago. It was June, and his brother, who is five years older, remembered that he and his parents spent much of the summer on their hands and knees hunting for hearing aids. They got into the habit of looking into Toby's ears almost constantly, remembering where they were when they saw the aids, so that when they looked again and the inevitable had occurred—that is, Toby had pulled them off and tossed them—they'd have a better idea of how far to backtrack.

"We pawed at many a sand pile, grassy park, and all over the house," his mother, Vicki, said. "The best was when he parked them in the elevator of his Fisher-Price parking garage. Luckily, they squealed, but it took many hours to find them, and I was sure they'd been flushed down the toilet."

When you're in the midst of a hearing aid crisis, it's hard to imagine you'll ever find the memory amusing. For most parents, though, that's exactly what happens: we take the experience and turn it into an anecdote. Even at the moment I learned that a dog had devoured

Elizabeth's hearing aid, I kept calm by repeating to myself, "This is going to be a great story someday." A few years later, when an FM boot disappeared, seemingly into thin air, and we spent a week unsuccessfully attempting to find it by retracing our steps, I told myself the same thing. Knowing we had replacement insurance certainly helped me to maintain a level head, but my experiences reminded me yet again of the power of humor. Both stories are guaranteed to get a laugh, and the lost boot tale has an added element of surprise. The day after I filed the insurance claim, Elizabeth's former kindergarten teacher found the boot in the first grade classroom, under the teacher's desk. As a result, our story had the happiest ending possible for everyone involved: we got to cancel the claim.

Chapter Six

ACCEPTING THE INCOMPREHENSIBLE

In one of my early efforts to understand what it would be like not to hear well, I stuck my fingers into my ears and tried to comprehend what was being said around me. If Elizabeth had been blind, I probably would have walked around with a scarf tied over my eyes. If she'd been unable to walk, I'd have tried getting around in a wheelchair. But hearing loss isn't something you can try on. Even with my ears plugged, I can hear my own voice clearly and my brain will automatically adjust to the reduced sound levels so I can focus in on what I want to hear.

Two things ultimately helped me understand how Elizabeth could hear: an audiotape that simulated hearing loss, and Elizabeth's audiogram coupled with one that showed which sounds fall at which frequency and decibel levels (see Figure 2–1).

The labels assigned to the degree of hearing loss—mild, moderate, moderately severe, severe, profound—are just that: labels. Two children can have similar audiograms but hear very differently. To best help your child, you need to know and understand the audio-gram—what it does and does not tell you—and the relationship of the audiogram to speech.

It was only after Elizabeth's audiologist charted her audiogram on the speech banana that I was able to better understand how her hearing worked—or, more precisely, how it didn't. Most speech sounds fell out of her hearing range. Unless whoever was talking spoke loudly and clearly, many of the speech sounds would have been barely audible to her. Given that words are made up of a series of sounds, it was safe to say that until she was aided, she hadn't been able to hear anything loudly or clearly. Again, I was left marveling at how she had managed to develop any kind of working vocabulary and comprehensible speech patterns—and feeling grateful for, in-stead of self-conscious about, my often loud speaking voice.

Hearing aids can and do help children with mild, moderate, and moderately severe losses. They can also benefit some children with severe hearing loss, but even aided, children with severe losses won't hear as well as aided children with more moderate losses. Parents whose children have profound hearing loss may elect to use manual communication in addition to, or instead of, oral communication. In general, hearing aids provide less benefit to children with profound hearing loss; indeed, they are the ones generally considered the best candidates for cochlear implants. But some children with cochlear implants, especially those implanted later in life after years of not hearing, will still elect to use manual communication and the serv-ices of an interpreter, translator, or transliterator.

What equipment or interpreters your child needs, what resources will benefit him, and how he will fare are highly individual. What is universal is that as parents of children who are hard of hearing we must make accommodations. The tangible ones, such as buying hearing aids, learning sign language, getting closed captioning for the television, buying an alarm clock that shakes the bed instead of buzzes, and getting either a TTY phone—(a teletypewriter for the deaf), a speakerphone, or a TDD (a telecommunication device for the deaf), are straightforward. If your audiologist can't help you find the services or equipment you need, consult one of the organizations in the Resources section.

The adjustments we must make to our expectations aren't as simple. Fears are common in the immediate aftermath of a diagnosis. Sometimes, in retrospect, they can seem irrational, unrealistic, or even amusing. "I remember my eyes welling up with tears on the way home from the audiologist," Elyse said. "My first thought was how tough it would be for Julie to get married."

Julie was four years old at the time.

"Are kids going to pick on him at school?" Arthur wondered after his son, Collin, was diagnosed with a moderate hearing loss.

Collin was six days old.

My worries took a while to crystallize because I was in denial for more than a month after Elizabeth's initial diagnosis. I had convinced myself the audiologist was wrong. If he was wrong, I could continue with all my hopes and dreams about my daughter—that she'd learn to play a musical instrument, excel at school, have lots of friends, graduate from college, and have a fabulous career in some white-collar profession like her parents and grandparents and aunts and uncles.

Dave, meanwhile, convinced himself that her future was bleak, that she might be mildly retarded, or, at the very least, that she might be a slow learner. There was no evidence that Elizabeth had any brain damage but, Dave pointed out, the inner ear was connected to the brain, and if that was damaged and we didn't know how, there was a chance her brain was damaged as well. I was furious with him; it was bad enough he had to think that way, but did he have to verbalize those thoughts and plant them in my head, too? And what if he was right? What did it say about us, that we were such snobs that we couldn't bear the thought of parenting an academically challenged child?

Initially, to ease my fears, and later as part of research for this book, I set out to understand all I could about hearing loss and how hard-of-hearing children learn. Much of that information is covered in Chapter Nine. Once Elizabeth got aided and began working with a speech pathologist and attending preschool, it became apparent that Dave and I could revise our expectations once again, this time upward. But as any parent discovers, even when hearing loss isn't involved, we're constantly revising our expectations. None of us can predict the future, and lives can change in a second.

Those initial fears inevitably give way to more pressing day-to-day concerns as we try to determine which of our children's behaviors stem from the hearing loss and which are personality traits or reactions to particular situations. Finding a balance between coddling our children and acknowledging how their hearing loss affects their lives is an ongoing challenge. Experts who work with and study children with hearing loss have noted that some tire easily, have a high level of stress, a poor self-esteem, a low threshold for frustration, and a slow response to directions. Admittedly, there are plenty of children with normal hearing who have those same traits. But understanding how hearing loss contributes to them may help you to better respond, if and when they become a factor in your child's life.

Listening Can Be Work!

Listening takes more effort when you're trying to hear above background noises that include such potential distractions as fans blowing, feet tapping, music playing, or people talking. That's why your hard-of-hearing child may be more tired when he comes home from school or social activities, why he may require downtime after participating in activities that involve other people, why he may be reluctant to bounce from one event to another, and why he may need more sleep.

When Elizabeth was in first grade, a lot of her friends stayed at school for lunch, and she wanted to as well. I thought it was silly; after all, we live only three blocks away and I was home all day, ready to make a nice, hot meal she could eat in the comfort of her own home. But for her, it was a social event, so I signed her up for one day a week.

At the end of the first month, I asked if I should sign her up for the rest of the year. "No," she told me. "I don't want to go back. It's too noisy."

Eventually Elizabeth will go to junior high school, farther away, and have to stay at school for lunch. If she tells me the cafeteria is too loud and asks for my help, I will speak to school officials and make accommodations so she can eat somewhere quiet. There are people who will argue that kids should tough it out and get used to the real world. Some of those people may well be hard of hearing. In some situations, I don't think accommodations are called for. For instance, if Elizabeth complained that she had too much homework and couldn't complete it all because of her hearing loss, I'd be hard-pressed to go to the teacher and ask for an exception. But wanting to eat in a quiet environment is not an unreasonable request. Where we parents can make accommodations, I think we owe it to our children to try, so that they can function at their best and reach their full potential.

Things Take Time ...

Auditory processing involves a number of steps, which include sound detection, discrimination, retrieval of relevant information from the brain, comprehension, remembering what's being said, and understanding it. For people with normal hearing, and even hard-of-hearing infants aided shortly after birth, auditory processing often develops automatically. Later-identified individuals, those with more severe hearing losses or those with disabilities in addition to hearing loss, may have to consciously learn the processes of sound awareness, discrimination, recognition, and comprehension. It's only natural that the process is slower than it is with a person who has normal hearing.

Elizabeth's teacher has told me she often has to repeat instructions for Elizabeth. At home, if I notice she isn't doing something I've asked, I'll tap her on the shoulder to make sure I have her attention.

Communication Can Sometimes Be Frustrating

Hearing loss is a communication disorder, and not being able to communicate can be stressful and frustrating. Compounding the situation is that the majority of children who wear hearing aids may look and act like everyone else. The result is that folks communicating with them assume they're hearing like everyone else.

A variety of factors affect a child's language comprehension ability, including distance from the person speaking, levels of room noise, and complexity of the language being used, according to leading audiology researcher Mark Ross, himself severely hard of hearing. In *Our Forgotten Children: Hard of Hearing Children in the Public Schools,* he writes, "Adults assume that [children] will comprehend a message because they can so evidently hear it. Other children may consider them less than desirable playmates for reasons that neither group really comprehends." The resulting disparities between what society expects and what hard-of-hearing children are capable of, as well as the conflicts between their needs and the way their needs are often ignored by what Ross calls "an insensitive and ignorant environment" can affect the children throughout their school years and beyond.

Paige got her first set of hearing aids in 1965 when she was three years old. They seemed to amplify everything, so she still had trouble picking out the main source of speech. Despite her loss—profound in her left ear, severe in her right—she was an A student. Socially, however, she considered herself a failure.

"What I remember is the frustration of never being able to connect with anyone," she said. "Playing games was hopeless. I could never follow the rules, ever. Somebody would stand up and say, 'These are the rules and you have to do this and this.' It was completely lost on me. What would have helped is if someone had backed up a bit and said, 'Hey, we're playing a game. Do you want to play? Here are the rules,' instead of throwing me into it."

It's heartbreaking to see your child excluded. I remember being on the playground late one afternoon, long after the final school bell had rung. Three girls from Elizabeth's class were playing together. They were the popular girls, the ones with whom she's never quite fit in, but they were the only people there, so she went to ask if she could join their game. I stood back and watched as she had a brief conversation with the girls, who then took off and ran away from her. Elizabeth came back to me, her head down, dejected. She told me they'd said she couldn't play. But had they? Or had she misheard? I sent her back again, and watched as the same scenario unfolded. Finally, the third time, I went to the girls and told them Elizabeth wanted to play, and could they please include her. They did.

When your child is too young to advocate for himself, it's important that you remember, and let those communicating with your child know that speech needs to be delivered at a slower pace and that the child and whoever is speaking need to be face to face. It's all the skills that are pretty much in place when you communicate with someone who is hard of hearing as an adult.

It's especially important to advocate for your child when he starts school. You'll learn more about how to do that in Chapters Eight and Nine. But whenever your child begins a new activity, whether it's school, sports, Girl Scouts or Boy Scouts, youth group, or even a birthday party, you should try to meet in advance with the person in charge to explain your child's hearing loss and what accommodations are needed.

Staying Positive

You don't need to have a hearing loss to suffer low self-esteem. But the fact is, if your child has a hearing loss, at some point he may feel bad about himself and about his hearing loss. In order to help him accept that this is something he'll likely have to deal with for the rest of his life, it's critical that you accept it, too.

Paige said she spent much of her childhood and early adult life pretending she didn't have a hearing loss. It wasn't that anyone came out and told her that a disability was bad. But when a doctor incorrectly concluded that Paige's hearing was normal, her mother's delighted reaction made it apparent that normal hearing made people happy and hearing loss was cause for gloom. "The underlying message was that it was bad," Paige said. "And the way I was treated by kids at school made it even more clear."

Paige's mother's reaction is understandable; it's a rare parent who hasn't sat in the audiologist's office praying the test results are wrong. But because children are especially sensitive to their parents' feelings and reactions, we need to be aware of and moderate how we cope with our child's hearing loss.

"A hearing aid doesn't have to be embarrassing—it's not," said Carren Stika, a clinical psychologist in San Diego who was diagnosed with a progressive hearing loss in her late teens and has a long track record of working with hearing-impaired children and their parents, both in private practice and through the advocacy organization Self Help for Hard of Hearing People (www.shhh.org).

In Carren's experience, the embarrassment is generally more a reflection of the parents, who feel their child is defective. Rather than focus on the hearing aid, Carren said, it's important to help a child build his self-esteem.

"Hearing loss doesn't have to be a curse," she said. "It doesn't mean you can't have a life or succeed. What it means is a parent has to be able to find out how can we help this child and how can we not make this into more than it has to be? How do we see our child beyond the hearing loss, that life and life's tasks and successes are multiple?

"A mild hearing loss or a moderate hearing loss or a severe hearing loss does not have to be a major disability as long as it's handled properly," she added. "It runs in close partnership with how those who are serving the child are responding to the hearing loss."

That doesn't mean you have to love the hearing aid or cochlear implant. In fact, you're likely to have a love-hate relationship with all your child's equipment, which, when it's working properly, can do wonders, and when it's not, will have the potential to make you crazy. What it does mean is that each of us has to find the balance between acknowledging our children's very real frustration when they come to us—as they will—with some variation of, "Why do I have to wear hearing aids? Nobody else does," while keeping them from wallowing in self-pity.

When 37-year-old Kim was growing up, she often removed her hearing aids. It was bad enough that she was the only kid in school who wore them, but they whistled constantly, which drew even more unwanted attention. The self-consciousness evaporated only when she began attending a residential school for the deaf, where nearly everyone wore hearing aids.

Putting your child in an environment where everyone is just like her—removing her from the mainstream—is a solution, but it's not going to work for everyone. And there are other ways to help your child realize she's not unique—or strange, weird, different, or whatever adjective she chooses to describe herself on a particular day.

One of the most critical factors is to make sure, from an early age, that your child has role models who wear hearing aids, explained audiologist Brad Ingrao. "They should know several adults who demonstrate that wearing hearing aids improves their ability to communicate and thereby to show the world their best. If they can look to these role models, they may be less likely to let the fact that other kids don't wear hearing aids really bother them."

Brad, who has a son who is deaf and uses American Sign Language, also stresses the importance of helping children understand their hearing loss and the power that their aids gives them to control their environment.

Toby, 23, who has worn hearing aids since he was two years old, said the best advice for parents is "have faith, be supportive, and don't panic. It's not the end of the world."

Toby is a graduate of a technical college in Toronto and a cameraman at a television station in the city. "I look at myself and I've done quite well for my age. I have friends who aren't doing much of anything. They're not deaf or anything, they just don't know what they want to do."

Jenny, who received a cochlear implant when she was 16 and is now a college student, said one of the best things her parents did for her and her sister, who is also deaf, was to support them and make sure their needs were met without putting unnecessary emphasis on their hearing losses.

"They came along with me to speech therapies, helped me to correct my speech, supported me when I wanted the cochlear implant, and, basically, made me feel very special," she said. "I believe it is extremely important that parents of hearing-impaired children treat their child just like any normal hearing child, and not highlight their disability. It does wonders for their self-esteem. I know being hard of hearing is not something to be ashamed of, or something to hide, but when you are ten years old, you tend to want to fit in with your peers at school and, therefore, it's important to be one of them."

Parents who also have normal-hearing children have another

challenge: to ensure that those children aren't shunted to the side because of the special needs of the hard-of-hearing child.

Terri, a mom in Virginia, found herself with little choice but to devote nearly all her time and attention to her hard-of-hearing baby, Caleb, who spent the first month of his life in the neonatal intensive care unit of a university hospital in the neighboring state of North Carolina.

Terri and her husband, Wayne, had two older daughters, 11-year-old Rachel and eight-year-old Sarah. Caleb had severe disabilities and his medical needs took nearly all of Terri's time. Her mother and her friends helped out a lot, but they couldn't make up for her absence in her daughters' lives.

The girls "would tell me they missed me or they needed me to 'love on them.' They'd come up to me and say, 'I need some loving, Mom,' " Terri recalled. "Sarah had to grow up so fast, and Rachel did, too. Wayne was working 60 to 70 hours a week and our life was in a whirlwind. They adjusted. They had to. There was no balance in our family during that first year. It was basically just a matter of trying to survive it all."

By the time he was three months old, Caleb was fitted with hearing aids and glasses. He traveled with an oxygen tank and he attracted a lot of attention. The girls' reactions to him were as profound as they were different. Sarah, the youngest, welcomed the attention and mothered Caleb. Rachel, the oldest, was scared of this baby who projectile vomited without warning. When they went out in public, she felt embarrassed.

"At that age, the one thing you don't want is attention all the time," Terri said. "Every time we went somewhere, we were stared at and people would just come up and want to know about him. People would walk by and touch him, blessing him."

Terri told Rachel to look her best "because we knew people would be looking at us. Not many people had seen a baby that little with hearing aids, glasses, and oxygen.

"Her life changed a lot," Terri said. "I couldn't be there like I was before. It was a very stressful time at our house. She managed to remain a straight-A student in all advanced classes. I don't know how. She loves Caleb, but I think she misses our other life. It was so much easier before, and we didn't even know it."

Psychotherapist Jeanne Safer, author of *The Normal One: Life with a Difficult or Damaged Sibling,* advises parents to allow nondisabled children to express negative feelings about a disabled sibling, even if it upsets the parents. "Don't require them always to 'understand'—they're children," she said.

She strongly recommends setting aside time for nondisabled siblings and letting them be the center of attention regularly. Praise their achievements so they realize they, too, are important.

"Let them have their own friends, their own activities, and their own moments to shine," she said.

Jeanne also counsels that normal-hearing siblings shouldn't be expected to share their parents' feelings or level of involvement with a disabled sibling. "Being a sibling is different from being a parent," she explained.

Ultimately, of course, parents will decide what works best for their families. California parents Alicia and Bill already had two toddlers at home when they learned that their baby Sylvia was deaf. After researching communication options, they decided Sylvia should receive a cochlear implant and learn oral skills.

"We have two other children and we had to take them into account," Alicia said. "We felt really, really strongly that we didn't want them to be responsible to translate for her. We felt that if we went for sign language, they'd have to constantly be translating for her, and we didn't want to put that on them. That's not fair to them."

Sylvia received a cochlear implant when she was 12-and-a-half-months old. Now, two years later, she has no problem speaking for herself, more proof to her parents that they made the right decision.

"We have long conversations," Alicia said proudly. "She's doing absolutely amazing."

Adjustment: A Lifelong Process

There is no one path to acceptance and adjustment, and neither is it a one-shot deal. As noted audiologists David Luterman and Mark Ross write in their book, *When Your Child Is Deaf,* "there are many fits and starts." Just when you think you've got everything under control, a piece of equipment will fail, something will get lost or broken, or a teacher, coach, or classmate will make an ignorant comment. Every time your child enters a new class or a new school, joins a team, goes to camp, or begins a new activity, you'll need to reexplain his hearing loss and what accommodations are necessary. You may feel as if you're repeating yourself, but the information is new to the people you're addressing, and they need to hear it as much as the last several thousand people for whom you've covered the territory. If your child has a progressive or fluctuating hearing loss, you'll have to adjust each time the audiogram changes.

Jill, whose son, Ian, was diagnosed at age seven with a progressive bilateral conductive hearing loss, had accepted the condition and incorporated the new reality of hearing aids, doctor's visits, and FM into the family routine. Then, when he was 12, Ian's doctors began to suspect he also had cochlear damage that would eventually leave him with no hearing. The news threw Jill into a tailspin.

The reality that the loss was gradual meant that the family would have time to adapt, but at the same time, Jill feared the news would devastate her son. "I know that for parents whose kids have been born deaf or who have lost hearing at a much younger age, this may sound harsh, but completely losing his hearing and knowing it is a certainty is going to be very hard on this kid, as well as us as parents," she said not long after the diagnosis.

She was only half right. When Ian learned his progressive sensorineural loss made him a candidate for a cochlear implant, he told his mother that was cool.

"He thinks it will be great to have 'bionic ears,' " Jill said. "Me? I cried when I heard the news. He took it completely in stride."

"Never give up!" said Carolyn, whose son Darrell, 17, was diagnosed at one year old with a profound loss and wore hearing aids before getting a cochlear implant. "Make your house and yard the fun place to go so lots of children will want to come and play. Educate the people around your child. Aim high. Never believe what the so-called 'professionals' think your child can or cannot achieve. We were told 'your son probably will never hear' even after ten years of wearing hearing aids, and 'he will graduate with the equivalent of a grade six education.' Our son will graduate four months after his peers—with a high school education."

"Dare to ask questions if you don't understand something," said Janet, whose son, Kevin, was left profoundly deaf after a bout with meningitis when he was a year old. He now has a cochlear implant. "At the end, the parents know the child better than any other person in the world. This doesn't mean not to be open to advice. The professionals always know a lot, but they don't always know better. We are the parents, and we are the ones making the decisions and taking the consequences for those decisions."

"Expect a roller-coaster ride of emotions as your child grows," another mother told me. "You'll go from one extreme to the other and back again. It's okay, but just keep going. Keep learning. Keep involved. And, more important than all that, let your child be a child first. Let them ride bikes, take dance lessons or gymnastics, swim and join sports, and anything else they have an interest in."

Karen, whose daughter, Christina, began wearing hearing aids for her severe bilateral loss at six months and received a cochlear implant at age seven, said the best advice she can give is that which was passed along to her when Christina was diagnosed: "Give yourself

CONNECTING WITH OTHER PARENTS

When the parents of children with hearing loss are asked about their most important resources for information and emotional support, they often report "other parents." Opportunities to connect with other families range from support groups sponsored by a university or speech and hearing center, to groups organized by the parents themselves. The internet has opened new doors for parent-to-parent communication, but most families still prefer direct contact. Some are able to combine the two by bringing kids and families together for occasional gatherings and then using email to communicate. Others prefer to connect with only one or two families as they work through the process of learning and acceptance. Ask your audiologist and other service providers for recommendations on how you can meet other parents. Even if there are no formal support groups in your area, many audiologists maintain a list of parents who have agreed to serve as a resource to other parents. Also, you will be able to connect with parents through many of the organizations and websites listed in the Resources section.

permission to grieve, for as long as you need, whenever you need it. Then, put your heart aside and get down to the business of making the most out of this situation. You will see after some time that you actually say out loud, 'It's okay. Hearing loss is not the end of the world.' "

Chapter Seven

HEARING LOSS AS A PART OF DAILY LIFE

In the initial days and weeks after a diagnosis, it's hard for many of us to believe our lives will get back to whatever sort of normal they were before. It seems unrealistic to imagine that hearing loss will someday cease to become the center of our universe, that it can and will become part of our routine, like brushing our teeth, grocery shopping, or doing the laundry.

Yet, it will. It has to, because our children are more than "walking hearing aids," a phrase coined by Jenny, the college student quoted in Chapter Six. When you think about it, it's ironic that the diagnosis seems so devastating; our initial reaction tends to be that everything about our child has changed for the worse when, in fact, the news should be cause for optimism. Our child may have been hearing poorly in some cases for years, and now she'll be able to hear and communicate that much better.

Admittedly, it's a lot easier for me to look at things that way now. When Elizabeth was diagnosed, what was particularly overwhelming was the realization that Dave and I had to revise our expectations for her, but because we had no experience with childhood hearing loss and therefore no idea what we were up against; we had no clue where to begin. We were fortunate in that we were referred almost immediately to the local rehabilitation hospital and provided with a team—an audiologist, a pediatric otolaryngologist, a speech pathologist, and a social worker—who helped us navigate through the paperwork from the different agencies that offered a variety of services for disabled children and their families. The social worker also referred us to local, national, and international support groups and agencies. Those groups and others are listed in the Resource section.

Not everyone will have a support team assembled for them. However, even if you have to do it on your own, it's critical that you find the people to help you and your child to understand and attend to the hearing loss and the role it will play in your lives. If your audiologist can't refer you to proper pediatric specialists and support groups, refer to the Resources section, which has a list of agencies and organizations designed to put parents in touch with the appropriate personnel or groups.

When it comes to emotional support, other parents who have been through what you're experiencing are your best resource. One of the most consistent pieces of advice I received from parents and professionals while researching this book was to get to know other parents of hard-of-hearing children, and to make sure your child gets to know other children and adults with hearing aids or cochlear implants. If you don't have the time or inclination to join a support group, or if none exist in your area, consider getting to know people through one of the internet listservs, chat rooms, or bulletin boards offered by some of the groups in the Resources section.

I tend to be outgoing, and so after I had finally accepted that Elizabeth's hearing loss was real and permanent, I began talking to just about everyone I saw with hearing aids. I struck up conversations with parents in the audiology clinic, with senior citizens standing in

line buying batteries at Radio Shack, and with a mother at Disney-
land whose two young children were wearing green and orange hearing aids (a revelation, as I'd assumed beige was the only available
color).

From these casual conversations, I learned all sorts of things,
among them that our prolonged odyssey to figure out what was
wrong with Elizabeth's hearing wasn't unusual, that kids with mild-
to-moderate hearing losses didn't necessarily go through batteries at
the same rate, and that even earmolds come in a variety of colors. Almost invariably, people were pleasant, helpful, interested, and, sometimes, downright chatty. Perhaps they were polite by nature, or
maybe I reminded them of a time when they, too, were struggling
with this new reality, and someone had also helped them.

Other parents can offer so much, from support and comfort to
practical suggestions. "One of the most useful things we did shortly
after our daughter's diagnosis was to have a family with a daughter
who was deaf over for dinner," said Matthew and Pamela, whose 21-
month-old daughter, Sophia, has a cochlear implant. "We asked them
a hundred questions or more and learned so much! Their daughter
was amazing. She's also a cochlear implant user and is making exceptional progress. Since then, we've also started attending a play-
group for children with hearing loss that meets once a month."

I looked into joining a support group, but when Elizabeth was
enrolled in preschool for hard-of-hearing children, I realized I already had one: the parents of her classmates. The teachers encouraged us to attend so we could see what our children were learning
and reinforce their lessons at home. Most of the parents worked full
time, so only two of us showed up regularly, myself and Gwen, the
grandmother of Nikki, the little girl whose speech had so impressed
Rachel, Elizabeth's speech-language pathologist. Nikki was the only
other girl in the class, and she and Elizabeth liked each other a lot.
They had similar interests—music, art, and animals—and they
played easily together. Neither seemed impatient about repeating

something if the other couldn't hear, which doesn't always happen with Elizabeth's hearing friends.

Gwen and I also developed a good friendship. During school, we would occasionally steal off to an observation room to trade stories, and when we got the girls together outside of school, the play dates were as rewarding for us as they were for the children.

Every few months, the parent liaison at the school organized a meeting where all the parents could get together, and it was there that I learned even more—that some kids were allergic to earmolds, that batteries didn't work as efficiently in cold weather, that other people's equipment broke down at least as often as ours did. From the parent liaison, the mother of a teenage son who was deaf, we learned that things wouldn't necessarily get easier as the years went on, but they would be, at the very least, different, and that the skills we were learning now would prepare us for what was to come.

How we come to accept and adjust to our child's hearing loss depends on so many factors: the age of our child at the time of the diagnosis, our family situation, our general outlook on life, where we live, what supports are available to us, whether we've had experience with other disabilities. One reason support groups, listservs, and chat rooms are so useful is that it's always helpful to hear about other people's experiences.

Becky: Hearing Loss Wasn't Such a Big Deal

"I think the thing that makes me different from everybody else is that I have an older child with a disability," said my neighbor Kathy, whose youngest daughter, Becky, six, was diagnosed at age three with a mild-to-moderate high-frequency hearing loss.

Kathy has five other daughters. Her second oldest, Elfi, who is 18, was born with spina bifida and had the first of more than a dozen operations when she was one day old.

"Becky's disability wasn't life threatening; Elfi's was," Kathy said. "We weren't sure she was going to come through right away; she had to have her back closed. There's an extreme loss of control when your child is having so many surgeries. It's a much more severe thing to cope with, I thought, than simply having to put in some hearing aids right away."

Although Kathy's instinct is to minimize the hearing loss, she has no intention of ignoring it. "If I'd known when she was six months old that she had a hearing loss, I would have gotten her hearing aids right away," she said. "Once we got them, her personality changed overnight. Gone was the frustration, the exhaustion. The fatigue started to melt away. There was no more collapsing on the floor in a ball. She was just so much happier."

Becky went to the same preschool program as Elizabeth, though she was in a different class. Because of provincial regulations, Becky didn't qualify for an FM system until she was in kindergarten. Kathy wasn't thrilled with the device to begin with; she felt the FM made everything too loud. "When I would go up to some of the other kids with their FMs and speak to them, they didn't hear me at all, and I could hear what they were hearing," she said.

Before Becky started kindergarten, at the same neighborhood school as Elizabeth, Kathy began lobbying for the school to purchase an FM sound field system for the kindergarten classroom. She researched and wrote a grant to help the school pay for it. The school now has two classrooms with FM systems: Elizabeth's and Becky's. The teachers have become FM fans because they can get the attention of all the students without having to strain their voices. In large part because of Kathy's efforts, the whole school will eventually be outfitted with the systems.

One reason Kathy put so much effort into arranging for the systems was that she didn't want Becky to stand out. "I've been through that and I know what a singled-out kid turns out like," she said. "It's really hard for them. Does Becky feel different? I don't think so—

not yet, anyway. She hasn't expressed that to me. She's never expressed any kind of remorse or sadness or those kind of things although my other daughter, who wears leg braces, has said to me, 'When am I going to be able to run?' Things like that just break your heart because you know that this is not going to be. It's not going to happen. And that whole experience has definitely colored how I am treating this experience."

When children ask why Becky has to wear hearing aids, Kathy likens them to glasses. "They're both aidable disabilities, as opposed to Elfi's, which is only partially aidable. She can't run, but Becky can play viola and go to dance class."

Cochlear Implants for Carter

Not long after learning her son, Carter, was profoundly deaf, Cheri, a mom in North Carolina, received a newsletter from the School for the Deaf in her area.

"They were spotlighting one of the students who had been named a shift manager at McDonald's," she recalled. "That's when it hit me—am I totally in denial?"

It wasn't that Cheri and her husband didn't appreciate that such a job "would be a huge feat for some children," she said. It's just that until that point, she'd been thinking about how Carter's deafness would affect his toddlerhood, his childhood, the next few years. It hadn't occurred to her to consider how it might affect his entire life and, at some point way off in the future, possibly limit his career options.

Eight months of trial hearing aid use showed amplification to be of little benefit, so Carter received a cochlear implant. Cheri and her husband knew the ideal scenario was for one of them to quit work to stay home to care for him, but that was simply not realistic for them. Instead, they kept their jobs and found day care for Carter.

"We're not made out of money, so we need our income, plus for my sanity, I needed it more than anything, so that put another huge demand on me," Cheri said. "I felt that was going to take me over the edge. I felt that if anything fails, it will all be on my head, but looking back, it would not have worked out as good as it has if we had taken another route, because that day care center has been awesome."

By the time he was four, Carter was speaking and hearing clearly enough to shush his parents when he was concentrating on hitting a golf ball with his toy clubs. "He is totally adjusted to his implant and acts like any other normal-hearing child," Cheri said. "He is very, very social, and well liked by his peers and his teachers."

That's not to say there haven't been setbacks. One of the most traumatic came when Carter's implant began failing intermittently after a year.

"It made me realize how much we depended on that implant," Cheri recalled. "I remember taking him down to X-ray to see if it was broken, and I had to tap him on the shoulder to communicate with him. Prior to that day, I could have taken him down there and said, 'Carter, come here,' and he would do what I told him. It was very humbling; it made me really appreciate what we have, although every night when we take it off, I realize we don't just take it for granted."

Because there is no guarantee that once an implant is removed the next one will be better, Cheri and her husband were faced with a tough decision: whether to take a chance with a new, more advanced model, or leave in the old one and hope it would work well enough. In the end, they opted to take a chance. The surgery was a success, but they worried Carter would have to start all over on the speech chart and language development. "Luckily he just whipped through all of them and he's made great progress with the second implant," Cheri said.

"As much as bad things have happened, I look at it and think, really, it could have been a lot worse," she said. "I think the main thing that keeps us going is that whenever we went to the hospital audiology clinic, we'd see some really tough cases of kids who have had 20 or 30 surgeries or they might not live or they have cancer. As bad as it was for Carter, at least it wasn't threatening his health."

The next reality check came when the couple's third child, Hailey, who was born two years after Carter, failed her newborn hearing screening. Initially Cheri wasn't upset. "I guess because we had traveled down that road, we knew that life would go on."

Then came the shocking news: Hailey had a severe-to-profound loss and would need hearing aids, not an implant.

"We said, 'Well, what do we do now?' " Cheri said, "and the audiologist said it was almost as if we were disappointed she had hearing. I said no, it was just that we knew how to proceed if she was totally deaf."

Hailey is spirited and independent. She's also bright, developing language skills appropriate to a child her age. "She's doing really well with her hearing aids," Cheri said. "She always responds to her name, and she's got a good vocabulary going."

And, like her brother, she has no qualms about asking her mother to pipe down. Part of her bedtime routine is to snuggle with Cheri and listen to a lullaby on her CD player. One night, Cheri began singing along, and Hailey said, "Shhhhh!"

Instead of being offended, Cheri laughed. "It was hilarious," she recalled. "I said, 'You know, I'll take that from her.' "

TJ and Casey: Living in a Small Town Meant Help Was a Long Time Coming

TJ was a few months past his third birthday when he was diagnosed with a moderate-to-severe bilateral sensorineural hearing loss. The staff at the local speech clinic offered his mom, Kathy, emotional support and all the literature at their disposal, but they couldn't provide TJ with hearing aids and the only audiologist in their small northern Ontario community didn't have an opening for months.

"I was quite frustrated with the system, having had to wait four months before getting a diagnosis and another three to four to get aids," Kathy recalled. "I started taking charge and called upon someone I knew who was a speech therapist in a larger city not far away. She was a lovely woman and well respected. She tactfully suggested I try another audiologist, and gave me the name and number, along with many other suggestions for hearing-impaired children. The phone call I made to that clinic changed our lives. Within three weeks of coming into contact with the audiologist there, the volume of information and support we received was a landslide compared to what we had received in the previous eight months."

TJ received his hearing aids two days before his fourth birthday. Several months later, his brother, Casey, was diagnosed with a similar hearing loss. Two days after the diagnosis, he celebrated his second birthday. Their older sister, Leah, has normal hearing.

"The emotions that came after TJ's diagnosis once again surfaced for Casey's," Kathy recalled. "Failure, guilt, especially since two of our three children were hearing impaired. After bathing the boys, then putting their 'ears' back in before holding them naked in my arms, a deep feeling of guilt would come over me. There is nothing like a beautiful, naked baby, but ones with hearing aids destroyed the beauty—in my mind, anyway. And in my mind, it was my fault. Thankfully, having come from a strong and beautiful family myself, this feeling has been slowly suppressed over the past three years, but it will always remain at the bottom of my heart."

TJ and Casey are bright and funny, and Kathy takes comfort watching them meet their daily challenges and solace in knowing that they've been blessed with a sister who's unfailingly willing to lend a hand, both at home and at school. Often teachers will ask Leah to help if the aids need to be checked or batteries replaced. When the boys were too young to put in the aids on their own, she did it for them.

Kathy's grateful for Leah's help. And rather than dwell on the burdens that a hearing loss brings, she's chosen to focus on the positive. "Our lives are richer because of TJ's and Casey's loss," she said. "They remind me daily of the gift that I have, but they don't."

Uprooting the Family

Katy was hospitalized with meningitis at 15 months. Her parents, Dee Ann and Lee, left their two other children with relatives back home, 150 miles away, and stayed in a Ronald McDonald house during the six weeks it took Katy to recover. The illness destroyed her sense of balance and left her with no hearing in one ear and a severe-to-profound loss in the other. Doctors told the family she would never play sports, ride a bike, ski, swim, or read past a fifth-grade level.

"Of course it was devastating news," Dee Ann said. "However, she was sick for so long, so we were very aware that the deafness was not the worst thing that could've happened."

Not long after the diagnosis, while Katy was still in the hospital, Dee Ann and Lee met the pastor of a local church, who was on an outing with a group of deaf teenagers.

"We nearly beat him down asking questions," Dee Ann said. "After a few minutes, he asked how to contact us later, and he said he would put together a group of parents for us to visit with. Two days later, we went to his house, and we became a little wary when we saw ten other cars. We didn't want some overpowering religious indoctrination. But that was not what happened. The pastor had assembled parents of deaf kids who communicated in different ways, had made mistakes in their children's education, had successful educational experiences, and had vastly different opinions and experiences. We listened and questioned and talked with those wonderful people for about four hours. Then we began our pursuit of the best option available for our daughter."

After spending months investigating educational opportunities, Dee Ann and Lee decided the best option was a school in Omaha, 400 miles from their home. They packed up the family and moved.

"Katy's hearing loss impacted our family in a major way because our life had to change completely," Dee Ann said. "We had been ranchers in a rural area, and because no help was available there, we had to move and change every aspect of our lives. It was maybe a little hard on the other children in the family, but they adjusted."

The move certainly benefited Katy. She got nearly all As in school, made the honor roll, played sports, played saxophone in the band, and has traveled as far as Japan on her own.

"She's not a great singer, but then, neither is anyone else in the family," Dee Ann said. "She actually did better in band than the other four kids, but ran out of time to practice because she wanted to be doing sports."

Now 19, she's a college student majoring in psychology at a small competitive liberal arts college in the Midwest. She's also captain of her college basketball team.

" The hardest thing for me is those rare moments when I ask myself, 'What if?' " Dee Ann said. "Katy has adapted so well, has had so many successes, that sometimes I forget about her constant struggle. But once, in a quiet moment when we were thinking about what if I could have one wish, she wished she could hear. It made me so sad, because for her it is constant.

"I think, although she has a world of friends and is outgoing and well liked, it has impacted her socially. If she didn't have her sports, she would have struggled more to find her niche. She can't whisper secrets like other girls do, she has to ask for clarification often, she misses out on parts of conversations. These are the kinds of things I grieve about in private. I do not dwell on them, but on occasion, I feel sad."

Toby: Learning to Speak Made the Difference

"I knew in my heart that there was something very wrong when my son was 20 to 22 months old," said Vicki, who lives in Ottawa, Ontario. "He did not speak, but worse, he clearly usually did not understand."

During the week he turned two, Toby was diagnosed with a moderate-to-severe bilateral sensorineural hearing loss. Two weeks later, Vicki and her husband, Glen, were invited to a meeting at the Children's Hospital of Eastern Ontario (CHEO), where Toby would receive his audiology care to the end of his teen years. They were invited to bring other relatives, and all four grandparents came. Also present were an audiologist, a social worker, and an auditory-verbal therapist (AVT).

Today, more than 20 years later, Vicki recalls that the meeting was vital to the family's understanding and acceptance of the diagnosis.

"CHEO has had a world-class AVT program for over 25 years," she said. "This program was explained to us on the day of the diagnosis, and quite honestly, I do not remember having other options explained to me, or that we ever seriously considered other options. We did have an acquaintance in our neighborhood who tried very hard to talk us into signing, but I never took her seriously because I couldn't really understand why we would do that when the other option seemed to make so much sense. She is the hearing daughter of signing deaf parents, and has always been and continues to be a very strong advocate for that community. But we were a hearing, speaking family, with one other son. It was just obvious to us that we would at least try speech—and why shouldn't it work?"

It did work. "Now that we know a great deal more about the choices, we are even more convinced that we made the right choice for our son," Vicki said. "Anything else for that child would have been a travesty. And furthermore, he tells us regularly that he is delighted that we made the choice we did, and that he cannot imagine being anything other than oral."

Toby developed into an avid athlete; he skateboards and plays hockey, baseball, and soccer. Because he doesn't use the FM during sports, he, his coaches, and teammates developed other strategies, among them yelling or using hand signals.

An extrovert, he also makes friends easily. Now twenty-three and working at a Toronto television station, he's a great source of pride to his parents.

"Our son is a fine young man who loves his work and who has good social and communication skills," his mother said. "We had many challenges along the way—what parent does not? When one looks at the pain, suffering, illness, grief, and unhappiness in the lives of so many, even most, what is moderate-to-severe hearing loss? Not such a big deal.

"Having said that, as long as I live, mostly at times when I least expect it, I will get a huge lump in my throat that our son is deaf and that he has to deal with this," she said. "This is not how we 'ordered' him, but that is how he came, and we are probably all better people for it. But I tell you, I cried throughout his college graduation ceremony!"

Chapter Eight

ADVOCATING FOR YOUR CHILD

Before I began researching this chapter, my concept of advocacy was telling people on the playground, in school, at social activities, or in any new situation that Elizabeth has a hearing loss. It was making clear that even though she wears hearing aids, she still doesn't hear as well as someone with normal hearing. It was letting people know that whoever is speaking will have to accommodate Elizabeth's needs. Generally that will involve facing her, speaking clearly or loudly to her—shouting isn't necessary but whispering is unacceptable—and checking to make sure she has understood what's been said.

After talking to parents and experts who had to battle for their children's rights and needs, I alternated between feeling embarrassed about my naiveté and grateful that things had gone so easily for Elizabeth that I'd been able to labor under my illusions for so long. At the same time, I came to understand that whether someone's efforts are as minor as a one-time request to an education specialist or as extreme as having to hire a lawyer for a court hearing, at its very basic level, advocacy is what I'd assumed from the beginning: it means doing what is necessary to make sure our children are treated fairly and afforded the same opportunities as their normal-hearing peers, whether on the playground, in school, at public gatherings, or by their health care providers.

Whether you realize it or not, you have already advocated for your child. Every time you take him to the audiologist because his earmolds don't seem to be fitting or the volume control on his hearing aids isn't functioning, you're advocating. Every time you've reminded the soccer coach that he has to turn on the FM before he addresses your daughter's team, you're advocating. Every time you've asked a teenager behind a fast food counter to repeat her question because your daughter, who wears hearing aids, doesn't hear well in crowded, noisy places, you've been an advocate.

Too many of us are misled into assuming advocacy is always a complicated process that requires lawyers, judges, professional experts, and years of legal battles. For some parents, sadly, that is the case. For more of us, I hope, advocacy will be a simpler, more direct process. For all of us with young children, it's something we'll likely deal with on some level every day, largely because our children don't always know when and how to speak up for themselves. One of the most important lessons we must teach them is how to do just that.

I'm usually quite confident and comfortable speaking up for what I believe in, largely because I've always felt my concerns were taken seriously. But when it came to acting as an advocate for Elizabeth, especially in the early days of her diagnosis, I was unpleasantly surprised to discover how often people didn't seem to hear what I was saying. The new teacher in Elizabeth's kindermusik class insisted on speaking in a whisper even though I told her repeatedly that Elizabeth couldn't hear unless she spoke up. The gym teacher, whom I had just reminded about Elizabeth's diagnosis, looked me straight in the eye and said, in all seriousness, "Oh, I think she can hear. I think she's just not paying attention."

At first I blamed myself. Maybe I wasn't convincing enough because I was having such a hard time accepting Elizabeth's hearing loss. But after talking to parents who had similar experiences and, more important, after dealing with people who did take my concerns seriously, I began to see there is no one way to advocate; different situations call for different approaches. Some people refuse to be convinced, others seem to listen with rapt attention and then proceed as if they didn't comprehend a word you said. Others, bless their hearts, do exactly as you ask. My job—any parent's job—is to learn to deal with each situation to make sure my child can hear and understand.

Unless Elizabeth has her hair pulled back so her hearing aids are visible, people meeting her have no idea she has a hearing loss. Sometimes even when her hair is pulled back and her hearing aids are visible, people don't notice. For the first few years after she began wearing hearing aids, whenever a stranger would say something to her in a crowded, noisy place and she didn't respond, I'd feel obligated to explain about the hearing loss. Now that she's nearly eight years old, I'm more likely to give her a chance to speak for herself. If she doesn't or she seems uncomfortable, I'll say something, but more and more, I'm starting to think that's intrusive and it's up to Elizabeth to decide when she wants to bring it up and to whom.

Some children are comfortable advocating for themselves at a young age. Others aren't, explained Diane Schmidt, who speaks to many parents as part of her job as supervisor of the media/graphics department at Boys Town National Research Hospital in Omaha, Nebraska, where she helped put together the excellent website www.babyhearing.org.

"I think mom and dad should be helping out in one way or another all the time, by which I mean you observe and step in when needed. If the child is handling the situation easily on their own, leave them alone. If they're struggling or shy, or the other person isn't responding well to them, step in and help. Most kids are really good at letting you know when they need a little help, whether it be by telling you or by a look or their body language. I think we just need to follow their lead."

If you're in a situation where your child needs to know everything that's going on, you may have to step in, even if your child feels he's in control. But it's also important to remember that sometimes we cause more problems and embarrassment by jumping in when our kids are confident they're handling everything. If you're finding that's happening on a regular basis, it's best to have a talk with your child in private, to explain why you feel the need to step in, and also to find out what he feels would work better.

Diane's 25-year-old daughter, Christin, is profoundly deaf. From the day Christin started school in a mainstream program, Diane talked to her about her rights in terms she could understand. Diane would frequently ask Christin how things were going with her interpreter, whether she could understand her clearly, if the interpreter was the one disciplining her in class if she wasn't paying attention (which was forbidden), and if the interpreter was interpreting everything the other children were saying. If there was any doubt, Diane would remind her that it was her right to have an interpreter who she could clearly understand and who was interpreting everything being said in the classroom. She'd encourage Christin to speak to the teacher of the deaf at the school, and she'd follow up in a few days by asking if Christin had done that.

"I didn't usually ask her to talk to the interpreter directly, because often they don't feel like a child has the right to tell them what to do or not to do, and the child goes away feeling that they shouldn't have said anything," Diane said.

If Christin hadn't talked to the teacher or was hesitant about doing so, Diane would offer to do it herself. Christin often preferred that option when she was younger. As she grew older and more confident, she'd sometimes speak to the teacher about a problem first, and then tell her mother.

When Christin was in middle school, she and her fellow deaf and hard-of-hearing classmates had an incompetent interpreter. The students couldn't understand her, and her behavior was unacceptable. Among other things, she'd sit crosslegged on top of a desk in front of her male junior high school students. The resource teacher for deaf students called Diane to ask if she would come into the school to observe the interpreter. The teacher said she had a gut feeling the woman wasn't qualified, and the administration responded better to parental concerns than to complaints from teachers.

Before Diane had a chance to speak to the resource teacher again, Christin came home and announced that she and her classmates had met and were going to bring their complaints to the teacher themselves. As a result of their efforts and parental complaints, the interpreter was removed, put on probation, and told she'd have to attend remedial signing classes consistently for a year.

When the special education director called Diane to explain the situation, Diane said she would not accept the interpreter working with Christin again, regardless of how much additional training she had.

"We had a rather heated discussion on this, but I insisted my child would not be the guinea pig during this interpreter's probation period," Diane said. "In the end, Christin never had her again, and before long, she was gone. But this is an example of how our kids can learn to advocate for themselves, which I think is our goal from day one. They need guidance and lots of support to do it, but they can and do learn how."

The Basics of Advocacy

Whether you're attempting to convince the cafeteria director to serve spinach for lunch every day or trying to secure preferential seating for your hard-of-hearing child in the classroom, the basics of advocacy are the same: start with the source. Just as you wouldn't go to the food supplier to complain about the lunch menu, your first step in advocating for your child in the classroom shouldn't be to make an appointment with the superintendent or the head of the school board.

Get to know your child's teachers. Perhaps they've had experience with hard-of-hearing children. If they haven't, make an appointment to sit down with them and explain your child's needs. Offer literature. For me, one of the most helpful books available was the third edition of *Our Forgotten Children: Hard of Hearing Pupils in the Public Schools,* edited by Julia Davis and published by Self Help for Hard of Hearing People (see the Resources section).

Many school districts have audiologists who are salaried employees; others are on contract to serve school-age children. As a group, educational audiologists are a special breed. They enjoy working in the educational environment and are often great advocates for kids and families. They can provide a vital link between the medical center audiologists and the classroom. The website for the Educational Audiology Association (www.edaud.org), although designed primarily for professionals, has links of interest to parents and also a directory of educational audiologists in the United States.

In the United States, children with special needs up to the age of 21 are protected by the Individuals with Disabilities Education Act (IDEA), which guarantees that all children with disabilities have access to a free appropriate public education that emphasizes special education and related services designed to meet their unique needs.

To receive federal funds under IDEA, each state must have an educational plan that complies with the law's standards and procedures. While the most significant features will be consistent, states vary in their procedural requirements. Your local education agency or state Department of Public Instruction can provide you with information about IDEA requirements for your state.

In Canada, federal disability laws are broader and scattered under several pieces of legislation, the most prominent being the Charter of

Rights and Freedoms. Because education falls under provincial jurisdiction, the best way to learn your child's rights is to check with the
Department of Education in your province or territory.

In the United States, if your child is being considered for special
services, you will be scheduled for a multidisciplinary team evaluation. Assuming your child meets eligibility criteria, the team will
work with you to develop an Individualized Family Service Plan
(IFSP). For children three and older, the plan is called an Individualized Education Plan (IEP). The IEP, which is required only in public
schools in the United States, will follow your child through his
school years, with updates and revisions as needed. Among the most
useful resources for learning more about IDEA and advocacy in general are the AG Bell Association, www.wrightslaw.com, and the
book *IDEA Advocacy for Children Who Are Deaf and Hard of
Hearing* by Bonnie Poitras Tucker, J.D. More information about all
is included in the Resources section.

In Canada, the rights of individuals with disabilities are outlined
in the Charter of Rights and Freedoms, but the accommodations
your child will receive will depend on where you live and where he
goes to school. Most school districts will have a document similar in
style to that of the IEP, although it is not considered a legal document. Like its U.S. counterpart, it is designed to identify your child's
educational needs and how the school will meet them in a given year.
The plan should be examined and revised at least once a year, or
more often if necessary.

It seems straightforward enough, but conflicts do arise. You may
not agree with what the school is offering your child, and the school
may not agree with what you believe your child needs. If that happens, the best approach is a nonconfrontational one. Provide evidence to back your claims, either in the form of studies or research
or letters from your child's audiologist, speech-language pathologist,
teacher of the deaf and hard of hearing, or other appropriate specialists. Perhaps the school officials truly are adversarial, but there

are good reasons not to lose your temper and start threatening the first time someone disagrees with you. Losing control is unprofessional and gives people an excuse to not take you seriously. It also keeps you from focusing on the important task, which is to ensure your child gets a solid education.

Bruce Goldstein is a Buffalo, New York, lawyer, whose specialization in disability law arose out of personal need. His two daughters were born deaf, and when they were getting ready to start school in the late 1970s, Bruce and his wife did extensive research to figure out where their children could get the best public education. IDEA had been in effect since 1976, the year the younger Goldstein daughter was born. "That's how I got into this law—I began investigating for them," Bruce said.

Since then, he has become a highly respected expert, sought after both by parents and school districts throughout North America. Some of his cases have set state and national precedent in disability law. His observations about advocacy in the education arena are insightful and valuable to all parents.

"You have to know who you're dealing with," he said. "In some school districts, you've got special ed directors who are child friendly, if you will, and then you've got others who are pure bureaucratic types. So you've got to try, as you would in any other situation where you're trying to persuade someone, to use some empathy and put yourself in the shoes of the other person. If you're dealing with a child-friendly person, you'd talk about the child and the importance of the child's progress. If you're dealing with a bureaucratic type, you want to emphasize that it's not going to cost much more, or cost anything more at all."

There are times when no matter how reasonable one party is, an impasse is inevitable. It may sound overly simple to say the world is made up of "good" school districts and "bad" school districts, but sometimes that's how it seems, Bruce said, adding that there are also plenty of shades of gray.

"The 'bad' districts will be operating the way they are either because they're trying to save money or out of ignorance or out of understaffing, so they'd have to do things in an assembly-line fashion," he explained. "They aren't prepared to give each child the time that is necessary, or they might be dealing out of ego or fighting over control with the parent, or they may just be working out of inertia."

Similarly, Bruce added, there are parents who develop a reputation for being difficult, "so from the school district's side, nothing you're going to do is going to satisfy them."

My husband would be the first person to tell you I'm opinionated and insist on doing everything my way. At home, maybe. But he's never seen me approach the principal at Elizabeth's school. When Elizabeth was in first grade, the school receptionist, Jan, whose own daughter has a hearing loss similar to Elizabeth's, told me to ask the principal if the school would pay for Elizabeth's FM batteries and repairs.

"She uses the FM for school," Jan told me. "We should be paying for the batteries and repairs."

I was skeptical and didn't want to look greedy, but after thinking about it for a few days, I asked Robin, the principal. "Fine," she said to me, and for the next year and a half, I submitted bills for every package of AA batteries I bought for the FM and every repair. Then one day, Jan told me that the budget was tight, so the school could no longer afford the expense. No problem, I said. We'd just go back to paying, and claiming the cost on our income tax.

Not long after that, we learned Elizabeth needed a new FM. Rhiannon, one of her audiologists, said the school should pay for it. "I'll call your principal," she said.

My chest tightened. "The school doesn't have enough money," I told her. If they couldn't afford a few hundred dollars for repairs and batteries, where were they going to find the $3,000 for a new FM?

"They can pay for it," Rhiannon said. "They receive extra money because of Elizabeth's hearing loss, and this is one of the things it's for. Don't worry. I'll take care of it."

I went home and had a long talk with Dave. His supplemental health insurance provided us with a five-year $1,000 allowance for hearing aids and related expenses. We'd blown that four years earlier, paying for Elizabeth's first hearing aids and her FM. In fact, we'd gone well over the budget and had paid for some of the equipment out of pocket. If necessary, we could have scraped together money for a new FM system, but if we waited another year, the health insurance would kick back in and it would be covered. But could we wait another year? The FM system seemed to break down every few months, and nearly every day I found myself having to press the boots to the hearing aids to guarantee a connection, or to fiddle with the antenna rings to avoid static.

The next day I went to the principal's office and said if the school couldn't afford the FM, Dave and I would find a way to pay for it. "Don't worry about it, Debby," Robin assured me. "We'll make it work. This is our responsibility, and we'll handle it."

When she called me into her office after hearing from Rhiannon and asked whether it would be okay to buy the less expensive FM, the one with wires instead of the more discreet wireless version Elizabeth was comfortable with, I balked. Sure it was more economical, but I knew from talking to other parents and audiologists that it was also much less desirable for a child who would rather not call extra attention to herself.

"No," I said. "She really needs the wireless, with the boots that don't have the rings attached. The one with the rings just isn't durable enough."

A week later, Elizabeth had the newest FM available. But there was a catch: Robin wanted it left at school when Elizabeth wasn't using it. Unlike the FM we'd gotten when Elizabeth was three, this one belonged to the school, and we couldn't use it at violin lessons, for soccer, at Hebrew school, or on vacations. I could understand that, but I still wanted it at home. Otherwise I'd have to do two equipment checks every day, one at home, and then one at school.

Plus, it would mean having to take Elizabeth's aids off when she got to school to put the FM boots on, which would be time consuming and, undoubtedly, annoying for both her and for me.

Peter, another of Elizabeth's audiologists, recommended that not only should we keep the FM at our house, we should be able to use it at our discretion. He told me about other families who used their school-owned FMs for nonschool events.

"Learning doesn't take place just between school hours," he reminded me.

He was right. I knew he was. But we had our own FM, fragile and aging though it was. I couldn't bring myself to insist that Robin let us use the new one just because it was new and in better condition. Sure, Elizabeth might have been entitled to use it during nonschool hours, but was it right to argue for something just because I could, not because she actually needed it? In the end, I decided, for me, it wasn't. However, I did tell Robin we needed to keep the FM at our house so I could do daily equipment checks, but that we wouldn't use it for anything other than school. She agreed without hesitation.

A year later, when I talked to Bruce Goldstein, I felt more validated in that decision. "Sometimes you have to look at the big picture and not try to get every little thing you might think you're entitled to," he told me. "When my daughters were going through the public school system, there were a number of occasions when my wife and I were aware the district wasn't implementing the IEP to the full extent, but on a number of occasions we didn't say anything because the more important thing was to keep good relations and make sure that things generally were being done properly. Look at anything in life, and how often is it really being done 100 percent to the hilt? So you look for substantially what's needed, rather than going for every last little item. You pick your fights."

Even though Bruce is a lawyer, a courtroom is his last choice as a venue for settling disputes. At least 95 percent of the time, he and his colleagues are able to settle a case without going to a hearing. "There are lots of different ways you can accomplish your goals, as long as you're practical in how you deal with it," he explained.

The best advice I've seen on how to conduct a dignified and successful advocacy campaign comes from Trish Freeman, a Kentucky mother who had to battle her insurance company before it would agree to pay for hearing aids for her two sons. When Trish's oldest son was three and her youngest two years old, they were diagnosed with mild and moderate losses, respectively. The losses turned out to be progressive, and the family had to buy new hearing aids at a rate of a pair a year. Within four years, both boys were profoundly deaf and the family found itself having to pay for its fourth pair of aids in as many years.

Until then, Trish said, she'd accepted her HMO's policy of not paying for hearing aids. "When it came time for the fourth one," she recalled, "I said, enough of this already. This is not right. We have this condition and it's affecting their health. I kept telling myself that if they were disabled because they had a physical disability, like a club foot, the insurance company would be paying for surgery, but they're not going to pay for children who can't hear? What's the difference? It's an arbitrary distinction they've made."

The HMO's rationale was that hearing aids aren't medically necessary. As a representative explained to Trish, the HMO considered hearing aids "life-enhancing services" and therefore not eligible for coverage.

For eight months, Trish wrote detailed, articulate letters to the HMO. She cited studies and evidence from the company's own certificate of coverage to highlight the flaws in its logic. Each appeal was turned down. Convincing the insurance company was beginning to look hopeless, but Trish couldn't bring herself to quit. The final step was a grievance hearing, and she was determined to have her say there.

Weeks went by and Trish hadn't heard from the company, so she called and asked the receptionist the date of the hearing. "You can't come," the receptionist informed her. "The committee will meet and they will review what you submit."

Trish was furious. "A hearing means your case will be heard, that you'll be able to present your case, not that you submit your documents in writing," she said. "I told the receptionist, 'You need to look up your definition of the word *hearing,* and if you don't intend people to come, you need to change the language in your certificate of coverage.'"

The receptionist spoke to the HMO's medical director, who made an exception and allowed Trish to attend the hearing. There, Trish spoke passionately about her sons' hearing loss and why her older son needed a new pair of sophisticated digital aids that would transpose the high-frequency sounds that he could barely hear into lower frequencies that he could. The committee—a pediatrician, an otolaryngologist, the medical director, and other physicians—listened quietly.

"Not a single one of them asked me a question," she said. "They all sat there looking at me with condescending looks on their faces, as if they were thinking, Oh, you poor thing. They just smiled at me and shook their heads and said, 'Thank you. You can go now.' I was dismissed. I didn't get to hear any of their discussions. I went home and promptly had a big glass of wine and told my husband, 'We'll still be paying for the hearing aids, but at least I tried.'"

Trish guessed wrong. A week later, the HMO sent her a letter saying they'd pay for the aids. But happy as she was with her victory, Trish was also still reeling from the experience. "It was an eye opener to the whole process," she said.

Trish is a pharmacist with a Ph.D. in pharmacology and the director of research and education for the American Pharmacy Services Corporation. She knows science, and she's accustomed to dealing with bureaucracies. But her eight-month struggle with her HMO over her sons' hearing aids, a struggle she waged without any legal help, nearly wore her down.

"Here I am, a health care professional. I have all these skills, and yet it was a daunting task for me," she said. Her biggest support came from the internet, specifically a site called Listen-Up (www.listen-up.org), which offers advice and template letters, including, now, her own, for parents in similar situations.

"I thought, other parents who are facing this situation, the majority of them are not likely to have the same skill set, and if it was a daunting task for me, imagine what it would be like for them. Most people would have just thrown their hands up. They would have said, 'This is impossible.' And that's not right. Other parents shouldn't have to go through this to get the services they need for their children."

When the opportunity to help those parents presented itself, Trish was ready. One night not long after the battle with the HMO had come to a successful conclusion, she picked up the latest issue of *Volta Voices,* the monthly magazine of the AG Bell Association for the Deaf and Hard of Hearing, one of the world's largest membership organizations and information centers on hearing loss. Her intent was to flip through the magazine before she fell asleep, but an article caught her attention. It was by a Maryland mother who was working to convince her state legislature to pass a law requiring insurance companies to cover hearing aids.

Somebody ought to do that in Kentucky, Trish thought to herself. And a little while later, after she'd turned off the light but still couldn't sleep, she decided she would be that somebody. "I had never even contemplated anything like that before, but all of a sudden I was motivated and empowered," she said.

She climbed out of bed that instant and drafted emails to the woman who had written the article and to the child advocate at the AG Bell Association. The next day, the two wrote back advising Trish to find a sponsor in the state legislature. A lifelong Kentuckian, she contacted Senator Vernie McGaha, who had been elected three years earlier. Vernie happened to have been Trish's high school band director and principal at the junior high while her mother was principal at the high school.

Not everyone is likely to have such connections, but it's important to remember that legislators are elected to serve constituents. Even if you don't know a legislator personally, you should be able to approach one. You can get a list of your representatives from your state or provincial legislature. Use email, the phone, or the postal service to contact those who have an interest in disabilities or special education or, if you have the time and energy, contact them all, until you find someone willing to take on your cause.

The AG Bell Association had sent Trish copies of the bills from Maryland and other states. She presented those to the senator. The bill they drafted was passed in the state Senate and made it out of the House committee, but the session ended before the House could vote on it. Ultimately, Trish said, "it was a blessing in disguise" because it gave her the time she needed to build a strong grassroots campaign.

A member of the Kentucky State Commission for the Deaf and Hard of Hearing, Trish sought representatives from every sector in the deaf and hard-of-hearing community—interpreters, vocational rehabilitation specialists, teachers of the hearing impaired, audiologists, parents, people who signed, the local AG Bell chapter—to serve on the study committee that would draft the new version of the bill. The idea was to cover every sector so each representative could be the contact person in his or her personal or professional community when it came time to generate support that would be needed to pass the bill.

The plan worked wonderfully. The 12 committee members met every few months and kept in touch mostly through email. The first time they met in person was to fine-tune the language of the bill. They agreed that companies should provide coverage for one hearing aid per impaired ear every 36 months, to a maximum of $1,800 per ear, up until the age of 18. They also wanted the law to require companies to pay for related services, such as earmolds and fitting fees.

The email network proved invaluable. If one of the legislators heard that a fellow House or Senate member had a problem with the bill, Trish would be notified, and she in turn would send a broadcast email to the study committee. Phones "would literally start ringing within minutes of my original email broadcast," Trish said. "It really was amazing to see it in action."

As the date of the vote drew closer, the committee's publicity machine geared up. Members provided flyers, sample letters, talking points, and newsletter articles for meetings at schools and appropriate organizations throughout the state. They encouraged interested parties to write letters to their newspapers supporting the bill. Trish contacted the media to drum up further interest. Capitalizing on the state's early childhood initiative "Education Pays" campaign, the committee came up with its own slogan, "Education should pay for all children, not just those with normal hearing!" which it repeated in letters to the media and legislators, and in flyers.

Among the people the committee invited to address the legislators were a mother whose child was diagnosed as hard of hearing at birth a month after Kentucky implemented a newborn hearing screening act, and a 15-year-old hard-of-hearing high school student with a 4.0 GPA who is active in sports. While the mother of the baby testified about her dismay at learning her child needed hearing aids and her insurance wouldn't pay for them, the 15-year-old boy had a happier story. Through work, his family had insurance that did pay for hearing aids. He was able to provide firsthand evidence that coverage had benefits that were academic, athletic, and social.

Senate Bill 152 passed on March 22, 2002, a year and a half after Trish had first contacted the senator. It went into effect on July 15, 2002. Ironically, the bill has no effect on the Freeman family; both of Trish's sons now have cochlear implants, which were automatically covered by her HMO.

But she wouldn't have traded the experience, both for the opportunity to help other parents and the chance to gain more insight into how childhood hearing loss is viewed by those who have no close experience with the condition.

"A lot of the stance of the medical community and insurance community is based on ignorance," she said. "They just don't have a clue, and it's our job to educate them about the negative outcomes—the negative health outcomes and the negative social outcomes associated with improperly managed hearing impairment. Put some earplugs in and spend the day struggling to hear, and struggling to communicate, and then see how you really feel about it."

If everybody was willing to accept proven facts and respond accordingly, advocacy would be a smooth process and disability-rights lawyers would be out of a job. But it's not only the medical and insurance companies that often operate out of ignorance. Sometimes, as Alicia, a California mother of three, learned the hard way, it's the very people who are supposed to be educating our children.

Alicia had a two-year-old son and a three-year-old daughter when her third child, a daughter, Sylvia, was born in 2001. When Sylvia was ten weeks old, she was diagnosed as profoundly deaf. Under IDEA, she was eligible for special services through her Special Education Local Plan Area (SELPA). Had she been over three years old, the services would have been provided through the local school district.

By the time the SELPA specialists arrived for their evaluations when Sylvia was three-and-a-half months old, Alicia and her husband had done enough research to know they wanted to raise her in an exclusively oral environment and arrange for her to have a cochlear implant when she was a year old.

"If Sylvia was our only daughter, then maybe we could move to a deaf community and really embrace signing and do all of these things, but she's not our only child, and we have to take everybody into account," Alicia said. "We honestly made a full-on effort to learn about signing, to learn about all the different methods, to make sure what we were thinking we wanted to do actually was what we wanted to do."

That's why it was especially frustrating for Alicia and her husband to see that the SELPA specialists weren't providing Sylvia with the kind of services they felt she needed. The teacher of the deaf and hard of hearing had Alicia put her daughter's hand on her throat to feel the vibration when she spoke. In Alicia's opinion, that was both outdated and inappropriate. "It wasn't an auditory method," she said. "[The teacher] didn't mean to do it; it was natural for her, because that's what she's used to. But it just wasn't a match."

The speech-language pathologist was used to working with children who had far less severe losses than Sylvia, children whose problems included stuttering and other speech disorders. She had very little experience with children who had or were about to have cochlear implants. Meanwhile, Alicia was taking classes at the John Tracy Clinic, a highly respected Los Angeles center that helps families with young children who are deaf and hard of hearing. The contrast between what Alicia was learning there about what Sylvia needed to reach her potential and the services Sylvia was receiving at home made her even more determined to find more suitable specialists.

As Sylvia approached her first birthday, Alicia found a local program she felt would better meet her daughter's needs. She and her husband met with the SELPA authorities to explain why they felt the program was more appropriate, but the SELPA wouldn't pay and insisted that its program, staffed by trained and accredited professionals, was sufficient.

Alicia and her husband continued to meet with the SELPA authorities. "When they said they weren't going to pay, I asked again," she said. "You need to try to compromise, you need to try to come up with creative solutions that work for everybody, or do whatever you can and try to work it out, because going to a hearing is not fun, and not good for anybody. That's the last resort. It's expensive, it's very emotionally taxing and draining, and it's hard on everybody. It creates more work for everybody—mother, school district, everybody."

In the end, Alicia and her husband felt they had no choice. "If you really see no other way, if there's nowhere else to go and in your heart of hearts you know what they're giving you isn't good enough, or right, and that's what you need to do, then that's what you need to do. It comes down to how strong a parent you are, and how strong of an advocate you are for your child. How much can you stomach, and how much does your child need whatever it is you're asking for. It's a scale, and you have to just balance it and see which one tips up and which one tips down."

After several unsuccessful meetings with the SELPA, Alicia and her husband decided they needed a lawyer. They contacted a local attorney and the AG Bell Association, which had a commitment to helping establish legal precedents for the rights of children who are deaf and hard of hearing. To that end, it will sometimes provide a lawyer for cases such as Alicia's. The association asked Bruce Goldstein to represent the family. Bruce filed a motion for a hearing.

The hearing was split into two sessions, each lasting less than a week, but the process from the time Bruce and his partner got involved lasted several months. In the end, the administrative law judge agreed with Alicia and her husband that the program offered by the SELPA was not appropriate and the one the family had found was. And yet despite her "victory," Alicia still feels a loss.

"After the court case is over and you still have to work with the school district for another 12 years, you're not starting off on a real good foot," she said. "Once the court case is over, that doesn't mean you're not working with them anymore, it just means you've created animosity."

It's doubtful a school district or the SELPA will try to retaliate against a family that's won a lawsuit, Bruce said. For one thing, it's illegal. For another, school districts are aware that parents who have won a hearing may use that venue again. "I've found generally that school districts are more agreeable if they've lost a hearing, just because they want to avoid any future hearings."

Cases such as Alicia's, where the focus is on the qualifications of the professionals, are more likely to stir up negative feelings than are, say, cases where parents are simply trying to get services for their children. "If you're attacking people's credentials or qualifications, that tends to be taken a little more personally," Bruce said.

So what does he recommend for parents who feel they've alienated their children's future educators long before the first day of kindergarten? Strive for the high ground, he advised. Try to keep emotion out of it. Once the hearing is over, he explained, "go back and do what's in the child's best interest in recognition that the district and the family are going to have to live together for some time."

Alicia's plan is to tread lightly, to choose her battles carefully. "I'm just going to have to work really hard to try to mend a bridge," she said. "I don't have a choice. I've got three kids going through the school district, and two are in the special ed system."

And it is possible to maintain a good relationship with your school district after a legal battle, even a protracted one, as Nebraska moms Michelle Janssen and Janet Petersen learned. In fact, both women said their relationship with the district improved after the nearly four years they spent trying to convince the authorities to hire Signing Exact English (SEE) interpreters to work with their children.

Michelle, whose daughter, Kendra, lost her hearing to meningitis at 14 months, said she doesn't like to ruffle feathers. In fact, Janet refers to her as "the nice one" of the pair. But Michelle also said that when the conflicts with the school system began, she was quick to become angry. If someone made her mad, she was likely to explode, "let them have a piece of my mind and then walk away."

Michelle credits Janet, who had two hard-of-hearing sons in school with Kendra, with helping her learn to rein in her temper. "She'd say, 'If you go in there and blow up at them, what good is that going to accomplish? They expect that. They don't expect you to say, No, you're not answering my question, this is the information

I need from you.' She has much more of an assertive personality. She calls it a pit bull personality," Michelle said.

They made quite a team, one who refused to back down and the other whose mission was to smooth things over. They joined forces when Kendra was in first grade and Janet's son Alex, who is profoundly deaf, was in second. Janet's son Nicholas, who has a severe-to-profound loss, was in sixth grade.

Their initial complaint was that the school's interpreters were unacceptable because their signing skills were limited. "It was like having a child in sixth grade with an interpreter who had preschool-level language skills," Janet said. "If I were to say, 'Oh gosh, look at that humongous building over there,' what they would be telling my child was, 'Look at that really big house.' Children are supposed to get their language expanded in a classroom as they progress, but if you have an interpreter whose language is limited, you have children coming out of school with limited language skills."

Both Michelle and Janet used SEE at home. The interpreters used a mixture of signing systems—primarily pidgin signs (a mix of English and American Sign Language) intermingled with SEE. The two mothers spent as much time as they could in their children's classrooms, always aware, Michelle said, that the mere act of observing ran the risk of appearing antagonistic. They also asked their children to keep them informed about what was happening in school. They kept records of what they considered substandard interpreting, and they met with the school district special education coordinator and teacher of the deaf to convince them to hire trained SEE interpreters. When their efforts failed, they filed a complaint against the district.

Nebraska Advocacy Services (NAS) represented Michelle and Janet in their case, Petersen v. Hastings Public Schools. The first step was a hearing before the Nebraska Department of Education, which ruled in favor of the school district. NAS then appealed to the U.S. District Court for the District of Nebraska, which upheld the ruling. The final appeal was to the U.S. Court of Appeals for the Eighth Circuit, which supported the previous two decisions, ruling that the district wasn't required to educate a child using strict SEE, but could use a modified SEE system.

Yet Michelle and Janet still feel like winners, and not just because they won the part of their complaint requesting that the school district use interpreters during nonacademic activities such as recess and sporting events. Their main goal—to have the district better train its interpreters and teachers of the deaf—was realized. Part of that was a function of the times; when the State of Nebraska closed its school for the deaf in 1998 and more deaf and hard-of-hearing students began attending local schools, some districts, including Hastings, began turning their special education programs over to state-run Educational Service Units. The Educational Service Unit in Hastings was staffed with people who welcomed input from Michelle and Janet.

"They wanted to do what was best for the children, and part of that was having a good relationship with the parents," Michelle said. "They knew our issue was language, and they trained their interpreters better and were very careful about who they hired, making sure that they had the proper skills. The program is excellent today."

It's natural to begin the advocacy process with high hopes and expectations, but it's equally important to be realistic. Listen to the people to whom you're advocating. Don't confuse compromise with weakness; compromise is a key part of the process. Your goal should be to ensure that your child receives the education, attention, or services that he needs, and to maintain a positive working relationship with the people charged with providing those services. If you find that you're constantly meeting resistance, or that a positive relationship is impossible, you may need to seek advice, either from other parents or from one of the many advocacy organizations listed in the Resources section. There *are* solutions to the problems you will encounter. Some will come more easily than others, but as with most things in life, patience, persistence, and a positive attitude will go a long way in helping you achieve your goals.

Chapter Nine

HELPING YOUR HARD-OF-HEARING CHILD LEARN

In the months immediately following Elizabeth's diagnosis, it seemed everything I read suggested that as a group, children with hearing loss are doomed to a bleak future. Every article seemed to cite the same studies, which had apparently all come up with nearly identical conclusions: hard-of-hearing children simply don't perform as well as their normal-hearing peers. Socially they have problems because they often miss important cues. Academically they lag behind because learning is language based and much of language is picked up incidentally—that is, it's overheard. Until a child with a hearing loss is properly aided, he is at a disadvantage that will continue unless and until he's able to make up lost ground.

The studies went on to suggest that once in school, even aided and equipped with personal FM systems, children with hearing loss would continue to have problems. It wasn't just contending with background noise from classmates, overhead lights, and heating systems; when they reached fourth grade and the emphasis was on words rather than pictures, they'd be even more lost and confused.

I didn't want to believe it. Elizabeth was a bright, curious little girl with a promising future. The only thing wrong with her was that she couldn't hear as well as other children. "My kid will beat the odds," I said to myself, all the while trying to ignore the other voice, the one that hissed, "Stop fooling yourself. It doesn't matter how smart your kid is. She's hearing impaired. Get real. Lower your expectations."

My first glimmer of hope that there really were exceptions to the studies' gloomy predictions came from two members of a local support group for hard-of-hearing children and their families. They reminded and reassured me that all children are different, and just because a child can't hear well doesn't mean he can't learn. Gradually I began to meet parents who had hard-of-hearing teenagers who were doing well in school. I also met and, on some of the websites listed in the Resources section, read about hard-of-hearing adults who were successful in their studies and careers despite having grown up wearing hearing aids—and not the sophisticated models of the late twentieth century that are designed to be discreet, efficient, and cut out as much background noise as possible. My in-laws went to a wedding reception and sat with a couple whose severely hard-of-hearing son was about to graduate from medical school, an example that made me realize perhaps the degree of hearing loss had less to do with academic success than I'd initially been led to believe.

One thing the success stories had in common was that the parents were actively involved in their child's education. They had researched forms of communication and chosen which was most appropriate for their child. They had gotten to know their child's teachers and made sure proper accommodations were in place in the classroom, whether that meant having the school supply a transliterator, interpreter or a teacher of the deaf and hard of hearing, or provide extra time for exams. They encouraged and supported their child at school and at home and stressed the importance of learning. While they didn't diminish the disadvantages that come with hearing loss, neither did they allow their child to use it as an excuse not to work to his potential.

Though it would be naive to assume every hard-of-hearing child is going to become a brain surgeon, there are things we, as parents, can and should do to ensure that our children get a proper education. Among the most important are that we have to understand their hearing loss and any other disabilities they may have, be involved throughout their school career, teach them to advocate for themselves, and ensure that proper accommodations are in place so that they have the same opportunity to learn as their normal-hearing classmates.

Hard of Hearing Is *Not* a Learning Disability

Some hard-of-hearing children have learning disabilities. Many hard-of-hearing children receive educational services from some of the same specialists who serve children with learning disabilities. But—and this is a big but—hearing loss is not a learning disability. Parents should not be confused into thinking the two automatically go hand in hand. Hearing loss is a physical condition. Not being able to hear well can certainly affect the way a child learns. That's why appropriate accommodations are essential. For families who choose to communicate using oral language, those accommodations begin with the right hearing technologies, such as hearing aids, cochlear implants, and FM systems. Once accommodations are in place, your child should be able to take full advantage of the educational system.

Hard-of-hearing children display the same range of intelligence as do normal-hearing children, said Christie Yoshinaga-Itano, a professor in the Department of Speech/Language & Hearing Sciences at the University of Colorado-Boulder. However, regardless of how bright hard-of-hearing children are, there are often large discrepancies between their nonverbal and verbal intelligence scores.

In people with sensory hearing loss, the cochlea doesn't work properly either because of a malformation or because the hair cells never formed, or formed but were subsequently damaged. A child with sensorineural hearing loss will, therefore, miss out on certain sounds. Hearing aids or a cochlear implant will help, but even with the best hearing technologies, noise and distance will present problems that prevent children with hearing loss from hearing like their normal-hearing peers.

Children who have frequent otitis media are also at risk for speech and language delays. Although their cochleas are unaffected, they don't hear clearly, which may result in speech and language delays and subsequent problems in school. Adults experiencing late-onset hearing loss can sometimes compensate for missing words or parts of words in conversation because those pathways already exist; language is already fully developed and it's easier to fill in gaps, as all of us do in noisy environments where we can't hear well. Children just learning language don't have that luxury, and it is critical that they get the full range of sounds to develop those neural pathways.

Properly fitted hearing aids or cochlear implants allow the brain to make use of sounds that would otherwise be missed. In short, they make sounds detectable: the sounds your child needs to hear—the teacher, a friend, or you—as well as the background noises, such as people chattering, dogs barking, and car horns honking, which often threaten to overwhelm the principal speaker's voice. For people with normal hearing, the brain automatically lowers background noise, allowing the listener to focus on what he or she wants to hear. Hearing aids and implants, for all their technological sophistication, will never work as well as a fully functioning auditory system. That means children wearing hearing aids or using a cochlear implant in a classroom, which by nature is full of background noise, will need special accommodations.

As noted earlier, in the United States, those accommodations are spelled out for the school-age child in an Individualized Education Plan. In Canada, the accommodations and the name of the document will vary depending on where you live. In either country, as a parent, you are expected to work with your child's teachers to determine what accommodations will best meet your child's educational needs and be included in the plan.

Children with hearing loss even in the severe range can often function well in a school environment with assisted learning devices such as a personal FM system or a sound field FM system. They also often benefit from preferential seating close to the primary speaker and away from noise sources such as computers, heating systems, pencil sharpeners, and doors that open into a hallway. Other accommodations may include being given extra time on tests and repeated or additional instructions. Children with the most severe hearing losses often need more accommodations. Options for these children may include:

• **Cued speech transliterator:** The transliterator constantly converts spoken information, verbatim, to visual information using hand shapes and locations near the mouth in an effort to enhance lip-reading. The transliterator, who should be beside or slightly in front of the teacher or primary source of information, provides the student with instant visual access to audible information.

• **Oral interpreter:** The oral interpreter will face your child and mouth the words spoken by the teacher or other students. Oral interpreters are used by some deaf or hard-of-hearing people who don't use sign language.

• **A sign language interpreter or translator:** The terms *interpreter* and *translator* are often used interchangeably when describing a person who translates between oral and manual forms of communication. Because *interpreter* is the most commonly used term, we will use that for the purposes of this definition. However, regardless of the term used, the job is basically the same: to take an oral form of communication and represent it on the hands, either in sign language or in a sign system, and to take the form of manual communication and translate it into oral language.

If your child uses a manual form of communication, an interpreter should be by his side in school, translating what he says into the oral language being used and what the teacher and other students say into his accepted form of manual communication. The interpreter's job is to ensure that your child has access to all that is being said, that the teacher and classmates have access to his input, and that he is able to participate in discussions.

The interpreter should be certified in the sign language or sign system used and should not change the information or apply her own interpretation to what is being said or signed. As with any profession, some interpreters are better than others. It's important to check your interpreter's credentials and references to make sure she is qualified for the job. In the United States, the Registry of Interpreters of the Deaf certifies American Sign Language (ASL) interpreters. In Canada, the certifying body for ASL is the Association of Visual Language Interpreters of Canada. The SEE Center for the Advancement of Deaf Children (www.seecenter.org) offers workshops and evaluations in Signing Exact English. See the Resources section for more information. It's also important to check with your child and his teachers to make sure the interpreter or translator is performing her duties appropriately.

• **Note taker:** In secondary schools and in the university setting it is often possible to arrange for note takers, usually other students willing to share their notes. This can be accomplished using double-sheet carbonized paper or by providing photocopies. This allows the student with hearing loss to focus on the teacher and supplemental visual aids.

- **Real-time captioning:** A real-time captioner uses a stenography-like machine to type the teacher's words into a computer, as the teacher is speaking. The captioning is displayed on a screen in front of the classroom, or on your child's personal computer screen, so your child can pick up information at the same time as the rest of the class.

- **Captioning:** Videos that are narrated by an unseen narrator are often difficult for hard-of-hearing students to follow. Captioning allows a student to follow the action by reading what's being said, instead of straining to listen to words that may not always be clear.

Children with hearing loss often look, act, and speak like their normal-hearing peers. For a parent having difficulty with acceptance of the hearing loss, having a child who appears to be like everyone else is a wonderful thing. But the fact remains that a child with a hearing loss has needs that are significantly different from those of his normal-hearing peers. Ultimately it's going to be better for everyone if those differences are apparent and attended to immediately. For instance, it's not unusual for undiagnosed hard-of-hearing children to be misdiagnosed with attention deficit disorder or other behavioral problems. Some of these children may indeed have attention problems, but often the root cause of their less-than-acceptable classroom behavior is that their needs aren't being met.

That was the case with Jill's son, Ian, whose mild hearing loss wasn't diagnosed until he was seven. Before that, his teachers were convinced he had a form of attention deficit disorder described as inattentive. That's because he wasn't hyperactive, he just didn't pay attention. After he began wearing hearing aids, but before he began using an FM system, his teacher still insisted he had behavioral problems. Her complaints were that he didn't pay attention and couldn't keep his eyes on his desk.

As it turned out, Ian's behavior was a reaction to his teacher; she paced back and forth when she spoke and often wrote on the black-board with her back to the class as she talked. Both postures made it nearly impossible for Ian to follow what was happening. His solution was to watch his classmates for clues. But when they were reading out loud, which the teacher often had them do, he couldn't hear them. Rather than disturb the class, he doodled, which the teacher considered yet another sign of his poor attention skills.

It took Ian's parents three years of fighting to get the district to meet their son's needs. In addition to the FM, Ian works every day with a teacher of the deaf and has a number of classroom accommodations, including extra time for schoolwork and on tests, one-on-one administering of any oral portions of work, and alternative test settings as needed and determined by the teacher of the deaf.

Now in eighth grade, Ian has recently been diagnosed with a progressive hearing loss that will leave him deaf. However, he still has enough hearing to use hearing aids and has become an honors student. As a benchmark to chart his progress, his teacher of the deaf had him take the Stanford Achievement Test. He scored higher than any student she'd had ever tested.

"He's not a genius," Jill said, "but after all the early failing he experienced in academics, it was great to have him score so well."

Well-behaved hard-of-hearing students are also often at a disadvantage, at least until they learn to advocate for themselves. Nicole is a nine-year-old fourth grade student at a public school in Edmonton. I've also taught her in Hebrew school for the past few years. She's a sweet, quiet girl who would rather doodle than speak up in class. She does well in Hebrew school and in public school. According to her mom, Pam, her grades "have not suffered yet due to her hearing impairment," but that "yet" is a key to Pam's fears.

"Sometimes I feel that this has led to her teacher not attending to her needs," Pam said. "I don't think she perceives Nicole to have special needs. In the long run, this will hurt Nicole."

The year Nicole was in second grade, she had a teacher who did not consistently use either the personal FM system or the sound field system in Nicole's classroom. Pam asked repeatedly, but even when she showed up in the classroom to pick Nicole up early for an appointment, more often than not the teacher wasn't wearing the microphone. Pam spoke to the principal, but the situation didn't improve. At the end of the school year, Pam enrolled Nicole and her younger sister, who has normal hearing, in a new school, where, as it turns out, the teachers have been much more supportive.

"Because of all the trouble I've had with Nicole's school, I'm not sure I'm the best one to give advice to others," Pam said. "I would say that we are the only ones who can be our child's advocate, and we have to take on that role wholeheartedly. We have to trust our instincts, encourage our child to communicate, and encourage open communication with the school and the teachers."

Open communication with your child's teachers is critical. Some parents choose to send a notebook back and forth as a way of keeping in touch with teachers and specialists. Others volunteer in the school, or schedule regular meetings. The arrangement you make will depend on your child, his teachers, and your respective schedules. Regardless of how you handle the relationship, your goal is to make sure that your child gets a solid education. That means working cooperatively with the professionals responsible for that education.

"My advice is to be the teacher's support, not adversary," said Karen, a Long Island, New York, mom whose daughter Christina received hearing aids at five months and a cochlear implant when she was seven. Now in elementary school, Christina is a B+ student who gets excellent support from her teachers and the principal. "It's a lot of extra work at home, but it's worth it to see her succeed," Karen said.

Karen brings Christina's schoolbooks home during the summer for review. She allows Christina to play with friends after school, as long as they do their homework first. She recommends setting aside time each day to sit down with your child to do homework. "Encourage reading and make school your number one priority," she said. "It will pay off."

Mary's daughter, Caitlin, hasn't had such a positive experience. Caitlin, who lives in western Canada, was ten when she was diagnosed with a moderate loss, which eventually turned out to be profound. Caitlin has had problems socially and academically, both before and since being aided. Because she couldn't hear her friends speaking, even when they were making plans in front of her, she'd miss out on what they were saying. As a result, she missed out on events. Teachers and peers would tell her, "You should learn to listen better."

One teacher didn't understand how to use the FM, and yelled into it. Another showed movies without captioning three or four times a week. The room was dark, so Caitlin couldn't do any other work, but the teacher wouldn't allow her to leave the room. It took a year of complaining to the principal, the administration, and various government officials before Mary could get someone to take her concerns seriously. The district is now allowing Caitlin to take some classes through correspondence, which Mary is convinced will help her improve her grades.

At the beginning of every school year, Mary writes letters to Caitlin's teachers, explaining the hearing loss, how it affects Caitlin, and what teachers can do to help her learn. She also meets with the teachers and the district's special needs coordinator. Caitlin, too, meets individually with the teachers. At the end of the school year, Mary meets with the school staff to choose her daughter's teachers for the following year and to request that certain helpful students are in the class, to help with note taking.

"My child's classmates, now that she is in high school, have accepted her hearing loss, but she still finds it difficult to make friends because people aren't willing to be patient and repeat things or take the time to help her," Mary said. "Some of her old friends from junior high completely ignore her and won't even acknowledge her."

Tina is five years old and has a profound unilateral hearing loss in her right ear. Children with unilateral hearing losses can have significant problems, especially with social interactions, in noisy settings, and in trying to determine where sounds are coming from. Tina is no exception. In fact, her mother, Laura, said that in some ways it would be easier if Tina were deaf in both ears.

"It's children like Tina who slip through the cracks because they are in the middle of the so-called 'norm' and 'deaf' community," Laura said. "If she didn't have a speech delay, she would never have had the help she's been able to obtain, and yet she still struggles with having only one good ear."

In school, Tina uses a personal FM system, but both socially and academically her kindergarten year was less than a success. Laura clashed with Tina's teachers and the school administration; neither could agree on what Tina needed. Socially, Laura had a hard time watching Tina's peers ignore her because they couldn't understand her and she couldn't find the right words to express herself.

"I'm worrying about her future and how she's going to cope," Laura said. "She's going to have to be a very strong individual, and at this time, she is very sensitive. I hope I can help her with that."

Children learn differently. Some hearing-impaired children excel in gym, others have a lousy sense of balance. Some have excellent handwriting and thrive in art class, others have poorly developed fine motor skills. Some love to read and have no trouble sounding out words, others will do anything to avoid cracking a book. Some love math, others struggle to add single-digit numbers. How your child fares in school depends on a wide range of factors, not just how well—or poorly—he hears.

The Preschool Program: Getting on the Right Track

About a month after Elizabeth received her hearing aids, she was assigned a speech-language pathologist (SLP) at the Glenrose Rehabilitation Hospital, where her audiologist and social worker were based. As we got more involved with Elizabeth's preschool education, and as her hearing aids began to take up more of our time, sometimes requiring weekly trips to the audiology clinic, I realized how fortunate we were to live in a big city with easy access to the services we needed. I couldn't imagine how we'd cope if we lived in a remote rural area and had to drive hours to get to a clinic.

Elizabeth's new speech pathologist was Rachel. She had a well-equipped office and classroom facilities at the Glenrose, but for her first meeting with Elizabeth, she came to our house. Her explanation: even though Elizabeth was the one with the hearing loss, we, her family, would play a role in helping her make up for the language skills she'd missed during her first three years. Together, we'd all work to bring her up to an age-appropriate level.

At first I feared that meant I'd have to spend hours each day going over flash cards with Elizabeth, or labeling every item in the house and conducting daily quizzes. As much as I wanted to help Elizabeth attain an age-appropriate vocabulary, I couldn't figure out where I'd find the time for that kind of intensive therapy. But while labeling certainly helps, and flash cards were truly useful, the big change in my life was that I suddenly became more aware of language. Where once I might have worked quietly or muttered under my breath as I cooked or cleaned or grocery shopped, I now made a conscious effort to talk as I went, to explain what I was doing, what we were seeing, and why.

Noah, with his normal hearing, would pick up most of his vocabulary as if by osmosis, simply by soaking up everything around him. Words like *hi, bye, kiss, macaroni, milk, cereal*—those words Elizabeth knew, because I'd said them to her over and over. "Here's your cereal and your milk," "Say bye to Grandma," "Give Daddy a kiss." I couldn't be so sure she'd know more incidental words, like *belt buckle, doorknob, happy,* and *sad*. Those were the sorts of words Rachel began helping her with in their early sessions, the spring that Elizabeth was three.

The following fall, Elizabeth was enrolled in the Glenrose Hospital's preschool program for children with hearing loss. There were five children in the class, all of them three years old or close to it. Two mornings a week, they met in a spacious, but cozy classroom divided into sections for reading, playing, music, vocabulary, and snacks.

First thing in the morning, Rachel inspected everyone's hearing aids and FM systems. At the same time, Brenda, the other SLP in the program, began one-on-one speech therapy sessions in a smaller room down the hall. The children used their free time to play, look at books, or sit on the lap of a parent, grandparent, or aide and listen to a story.

Once class was in session, the five children sat in a row of chairs while Rachel took attendance. When their names were called, they had to respond. It was good training for elementary school, but its intended purpose was to teach the children to listen for their name and respond appropriately. Late-diagnosed children, so accustomed to not hearing, often tune out without even thinking about it. They need to be taught how to listen, something that comes naturally to normal-hearing children (though parents might often think otherwise).

After attendance, the children continued sitting while Rachel read them a story or reviewed new words, always using pictures to reinforce the vocabulary. Sometimes the three boys in the class moved around and bothered each other, but within a few months, fidgeting happened rarely, if at all. By and large, the five children were unwaveringly attentive.

Just how remarkable this was became clear to me a year later, when Elizabeth was in kindergarten. Because her birthday was close to the cutoff date, she was at least a half-year younger than some of her classmates. And yet most of them seemed much less able to sit still and cooperate than her hard-of-hearing classmates had been.

"They knew they had to listen," Brenda explained to me when I asked her about it a few years later. Few children are in such structured preschool programs that put so much emphasis on listening. "We're expecting active participation in listening, and a response. In a playschool, you don't necessarily get an opportunity to answer a question; you're given that opportunity, but not everybody gets picked. In our program, everybody got picked. When our kids get to elementary school, the teachers love them because they know how to sit and pay attention and focus."

After vocabulary, the children did a craft, something that reinforced whatever concept they were learning. Elizabeth still has on her wall one of the first crafts she did in preschool. It's a house, and in each room, she had to paste the appropriate furniture—the stove and fridge in the kitchen, the toilet and sink and tub in the bathroom, the bed and desk and dresser in the bedroom. It sounds so obvious, and to children who hear and pick up language incidentally, it is. Children who are hard of hearing need these things pointed out and reinforced over and over, until it becomes second nature to them.

The preschool program also included physical education, music, and drama. Rachel and Brenda videotaped the kids' performances in *We're Going on a Bear Hunt, The Three Little Pigs,* and *The Very Hungry Caterpillar,* so they could have permanent records of their acting debuts.

When, at the end of the preschool year, Dave and I were informed that Elizabeth had tested at or above her age level in speech and language and therefore didn't need to come back to the program the following year, I cried. Elizabeth had gotten a first-rate education in the preschool program. I doubted she'd ever again be in a situation with such a favorable teacher-to-student ratio—five children, a teacher, an aide, an SLP, and at least one parent and grandparent at every session to help out.

"This is a good thing," Rachel and Brenda insisted, as they handed me a box of tissues. "She's ready to be mainstreamed."

The question for Dave and me was, mainstreamed in what? It was nearly the end of June. The other preschool programs in the city were closed for the summer, so it was too late to even observe them. It was also too late to get Elizabeth into a private kindergarten, as admissions had closed months earlier.

Our neighborhood playschool, where Elizabeth had gone one day a week in addition to the Glenrose program, was strictly for play. The focus was on fun, crafts, and games. After a year where she had thrived in a highly structured environment, Dave and I worried that a whole year of fun and games would be a step backward, not to mention less than stimulating for her.

After spending most of the summer seeking the opinions of everyone we could think of, including a friend who is a child psychiatrist and had been saying since May that Elizabeth was ready for kindergarten, we decided to sign her up for kindergarten at our neighborhood school. She wouldn't turn five until mid-January, but our school district's cutoff date is March 1, so technically her age wasn't a problem. And Dave and I, whose birthdays are in December and November, had both started school early and managed to do well. But would Elizabeth be able to keep up?

By the time we made our decision, the neighborhood school was closed for the summer. We spent most of August away, returning home a week before Labor Day, at which time I went to the school to register Elizabeth. The administrative assistant handed me a registration form, and I began to fill it out.

"Elizabeth is hearing impaired," I explained to the principal. "She has a personal FM system. I can come and show the teacher how to use it."

That's when the administrative assistant spoke up. "My daughter is hearing impaired," she said, smiling warmly at me. "She has an FM, too."

I felt my eyes well up with tears. The administrative assistant had a daughter who wore hearing aids? In such a small school, there would be someone who would understand not only how to help Elizabeth, but what I was going through as well? I couldn't believe my good fortune. And it got better: one of the two teachers who job-shared in the kindergarten/grade one classroom had taught at the provincial School for the Deaf, and had also taught in a mainstream school with hard-of-hearing children.

In the years since Elizabeth has been in school, the administrative assistant, Jan, has become a friend, a shoulder to lean on, and the person Elizabeth goes to when she needs help with equipment checks and battery changes. Because Jan's daughter, Melissa, is ten years older than Elizabeth, Jan has already been down the road on which I'm just starting. She's the person who let me know when it was time to start encouraging Elizabeth to take responsibility for battery changes, and she's already warned me of what I can expect when Elizabeth hits high school and will probably protest about using her FM.

Our fears that Elizabeth wasn't academically ready for school were unfounded. Her teachers made that clear to us throughout kindergarten, and as the years have gone by, it's obvious they're right. Elizabeth is a good student, not at the top of her class, but not at the bottom, either. She is responsible and conscientious and actually enjoys her schoolwork. She likes art, music, and reading, but her favorite subjects seem to change. One week she likes language arts and writing stories, the next week she likes math.

That's not to say she hasn't had any problems. Her spelling is inconsistent and she doesn't always follow directions properly, but no one, from her teachers to the district's educational consultant for the deaf and hard of hearing, has been able to say for sure whether that's a function of her age and development or her hearing loss. I'm tempted to go more with the former, and not just because her teachers have assured us that such problems are common among primary school students. Halfway through second grade, the educational consultant for the deaf and hard of hearing came to school to observe Elizabeth and test her. On the Kaufman Test of Educational Achievement, she tested above her age level in spelling and math computation.

Danny: Following the Academic Path Set by His Hearing Brother

Danny was born with what's known as a Mondini malformation. He has no cochlea in his right ear and a partial formation in his left. He was diagnosed as profoundly deaf when he was about a year old. Five months before his second birthday, he received a cochlear implant. Until then, he had been largely silent. "The only time we heard his voice was when he laughed or cried," said his mother, Jennifer, an occupational therapist.

Once Danny received his implant, a teacher from the Boys Town National Hospital Early Education Program came to the family's house several times a week to work with Danny and the family. Her goal was to alert Danny to sound and help him and his family with his communication and language skills.

Six months after he was implanted, Danny was enrolled in a toddler program at Boys Town, where the emphasis was on total communication. Eventually his parents signed him up for two other separate programs. At the Omaha Hearing School, which he attended part time for three years, he focused on auditory training. At the Jewish Community Center in Omaha, which he attended part time for two years, he received an introduction to the Jewish education that is part of his family heritage.

By the time Danny entered kindergarten shortly before his sixth birthday, he'd had three years of preschool in three different programs. He'd been reading for almost two years, and was eager to learn more. To further ease his transition into the public school system, the district put together a sign language class for his kindergarten classmates. Fifteen students showed up for the class, which took place during the summer. Danny and his mother helped teach. The class wasn't intended to make the students proficient. Rather, it was an introduction designed to provide a comfort level so the youngsters would understand the basics of sign language and not spend class time trying to figure out who Danny's interpreter was and what she was doing. It also had the perhaps unexpected benefit of showing Danny's classmates that even though he didn't hear well, he had something to offer.

That he was smart was never in question. He surprised even his family when, at four, he began to read to his mother. She hadn't taught him. In fact, she always worried he'd have trouble with reading because phonetics is sound based. But because reading is important to the family, she read to him constantly, finger-spelling words for which there were no signs in Signing Exact English. One day she finger-spelled b-u-s, and Danny, unprompted, said, "Bus."

Soon the family began holding finger-spelling contests, where Danny competed with his brother, who is two-and-a-half years older, and his dad. "He was just great," Jennifer said. "I would finger-spell, say, plumber, and he would come back and say 'Plumb-ber.' Having never heard the word, he didn't know not to pronounce the 'b.' "

Entering kindergarten, Danny tested above average in all areas except for math, where he was average. Now in first grade, he is having trouble with math. On a recent diagnostic test, out of 20 possible right answers, Danny scored only eight. Jennifer has asked the teacher to send home more worksheets, and she looks for opportunities at home to work math into whatever they're doing. For instance, for Danny's seventh birthday party, Jennifer brought home three packages of goody bags with eight bags in each package. Before Danny began filling the bags, she asked him to figure out how many there were.

Jennifer has spoken with the district's consultant for the deaf and hard of hearing about Danny's math problems, but it's not clear whether the problems stem from his hearing loss or whether he'd have trouble with math even if his hearing were normal. The consultant has suggested that some of the information he needs may be getting lost in translation, and that because he is such a visual learner, math concepts are more difficult when they are just explained. Danny does much better if he can see the problem—laying out coins that are to be added up, for example. His parents and the consultant have discussed taking him out of class a couple of times a week to work on math. He is already pulled out of class two or three times a week for speech therapy.

"I don't want him to fall behind, because once a deaf kid falls behind, it's so much harder to catch up," Jennifer said.

The fear of Danny falling behind is not a new concern. Jennifer and her husband, John, worried even before Danny went to kindergarten about the effects of going from small specialized programs with five children to a large public school class with more than 20. But they felt they didn't have a choice. The small programs for hard-of-hearing children weren't available for kindergartners.

Danny could have attended a school in another district, where most of the deaf children in the area go. However, the district had recently undergone massive budget cuts, and the family felt the services weren't as good as those offered in their own district. Also, the program there relied strongly on signing. Danny is oral; he likes using his voice and doesn't like depending on signs. Jennifer and John also decided against sending him to a public school with deaf children who don't use interpreters. Ultimately they opted to send him to the neighborhood school where his brother is a student.

When Danny was in kindergarten, he spent five half-days a week at the neighborhood school, and the rest of the time at the Omaha

Hearing School. By first grade, however, he was ready to be mainstreamed full time at the neighborhood school.

Before Danny began kindergarten, the school district hired an interpreter for him. The following year, that interpreter got a new job and Danny got a new interpreter. As with his first one, Jennifer is pleased with her performance. "She tries to interpret side conversations that are going on, but she steps back if she sees he's getting it and not needing her. He's learned to hear things with his implant. If the teacher is reading a story or giving instructions, she's right up there interpreting. She says half the time he's watching her and half the time he's watching the teacher. If they're all sitting on the floor and somebody behind him makes a comment, he won't know that, so she's there to fill in for him."

The interpreter doesn't always stay with him at recess or on the playground after lunch, however. "I've always said I don't want her to be Danny's little buddy," Jennifer said. "In the past I've said for unstructured time, I didn't want an interpreter. You don't want the kids to think you always have to have this person by your side, and I was afraid he'd end up interacting with the interpreter instead of with the kids."

A few months into first grade, Danny began complaining that he had no one to play with at recess. The teacher, too, had noticed that the first graders were beginning to pair off with best friends and was planning to talk to the class about that. In the meantime, Danny was lonely, and Jennifer was concerned. So one day she went to school to see for herself what was happening on the playground. What she saw was that the girls Danny wanted to play with were going through the phase where they would run away from a boy if they thought he liked them. Danny, whether because of his hearing loss or his age, didn't understand.

"Some things are still getting lost on him," Jennifer said. "He's still not getting all the social situations. I worry more about that than the academic situations, because the interpreter will always be there for the academic situations to make sure he doesn't miss anything."

Jennifer has invited classmates to the house to play with Danny, and he's been invited on play dates as well. "They all like him and think favorably of him, I think, but when he's on the playground, he's not somebody they're clicking with," she said.

His closest school friend is a boy in kindergarten whose mom is good friends with Jennifer. "This little boy doesn't even care that sometimes Danny doesn't understand him," she said. "If his peers don't get him right off, they don't take the time to repair the communication. They simply walk away and don't take the time to make sure he is understood or make sure he is understanding them. There are maybe one or two girls who will get in front of him and repeat things—they're very good at repairing a communication breakdown—but for the most part, the boys I've seen playing with him will just give up and walk away."

At recess, when all the boys go off to play soccer, Danny doesn't join them. Because of his hearing loss, his sense of balance isn't strong. Unlike his brother, a natural athlete, Danny's not comfortable playing sports. Jennifer and John don't push him, although they encourage him to participate in clinics for noncompetitive sports, such as tennis and basketball. Their hope is that in addition to helping Danny with balance and coordination, the experience will teach him that sports are fun, and give him the confidence to participate more often.

On the other hand, Jennifer said, "academically I expect him to have just as normal a life as his brother and sister, without denying there is a disability going on. He has strengths in other areas—he's very creative and he likes to build things."

Not long after his sixth birthday, Danny asked to take piano lessons, as his brother had been for four years. Jennifer debated before deciding to go ahead. "Why would I do it for the other two and not for him?" she says. "I don't want his life to be different because of my preconceived notions that he can't do something. We'll see. If it's just a frustration and he isn't getting anywhere, we won't continue. But I've already seen that it's working out."

Julie: Defying the Odds

Julie's parents took her to an audiologist for her first hearing test when she was three, but it wasn't until she was four that she received an accurate diagnosis. She had a moderate-to-profound sensorineural loss in her right ear and a severe-to-profound mixed loss in her left. It took a month for the audiologist to fit her with appropriate hearing aids. In the meantime, her mother, Elyse, who knew nothing about hearing losses or the educational needs of children, recalled, "I was scared out of my mind. The experts told me she had too much hearing to go to a deaf school, and even if she went to a deaf school, she'd come out with a fourth-grade reading level."

After much research, Elyse and her husband, Larry, decided to send Julie to their local public school. The district provided Julie with an itinerant teacher for the deaf, who spent three hours a week in the classroom with her, or took her out of class to work with her privately. Julie's Individualized Education Plan said the school must provide captioning for videos, extra time for tests, and preferential seating, and that directions must be reread or simplified as needed. Early in Julie's school years, Elyse lobbied the district to buy a wireless FM instead of the less expensive and less effective older version it would have preferred to purchase.

Now in eighth grade, Julie is an A student who scores in the superior range in district-wide language arts exams and is an avid reader. She got only one B at the end of her seventh-grade year, in social studies. To this day, her mother is grateful for and pleased with her daughter's academic success. But it hasn't always come easily.

Julie's parents know at the end of each academic year who her teacher will be for the coming year, and what friends will be in her class. But on the first day of second grade, the principal called Elyse to inform her that Julie would be getting a new teacher. The problem: the teacher whose class she was supposed to be in refused to wear the FM microphone. A cancer survivor, the teacher had gone through chemotherapy the year before and was afraid the microphone would emit radiation!

It was an irrational fear, as the FM emits nothing harmful, but it nonetheless resulted in upheaval at the beginning of Julie's school year. In fifth grade, Julie failed math in the first marking period. Elyse believes it's because Julie didn't feel prepared and wasn't up to the challenge, coming off a year with a teacher who had spoken in a monotone that she'd found hard to understand. After the first report cards went home, Julie worked hard with her itinerant teacher and stayed after school two days a week for a small class with other students who needed extra help. By the end of the year, she earned a B.

There have been problems, too, with broken equipment and with videos that aren't captioned. "The first time I heard about the captioning, I called and I was nice," Elyse said. "I'm nice the first time. I'm nice the second time. By the third time, it's enough already. When a person can't hear right and people are talking and there's music in the background, or the narrator is talking at warp speed, my kid's not getting all that knowledge and it's against the law. Now Julie's becoming an advocate for herself. She tells the teacher when it's not captioned."

However, all the telling won't help when the teacher doesn't get it, which has happened in the past. "The first time, the teacher said, 'Well, Emily heard it without the captioning.' You don't compare kids. How ignorant is that? And the shame of it was, he was a very, very nice guy, but very stupid when it came to hearing losses."

Elyse, who is now an aide in a Long Island, New York, elementary school, understands the pressures the teachers are under.

"They're overloaded," she said. "They're pulled in this direction and that direction, and the meetings and the stress and the parents. They are pushed to the max. I know that personally. But if I showed you half a movie and gave you a test, would that be fair?"

Elyse wrote to the principal, who called and told her he would take care of the problem. If the movie isn't captioned, Julie is now allowed to take the video home, or she is given a book that contains the facts she needs to learn. "There are ways around it," Elyse said.

Socially, however, there aren't a lot of ways to overcome a hearing loss. In one-on-one situations, Julie does well, but in larger groups, she has trouble hearing and keeping up. Strong willed and outgoing, she prefers to dominate a conversation, perhaps, Elyse said, "because it's the only way you can hear what's going on." But it's not always a successful method, especially when there's lots of noise, which there is in large groups.

"She's got one or two girls who like her, and she likes them, so she has a teeny little clique," Elyse said. "She has friends, and she's happy."

The summer before Julie entered eighth grade, her parents arranged for her to have a cochlear implant in her left ear. She had become a candidate when the hearing in her right ear—her better ear—deteriorated during elementary school. The implant was turned on in late September, but the mapping process is lengthy. In order to hear and understand in school, Julie continued using a hearing aid in her right ear. Cochlear implant experts continue to debate the benefits of using an aid and an implant, but Julie will likely use both, except during the mapping process.

"Implanting borderline kids is relatively new," Elyse said, "but for now, she's doing fine at school. I don't have to hover. She's pretty responsible, and she's a good student."

Melissa: School Was a Constant Struggle But Mom Learned an Important Lesson: Ask Questions Until You Get Answers

Melissa was diagnosed with a mild-to-moderate loss when she was about two and a half, after a day care worker noticed she didn't seem to be able to hear when someone called her from across the room. Her mother, my friend Jan, who was by then separated from Melissa's dad, got her the help she needed right away, "but it was a roller coaster for a very long time," she recalled.

"You'd have these highs—Melissa is doing so well, she's got her speech patterns fixed, she's saying everything the way she's supposed to say it, she's not going to have any problems with her speech. And then it would be, but she has trouble with concepts, she has trouble with word recognition, she has trouble with letter recognition. So it went back and forth between she's doing great, and, oh, she's not doing great. I was constantly feeling, where am I and what do I do now?"

Like Elizabeth, Melissa went to the Glenrose Rehabilitation Hospital in Edmonton for hearing tests and speech therapy. The professionals spoke in technical terms Jan often found difficult to decipher, and they sent her reports predicting future problems she could expect Melissa to encounter, but which made no sense to her at the time.

By the time Melissa reached first grade, the problems were beginning. She couldn't sound out words. Even with her hearing aids, certain sounds didn't register, making phonetic reading difficult.

"You could say, 'Yes, that's typical of a hearing-impaired child,' " Jan said. "But you can have the kid sitting next to her who's not hearing impaired who has the same reading problems. So you don't really know why it's happening."

Melissa learned to read, but unlike her mother, who calls herself a readaholic, she never learned to love it. Jan believes that had a lasting effect on her academic career. "You know that kids with hearing loss are going to have trouble with vocabulary; they're only going to want to learn the words that can help them get their point across in the fastest and simplest way. They're not going to want to learn 12 words for silly."

At Melissa's elementary school, all sorts of promises were made, from the guarantee of extra help in language arts to the promises of an Individualized Program Plan, "but it never came to pass," Jan said.

Not only did school officials renege on their promises, she said, but judging from the comments on Melissa's progress reports— "Melissa needs to study more" and "Melissa needs to put more effort into preparing for exams"—they seemed to have forgotten she had a hearing loss.

By the time Melissa was in sixth grade, her FM was so old Jan was told it wasn't worth repairing. The school refused to buy a new system, but it did agree to purchase a secondhand one on the condition that Jan reimburse them before Melissa moved on to junior high school. She agreed only because she wanted to make sure Melissa would get an FM as quickly as possible.

Then she called the district's audiology consultant, who informed her that the school was responsible for purchasing equipment required for instructional use and that it could not refuse or blackmail parents into paying for it. Jan told the elementary school principal she wouldn't reimburse the school. "I told them if they wanted to pursue it, they could talk to the audiology consultant," she recalled. "I never heard another word about it."

In seventh grade, Melissa used an FM owned by the junior high school. She also had time with an aide every day. But the following year, the aide position was eliminated due to budget cuts, and the FM broke and was going to take weeks to repair. There is a provincial agency that helps parents purchase FM systems for their children, but only if the systems will be used outside of school. So Jan sent the agency a proposal.

"I had to come up with situations where she would use it outside of school, even though I knew those situations weren't likely," Jan said. "But Melissa needed the FM, and we couldn't afford to pay for it ourselves." The proposal was accepted, and Melissa got a new FM.

However, her academic problems persisted. Though she scored well on class work, she consistently failed tests because she didn't understand the questions. Jan was convinced it was because she had never learned to read properly. The principal offered to have someone read the exam questions to Melissa, but what Jan wanted was to have the questions rephrased. She was repeatedly told it could not be done.

Jan, who was working for the school board's Department of Continuing Education, was beginning to feel like a pest. She was pushing the principal to have Melissa tested for learning disabilities, but he wasn't moving very quickly. When she finally did get a positive response, it was because the principal was out of town and his email was automatically forwarded to one of the counselors, who emailed back promptly and said, "No problem. I'll set that up right away."

"So that's a really important lesson," Jan said. "If you keep banging on the door and you're not getting in, try a different door. It turned out you don't talk to the principals of the schools. Once you get to junior high you talk to the counselors. And where I made my mistake in the first two years of junior high school was I kept talking to the principal. He'd sit there and nod and he wouldn't do anything. He never said, 'Go talk to the counselor,' and he never passed my complaint on to the counselor."

Jan's next eye-opening experience came before Melissa started high school. She received a call from a high school counselor recommending Melissa enter a program for students who had been in a junior high program for students with learning disabilities.

"I said, 'She's not coming out of a program for students with learning disabilities,' and the counselor said, 'Yes, she is,' and I said, 'She's not learning disabled, she's hearing impaired,' and the counselor said, 'What?' That's how I learned she wasn't coded properly. You, as a parent, have no way of knowing how your child is coded unless you check. And you have to check."

When Melissa was tested in ninth grade, Jan learned she had poor short- and long-term memory. To accommodate for that, in high school Melissa focused on only two core subjects at a time, so the material was compacted into a shorter time frame. When final exam time rolled around, instead of having to remember material from September to June, she had to remember only from September to December, and then from January to June.

"High school was definitely the best experience in terms of our relationship with teachers," Jan said. "At this point, they could see she was a hard-working, intelligent girl who had some kind of road-blocks to comprehension."

She was also a dedicated athlete, winning Canadian championships in five-pin bowling both as a team member and an individual. She graduated from high school in 2003, a solid C student. The following fall, she started a job in the purchasing department of an office supply company, doing data entry. Her plan is to save enough money to attend a technical school, though she's not yet sure what she'd like to study.

The years of doing poorly in school brought Jan and Melissa closer, especially the three years in junior high when Melissa came home saying, "I'm stupid. I'm never going to have a good life. I can't pass anything and I can't learn anything."

"Those were the years we really bonded, because we stuck together," Jan said. Adding to Melissa's academic problems was that some of the girls she'd been friends with were becoming cliquey in the way that junior high school girls often do. Melissa still had some friends, but she was already feeling sensitive, and the rejection from her friends didn't help.

"I felt awful, but I wasn't going to let her sink into that 'oh feel sorry for me' stuff, either," Jan said. "I said, 'Look, there are a lot of people in this world who are not academically proficient, and if you don't know what that means, you can look it up. But you don't have to be a university graduate to have a good life. There's lots of people out there who never even went to school that have a good life. You'll have the life that you make for yourself, and if that's in school or that's digging ditches or whatever, you'll be happy.' "

As for Jan, she wishes she'd been better prepared. She's generous and warm and helpful by nature, but I'm convinced part of what's led her to reach out to me and Elizabeth is that she doesn't want others to go blindly down the same path she had to carve out for herself and Melissa.

More than once she's told me, "Being aware of what could possibly be ahead of you puts you light-years ahead of where I was. I had no idea Melissa was going to have problems of this magnitude. I didn't even know where to turn to deal with it. Now that I've been on both sides, as a parent and working in a school, I'd say you have to keep pushing."

Chapter Ten

ADVICE FROM THE TRENCHES

One of the reasons I set out to write this book was to find answers to the questions that had stumped me when Elizabeth was first diagnosed. But it eventually became apparent that understanding how her inner ear worked and the difference between digital and analog hearing aids wasn't enough. What I really wanted to know was: How is the hearing loss going to affect her over the course of her life? Will she be happy? Will she be productive? Will she have good friends? What can I do to make sure everything turns out okay for her?

For those questions, of course, there are no answers. Nobody has them, even when hearing loss isn't involved. So, I decided, if I couldn't predict Elizabeth's future, I'd talk to adults who grew up wearing hearing aids. I'd ask what their parents had done to help or hinder them, and what they wished the hearing people in their lives had understood about hearing loss. Our children will no doubt have different lives than the adults profiled here, but in the absence of a crystal ball, their stories provide helpful insights.

One of the most important things we can do as parents is to help our children develop confidence—it's something we must do regardless of their hearing. I'd like to think I knew that implicitly before I began interviewing hard-of-hearing adults, but they definitely drove that point home. Two that did so with particular clarity were Paige, an assistant professor in the Department of Medicine at the University of Alberta, and Toby, the Toronto TV cameraman.

For every Paige, a social outcast who never had a close friend until she was 12 but who excelled in school, loved books, and read herself to sleep every night, there's a Toby. Toby is a well-liked bundle of energy. He almost failed fifth grade and spent the next three years in special ed classes. Rather than feeling sorry for himself, he took advantage of the smaller classes and caring teachers. Given a chance to phase back into "the regular mainstream" in high school, which he said "was kind of like getting called up to the majors," he opted to stay in special ed for math and English.

On the surface, Toby and Paige appear to have nothing in common except hearing loss. She's a preppy-looking academic with a wall full of advanced degrees, a happy marriage, and a child. He's a 23-year-old barely out of his baggy-pants-and-dyed-hair skateboarding phase, sharing a house with a bunch of other young adults in downtown Toronto.

Yet when I asked both of them, in separate interviews, what advice they'd give parents of newly diagnosed hearing-impaired children, they told me the same thing: "It's not the end of the world."

"It's not something I'd change about myself, really," Toby said. "I don't mind it. It's just who I am. If I'm in loud places, it's hard for me to hear, but it's normal for me. People ask, 'How do you get by? How do you hear?' It's like people who don't see quite as well. You kind of get used to it and move on."

Added Paige, "Those two words, *hearing impaired,* are so tiny, so small, compared to what the mind of a child can do. There is a sense, of course, that the social interaction is missing for those kids, but re-

member, as they go along in life, the people who really care are the
ones who are going to be their friends. If they're born into a family
that really cares about them, and shows their appreciation and is
very patient with them and enjoys their company and their insight
and their input into things, then I think it's very much more likely
that they can go ahead."

Toby was diagnosed with hearing loss just before his second
birthday. His mother, Vicki, took him to the audiologist and to
speech therapy. At home, she labeled everything from cups to doors
to help him expand his minuscule vocabulary.

"I owe so much to my mom," he said. "Only about five or six
years ago did I really realize how hard she worked, how dedicated
she was. It does pay off in the end."

Paige

On a Friday afternoon in late November, Paige sits at her desk, surrounded by scientific articles she needs to read before writing her latest grant proposal. She's a principal investigator in a large research
group studying chronic obstructive pulmonary disease and asthma.
Her specialty is determining how white blood cells called neutrophils
and eosinophils contribute to these and other lung diseases.

Her office is a hub of activity. Emails flash on the computer monitor, which is within easy eyeshot of a framed photo of her husband
and their nine-year-old daughter. When the phone rings, it's her husband, calling to let her know they've been invited to a friend's for
Christmas dinner. Researchers knock on the door periodically, eager
to share news of their latest finds.

"I'm getting to the stage where people are starting to sit up and
notice what I'm doing, and it's just so sweet," she said. "I never expected to go this far with hearing loss."

Paige has a profound sensorineural loss in her left ear and a severe loss in her right. That she has a career she loves and a solid marriage and family life are a testament to her innate intelligence, self-described aggressive personality, and mother who consistently bolstered her self-esteem, giving her confidence so that even when classmates ignored her and made her school years a misery, she knew she had something going for her.

"The thing my mother did was she kept on telling me that I was very bright and very clever," Paige said. "I believed it, and I think that helped."

But that doesn't mean her early years were easy. For Paige, who was born in 1962, they were pretty much a nightmare. Although she was apparently born with normal hearing, by the time she was a year old, her vocabulary had stopped developing. Her parents were separated by then, and her mother bore the responsibility for getting a diagnosis.

The first doctor they visited concluded Paige was either mentally retarded or autistic. She managed to fool nearly every doctor who tested her, either by lip-reading or picking up clues from her mother, on whose lap she sat for every hearing test. It was only when a specialist sent her mother out of the sound booth and covered his mouth during the test that Paige was given an accurate diagnosis. By then she was nearly eight, and she'd been wearing hearing aids for almost five years, although they were probably not appropriately fitted. They made everything louder, which she found overwhelming. She hated them. On more than one occasion she pulled them out of her ears and hurled them across a room. Once she bit into them so hard she left teeth marks in the plastic casing.

Her relationships with peers weren't much better. In day care, she stole vitamins out of the other kids' lunches, and in grade school, she was one rung above the least popular kid in class. In middle school, girls would walk away when they saw her coming. Once she went to someone's house to play, and the girl kept her waiting on the porch for a half hour, finally emerging to announce, "I've got a lot of fish bones stuck in my throat and I just don't feel very good, so I don't want to play right now."

It wasn't until she was 12 and her family moved to New Zealand that Paige finally began making friends. To this day, she thinks it had more to do with the accepting nature of the kids in her adopted country than with any change in her personality.

"They didn't have a problem with eccentricity or odd speech patterns or odd anything," she said. "They thought I had a strong American accent while I was there, and I was just the American kid and that was kind of interesting for them. It was a novelty."

Paige was born in Dallas, Texas, and by the time she moved to New Zealand, she'd also lived in Pasadena, California; Santa Fe, New Mexico; and Philadelphia, Pennsylvania. She never received special services in school because of her hearing loss. There were no FM systems, no itinerant teachers of the deaf and hard of hearing to provide one-on-one tutorials. Often she had trouble following what was being said and where discussions were going. She relied strongly on visual cues and grew to appreciate the loud, clear, and slow speech patterns of her teachers, particularly the ones in the United States.

The teachers, too, recognized her ability. Halfway though kindergarten, the teacher put her into first grade, sensing she was bored and would benefit from learning to read. Paige learned within two weeks, and she loved it.

"I would read until I fell asleep every night, because this was where my information flow was," she said. "The rest of the day, it was kind of patchy, and reading was nice and continuous. It's logical. There are no missing bits, all the words are there. And you can control it."

Her weaknesses were comprehension, understanding new concepts, and retaining information. Math was a consistent problem; she needed help with addition, and one summer she forgot how to do long division. To this day, she considers herself a slow learner and is convinced her hearing loss has something to do with that.

"It's almost like a part of your brain really needs the auditory information to come in to make it work," she said. "When you don't get speech coming in, somehow your ability to process the information through speech is missing. You can read and understand information very well, though, and that's a very good compensatory mechanism. If I were a parent of a hard-of-hearing child, I would spend a lot of time getting my child really quickly up to speed on reading. I'd throw books at her right and left."

Paige's family returned to New Mexico when she was 15. At the time, she was excited, looking forward to returning home. "By this point, I'd forgotten what it was like," she said. "We went back, and within one week, I regretted it. I was in my junior year of high school, and it was just awful. No one wanted to play with me again, and this was a different group of people. The ones who were in class with me before had all gone off to different schools."

When the school year ended, Paige struck a deal with the guidance counselor to finish her credits at a local college. Eventually she moved back to New Zealand, where she graduated from Victoria University and eventually entered the Ph.D. program at the Wellington School of Medicine at the University of Otago. Neither university had an Office of Students with Disabilities, so Paige came up with her own system for success.

"I copied people's notes because I couldn't hear the lecturer and write notes at the same time," she said. "I befriended students in my most charming manner possible, and they were very nice. I never got a no. They were all really helpful."

As a child, Paige avoided telling people she had a hearing loss. Her husband, an engineer she met and married during graduate school, has encouraged her to be more open about it.

"He says people treat me like an idiot otherwise," she admitted.

But what really helped her overcome her sense of shame about her loss was meeting a highly respected European scientist who is going blind.

"When he gives presentations, he has to say, 'Please tell me if the slide is upside down, because I can't tell.' When I told people this story, they thought it was a joke, but it's not. It was like he was giving people a chance to understand his disability. He was letting them into his world, in a sense. When I sat down with him, I said, 'I was amazed at how you could say that without feeling humiliated in front of all those people,' and he said, 'Oh no, you should use it, because not only do they get less confused at why things aren't working the way they think they should, you're helping them to become more patient and understanding. So we become the teachers of other people.' "

Down to earth and realistic, Paige isn't the sort to put a cheerful spin on something just to make it easier to accept. So when she offers her take on the positive aspects of hearing loss, it's hard not to take them seriously. For instance, she said, she experiences a wonderful sense of peace and calm when she removes her hearing aids before going to sleep. And during the waking hours, there are also benefits.

"It opens doors in ways you might not have imagined," she said. "For example, if I walk into a group of people and start talking to a few of them and some of them talk back to me and they're not clear, and I say, 'Listen, I have a hearing loss. I can't understand what you're saying, it's very crowded, and I need you to slow down, face me, and articulate your words,' and they go, 'Oohghhsoxlb,' and walk off. I say to myself, 'There you are. You've just done self-selection. You are not a patient and considerate and compassionate human being.' I wind up going with the patient, compassionate, kind types, because they're the ones that actually face me and speak clearly. I end up gravitating toward the really nice people."

That lesson won't be so obvious to a child at a small school where the pool of potential friends is limited. "As you get older and start working, you can move yourself in directions where the people are better at opening up and being kind to you," Paige said. "What you find as a hearing-impaired person is that gradually, gradually, gradually, you are with a group of people who are wonderful, because they're the people who are making the effort to reach out and communicate."

Toby

If you're convinced that the biggest disadvantage to wearing hearing aids is the stigma, you've probably never worn hearing aids. So before you risk prejudicing your hard-of-hearing child with unfounded worries, consider what Toby—who has worn hearing aids for 21 of his 23 years—has to say: "Sweat is the biggest disadvantage of having hearing aids. Water-resistant aids would be a dream. Waterproof aids would be even better."

Mind you, Toby is an avid athlete who grew up playing just about every sport imaginable and continues to play hockey year round, but sweat is a universal problem, so common that audiology clinics generally carry at least one device to protect equipment from moisture. But Toby has yet to find the ideal product, so when he plays hockey, he wears only one aid. If he misses out on rink chatter, that's fine with him.

"Half the time you don't even want to hear what people are saying," he said. "It doesn't bother me that much."

Not that Toby is a recluse. In fact, he's an outgoing young man who shares a house with ten people and likes going out drinking with his buddies. If he misses out on conversations, he'll ask the speaker to repeat what he's said, up to ten times if necessary, though generally he settles for three.

"My lip-reading isn't that good," he said. "I'm always running into people who mumble or don't move their lips correctly. I live in Toronto, and accents are a tricky business, too. Usually what I do is stick my ear in the speaker's mouth and they usually yell and I usually hear it. It can be bad, but I'm not a big fan of crowded places anyway. I don't go out to loud bars. If anything, the one disadvantage when I go out is that it's hard to hear, but I just go with it, and that's about it. You can't really change much."

It's become something of a cliché to say that life works best if you accept what you can't change and change what you can, but that philosophy seems to have worked for Toby. Consider his early academic career. He was a poor student, though he's reluctant to blame that on his hearing loss. "My brother was the same way, so maybe it was genetic," he reasoned.

Whatever the cause, Toby was a hyperactive boy who would rather have been playing hockey or soccer or riding his bike than sitting quietly at a desk in a classroom. "In grade five, I had a really tough year. I nearly got put back, so I did special ed in grade six, seven, and eight, and it made all the difference for me."

The special ed classes were small, and Toby benefited from the extra attention. Rather than dwelling on the negative and feeling badly about being put in special ed, he focused on learning as much as he could.

"All the special ed teachers were so cool. They were patient and easygoing. That made you want to go to school and go to class and learn more," he said. "By grade seven, I was doing all right, and by the time I got to high school, my grades went up. I think I started trying harder. I think the motivation was realizing that this was when school really counted."

The school board provided Toby with an FM system, which he said he began "getting fed up with" halfway through elementary school. That was understandable; the FM of the era consisted of a box attached to the body with four straps that Toby likened to "a strap-on-bomb-type device." In fifth grade, he received a more modern model with boots that attached to his hearing aids, but by high school he was ready to abandon the system altogether.

"I'd always be sitting at the front, and it became more of a hassle to put it away every night and to get it from every teacher at the end of the class," he said. In college, he opted to forego the FM in favor of sitting in the front of the room.

"I have a moderate-to-severe hearing loss, but I can still hear people pretty good, and if there's no yapping in the class, I can hear fine," he said. "In real life, I'm not going to have an FM. I don't want one and I don't need one, and I'm not going to get one unless I fork over a ton of money."

About a half-dozen kids at Toby's elementary school wore hearing aids, and when he started kindergarten, he was just one of the younger kids with a hearing loss.

"It was kind of accepted throughout the school," he said. "I was never picked on, and by grade seven or eight, it was a normal thing. By high school, everyone grows up, they figure out what hearing aids are, and that's that. I used it to my advantage, if anything, when I was a kid."

The FM system made Toby more attractive to his classmates. By third grade, they'd figured out that if they put their ears up to his, they could hear everything the teacher said when she left the room if she forgot to turn off the microphone, which she generally did.

At a hockey game when he was 16, he used his hearing loss to help his team. "I was mad and I shot the puck after the whistle, and the ref gave me a penalty," he recalled. "I heard my coach yell, 'He can't hear, he can't hear, he wears hearing aids,' and I thought, I have to use this to my advantage. The ref said, 'Can you hear?' and I said, 'No.' Later my coach told me he knew I'd heard the whistle, but he figured it was worth a try. That was the only time I got away with it."

It wasn't, however, the only time someone asked him if he couldn't hear. One summer when he was in his late teens, he worked at a gas station. During rush hour on a busy afternoon when the streets were clogged with noisy traffic, a woman pulled up and asked for 20 dollars worth of gas. The problem was, Toby couldn't understand what kind of gas she wanted. "She was mumbling and she had her radio on," he recalled.

He kept asking her and she kept answering and he kept not understanding. Finally she lost her temper and yelled, "What are you, deaf?"

"As a matter of fact," Toby replied, "I am."

The woman was so embarrassed she drove off without bothering to fill up. Toby and his fellow pump jockeys got a good laugh out of it. "I mean, what else could you do?" he said.

Given the chance to address a group of parents of newly diagnosed hard-of-hearing children, Toby knows exactly what he'd say.

"Be supportive, be patient, be anything a parent would be. Just know your child can do all things. Parents shouldn't feel too bummed or sad or think because their kid has a hearing impairment they won't be able to do anything. I look at myself, and I know a couple of other guys who have hearing aids and are doing quite well for themselves. Anything's possible."

Katy

Katy was born with normal hearing, but a bout of meningitis just before her second birthday left her with no hearing in one ear and a severe-to-profound loss in the other. The family moved from their farm to Omaha, Nebraska, 400 miles away so Katy could get the services she'd need to succeed in school and in life.

Katy's parents were adamant about making sure her hearing loss was recognized, and that with a little help, she could be a normal student. They attended her annual Individualized Education Plan meeting, which allowed them to teach her teachers and the school faculty about the accommodations she would need.

"Sometimes I felt embarrassed that I was being earmarked, but looking back, I realize how much my parents actually helped me by doing the things they did," she said. "In restaurants, I would make them order for me to make it less embarrassing when I couldn't understand the waiter or waitress. But around middle school, they started making me do things myself, which helped me to become more independent with my hearing loss."

Katy was an A student in high school and is a psychology major and captain of her basketball team at a small competitive liberal arts college in the Midwest. Although she has traveled on her own, as far as Japan, college marks the first time she's been away from her parents for an extended period of time. It's made her realize even more strongly that their intervention made social situations easier for her.

Trying to decide when to tell people about her hearing loss and when to keep quiet about it has always been a big issue for Katy. She doesn't like drawing attention to herself because she doesn't want people to see her as different, so usually she keeps quiet and tries to follow what's being said.

But college is teaching her when to speak up for herself. Not long ago, when a class she was taking broke into small discussion groups, the room suddenly filled with distracting background noise. Katy couldn't make out anything that was being said. She asked that her group be allowed to go into the hall, where it was quiet.

Her preferred method, though, is to let people notice her hearing aid. "It may not be the best way, but it's the most comfortable for me."

Another tactic she's now trying is to move to the right of people, situating herself so that her "good" left ear is closer to the sound source. "A lot of my friends have caught on to this and will often help accommodate me and make it easier for me," she said.

"I feel like I have to make the extra effort to make people comfortable, which may be why I don't bring up my hearing right away, because people sometimes get nervous and overarticulate or talk extremely loudly. I generally like to joke about it and talk about it once I get to know people better, to let them know I'm okay with it, and that I'm okay talking about it, so they can feel more comfortable about asking me."

Katy says her hearing loss has forced her to be assertive, but being assertive off the basketball court is not something that comes naturally. There have been many times when she hasn't been able to hear, but has pretended she could.

"In classroom situations, I get frustrated and mad at myself that I don't often have the courage to speak up, but I also feel that maybe I'm not trying hard enough, although this is something I'm getting better at. In conversations with friends, I think I've been doing it for so long I barely realize it anymore. I usually just try to follow as best I can and fill in what I missed, kind of like fill in the blank. The funny thing is, my closest friends realize I do this and they'll stop and say, 'You didn't hear me, did you,' even though I'd been nodding all along. So we laugh about it, and then they fill me in on what I'm missing."

Slowly Katy has been gaining the confidence and developing the comfort level to let people know, when she thinks it's necessary, that she's hard of hearing. "I've come to realize that people don't see you as all that different, because what counts most is your personality."

Katy doesn't remember anyone making fun of her because of her hearing loss when she was growing up, but she does recall people saying that her speech sounded weird. That made her self-conscious about speaking, but she's come to realize that "the more I think about it, the more it hinders me."

The hearing loss also means she has to work harder to succeed in school, which, she said, can be frustrating. It's also painful, she said, in places such as the school lunchroom or a busy restaurant where there is a lot of background noise.

But Katy comes from a family that tends to dwell on the positive, and over the years, her hearing loss has provided a surprising number of opportunities for a good laugh. When she was a child and her parents got mad at her, she knew she'd get a smile if she turned off her aid so she didn't have to listen to them yelling. Once, in a basketball game, she scored two points after her hearing aid tumbled to the floor and everyone in the gym thought her ear had fallen off.

"The ref didn't know what to do, so he just stood there along with everyone else, and I dribbled in for a wide open lay-up."

Living with hearing loss has taught Katy to laugh instead of mope when things don't go her way. "I can turn awkward situations into funny ones by making a joke about it. It's not disrespectful or anything, but I really feel like there is a lot of humor to be found in my hearing loss. And when I think of how much worse it could have been, with meningitis cases killing kids or causing them to be deaf and blind, I realize how lucky I am."

David

David, who is a math professor at Howard University in Washington, D.C., lost his hearing after contracting meningitis. His diagnosis: profound bilateral hearing loss. But because he could detect some low frequencies in his left ear, his parents had him fitted with a hearing aid. It was 1955 and David was almost five years old. Hearing aids weren't nearly as sleek and sophisticated as they are today. David had to wear a "box" strapped to his chest. A wire connected the box to an earmold and receiver.

"I refused to wear it until my mother took me around to several families on our block in Chicago and had me show them my new device," he recalled. "They cheered and congratulated me on having it. This made it, if nothing else, a symbol of my ties to the community and motivated me to wear it faithfully. Wearing it pretty much all my waking hours for the next several years gave me a chance to learn to use my amplified residual hearing. Ever since, I've worn a hearing aid because it's so much less difficult to understand people when I do."

Understanding is David's biggest challenge, what he considers the greatest drawback to hearing loss. "It takes a lot of work and often can't be done anyway. I can't hear my children talking to each other. Foreign languages, even ones I can read and write, are impossible for me to speak or understand when spoken. One of my brothers is a professional actor. I can appreciate his body language, but not his voice. Deafness *is* a negative thing that cuts me off from a lot of good stuff."

It also had a direct effect on his siblings, all but one of whom were born after David lost his hearing. "Each of them learned how to speak to me while learning how to speak in the first place, and each became consciously aware, at about age four, that my hearing was limited."

David doesn't think his siblings resented his hearing loss, but he also doesn't deny that it greatly shaped his early relationship with the brother who is closest to his age. Two years old when David became deaf, "he surely did not get as much of our parents' attention as he should have because they were distracted by my crisis, which shadows his earliest memories," David recalled.

The two attended a Catholic elementary school in a rough neighborhood far from theirs, the only school that was willing to accommodate David's disability. "He knew I wasn't aware of many things because I couldn't hear them happening or developing, and he felt responsible for me. That was a serious burden at such a young age. But for all the others, I was a revered big brother."

It wasn't until he was seven or eight that David was able to understand people to a useful degree, and only if they were speaking directly to him, facing him, and standing in good light in a place without too much background noise. He also had to give them his full attention.

"Even then I can fail to understand," he said, "but under such circumstances, it's usually pretty evident from my responses whether I'm getting it or not."

A bigger problem is that people don't and often can't realize that what they're saying directly to him is all he can understand, that he doesn't hear the many other things normal-hearing people do.

"I don't hear what people across the dinner table from me say to each other. I don't overhear. I don't hear things addressed to the group in general, unless I happen to be in the right location at the right time, so it's as if they were addressed directly to me," he said. "I seldom even hear my name called if someone's trying to get my attention. Normal-hearing people hear these things and much more, a lot of which I'm probably not even aware of. They take what they hear for granted, and assume that I do, too—an assumption so unconscious that the conscious knowledge that I'm deaf often does not affect it. Indeed, since people with normal hearing are *always* hearing sounds—ears can't be closed the way eyes can—the very concept of *not* hearing, deafness, can be quite hard to imagine in any concrete, useful way."

Telling people about his hearing loss isn't an issue for David; if they don't notice his hearing aid, they can usually tell because it's obvious he isn't following the conversation. The bigger issue is whether to call special attention to it. In general, he does that only when he needs accommodations—for example, taking a particular seat at a lunch table or in a lecture hall so that he can lip-read.

He tells his students at the first class meeting, right after announcing his office location and hours and exam and grading policies. "I inform the class that I'm deaf, I lip-read, and I don't hear my name called so that to ask questions they must raise their hands," he said.

For most students, and most people in general, he said, his deafness is "strictly a practical matter. They just want me to be able to communicate with them reasonably and effectively, to understand the questions they ask and answer them usefully and without too much unusual effort."

Raising hands in class is acceptable; having to write out questions probably wouldn't be, he said.

Several times during his teaching career, students have tried to blame their failing grades on David's deafness. It's never worked. "Since other students in the same classes, not to mention the students in my other classes, had no such problems, the departmental chair— and it was a different one each time, as I recall—was completely unsympathetic to the complaining students."

Having a teacher who can't hear you whisper and whose insistence that you remain quiet during lectures and raise a hand before speaking can also prove to be motivating, as it did for at least one of David's students. "After struggling very hard but managing to get an A in the end, he came to my office and said, 'I knew you learned that stuff without even being able to hear it. I could hear it. I had no excuse not to learn it.'"

It would be nice, David said, if more people understood what he calls "the ambiguity of damaged or absent hearing, how it cannot be overcome by simply increasing the volume, how it imposes something analogous to foggy tunnel vision, but also how, if you've lived with it for a long time, you've probably learned to deal with it."

David sometimes encounters people who are more sensitive to hearing loss, who seem to genuinely understand how he misses much of what the hearing world hears. "Some of these people fear that I suffer over it, such as by feeling left out," he said. "In fact, I feel I'm living quite a satisfactory life with what I do get. The glass is, so to speak, one-quarter full rather than three-quarters empty."

AFTERWORD

In the five-and-a-half years since Elizabeth began wearing hearing aids, our family life has changed more than I could have imagined. I realize the same can be said by any parent over the course of five years, regardless of his or her child's hearing. But what's taken me by surprise is that as I was learning more about pediatric hearing loss and how to help children and families affected by it, my daily responsibilities regarding Elizabeth's hearing were diminishing.

No longer do I have to remove her hearing aids every night and clean and test them in the morning. She takes them off before bed and in the morning puts them in, usually before I have a chance to do it. When her batteries die, she changes them. When her ears feel waxy, she wipes them with a damp cloth.

The same won't necessarily hold true for every child; some become independent earlier, while those for whom hearing loss is part of a larger spectrum of health problems may never become fully independent. Regardless of your child's situation, though, the one thing you can count on is that nothing will remain static.

What Jack and I hope we've done here is provide you with a useful introduction to the world of hearing loss in children. As your child grows, needs will change and, as a result, so will your responsibilities. There will be pieces you'll still have to put together, but as we've shown here, there are many people and organizations to help you along the way. We wish you the best in this journey.

GLOSSARY

Acute otitis media: An infection of the middle ear that often includes pain, fever, and conductive hearing loss.

Air conduction pathway: The transmission of sound through the outer and middle ear to the cochlea.

Air conduction threshold: The hearing threshold for a pure-tone delivered from an earphone or insert receiver.

Amplification: An increase in the intensity (loudness) of sounds provided by a hearing aid.

Analog: A type of hearing aid that provides amplification by continuous changes in sound processing.

Audiogram: Graphic representation of hearing thresholds plotted on a chart to show the softest sound a person can detect at various frequencies from low pitch to high pitch.

Audiologist: A health care professional whose practices include prevention, evaluation, and rehabilitation of hearing impairment and related communication disorders.

Auditory brainstem responses (ABR): Neurological responses produced by the auditory nerve and brainstem in response to sound. Audiologists measure ABRs to screen for hearing loss, estimate hearing threshold levels, and evaluate auditory processing.

Auditory neuropathy: A term used to describe a pattern of symptoms in which behavioral or ABR measures suggest significant hearing loss while measures of cochlear function such as otoacoustic emissions appear normal.

Auditory processing disorder: A disorder of auditory processing resulting from disease, trauma, or abnormal development of the auditory system.

Behavioral hearing tests: Assessment procedures that involve observable responses to sound.

Binaural hearing: Hearing with both ears.

Bilateral hearing loss: Reduction of hearing sensitivity in both ears.

Bone conduction: A hearing test that involves transmitting sound to the inner ear via a small vibrator applied to the skull.

Bone conduction threshold: The threshold of hearing sensitivity to pure-tones delivered from a bone-conduction vibrator.

Cerumen: Substance secreted from glands in the ear canal, commonly referred to as ear wax.

Cochlea: Auditory portion of the inner ear, consisting of fluid-filled channels containing hair cell receptors.

Cochlear implant: A device consisting of an electrode array surgically implanted in the cochlea. It delivers electrical signals to the auditory nerve from an external processor, enabling people with severe to profound hearing loss to perceive sound.

Conductive hearing loss: Reduction in hearing sensitivity due to reduced sound transmission because of abnormality in the external ear canal, ear drum, or middle ear.

Digital: A type of hearing aid that provides amplification by changing the incoming sound into streams of data.

Ear infection: *See* acute otitis media.

Earmold: A custom-fitted device to deliver sound from a behind-the-ear hearing aid into the ear canal. It also helps to hold the hearing aid in place.

Eustachian tube: The passageway leading from the throat to the anterior wall of the middle ear, which opens during yawning and swallowing to equalize middle-ear air pressure.

Frequency: Also known as Hertz (Hz), it is the number of cycles occurring in one second. It corresponds to a listener's perception of pitch.

Hair cells: Sensory cells in the inner ear where nerve endings attach to the auditory nerve.

Hearing Level (HL): The decibel level of sound as it relates to normal hearing.

Masking noise: Sound used by an audiologist to prevent one ear from hearing while the other is being tested.

Meningitis: A bacterial or viral inflammation that can cause auditory disorders due to infection or inflammation of the inner ear or auditory nerve.

Mixed hearing loss: Hearing loss with both conductive and sensorineural components.

Objective test procedure: Measurement of hearing sensitivity based on predictions made from physiologic responses such as ABR. The child's participation is not required.

Otitis externa: Inflammation of the ear canal. It may be accompanied by pain, swelling, and secretions.

Otitis media (OM): Inflammation of the middle ear.

Otitis media with effusion (OME): Inflammation of the middle ear with an accumulation of fluid behind the eardrum in the middle-ear space.

Otoacoustic emissions (OAE): Low-level sounds produced by the cochlea and used by audiologists as a test of inner ear (cochlear) function.

Otolaryngologist: Physician who specializes in the diagnosis and treatment of diseases of the ear, nose, and throat, including related diseases affecting the head and neck.

Otorrhea: Any substance discharged from the external ear.

Otoscope: A device that provides light and magnification for visual examination of the ear canal and ear drum.

Ototoxic: Medications potentially harmful to the auditory system.

Recessive genetic condition: Inherited condition in which both parents carry an abnormal gene. For each pregnancy there is a 25 percent chance of the baby being affected.

Pure tone: A single frequency used by audiologists to evaluate hearing sensitivity.

Pure tone audiometer: An instrument for presenting pure tone sounds of different frequencies.

Pure tone air conduction audiometry: Measurement of hearing thresholds to pure tones presented through earphones or insert receivers.

Pure tone bone conduction audiometry: Measurement of hearing thresholds to pure tones presented from a small vibrator placed against the skull.

Pure tone screening: Test used to determine hearing sensitivity to pure tones at a fixed hearing level, typically 20dB HL.

Pure tone threshold audiometry: Determination of lowest level a pure tone can be detected about 50 percent of the time.

Residual hearing: The amount of functional hearing available to a person with a sensorineural hearing loss.

Rubella: A viral infection characterized by fever and a skin rash resembling measles; may result in abnormalities in the unborn child, including sensorineural hearing loss (also known as German measles).

Sensorineural hearing loss: Loss of hearing sensitivity due to disorders involving the cochlea and/or the auditory nerve.

Serous otitis media: Inflammation of the middle ear with an accumulation of thin, watery (serous) fluid.

Signal-to-noise ratio: The relationship of a primary signal to the level of background noise. People with hearing loss need a better signal-to-noise ratio than people with normal hearing.

Sound bore: A channel through the earmold where sound is received from the hearing aid and delivered to the ear canal.

Speech-language pathologist: Health care professional whose professional practice includes evaluation, rehabilitation, and prevention of speech and language disorders.

Threshold: In audiometry, the softest sounds (usually pure tones or speech) a person can detect.

Tympanic membrane: A thin membrane at the end of the ear canal that vibrates in response to incoming sounds, which are then transmitted to the middle and inner ear.

Tympanogram: Graph that shows how well the eardrum and middle ear respond to sound; can be used to identify middle ear disorders that require medical attention.

Tympanometer: Instrument used to screen for middle-ear disorders such as otitis media.

Tympanostomy tube: Small tube inserted in the tympanic membrane to equalize air pressure in the middle ear; also known as a pressure equalization tube.

Unilateral hearing loss: Loss of hearing sensitivity in one ear only.

RESOURCES

AAP "Champion" Screening Initiative:
The American Academy of Pediatrics' screening initiative is designed to improve the quality of newborn hearing screening, diagnosis, and intervention programs by increasing the appropriate involvement of primary care pediatricians and other physicians who care for children and by linking follow-up services more closely to the newborn's medical home, as defined by the Joint Committee on Infant Hearing.

The American Academy of Pediatrics
141 Northwest Point Boulevard
Elk Grove Village, Illinois 60007–1098
1-847-434-4000
www.aap.org/new/univnewhearscreen.htm

Alexander Graham Bell Association for the Deaf and Hard of Hearing, Inc. (A.G. Bell):
The Alexander Graham Bell Association for the Deaf and Hard of Hearing is one of the world's largest membership organizations and information centers on hearing loss and the auditory approach. AG Bell promotes the use of spoken lan-

guage by children and adults with hearing loss. Through advocacy, publications, financial aid and scholarships, and numerous programs and services, AG Bell promotes its mission: advocating independence through listening and talking.

3417 Volta Place, NW
Washington, DC 20007
1-866-337-5220
www.agbell.org

American Academy of Audiology (AAA):

With more than 8,900 members, the AAA is the world's largest professional organization of, for, and by audiologists. The AAA promotes quality hearing and balance as care for adults and children by advancing the profession of audiology through leadership, advocacy, education, public awareness, and support of research.

11730 Plaza America Drive, Suite 300
Reston, Virginia 20190
1-800-AAA-2336
www.audiology.org

American Academy of Otolaryngology-Head and Neck Surgery:

The academy represents more than 10,000 otolaryngologist-head and neck surgeons who diagnose and treat disorders of the ears, nose, throat, and related structures of the head and neck.

One Prince Street
Alexandria, Virginia 22314–3357
1-703-836-4444
www.entnet.org

American Association of the Deaf-Blind (AADB):

AADB is a national consumer advocacy organization for people who have combined hearing and vision impairments.

345 North Monmouth Avenue
Monmouth, Oregon 97361
1-800-438-9376
http://www.tr.wou.edu/dblink/index2.htm

American Society for Deaf Children (ASDC):
ASDC's primary mission is to advocate for the highest quality programs and services for parents so they are able to make informed choices to meet their children's educational, communication, personal, and social needs.

American Society for Deaf Children
P.O. Box 3355
Gettysburg, Pennsylvania 17325
1-800-942-ASDC (Parent Hotline)
www.deafchildren.org

American Speech-Language-Hearing Association (ASHA):
ASHA's mission is to ensure that all people with speech, language, and hearing disorders have access to quality services to help them communicate more effectively. ASHA's website also contains a directory of audiologists and speech pathologists.

10801 Rockville Pike
Rockville, Maryland 20852
1-800-638-8255
www.asha.org

Auditory-Verbal International, Inc. (AVI):
AVI is a private, nonprofit international membership organization whose principal objective is to promote listening and speaking as a way of life for children who are deaf or hard of hearing. AVI's goals are to heighten public awareness of the auditory-verbal approach, ensure certification standards for auditory-verbal clinicians and teachers, provide quality educational opportunities for parents and professionals, and facilitate networking among the professional and lay communities.

2121 Eisenhower Avenue, Suite 402
Alexandria, Virginia 22314
1-703-739-1049
www.auditory-verbal.org

BEGINNINGS for Parents of Children Who Are Deaf or Hard of Hearing, Inc.:
BEGINNINGS was established in 1987 to provide emotional support and access to information for families with deaf or hard-of-hearing children, from birth through age 21. The organization provides an impartial approach to meeting the diverse needs of these families and the professionals who serve them. (Services are also available to deaf parents who have hearing children.) The mission of BEGINNINGS is to help parents be informed, empowered, and supported as they make decisions about their child. The BEGINNINGS website, which serves families and professionals, includes topics such as early intervention, communication options, audiology and assistive technology, and school issues.

P.O. Box 17646
Raleigh, North Carolina 27619
1-919-850-2746
www.beginningssvcs.com

Canadian Academy of Audiology:
The Canadian Academy of Audiology is a professional organization dedicated to enhancing the profession of audiology, and providing quality hearing health care and education to those with, or at risk for, hearing and/or vestibular disorders. The Academy further strives to represent the audiological community on relevant national issues in a timely, organized manner.

250 Consumers Road, Suite 301
Toronto, Ontario M2J 4V6
1-416-494-6672 / 1-800-264-5106
www.canadianaudiology.ca

Canadian Association of Speech Language Pathologists and Audiologists (CASLPA):
With over 4,600 members, CASLPA is the single national body that supports the needs, interests, and development of speech-language pathologists and audiologists across Canada.

401 – 200 Elgin Street
Ottawa, Ontario K2P IL5
1-613-567-9968
www.caslpa.ca/english/index.asp

The Canadian Hard-of-Hearing Association (CHHA):
CHHA is a consumer-based organization formed in 1982 by and for hard-of-hearing Canadians. CHHA works cooperatively with professionals, service providers, and government bodies, and provides information about hard-of-hearing issues and solutions. CHHA is the national voice of hard-of-hearing Canadians. It provides a vehicle for hard-of-hearing and deafened people to make their needs known and to work at ensuring that those needs are identified and addressed. The philosophy of CHHA is to produce knowledgeable hard-of-hearing consumers who understand how to have their needs met. Its mission is to raise public awareness concerning issues that are important for persons who are hard of hearing, to promote their integration in Canadian society, to remove any barriers to their participation, and to generally make every community in Canada a better place for persons who are hard of hearing.

2435 Holly Lane
Suite 205
Ottawa, Ontario K1V 7P2
1-613-526-1584
www.chha.ca

The Canadian Hearing Society:
The Canadian Hearing Society provides services that enhance the independence of deaf, deafened, and hard-of-hearing people, and that encourage prevention of hearing loss.

271 Spadina Road
Toronto, Ontario M5R 2V3
1-416-928-2500
www.chs.ca

Captioned Media Program:
This free-loan media and open-captioned program is funded by the U.S. Department of Education. Deaf and hard-of-hearing persons, teachers, parents, and others may borrow materials without having to pay rental, postage, or registration fees. Other services include free information about captioning and assistance to captioning companies on request.

Captioned Media Program
National Association of the Deaf
1447 East Main Street
Spartanburg, South Carolina 29307
1-800-237-6213
www.cfv.org

Center for Hearing Loss in Children, Boys Town National Research Hospital:
The Boys Town National Research Hospital is a nationally oriented clinical and research facility dedicated to the study and treatment of children's communication disorders. The efforts of the hospital's multidisciplinary staff are closely coordinated with the programs of the Center for Hearing Loss in Children.

Boys Town National Research Hospital
555 North Thirtieth Street
Omaha, Nebraska 68131
1-402-498-6615
www.boystownhospital.org/parents/info/index.asp

Cochlear Implant Association, Inc. (CIAI):

Formerly Cochlear Implant Club International, Inc., CIAI is a nonprofit organization for cochlear implant recipients, their families, professionals, and other individuals interested in cochlear implants. CIAI provides support, information, and access to local support groups for adults and children who have cochlear implants, or who are interested in learning about cochlear implants. CIAI also advocates for the rights of and services for people with hearing loss.

5335 Wisconsin Avenue, NW
Suite 440
Washington, DC 20015–2052
1-202-895-2781
www.cici.org

Council for Exceptional Children: (CEC)

The Council for Exceptional Children (CEC) is an international professional organization dedicated to improving educational outcomes for individuals including students with disabilities, and/or the gifted. CEC advocates for appropriate governmental policies, sets professional standards, provides continual professional development, advocates for newly and historically underserved individuals, and helps professionals obtain conditions and resources necessary for effective professional practice.

1110 North Glebe Road
Suite 300
Arlington, Virginia 22201–5704
Toll-free: 1-888-CEC-SPED
Local: 1-703-620-3660
TTY: 1-866-915-5000 (text only)
Fax: 1-703-264-9494

CEC Canada (CCEC)
Box 56012
Stoney Creek, Ontario L8G 5C9
Phone and Fax: 1-204-452-1985
www.cec.sped.org

Deafness Research Foundation (DRF):
DRF is the leading source of private funding for basic and clinical research in hearing science. The DRF is committed to making lifelong hearing health a national priority by funding research and implementing education projects in both the government and private sectors.

1050 Seventeenth Street, NW
Suite 701
Washington, DC 20036
1-202-289-5850
www.drf.org

The Deaf Resource Library:
The Deaf Resource Library is a virtual library, an online collection of reference material and links intended to educate and inform people about deaf cultures in Japan and the United States, as well as deaf and hard-of-hearing related topics.

www.deaflibrary.org

Early Listening Function (ELF) and Children's Home Inventory of Listening Difficulties (CHILD):
These are two separate "functional assessment" tools that help parents and caretakers systematically observe a hard-of-hearing child in typical daily situations to better understand the implications of hearing loss and the importance of amplification. Both tools, which are documents designed to be filled in by parents or caretakers, were developed by audiologist Karen Anderson and can be downloaded in PDF form. www.phonak.com/professional/pediatrics/diagnostic.htm

EDEN, the Electronic Deaf Education Network:
A comprehensive and informative website developed and maintained by Brad Ingrao, an audiologist whose son is deaf. EDEN offers parents support, ideas, and information from a variety of sources with a wealth of knowledge about how to help children who are hard of hearing or deaf. The website also has a chat room and a library.

www.info@bradingrao.com

Educational Audiology Association (EAA):

The EAA is an international organization of audiologists and related professionals who deliver a full spectrum of hearing services to all children, particularly those in educational settings. The mission of EAA is to act as the primary resource and active advocate for its members through its publications and products, continuing educational activities, networking opportunities, and other professional endeavors.

13153 North Dale Mabry Highway
Suite 105
Tampa, Florida 33618
1-800-460-7322
www.edaud.org

Hands and Voices:

Hands and Voices is a parent-driven, nonprofit organization dedicated to providing unbiased support to families with children who are deaf or hard of hearing. This organization provides support activities and information concerning deaf and hard-of-hearing issues to parents and professionals that may include outreach events, educational seminars, advocacy, lobbying efforts, parent-to-parent networking, and a newsletter. Hands and Voices also strives to connect families with resources and information to make informed decisions around the issues of deafness or hearing loss.

P.O. Box 371926
Denver, Colorado 80237
1-303-300-9763
www.handsandvoices.org

Hearing Ear Dogs of Canada:

The Lions Foundation of Canada trains dog guides to meet the needs of Canadians with hearing and other medically and physically limiting disabilities. All programs are offered at no charge to the client, but future care and maintenance become the responsibility of the guide dog recipient.

P.O. Box 907
Oakville, Ontario L6J 5E8
1-905-842-2891
www.dogguides.com/programs/programs03.htm

The Hearing Exchange:

The Hearing Exchange is an online community for exchanging ideas and information on hearing loss. This site is a useful tool for parents of a child who is hard of hearing or deaf, or for a professional who works with hard-of-hearing children or adults. No matter what method of communication the family has chosen, they will likely find interesting and supportive information at this site.

P.O. Box 689
Jericho, New York 11753
1-516-938-5475
www.hearingexchange.com

The Hearing Foundation of Canada:

The Hearing Foundation of Canada is a national charitable organization established in 1979 and led by a volunteer board of directors drawn from the business and medical communities, many of whom have personal experience with hearing loss. This organization is committed to eliminating the devastating effects of hearing loss on the quality of life of Canadians, particularly youth, by promoting prevention, early diagnosis, leading-edge medical research, and successful intervention.

330 Bay Street
Suite 1402
Toronto, Ontario M5H 2S8
1-416-364-4060
www.hearingfoundation.ca

International Hearing Society (IHS):

IHS is the nonprofit, professional association that represents hearing instrument specialists in the United States, Canada, Japan, and several other countries. IHS advocates and supports the highest standard of professional competency, business integrity, and excellence in serving the hearing impaired.

16880 Middlebelt Road
Livonia, Michigan 48154
1-734-522-7200
www.ihsinfo.org

John Tracy Clinic:

John Tracy Clinic provides, worldwide and without charge, parent-centered services to foster communication skills in young children with a hearing loss. The clinic also offers services to help the professional community understand how to work with deaf children. This site has a useful and informative FAQ page.

806 West Adams Boulevard
Los Angeles, California 90007
1-213-748-5481
www.johntracyclinic.org

The Listen Foundation:

The Listen Foundation has supported families who would otherwise not have access to the equipment and therapy that their children need in order to become listening, speaking adults, enabling them to reach their full potential as productive members of society.

6950 East Belleview Avenue, #102
Englewood, Colorado 80111
1-303-781-9440
www.listenfoundation.org

Listen-Up:

Listen-Up provides information, answers, help, ideas, and resources related to hearing loss. Whether you're interested in auditory processing or buying a special alarm clock, the site will point you in the right direction. The web master has dedicated years to gathering information and developing products geared to the special needs of hearing-impaired children and their families, and professionals who serve them.

www.listen-up.org/index.htm

Marion Downs National Center for Infant Hearing:

The Marion Downs National Center for Infant Hearing at the University of Colorado at Boulder is a center for coordinating statewide systems for screening, diagnosis, and intervention for newborns and infants with hearing loss.

Marion Downs Center
University of Colorado at Boulder
Department of Speech, Language, and Hearing Science
Campus Box 409
Boulder, Colorado 80309–0409
www.colorado.edu/slhs/mdnc/

My Baby's Hearing: (www.babyhearing.org)

Boys Town National Research Hospital formed this website as an informative resource for parents of babies with hearing loss, but it provides a wealth of information for caregivers of infants with hearing loss as well. Not only does this website teach about the ear and how it works, it also describes different types of hearing loss a baby may have and discusses causes for these hearing losses. It answers many questions about the various styles of hearing aids and assistive devices available for young children today. There is a small section that discusses cochlear implants as an option for some babies with hearing loss. This website teaches parents what type of testing to expect for their child in future months and years. The website also helps parents read and understand the audiogram.

Boys Town National Research Hospital
555 North Thirtieth Street
Omaha, Nebraska 68131
1-402-498-6615
www.babyhearing.org

National Association of the Deaf (NAD):

NAD, established in 1880, is the oldest and largest constituency organization safeguarding the accessibility and civil rights of 28 million deaf and hard-of-hearing Americans in education, employment, health care, and telecommunications.

814 Thayer Avenue
Silver Spring, Maryland 20910–4500

1-301-587-1788

www.nad.org

National Center for Hearing Assessment and Management (NCHAM):
The NCHAM site contains a wealth of information and resources concerning the many dimensions of early hearing detection and intervention, including resources available in each state.

National Center for Hearing Assessment and Management (NCHAM)

Utah State University

2880 Old Main Hill

Logan, Utah 84322

1-435-797-3584

www.infanthearing.org

National Centre for Audiology, Canada (NCA):
NCA is one of Canada's preeminent centers of excellence in the field of hearing health care and houses Canada's largest educational and research programs in the field. NCA's responsibilities include continuing education and technical assistance for audiologists; research on hearing and hearing instruments; state-of-the-art clinical services; consultation with government agencies; professional and consumer associations; and other agencies to improve hearing health care services and public education about hearing and hearing loss; and dissemination of knowledge about hearing loss and its prevention and treatment.

National Centre for Audiology

Room 2262

Elborn College, University of Western Ontario

1201 Western Road

London, Ontario N6G 1H1

1-519-661-3901

www.uwo.ca/nca/

National Cued Speech Organization:

The National Cued Speech Association is a nonprofit membership organization founded in 1982 to promote and support the effective use of cued speech. This organization raises awareness of cued speech and its applications, provides educational services, assists local affiliate chapters, standards for cued speech, and certifies cued speech instructors and transliterators.

Ascension Parish School
10525 Buxton Road
St. Amant, Louisiana 70774
www.cuedspeech.org

National Deaf Education Network and Clearinghouse:

Gallaudet University's Laurent Clerc National Deaf Education Center shares the concerns of parents and professionals about the achievement of deaf and hard-of-hearing students in different learning environments across the country. The Clerc Center has been mandated by Congress to develop, evaluate, and disseminate innovative curricula, instructional techniques and strategies, and materials. The aim of the Clerc Center is to improve the quality of education for deaf and hard-of-hearing children and youth from birth through age 21.

Laurent Clerc National Deaf Education Center
Gallaudet University
800 Florida Avenue, NE
Washington, DC 20002
1-202-651-5226
http://clerccenter.gallaudet.edu

National Early Childhood Technical Assistance Center (NECTAC):

The NECTAC website supports the implementation of the early childhood provisions of the Individuals with Disabilities Education Act. This technical assistance focuses on early childhood research, "best practices," and policy and legal issues. The mission of the center is to strengthen service systems to ensure that children with disabilities (birth to age five) and their families receive and benefit from high-quality, culturally appropriate, and family-centered supports and services. Through the website, the knowledge base of early intervention and early childhood special education is made available in a variety of formats.

NECTAC
Campus Box 8040, UNC-CH
Chapel Hill, North Carolina 27599–8040
1-919-962-2001
www.nectac.org

National Institute on Deafness and Other Communication Disorders (NIDCD):
The NIDCD sponsors research on disorders of human communication, including hearing, balance, smell, taste, voice, speech, and language. This interactive site includes a nice section for teachers and children.

31 Center Drive, MSC 2320
Bethesda, Maryland 20892–2320
1-301-496-7243
www.nidcd.nih.gov

Oral Deaf Education:
This organization is dedicated to helping deaf children learn to talk. The new technology available today through modern hearing aids and cochlear implants provides enough access to sound that, with appropriate instruction at Oral Deaf Education Schools, most deaf children can learn to talk.

www.oraldeafed.org

Parents of Deaf /Hard-of-Hearing Children
Parents of Deaf HH is a listserv of parents of deaf and hard-of-hearing children. This online support group is a useful tool for parents who have questions or need encouragement while raising their deaf or hard-of-hearing child.

PARENTDEAF-HH@LISTSERV.KENT.EDU

Raising Deaf Kids:
The Children's Hospital of Philadelphia formed this website as a resource for parents and caregivers of children who are hard of hearing or deaf. This

website, which can also be viewed in Spanish, answers questions about hearing loss, gives excellent communication tips, and aids parents in making communication decisions. It also contains links to a number of resources (organizations, books, and websites) that may be useful to parents or caregivers of children with hearing loss.

Deafness and Family Communication Center
The Children's Hospital of Philadelphia
3535 Market Street, Ninth floor
Philadelphia, Pennsylvania 19104
1-215-590-7440
www.raisingdeafkids.org

SEE Center for the Advancement of Deaf Children:

The SEE Center is a nonprofit organization that works with parents and educators of deaf and hard-of-hearing children. The center promotes early identification and intervention and provides information about and workshops on the use of the sign language system Signing Exact English.

P.O. Box 1181
Los Alamitos, California 90720
1-562-795-6614
www.seecenter.org

Self Help for Hard of Hearing People (SHHH):

SHHH is the United States' largest organization for people with hearing loss. It exists to open the world of communication for people with hearing loss through information, education, advocacy, and support. Their website contains information about state and local SHHH chapters in the United States.

www.shhh.org

Ski-Hi Institute:

The Ski-Hi Institute is a group of parents and professionals whose goal is to enhance the lives of young children with special needs and their families. Many programs have been developed at the Ski-Hi Institute for children who are deaf/hard of hearing, blind/visually impaired, deaf-blind, multi-disabled, or have any special needs.

6500 Old Main Hill
Logan, Utah 84322–6500
1-435-797-5600
www.coe.usu.edu/skihi

The Society for the Educational Advancement of the Hearing Impaired (SEAHI):
SEAHI is an Alberta-based society of parents with deaf and hard-of-hearing children. The aim of this organization is to inform other parents and be informed about communication and educational issues for English-based methods of communication.

12310 105 Avenue
Edmonton, Alberta T5N 0Y4
1-780-717-0419
www.seahi.org/SEAHI

"Speaking for Myself." in English and Spanish by the Oberkotter Foundation:
This program promotes spoken language. The foundation's website offers specific information about oral-deaf schools and their programs and services. The foundation's library, which is accessible through the website, provides more general information on oral deaf education.

www.oraldeafed.org

Strategies for Teaching Children:
This website, part of the West Virginia University website, introduces strategies for teaching children with hearing impairments.

www.as.wvu.edu/~scidis/hearing.html

VOICE for Hearing-Impaired Children:
The mission of this organization is to ensure that all hearing-impaired children have the right to develop their ability to listen and speak and have access to services that will enable them to listen and speak. VOICE is based

in Toronto, Canada, and assists in making effective decisions by providing information regarding the available choices and the ongoing support required for these choices. VOICE promotes parental choice regarding communicative approaches for deaf children with the auditory-verbal approach as the first option. Their website provides a forum for parents to discuss their individual concerns and support one another.

161 Eglinton Avenue East
Suite 701
Toronto, Ontario M4P 1J5
1-416-487-7719
http://voicefordeafkids.com

Where Do We Go From Hear?:
This site was created by a mother of a severely deaf child to provide information for families of infants and children diagnosed with a hearing loss and the professionals who work with these individuals.

www.gohear.org

Wrightslaw:
This website is an excellent resource for accurate, up-to-date information about special education law and advocacy for children with special needs. It was developed and is maintained by Pete and Pam Wright. He's a lawyer who represents children with special needs and she's a psychotherapist. They have co-written advocacy books and resources including *Wrightslaw: From Emotions to Advocacy—The Special Education Survival Guide (2002),* published by Harbor House Law Press.

www.wrightslaw.com

RECOMMENDED READINGS

It's not always easy to find books about hearing loss in children. Local bookstores may carry one or two titles, but I've found that the best place to look is the A.G. Bell website (www.agbell.org). (The address is listed in the Resources section.) The following list, while by no means comprehensive, includes books that some of my parenting friends and I have found particularly helpful.

Candlish, Patricia Ann Morgan, M.L.S. *Not Deaf Enough: Raising a Child Who Is Hard of Hearing with Hugs, Humor, and Imagination.* Washington, DC: Alexander Graham Bell Association for the Deaf and Hard of Hearing, Inc., 1996.

Davis, Julia M., Ph.D., ed. *Our Forgotten Children: Hard of Hearing Pupils in the Schools.* Third ed. Bethesda, MD: Self Help for Hard of Hearing People Publications, 2001.

Luterman, D., and Ross, M. *When Your Child Is Deaf: A Guide for Parents.* Baltimore: York Press, 1991.

Schwartz, Sue, Ph.D., *Choices in Deafness: A Parents' Guide to Communication Options.* Bethesda, MD: Woodbine House, 1996.

Tucker, Bonnie Poitras, J.D., *Idea Advocacy for Children Who Are Deaf or Hard of Hearing*. San Diego: Singular Publishing Group, Inc., 1997.

Wayner, D. S., Ph.D., and E. I. Rupert, M.Ed. *Voices from a Quieter Land: Insights Into the Impact of Hearing Impairment*. Austin, TX: Hear Again, 2001.

Wayner, Donna S., Ph.D., *Hearing and Learning: A Guide for Helping Children*. Austin, TX: Hear Again, 2001.

Wright, P., and Wright, M., *Wrightslaw: From Emotions to Advocacy—The Special Education Survival Guide*. Hatfield, VA: Harbor House Law Press, 2002.

INDEX

career options limited by, 107
child going through phase toward, 156
child tired from, 90–91
child's behavior and, 5–6, 11–12, 90
cochlear implants for, xvi, 68
common experience of, 24–26
comprehension with, 180
conditions occurring with, 41
conductive, 24, 99
confidence gained with, 169
Connexin 26 as cause, 28–30, 44
coping with, 105–7
daily life with, 102–14
defiance misinterpreted with, 7
degrees assigned to, 87
detecting, 7
determination of, 39
educating about, 100, 117
environment noisy with, 53, 62, 91
expectations exceeded for, 168
friends accommodating for, 177
hearing aids for, xvi, 12–13, 88
humor and, 179
implications at birth of, 19
independence with, 177
infant signs of, 2
learning cause of, 30
life changed by, 112
marriages stressed by, xix
meningitis causing, xix, 14, 111, 134, 176, 179
middle-ear problems as, 32–33
needs different with, 143
openness about, 171
otitis media causing, 35
overhearing absent with, 181
overview of, 14–20
parents advocating for child with, 93–94, 115–36, 140, 168
parents' reactions to, 94
parents' role in, 23
permanent, 25
personality change from, 106
physical condition as, 139
poor student with, 174
potential of, 176
preschool programs for, xix, 147–53
problems continued with, 137–38
problems stemming from, 155
progress with, xii
progressive, 99, 144
reality of, xviii
recessive genes in, 28
search for causes of, 26–30
self-consciousness about, 95

self-esteem lowered from, 94–95
sensorineural as, 14
severity in, 23
signal-to-noise ratio and, 62
slow learner with, 171
social acceptance with, 93–94
social impact of, 112
socially overcoming, 160
sound frequencies perceived with, 15
specialist for, 40–44
speech therapy helping, 15
support groups for, 101, 103
unilateral, 65, 146–47, 188
unnecessary emphasis on, 96
vision with, 44
visual cues with, 32
vocabulary problems with, 162
world not ending with, 167
Hearing problem
behavior resulting from, 5–6, 11–12, 90
negative social outcome from, 131
Hearing test, 7
accurate diagnosis for, 169
goal of, 39–40
pure tone audiometry used in, 37
sensitivity determined with, 57
technological improvements in, 37
Hearing thresholds, 18
Heredity, 43
Hertz (Hz), 16
High-frequency loss, 27
HMO
bureaucratic struggle with, 127–28
coverage language for, 127
policies of, 126

IDEA. *See* Individuals with Disabilities Education Act
IDEA Advocacy for Children who are Deaf and Hard of Hearing, 121
IEP. *See* Individualized Education Plan
Immaturity, 6
Incus, 20
Individualized Education Plan (IEP)
accommodations required with, 176
eligibility ages for, 121
implementing of, 125, 158
Individualized Family Service Plan (IFSP), 121
Individuals with Disabilities Education Act (IDEA), 120, 131
Infants
earmolds outgrown by, 77
hearing loss indications in, 2
physiologic tests for, 57–58
trouble talking as, 3